# THE SCRUM FIELD GUIDE

# The Agile Software Development Series

## Alistair Cockburn and Jim Highsmith, Series Editors

⋏⋏ Addison-Wesley

Visit **informit.com/agileseries** for a complete list of available publications.

---

Agile software development centers on four values, which are identified in the Agile Alliance's Manifesto*:

1. Individuals and interactions over processes and tools
2. Working software over comprehensive documentation
3. Customer collaboration over contract negotiation
4. Responding to change over following a plan

The development of Agile software requires innovation and responsiveness, based on generating and sharing knowledge within a development team and with the customer. Agile software developers draw on the strengths of customers, users, and developers to find just enough process to balance quality and agility.

The books in The Agile Software Development Series focus on sharing the experiences of such Agile developers. Individual books address individual techniques (such as Use Cases), group techniques (such as collaborative decision making), and proven solutions to different problems from a variety of organizational cultures. The result is a core of Agile best practices that will enrich your experiences and improve your work.

* © 2001, Authors of the Agile Manifesto

⋏⋏ Addison-Wesley    **informIT.com**  |  **Safari** Books Online

# THE SCRUM FIELD GUIDE

## PRACTICAL ADVICE FOR YOUR FIRST YEAR

MITCH LACEY

✦ Addison-Wesley

Upper Saddle River, NJ • Boston • Indianapolis • San Francisco
New York • Toronto • Montreal • London • Munich • Paris • Madrid
Capetown • Sydney • Tokyo • Singapore • Mexico City

Many of the designations used by manufacturers and sellers to distinguish their products are claimed as trademarks. Where those designations appear in this book, and the publisher was aware of a trademark claim, the designations have been printed with initial capital letters or in all capitals.

The author and publisher have taken care in the preparation of this book, but make no expressed or implied warranty of any kind and assume no responsibility for errors or omissions. No liability is assumed for incidental or consequential damages in connection with or arising out of the use of the information or programs contained herein.

The publisher offers excellent discounts on this book when ordered in quantity for bulk purchases or special sales, which may include electronic versions and/or custom covers and content particular to your business, training goals, marketing focus, and branding interests. For more information, please contact:

U.S. Corporate and Government Sales
(800) 382-3419
corpsales@pearsontechgroup.com

For sales outside the United States please contact:

International Sales
international@pearson.com

Visit us on the Web: informit.com/aw

*Library of Congress Cataloging-in-Publication Data*
Lacey, Mitch.
  The scrum field guide : practical advice for your first year / Mitch
Lacey.—1st ed.
       p.   cm.
  Includes index.
  ISBN 0-321-55415-9 (pbk. : alk. paper)
1.  Agile software development. 2.  Scrum (Computer software development)
I. Title.
  QA76.76.D47L326 2012
  005.1—dc23                                              2011040008

ISBN-13: 978-0-321-55415-4
ISBN-10:      0-321-55415-9
Text printed in the United States on recycled paper at RR Donnelley in Crawfordsville, Indiana.
Second printing, October 2013

*This book is dedicated to two teams; The first team is my family. My wife, Bernice, and my kids, Ashley, Carter, and Emma—without their support and constantly asking "are you done yet?" this book would not be here. They kept me focused and supported me throughout.*

*The second team is the group of guys from the Falcon project while at Microsoft. John Boal, Donavan Hoepcke, Bart Hsu, Mike Puleio, Mon Leelaphisut, and Michael Corrigan (our boss), thank you for having the courage to leap with me. You guys made this book a reality.*

# CONTENTS

# FOREWORD
## BY JIM HIGHSMITH

"Scrum is elegantly deceptive. It is one of the easiest frameworks to understand yet one of the hardest frameworks to implement well." So begins Chapter 1 of this thought-provoking and valuable guide to Scrum. I've seen too many organizations get caught up in the assumed simplicity of Scrum—they never seem to make it past Scrum 101 to a mature view of Scrum. They practice "rule-based" agility and don't appear to see the irony. They don't understand that change, particularly in larger organizations, will be difficult—the path bumpy—no matter how devoted they are to implementation—and that a few simple rules just aren't enough. This guide helps you move beyond Scrum 101 to a mature, realistic implementation. It isn't about the basic Scrum framework (except for an appendix); it's about all the harder, but practical, aspects of making the Scrum framework work for you and your team.

When it comes to agile transitions two hot buttons are often overlooked in attempts to get Scrum (or other frameworks) up and running—release planning and technical practices. Mitch is very clear from the beginning that technical practices are critical to effective Scrum implementations. As he points out, it's impossible to achieve the goal of shippable software every sprint without implementing solid technical practices. His basic list—test-driven development, refactoring, continuous integration and frequent check-ins, pair programming, and integration and automated acceptance testing—defines a great starting place for technical practices.

I had to laugh at the story conversation in the Chapter 11, "Release Planning" (each chapter has a lead-in story that illustrates the issues to be addressed). "But Stephen, we're using Scrum. I can't tell you exactly when we'll be done." Stephen, of course, was the manager who needed project completion information for his management chain. One of the key mindsets required to be an effective agile leader is what I call "And" management, the ability to find common ground between two seemingly opposite forces. One of these common paradoxes in Scrum projects is that between "predictability" and "adaptability." Traditionalists tend to come down on the side of predictability, while some agilists come down on the adaptability side. The secret, of course, is to balance the two—figuring out how to do appropriate levels of both. In his chapter on release planning, Mitch gives us some good guidelines on how to approach this paradox in a practical "And" management fashion.

In a recent conversation a colleague mentioned the two things he considered critical in a nascent Scrum implementation—learning and quick wins. Mitch addresses both of these in Chapter 2, "Getting People on Board" (indicating how important they are), when he delves into change management and developing the capability to learn and adapt as the transition to Scrum continues. Getting quick wins is one of the points Mitch describes as part of John Kotter's popular change management system.

Another plus of this book is the short chapters, each devoted to a topic that helps turn the basic Scrum framework into a workable framework by advocating key practices. These run the gamut from discussing Scrum values, to defining roles, to calculating velocity, to determining sprint lengths, to decomposing stories, to conducting customer reviews. There is also a fascinating chapter on defining what "done" means—Chapter 7, "How Do We Know When We Are Done?"—a necessity for effective Scrum projects.

For anyone who is implementing Scrum, or any other agile method for that matter, Mitch's book will definitely help you make the transition from elegantly simple to effective, practical results. It may not make the hard stuff easy, but at least you will understand what the hard stuff is all about.

—Jim Highsmith
Executive Consultant, ThoughtWorks

# FOREWORD
## BY JEFF SUTHERLAND

Mitch and I have worked together for many years training developers in Scrum. Studying this book can help users overcome the biggest challenges that have occurred in the last ten years as agile practices (75 percent of which are Scrum) have become the primary mode of software development worldwide.

Ten years after the Agile Manifesto was published, some of the original signatories and a larger group of agile thought leaders met at Snowbird, Utah, this time to do a retrospective on ten years of agile software development. They celebrated the success of the agile approach to product development and reviewed the key impediments to building on that success. And they came to unanimous agreement on four key success factors for the next ten years.

1. Demand technical excellence.
2. Promote individual change and lead organizational change.
3. Organize knowledge and improve education.
4. Maximize value creation across the entire process.

Let's see how Mitch's book can help you become an agile leader.

## Demand Technical Excellence

The key factor driving the explosion of the Internet, and the applications on smartphones, has been deploying applications in short increments and getting rapid feedback from end users. This is formalized in agility by developing product in short sprints, always a month or less and most often two weeks in length. We framed this issue in the Agile Manifesto by saying that "we value working software over comprehensive documentation."

The Ten Year Agile Retrospective of the Manifesto concluded that the majority of agile teams are still having difficulty developing product in short sprints (usually because the management, the business, the customers, and the development teams do not demand technical excellence).

Engineering practices are fundamental to software development and 17 percent of Scrum teams implement Scrum with XP engineering practices. The first Scrum team did this in 1993 before XP was born. It is only common sense to professional engineers.

Mitch says in the first chapter that he considers certain XP practices mandatory—sustainable pace, collective code ownership, pair programming, test-driven development, continuous integration, coding standards, and refactoring. These are fundamental to technical excellence, and the 61 percent of agile teams using Scrum without implementing these practices should study Mitch's book carefully and follow his guidance. This is the reason they do not have shippable code at the end of their sprints!

There is much more guidance in Mitch's book on technical excellence, and agile leaders, whether they be in management or engineering, need to demand the technical excellence that Mitch articulates so well.

# Promote Individual Change and Lead Organizational Change

Agile adoption requires rapid response to changing requirements along with technical excellence. This was the fourth principle of the Agile Manifesto—"respond to change over following a plan." However, individuals adapting to change is not enough. Organizations must be structured for agile response to change. If not, they prevent the formation of, or destroy, high-performing teams because of failure to remove impediments that block progress.

Mitch steps through the Harvard Business School key success factors for change. There needs to be a sense of urgency. Change is impossible without it. Agile leaders need to live it. A guiding coalition for institutional transformation is essential. Agile leaders need to make sure management is educated, trained, on board, and participating in the Scrum implementation.

Creating a vision and empowering others is fundamental. Arbitrary decisions and command and control mandates will kill agile performance. Agile leaders need to avoid these disasters by planning for short term wins, consolidating improvements, removing impediments, and institutionalizing new approaches. Agile leaders need to be part of management or train management as well as engineering, and Mitch's book can help you see what you need to do and how to do it.

# Organize Knowledge and Improve Education

A large body of knowledge on teams and productivity is relatively unknown to most managers and many developers. Mitch talks about these issues throughout the book.

## Software Development Is Inherently Unpredictable

Few people are aware of Ziv's Law, that software development is unpredictable. The large failure rate on projects worldwide is largely due to lack of understanding of this problem and the proper approach to deal with it. Mitch describes the need to inspect and adapt to constant change. The strategies in this book help you avoid many pitfalls and remove many blocks to your Scrum implementation.

## Users Do Not Know What They Want Until They See Working Software

Traditional project management erroneously assumes that users know what they want before software is built. This problem was formalized as "Humphrey's Law," yet this law is systematically ignored in university and industry training of managers and project leaders. This book can help you work with this issue and avoid being blindsided.

## The Structure of the Organization Will Be Embedded in the Code

A third example of a major problem that is not generally understood is "Conway's Law." The structure of the organization will be reflected in the code. A traditional hierarchical organizational structure negatively impacts object-oriented design resulting in brittle code, bad architecture, poor maintainability and adaptability, along with excessive costs and high failure rates. Mitch spends a lot of time explaining how to get the Scrum organization right. Listen carefully.

## Maximize Value Creation Across the Entire Process

Agile practices can easily double or triple the productivity of a software development team if the product backlog is ready and software is done at the end of a sprint. This heightened productivity creates problems in the rest of the organization. Their lack of agility will become obvious and cause pain.

## Lack of Agility in Operations and Infrastructure

As soon as talent and resources are applied to improve product backlog the flow of software to production will at least double and in some cases be 5–10 times higher. This exposes the fact that development operations and infrastructure are crippling production and must be fixed.

## Lack of Agility in Management, Sales, Marketing, and Product Management

At the front end of the process, business goals, strategies, and objectives are often not clear. This results in a flat or decaying revenue stream even when production of software doubles.

For this reason, everyone in an organization needs to be educated and trained on how to optimize performance across the whole value stream. Agile individuals need to lead this educational process by improving their ability to organize knowledge and train the whole organization.

## The Bottom Line

Many Scrum implementations make only minor improvements and find it difficult to remove impediments that embroil them in constant struggle. Work can be better than this. All teams can be good, and many can be great! Work can be fun, business can be profitable, and customers can be really happy!

If you are starting out, Mitch's book can help you. If you are struggling along the way, this book can help you even more. And if you are already great, Mitch can help you be greater. Improvement never ends, and Mitch's insight is truly helpful.

—Jeff Sutherland
   Scrum Inc.

# PREFACE

When my daughter Emma was born in late 2004, I felt out of my depth. We seemed to be at the doctor's office much more than we had been with our other children. I kept asking my wife, "Is this normal?" One night, I found my wife's copy of *What to Expect the First Year* on my pillow with a note from her, "Read this. You'll feel better."

And I did. Knowing that everything we were experiencing was normal for my child, even if it wasn't typical for me, or observed before, made me feel more confident and secure. This was right around the same time I was starting to experiment with Scrum and agile. As I started to encounter obstacles and run into unfamiliar situations, I began to realize that what I really needed was a *What to Expect* book for the first year of Scrum and XP.

The problem is, unlike a *What to Expect* book, I can't tell you exactly what your team should be doing or worrying about during months 1–3 or 9–12. Teams, unlike children, don't develop at a predictable rate. Instead, they often tumble, stumble, and bumble their way through their first year, taking two steps forward and one step back as they learn to function as a team, adopt agile engineering practices, build trust with their customers, and work in an incremental and iterative fashion.

With this in mind, I chose to structure this book with more of a "I've got a pain here, what should I do" approach. I've collected stories about teams I've been a part of or witnessed in their first year of agile life. As I continued down my agile path, I noticed the stories, the patterns in the companies, were usually similar. I would implement an idea in one company and tweak it for the next. In repeating this process, I ended up with a collection of real-world solutions that I now carry in my virtual tool belt. In this book, I share some of the most common pains and solutions with you. When your team is hurting or in trouble, you can turn to the chapter that most closely matches your symptoms and find, if not a cure, at least a way to relieve the pain.

*The Scrum Field Guide* is meant to help you fine-tune your own implementation, navigate some of the unfamiliar terrain, and more easily scale the hurdles we all encounter along the way.

## Who Should Read This Book

If you are thinking about getting starting with Scrum or agile, are at the beginning of your journey, or if you have been at it a year or so but feel like you've gotten lost along the way, this book is for you. I'm officially targeting companies that are within six months of starting a project to those that are a year into their implementation, an 18-month window.

This is a book for people who are pragmatic. If you want theory and esoteric discussions, grab another of the many excellent books on Scrum and agile. If, on the other hand, you want practical advice and real data based on my experience running projects both at Microsoft and while coaching teams and consulting at large Fortune 100 companies, this book fits the bill.

# How to Read This Book

The book is designed for you to be able to read any chapter, in any order, at any time. Each chapter starts out with a story, pulled from a team, company, or project that I worked on or coached. As you might expect, I've changed the names to protect the innocent (and even the guilty). Once you read the story, which will likely sound familiar, I walk you through the model. The model is what I use in the field to help address the issues evident in the story. Some of the models might feel uncomfortable, or you might believe they won't work for your company. I urge you to fight the instinct to ignore the advice or modify the model. Try it at least three times and see what happens. You might be surprised. At the end of each chapter, I summarize the keys to success, those factors that can either make or break your implementation.

This book is organized in four parts.

Part I, "Getting Prepared," gives you advice on getting started with Scrum, helping you set up for success. If you are just thinking about Scrum or have just begun to use it, start there.

Part II, "Field Basics," discusses items that, once you get started down the agile path, help you over some of the initial stumbling blocks that teams and organizations encounter. If you've gotten your feet wet with Scrum but are running into issues, you might start here.

Part III, "First Aid," is where we deal with some of the larger, deeper issues that companies face, like adding people to projects or fixing dysfunctional daily standup meetings. These are situations you'll likely find yourself in at one point or another during your first year. These chapters help you triage and treat the situation, allowing your team to return to a healthy state.

The last part, Part IV, "Advanced Survival Techniques," contains a series of items that people seem to struggle with regardless of where they are in their adoption, things such as costing projects, writing contacts, and addressing documentation in agile and Scrum projects.

If you are starting from scratch and have no idea what Scrum is, I've included a short description in the appendix at the back of the book to help familiarize you with the terms. You might also want to do some more reading on Scrum before diving into this book.

## Why You Should Read This Book

Regardless of where we are on our agile journey, we all need a friendly reminder that what we are experiencing is normal, some suggestions on how to deal with it, and a few keys for success. This book gives you all that in a format that allows you to read only the chapter you need, an entire section, or the whole thing. Its real-life situations will resonate with you, and its solutions can be applied by any team. Turn the page and read the stories. This field guide will become a trusted companion as you experience the highs and lows of Scrum and Extreme Programming.

## Supplemental Material for this Book

Throughout this book, you may find yourself thinking, "I wish I had a tool or downloadable template to help me implement that concept." In many cases, you do. If you go to http://www.mitchlacey.com/supplements/ you will find a list of various files, images, spreadsheets, and tools that I use in my everyday Scrum projects. While some of the information is refined, most of the stuff is pretty raw. Why? For my projects, I don't need it to be pretty; I need it functional. What you will get from my website will be raw, true, and from the trenches, but it works.

# ACKNOWLEDGMENTS

When I first had the idea for this book, it was raw. Little did I know that I was attempting to boil the ocean. My wife, Bernice, kept me grounded, as did my kids. Without their strength, this book would not be here today.

David Anderson, Ward Cunningham, and Jim Newkirk were all instrumental in helping me and my first team get off the ground at Microsoft. Each of them worked there at the time and coached us through some rough periods. I still look back at my notes from an early session with Ward, with a question highlighted saying "can't we just skip TDD?" Each of these three people helped turn our team of misfits into something that was really special. David, Ward, and Jim—thank you.

I thank Mike Cohn and Esther Derby for letting me bounce the original ideas off them at Agile 2006. Mike continued his support, and we often joked that my book would be out before his *Succeeding with Agile* book. When that didn't happen, he proposed that a better goal might be for me to finish before he was a grandfather. Well, Mike, I made it—and don't let the fact that your oldest daughter is still in high school lessen my accomplishment!

I could not have done this without the help of Rebecca Traeger, the best editor on the planet. She kept me on track, focused, and helped me turn my raw thoughts and words into cohesive chapters.

In the first printing, I made a big mistake and forgot to acknowledge my good friend and frequent reviewer Peter Provost. (Just goes to show that no matter how perfect something seems, there is always room for improvement.) Peter's honest feedback helped me tremendously, from the first draft to the last.

I would also like to once again thank the following friends, each of whom helped craft this book into what it is today. Everyone listed here has given me invaluable feedback and contributed many hours either listening to me formulate thoughts or reading early drafts. I cannot thank each of you enough, including Tiago Andrade e Silva, Adam Barr, my artists Tyler Barton and Tor Imsland, Martin Beechen, Arlo Belshee, Jelle Bens, John Boal, Jedidja Bourgeois, Stephen Brudz, Brian Button, Mike Cohn, Michael Corrigan, Scott Densmore, Esther Derby, Stein Dolan, Jesse Fewell, Marc Fisher, Paul Hammond, Bill Hanlon, Christian Hassa, Jim Highsmith, Donavan Hoepcke, Bart Hsu, Wilhelm Hummer, Ron Jeffries, Lynn Keele, Clinton Keith, James Kovaks, Rocky Mazzeo, Steve McConnell, Jeff McKenna, Ade Miller, Raul Miller, Jim Morris, Jim Newkirk, Jacob Ozolins, Michael Paterson, Bart Pietrzak, Dave Prior, Michael Puleio, René Rosendahl, Ken Schwaber, Tammy Shepherd, Lisa Shoop, Michele Sliger, Ted St. Clair, Jeff Sutherland, Bas Vodde, and Brad Wilson.

I'd also like to thank the team at Addison-Wesley, including Chris Zahn and Chris Guzikowski. Chris Zahn made me question just about everything I wrote, which put the words in a different light for me. Chris Guzikowski didn't fire me even when I missed the two-year-over-planned date. I appreciate all that your team did to help guide me through the process.

Books don't just pop out of your head and onto paper. They, like most projects I've ever encountered, are truly a team effort. The people I have mentioned (and likely a few that I forgot) have listened to me, told me where I was going astray, given me ideas to experiment with on my teams and with clients, and been there for me when I needed reviews. I imagine they are as glad as I am that this book is finally in print. I hope that after you read this, you too will join me in thanking them for helping to make this guide a reality.

# ABOUT THE AUTHOR

**Mitch Lacey** is an agile practitioner and consultant and is the founder of Mitch Lacey & Associates, Inc., a software consulting and training firm. Mitch specializes in helping companies realize gains in efficiency by adopting agile principles and practices such as Scrum and Extreme Programming.

Mitch is a self-described "tech nerd" who started his technology career in 1991 at Accolade Software, a computer gaming company. After working as a software test engineer, a test manager, a developer, and a variety of other jobs in between, he settled on his true calling, project and program management.

Mitch was a formally trained program manager before adding agile to his project tool belt. He began developing agile skills at Microsoft Corporation, where his team successfully released core enterprise services for Windows Live. Mitch's first agile team was coached by Ward Cunningham, Jim Newkirk, and David Anderson. Mitch cut his agile teeth working as a product owner or ScrumMaster on a variety of projects. He continued to grow his skills to the point where he was able to help other teams adopt agile practices. Today, with more than 16 years of experience under his belt, Mitch continues to develop his craft by experimenting and practicing with project teams at many different organizations.

As a Certified Scrum Trainer (CST) and a PMI Project Management Professional (PMP), Mitch shares his experience in project and client management through Certified ScrumMaster courses, agile coaching engagements, conference presentations, blogs, and white papers. Mitch works with companies across the world, from Austria to Colombia, California to Florida, Portugal to Turkey, and just about everywhere in between.

Mitch has presented at a variety of conferences worldwide, is the conference chair for Agile 2012, and sat on the board of directors of the Scrum Alliance and the Agile Alliance

For more information, visit www.mitchlacey.com where you will find Mitch's blog as well as a variety of articles, tools, and videos that will help you with your Scrum and agile adoption. He can also be found on Twitter at @mglacey and by email at mitch@mitchlacey.com.

# Chapter 1

# SCRUM: SIMPLE, NOT EASY

Scrum is elegantly deceptive. It is one of the easiest frameworks to understand yet one of the hardest frameworks to implement well. I say "implement well" because Scrum's inherent simplicity can seduce us into thinking it is easy to do, when in reality it can take years to do it well. Scrum seems to go against all that we have learned in our many, many years of waterfall development. It stands to reason that it will take us a while to unlearn our bad habits and adjust to a new reality.

In the appendix of this book I explain the mechanics of Scrum. If you are not familiar with Scrum and how it works, I suggest you start there. If you already have some background on what Scrum is, you know that the mechanics are fairly straightforward. So straightforward, in fact, that many mistakenly believe they "get it" and can begin immediately modifying Scrum to better fit their situation. Too often they instead find themselves lost or wounded, and in need of assistance, which is where this book comes in. The story that follows illustrates how quickly things fall apart when Scrum is implemented without understanding and without a solid grounding in the core agile concepts that make Scrum work.

## The Story

Jeff was as an agile coach helping teams adopt Scrum inside a large software company. One day, he received an email from Suzy, a program manager in his division.

"Jeff, please help. We've been doing Scrum for about six months and our code quality isn't improving the way I'd like. I think we need you to come and talk to us about pair programming. Next Monday is the beginning of our planning week. Can you come then?"

Jeff sat back in his chair. Talking about pair programming was relatively simple. He could bring his friend Julie, a great developer and seasoned agile practitioner. No problem. Yet two words from the email kept repeating in his head. Planning *week*? Scrum calls for two sprint planning meetings that last no more than four hours each. And this team took a week? Something told him they had more to work on than just pair programming. It was going to be an interesting Monday.

On Monday, Jeff and Julie arrived at the meeting and found Suzy and her team of eight in the conference room together. After a brief introduction by Suzy, Jeff and Julie introduced themselves and began to ask about the code quality issues Suzy had told them about.

The team was quick to answer. The lead tester, Mike, went first, "The reason our code is poor quality is because we have *no* time to test. The developers write the code right up until the last day during our four-week sprint. The coding and testing sprint is supposed to be for coding *and* testing. But our testing is either shoved right to the end of the sprint or it bleeds into the integration sprint."

Julie interrupted. "I'm sorry, Mike, did you say the integration sprint?" She looked at Suzy, who nodded.

"Oh. I didn't explain our modifications, did I?" said Suzy. "See, we know that Scrum calls for a release every four weeks, but that's just not possible for the kind of work we do. I mean, before trying Scrum, we tried to release quarterly and that was a complete disaster! So what we did was change Scrum to fit our process and reality better." Suzy went to the whiteboard and began to write.

"First we have our sprint planning week, followed by our four-week *actual* sprint, where the developers write the code and the testers write the test cases. After that, we do our integration, then we deploy. Of course, I usually add a week of buffer, too, just in case," said Suzy.

When she finished, she had just about filled up the whiteboard.

- WEEK 1: PLANNING
- WEEKS 2–5: DEVELOPERS CODE; TESTERS WRITE CASES AND DO LIGHT TESTING
- WEEKS 6–7: INTEGRATION
- WEEK 8: DEPLOYMENT TO LIVE SITE
- WEEK 9: BUFFER, JUST IN CASE

Jeff and Julie looked at each other, and then back at Suzy. The rest of the team looked bored. Jeff asked the obvious question, "Suzy, are your sprints really eight or nine weeks long?"

"That's right," said Suzy. "You sound surprised. I know it's not 'out-of-the-box Scrum' but it works for us. I'm thinking we may need to add another week, you know, for writing specs and test plans. We're having trouble fitting that in. Right now, we do that during our buffer week, but I really hate to cut into our cushion."

"Ok, we'll come back to that," said Julie. She looked at Jeff, who held his hands up as if to say, "Whatcha gonna do?" Julie continued, "Mike, you were saying that you don't have time to test."

Wyatt spoke up before Mike could answer, "Don't listen to Mike. They have plenty of time to test. We're the ones who never have enough time. We bust it every sprint to get as much coding done as we can. So what if it takes us all four weeks? That's how long it takes." Wyatt looked at Mike and continued, "All you and the rest of the testers have done since we started using Scrum is complain that you have no time. Maybe Scrum is the problem."

Jeff and Julie exchanged glances.

Suzy interjected, "Team, come on, we're not here to complain about Scrum. We're here to get our code quality up." She paused and took a deep breath. "I've been saying this for six months," she said to Jeff and Julie with a quick roll of her eyes.

Jeff nodded. "I can tell you're frustrated. And I can tell Wyatt and Mike are frustrated. Can I explore this a bit with the team? See if I can get to the root of the problem?" Suzie nodded enthusiastically.

Jeff began with his first standard assessment question. "OK. Both Scrum and Extreme Programming (XP) call for daily checkpoints. In Scrum these are the daily Scrum meetings. How would you rate your daily Scrum meetings?" Jeff asked the team.

Mike laughed. "*Daily* meeting? Are you kidding? We don't have time for those. We meet twice a week for an hour. And that's bad enough."

"OK, Mike. Tell me about those meetings," said Jeff.

"Well, first off we say the same thing every single time. Developers say they are working on tasks, and we say we are building test cases. Big news, there. Then we spend 20 minutes or so triaging our bug list, which boils down to going through the list and saying 'this bug is per the design' or 'we'll fix that one in the next sprint.' Of course, we never do fix them. It's just a big dysfunctional mess," said Mike.

Suzy was now becoming visibly angry, so Jeff gave her the opportunity to speak.

"Thanks, Mike. Suzy, what are your thoughts?" asked Jeff.

"Mike's right about one thing. Daily meetings won't work for us. We *have* to do the meeting every other day. My schedule is too busy to meet every day, and some team members are on other projects. I know it's not ideal, but it's what we need to do. What gets me is that the team fights me on even having them twice a week—they think it is too much overhead. You heard the way Mike was talking just then. They all complain about the meetings, the schedule, the lack of time! But I can't help the fact that management is pushing us to release more often. Plus, like I keep telling them, it's *my* project. *I* am setting the plan, and *I* am setting the structure. Tell them, Jeff. I'm the ScrumMaster. They should do what I say, right?" demanded Suzy.

Jeff gave a noncommittal shrug and bit his tongue. He was starting to realize how little they understood about Scrum. He glanced at Julie and gave her one of those *they don't get it* looks. Julie acknowledged it with a slight nod. Jeff continued with his assessment.

"Ok, I hear you. Let's not get ahead of ourselves. It sounds like one potential issue might be that your daily standup meetings are not daily, not productive, and last too long. We can fix that. Let's skip that for now and bring our thought process up a level. Tell me what brought you to eight-week sprints."

Wyatt spoke up. "I've been here over ten years and believe me, I've seen every new fad there is. They come and they go. But I drank the Kool-Aid this time and really thought Scrum might be different. What a joke! This whole thing started because management was pushing us to release more quickly. We had gotten down to quarterly releases—going from yearly to quarterly hurt, let me tell you, but we were doing it. But that wasn't quick enough for management, was it?" Wyatt paused and looked around the room for confirmation.

He continued, "So, Suzy and I were sitting at lunch one day and happened to meet up with a colleague of mine who works in another division. He told us his team was using Scrum and how they were delivering every four weeks and how happy the people were. He said their quality was through the roof. The management team had not been this happy in years and the customers were ecstatic. This guy was like me, a skeptic, you know? So I thought, if he says it works, it must work. Suzy and I spent the afternoon with him, learning all about Scrum. Seemed simple enough, but it had some problems. First off, those daily meetings. Who has time for that? Simple fix was to make them twice weekly. Then, it was obvious that a four-week cycle would not work for us—after all, we could barely do a quarterly cycle, so we decided to double it at eight weeks. From there, we broke our workflow down into eight weeks. It was just a matter of shrinking everything down. After all, Scrum is just another incremental process."

Jeff and Julie glanced at each other again.

Wyatt continued, "I see that look. But I'm telling you, we know our team and our product. There's no way Scrum would work for us the way it comes out of the box. So, we did what any software team would do, we customized it to suit our needs. The way we have it structured fits best with how we've done things in the past."

"Right," confirmed Suzy. "I mean, Scrum is just a way for project managers to manage the work, only shorter."

Jeff sat back. The assessment questions he had prepared weren't designed for a situation like this. He wasn't sure what to say at this point. Julie stepped in to help, "Do you have a common definition of done, Wyatt?"

"Sure we do. We have our design review meeting after the first week. Then, at the end of week five, we have our code complete milestone. At the end of integration, we are test and integration complete. Once we hit these milestones, we release to the live site. It's really not that hard to understand," said Wyatt.

"No, it's simple. I get it," said Julie reassuringly. "So, team, Wyatt, Mike, and Suzy have explained your process. The way I understand it you have twice weekly standups, an eight- (sometimes nine-) week sprint, and have check points at certain key stages to let you know you are done. How is it working for you? Are you having fun? Is your code quality a lot better?" asked Julie.

"Well, it's not bad," said Wyatt.

"Not bad?" said Suzy. "It's awful."

"Well, it's not our fault it's awful! We try to test, but, like I said, there's just no time!" screamed Mike. The rest of the team stared at the table. They weren't getting involved in this fight.

"I'm not blaming you, Mike, though I could. Nope. The real problem is Scrum," said Wyatt. "It's a stupid process and it doesn't work."

"Not that again," said Suzy. "How many times do we have to have this argument? We go through this at every retrospective."

"Retrospective?" interjected Wyatt. "That's just a fancy name for a two-day bitch session. Retrospectives don't change anything. Scrum doesn't change anything. I take that back. It does change one thing—it makes us all miserable."

"Wyatt, this was your idea, too. Why did you sign up to do Scrum if all you were going to do was sabotage it?" asked Suzy heatedly.

Jeff stood up. It was time to stop asking questions and start getting this team to face the truth.

"Look, it's not anyone's fault and it's not Scrum's fault either. To me, and I'm sure Julie agrees, it sounds like you're not really *doing* Scrum. What you're doing is what you've always done, only squeezed into an eight-week cycle. You're just calling it Scrum."

Wyatt and Suzy started to argue, but Julie put her hand up to stop them. "Let me ask one question. This is for the whole team. Wyatt, Suzy, Mike, please don't answer." Julie looked down the table at each team member before continuing, "Has this new way of working made your lives miserable or was it always like this, but just maybe not as obvious?" asked Julie.

Everyone looked down, their chins to their chests in deep thought.

"It sucked before, too," said a voice from the back.

"Yeah," said another team member. "I just never knew how much it sucked before."

There was a dead silence in the room as self-realization started to dawn on them.

Wyatt sighed and said, "You're right. It was not any better before; it just wasn't as obvious. We only felt the pain every quarter. Now we feel it every 8 weeks."

Mike chimed in, "You know, looking back on the last six months, we have uncovered a lot of stuff that we could and should fix, but we haven't done anything about it. Not really."

Suzy interrupted.

"Guys, I'm really tired. Can we postpone this for a few days, reconvene next week?" she asked.

The team nodded. They *were* tired.

Suzy left the meeting knowing things were bad. She spent the weekend and the early part of the next week thinking about how to move things forward. She invited Jeff and Julie back for another meeting, one she hoped would set a new tone for the team.

"I'm sorry, everyone," she said to open up the meeting. "I knew things were rough, but I didn't know it was this bad. I originally asked Jeff and Julie to help us with pair programming because I thought that would fix our quality issues. Clearly I have been blind to our real needs and for that I apologize. We've gone about this all wrong. It's not Scrum that has failed; we have failed to use Scrum. I'd like to ask you all if we can start over. I think Jeff and Julie can help us do that," said Suzy.

Wyatt nodded and looked at the team, "I know I can be a jerk. I've been here so long sometimes I think I own the place, but I don't. I know I can get better. I'll stop complaining and give it a real chance to work, but only on one condition."

"What's that?" asked Jeff.

"That we do it for real," said Wyatt. "No more customizations. And we need a coach, someone who can show us what to do. This hasn't been nearly as easy as it looked."

Mike looked up. "I have a condition, too. We fix the problems. Really fix them, not blame each other for them." He held out a hand to Wyatt. "Think we can do it?"

Wyatt looked at Mike, looked at his hand, and then shook it, "I think we are up for the challenge. If Jeff will still help us, that is," he said mockingly, raising his eyebrows at Jeff.

Everyone laughed—the first laugh they'd had as a team in quite a while. It was a start. They went around the table, all verbally committing to trying Scrum, for real this time. Jeff and Julie left the meeting a short time later, feeling like they'd accomplished quite a lot but knowing there was much more left to do.

"What are you going to do now, Jeff?" asked Julie.

"The first thing I'm going to do is to teach them what Scrum is—its values, the framework, the shift in mindset that they are going to need to go through," said Jeff.

"Don't forget to show them how it manages risk and helps identify the problems," said Julie.

"Exactly. I'll start with the basics and work my way through the obstacles as they pop up. It'll be a struggle at times, but they can do it. No pain, no gain, right?"

# Scrum

Scrum seems pretty basic. But what many people don't understand is that, to do it well, you must fundamentally change the way you develop software. And that's not easy. You're going to struggle. You're going to encounter obstacles. The team in our story found that out the hard way, and if you've picked up this book, you've probably discovered it too. To understand why something so simple can be so hard, let's look more closely at Scrum.

## What Is Scrum?

*Jeopardy* has always been one of my favorite TV game shows. I keep wishing for the software development edition where we have categories like *Methodologies and Frameworks, Common Causes of Software Failure, Famous Software Architects,* or *Stupid Quotes from Smart People.* I can think of dozens of questions that would fill these categories, such as, "Name the person who is thought to have said: *Be nice to nerds. Chances are you'll end up working for one.*" I envision a question under *Methodologies and Frameworks* to be, "Named after a Rugby term, this project management framework delivers working software every two to four weeks." One common answer that would likely be accepted, in the form of a question of course, would be *What is ... Scrum?*

So what is Scrum really? Scrum is *not* a methodology or set of engineering practices. It is, instead, a lightweight framework designed to manage software and product development. Ken Schwaber and Jeff Sutherland [Schwaber 01] describe Scrum like this:

> *Scrum (n): A framework within which people can address complex adaptive problems, while productively and creatively delivering products of the highest possible value. Scrum is:*
>
> - *Lightweight*
> - *Simple to understand*
> - *Extremely difficult to master*
>
> *Scrum is a process framework that has been used to manage complex product development since the early 1990s. Scrum is not a process or a technique for building products; rather, it is a framework within which you can employ various processes and techniques. Scrum makes clear the relative efficacy of your product management and development practices so that you can improve.*

Scrum relies on a fixed cadence of iterative cycles called *sprints*. Each sprint begins with a planning meeting and ends with a demonstration of potentially shippable product. Scrum is characterized by a high level of feedback and transparency, both within the team and outside it. Its short cycles and collaborative nature make it ideal for projects with rapidly changing and/or highly emergent requirements.

Scrum is built on five core values and has three distinct roles, three artifacts, and three (or four) meetings. More detail on the mechanics of Scrum may be found in Appendix A, "Scrum Framework."

## Implementing Scrum

While Scrum might appear simple to implement, it is actually challenging. Why? Because doing so requires more than just putting the right mechanics into place and then pressing a button. Implementing Scrum correctly requires teams to be willing to make the following changes:

- Develop an understanding of Scrum's underlying values.
- Undergo an often enormous shift in mindset.
- Plan for change to occur and adapt when it does.
- Deal with newly exposed or emerging issues.
- Incorporate agile engineering practices.

## Scrum Is Built on Values

Any framework worth using is built on principles and values. Each of the original agile practices—XP, Scrum, DSDM, Crystal, and FDD—as well as Kanban and Lean, has a set of core values. These values guide us, provide clarity in times of ambiguity, and, most importantly, help us understand *why we do what we do.* As you read in the story above, the team was attempting to go through the motions of Scrum, but they did not understand why. What they lacked was a clear understanding of the values behind the Scrum framework: focus, respect, commitment, courage, and openness [Schwaber 02].

*Focus.*   To focus means to concentrate, to direct attention on something. In Scrum, the team must have focus if it is to accomplish everything that needs to be done to deliver a potentially releasable increment of functionality. Focus means working on one project at a time. It may mean having dedicated "team time," where the entire team is off email, instant messaging, mobile phones, and meetings. Focus is doing whatever it takes to allow the team to concentrate on the delivery at hand for the entire length of any given sprint.

*Respect.*   We have all heard that respect is earned, not granted. In Scrum, this is especially true. Respect for one's teammates, or lack thereof, can make or break a project. High-performing Scrum teams trust each other enough to admit to obstacles. They have faith that when one team member commits to a task, that team member will follow through. There is no *us* versus *them* on a true Scrum team. In the story that opened this chapter, testers and developers were clearly at odds and had little respect for each other. The team was lucky, though, in that the people had not yet lost all respect for each other, as is evidenced by their ability to come together in the end.

*Commitment.*   A commitment is a pledge or promise, an obligation to deliver. Commitments should not be made lightly—they should be made with as much information as possible. The team makes a commitment to the organization and to each other during each sprint planning meeting. At the end of sprint planning, each team member should have the same level of understanding about what the team is committing to accomplish during that sprint.

*Courage.*   Courage is the ability to face difficulty in spite of your fears. Alleviating these fears is one of the best ways teams and organizations can help team members be courageous. A team that has demonstrated understanding in the face of frank discussion and an organization that has proven that it will listen to bad news objectively helps give individuals the courage to speak their minds. Remember, when teams lack the courage to do what they feel is right, the right thing will likely not be done.

*Openness.*   Openness enables us to be receptive to new ideas. Nowhere is a team's openness more apparent than in the sprint retrospectives. Having the willingness to receive new ideas, perceptions, and ways of thinking helps us grow into a learning organization and a high-performing team.

## Scrum Requires a Shift in Mindset

Albert Einstein said, "We can't solve problems by using the same kind of thinking we used when we created them." One of the biggest impediments to a successful adoption of Scrum, or any agile method for that matter, is the inability to have a shift in mindset, the inability to use a new way of thinking to solve problems. As a result, Scrum and all agile practices require a certain degree of open mindedness, at least for the first three to six months. When I worked on my first Scrum project, it took nearly a year before I truly understood what Scrum was about.

During that year, I learned that Scrum was a powerful but potentially dangerous tool. Did you ever see that old show *Home Improvement*? The main character, Tim "The Toolman" Taylor, would always get into trouble with a shiny new tool when he failed to take safety precautions, rigged it to be used in ways it was never intended, or simply bit off more than he could chew. Scrum is the same way. If not operated according to instructions, especially at first, Scrum can make your project go horribly wrong, fast. Too many teams take a rudimentary understanding and decide they know better; their situation is different; they've got this thing figured out.

Take my advice: Get to know Scrum before you decide it needs to be customized. Use it as intended, "out-of-the-box," if you will. Spend time learning as much as you can about it. Set aside some room in your brain to let this knowledge grow, to steep like a cup of tea. To my software audience I say, set aside some memory address space in your brain to let this knowledge sit. Do not—I repeat, do not—try to combine Scrum with other tools you are familiar with just yet; now is not the time. Only when you have mastered one tool can you learn to use it with others successfully. Above all, have the strength and discipline to give it a fair shot, even (and especially) when it is difficult and challenging. You may be surprised at how little you need to change Scrum and how much you end up changing your mind. You might think this goes against the first value of the Agile Manifesto, *Individuals and interactions over processes and tools*. On the contrary, it is the individuals and interactions that enable you to learn to use Scrum (or any other agile practice), and sticking to it helps you make an informed decision on what works.

## Scrum Takes the Shortest Path, Not the Set Path

The longest path through a project is known as the critical, or rate-limiting, path. We build a plan around the critical path and follow the plan, from point A to point B. Along this path, issues and problems surface: issues like the stakeholders not knowing exactly what they wanted when the plan was built, having business goals change as the product moves through its life cycle, having the project respond to internal and external forces, such as a competitor's release, and other details that are often revealed during development. These are all things that happen on nearly every project; software projects are not alone.

With a traditional planning method, when these issues arise we are still forced to go from A to B, making sacrifices along the way—sacrifices in quality, functionality, and customer satisfaction. Once we finally reach point B, we begin to triage the baggage we have accumulated and begin building our plan to get to C, the place we discovered we needed to reach but could not, simply because the plan would not allow us to (see Figure 1-1).

In Scrum, we acknowledge that issues like the ones identified above are going to happen—they are a fact of life. Instead of building the perfect plan to mitigate as many of them as we can, we embrace the fact that they will occur and build in mechanisms to allow for them to be handled during the project as they surface so that we don't have to make a pit stop at B; we can go directly to C.

We do this by putting in daily, weekly, and monthly checkpoints with people at various levels (team, management, customers) to ensure we are on track and building the right functionality to meet the vision. Instead of betting on an all-encompassing requirements-gathering phase, we gather requirements over time, adjusting and refining them as new information is revealed during development. Because we can do this, the project is allowed to adapt to the needs of the business and external market conditions, providing us the shortest path to success (see Figure 1-2).

Success does not come without some cost, though. In the perfect-plan model, we have the perception (often false) of knowing the exact date the project will be done. This perception is hard to give up. In reality, though, we all know that either the schedule slips, features (whether they are the most important features or not) are cut to meet the schedule, or quality suffers to squeeze in a set amount of functionality by a predetermined date. In the end, all these sacrifices cost the business in time, quality, and money.

With Scrum, we don't promise to deliver a set amount of functionality by a certain date. We vary either the end date or the set of functionality. On some projects, we promise to deliver an approximate amount of functionality by a set date. We do this by locking in the cost (what the customer can spend per sprint) and schedule

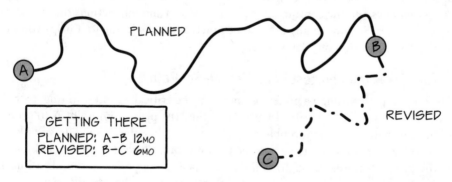

**FIGURE 1-1**   The traditional planning method

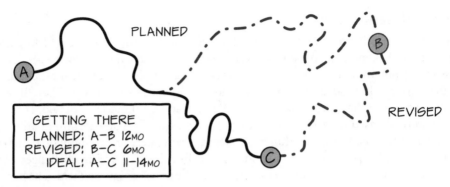

**FIGURE 1-2**   Scrum planning method

(when the project will end and how many sprints will be run) up front. We then estimate how many features we can complete within those constraints. Because Scrum projects always do the highest-priority work first, any features that do not get completed by the end of the project are the features that are of low value and likely less important to the overall success of the project.

On other projects, where features are more important than a set completion date, we might lock in features, but allow the date (and consequently the cost) to fluctuate. We promise to deliver a set amount of functionality by an approximate date, or date range. When changes occur (new features are added or existing feature requests are better understood), the customer understands that he must make a choice between delivering that functionality in the agreed-upon time or extending the schedule to accommodate the desired functionality.

This is a large deviation from a traditional approach, where the features are captured up front and then the teams are asked to estimate the time and cost constraints needed to deliver them, often only to have the cost and time constraints reduced while being asked to commit to the same feature set.

Figure 1-3 summarizes the differences between the two approaches.

It is also a huge shift in mindset, which is why trust in and alignment with the values discussed in this chapter are so important.

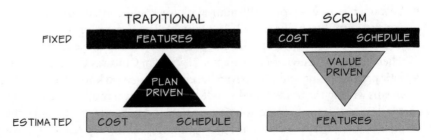

**FIGURE 1-3**   Contrasting the planning methods

## Scrum Unearths Issues

Scrum exposes issues, those that were long ago swept under the rug and forgotten and those that some people did not know existed. It also exposes new issues. These issues are not limited to coding or teamwork. For example, one of the most common questions that I see surface is, "How should we compensate our people?" or "It takes *how long* to run the acceptance test suite?" In a traditional model, a developer might be rewarded based on getting his coding done on time and at a certain quality bar. How does this map to a cross-functional team, where there are no individual metrics on functional areas? It is organizational norms like this that Scrum challenges, forcing management to make hard choices: address the issues or ignore them. The benefit of Scrum, however, is that once these behaviors and patterns become visible it is difficult to ignore them.

## Scrum Should Marry

Scrum is a project management framework. As such, it tells you how to manage your project, but does not contain the specific engineering practices that enable you to deliver potentially shippable software every two to four weeks. For that, you need Scrum's Prince Charming: Extreme Programming (XP). While Scrum and XP have a great deal in common (e.g., XP has a planning game; Scrum has planning meetings), XP contains some different practices that complement Scrum beautifully, such as continuous integration, test first, and pair programming.

While implementing Scrum by itself helps teams, marrying Scrum and XP yields tremendous results. That's not to say that you should jump into XP practices before you have a solid Scrum foundation—be careful about introducing too much change all at once. Once your team is experienced with the roles, artifacts, and meetings of Scrum, they are ready to start integrating XP practices, but beware—doing agile project management while using waterfall engineering practices is often a volatile mix, causing more problems than it attempts to solve. This may take a day, a week, or a month; it all depends on the team's tolerance for change. However, once XP is introduced, the true magic occurs.

The XP practices that I consider mandatory for the projects that I work on are as follows:

- **Sustainable pace**—Work a 40-hour work week and consistently work at 85 percent output (see Chapter 23, "Sustainable Pace," for more).
- **Collective code ownership**—The whole team works on the entire code base. There is no single owner (see Chapter 21, "When Cultures Collide," for more).
- **Pair programming and test-driven development**—Also known as test first, this means writing the test before the code with the typical model of red to indicate a failing test, green to indicate a passing test, and then refactor to make the code better. Always work toward green, no exceptions (see Chapter 19, "Keeping People Engaged with Pair Programming," for more).

- **Continuous integration**—CI enables us to have a continuous picture of how the codebase is behaving and performing. Check in your code, at a minimum, daily. Strive to go home in a green state every day, just like having each test in test-driven development (TDD) be green.
- **Coding standards**—Often overlooked, not having coding standards wreaks havoc on collective code ownership as each team member implements his or her own personal style. Create them, publish them, and hang them on the wall to remind everyone.
- **Refactoring**—Since up-front design and architecture are minimized (not removed) and the system is developed for today, the code must be refactored. Without refactoring, changing requirements can result in big up-front designs that are not adaptive to business needs.

Potentially shippable—these two words often cause teams many headaches and, as my friend Chris Sterling wrote in a blog post, are one of the forgotten Scrum elements [STERLING]. To truly reach a shippable shape, teams need to change not only their project management process but the way they develop software. Otherwise, all the issues presented in our story—poor quality, no time to test, and inability to deliver—will remain and will sink the project. Integrating XP practices is the best way I've found to bring about true and lasting change.

## When Is Scrum Right for Me?

We've established that implementing Scrum is much more complicated than it might appear. So should you even try it? It depends.

I have several friends who work in the construction industry. I often ask them to assist me on small house projects in return for dinner, and they are happy to oblige me. One thing I notice every time they come over is the plethora of tools they have on their belts. I asked Joachim once if he carries a standard set or if he custom builds his belt for each job his crew works on. He told me he always has his basics (a tape measure, pencil, and safety glasses), but almost everything else depends on the job. If he is doing framing work, he'll load his belt with the tools needed for framing. When he is doing finish carpentry or tiling, he uses a different set. At the same time, though, the tools that are not on his belt are always close by in the truck. How does this apply to Scrum?

I view Scrum as a tool in a person's tool belt. Like any good contractor, a person should use Scrum when it's appropriate, which might not be 100 percent of the time. Just as we would not use a screwdriver to secure a nail, we should not use Scrum on a project that does not require it. So when *should* we use Scrum?

Software projects generally fall into four different areas: simple, complicated, complex, and anarchy (see Figure 1-4), as adopted from Ralph Stacey's *Strategic Management and Organisational Dynamics, 2nd edition* [STACEY]. Simple projects are made up primarily of knowns: Similar projects have been done over and over

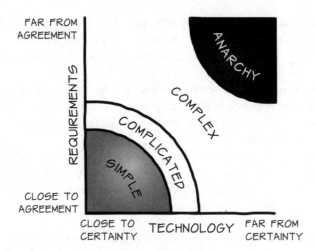

**FIGURE 1-4**   The relationship between requirements, technology, and type of project

so everyone agrees on what is needed and the technology is well understood. Simple projects are easy to implement and understand.

As we move farther out from the simple zone, however, things become a little fuzzier. Our requirements, our technology—or both—may not be as stable as we had hoped. Perhaps people are not as certain about what the final product will look like. Maybe the technology is new or untried. In this area, the area of complicated and complex, we encounter a substantial amount of change. Projects here are much more difficult to implement and predict. Then, as we move beyond complex toward anarchy, we begin to have truly unknown unknowns. When projects or companies are in this state, they should focus on fixing the problems that put them there instead of building a system.

What this all means is that if you are anywhere but the simple area, you will have change in your project—change in requirements, technology, or both. I have used Scrum and XP on simple projects, and more often than not, I found it overkill. However, as you move away from agreement and certainty, you want to use Scrum and XP, as doing so helps you adapt to the changing business requirements that are sure to come.

## Change Is Hard

Scrum is all about change. Some people embrace change and some avoid it like the plague. Both responses are perfectly natural. In software, we typically avoid change not because we are afraid of it, but because we have been conditioned to provide the right thing the first time. We equate change to "bugs" or features that we missed when we were developing the product—to us, a change request suggests we have failed in some way. What we often don't understand is that change is inevitable. We cannot

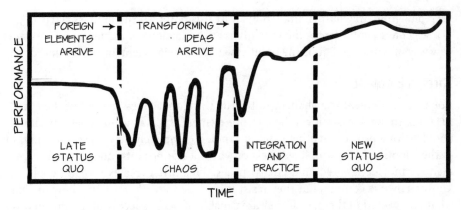

**FIGURE 1-5**  Satir's Stages of Change

predict the future; we cannot be expected to know about sudden market shifts or a competitor's newest release before they happen. To be successful, we must learn to embrace change. Scrum gives us the tools to do this, but moving to a place where change is integrated into our process is a difficult journey.

The team in our story wanted to use Scrum but was fearful of leaping into the unknown. They tried, in vain, to hold on to familiar patterns and prevent mistakes by modifying the process and adding planning and integration sprints. Instead of keeping them from failing, these modifications actually *caused* problems and made things much worse.

Understanding common reactions to change is key to a successful Scrum implementation. Virginia Satir was a family therapist who, through clinical studies, identified a common pattern in the way people experience change. These stages include the late status quo, the introduction of a foreign element, chaos, integration and practice, and the new status quo. These patterns of behavior are known as Satir's Stages of Change [SATIR], which are visually represented in Figure 1-5.

I find that these stages are fairly constant, no matter what level of change a person takes on. My mother tried to quit smoking when I was growing up and I observed these patterns. I also have observed them with kids when trying to ride a bicycle for the first time. Let's look at how Scrum teams move through these stages.

## Late Status Quo

When people are in the status quo, they are comfortable. Often, people find excuses to stay in the status quo because it is the world they are familiar with. People tend to ignore the need for change and just keep doing the same thing, only better, harder, or more diligently. An all-too-familiar example of the status quo is the death march, where teams soldier on toward certain failure while working longer hours and making unwanted sacrifices to quality to try to meet a deadline. Eventually, everyone begins to complain about the futility of believing that all can be made well if we just keep plugging away harder and stronger. At this point, a critical mass starts to grow, as a select few people tire of the way things are being done or management institutes a new way of working. This is the point at which a foreign element is introduced.

## Foreign Element

The foreign element is a challenge; it is the thing that takes you out of the Late Status Quo. In some cases it can be a minor element, such as using a new specification template for a project. In other cases, it can be a completely new way of working, such as the adoption of Scrum. Regardless of which it is, once introduced, the foreign element cannot be ignored, and chaos ensues. This often creates fear in people. They know change is coming, but they resist it because they do not know how to change, what is expected of them, or if they are capable of being successful in "this new way" as they were in the old, familiar way.

## Chaos

Chaos comes when the status quo is interrupted by the foreign element. While the degree of chaos depends on the nature of the foreign element, in the case of a large-scale change, it can feel as if everything familiar has vanished. Even those who are most certain about the need for a new way of doing things are forced to work in a way that feels unfamiliar and uncomfortable. People in this state are nervous and uncertain and often feel vulnerable. They are afraid of making a wrong move. As a result, anxiety builds and performance varies widely. As the group works through this stage, things will get worse before they get better, but they indeed will get better. The end of chaos comes with the identification of a transforming idea.

What transforming idea will end the chaos that Scrum initially introduces? It varies from team to team, but the overall theme is usually the general thought, "Hey, this is not that bad. We can do this." People start to see the connection between the foreign element and the way things can be in the future. The connection is made.

## Practice and Integration

My kids play sports. Every time they complain about attending practice, I remind them that someone else is practicing right now, practicing to beat them when their two teams meet. Practice in software development is equally essential. Without practice, the foreign element will never become familiar, second nature, an ingrained habit.

As a team begins to learn the practices and understand the principles of Scrum, it begins to realize Scrum's benefits. As these benefits emerge, the team members gradually embrace their new reality. Chaos begins to fade as the team moves toward a new equilibrium. Trust, relationships, and identities emerge in the team and in the group at large. As people learn to work together in a new way, performance starts to improve, often exceeding levels seen prior to the change. Don't take these early gains as a sign that the team is now "fine." On the contrary, teams in this stage need more nurturing and caring than they will later. While it's true that people are gaining confidence in their work, they may still feel vulnerable, even though it may not be visible. The newfound success is tenuous and delicate and should be treated appropriately. Still, with each success, the prospects of what can be accomplished start to emerge. For most, it might feel like nirvana; for a select few it may always feel somewhat chaotic.

### New Status Quo

As the team members become skilled and comfortable with the transforming idea, they begin to outpace their previous results. They feel rested and have the sense of accomplishment that comes from going through a transformational event together. This stage enables people to explore new ways to improve, to feel they have a right to make things better, and to work together to create a learning organization. The freedom to continue to practice in a safe environment is key here. Just like in sports, you never get so good that you don't need to practice or learn new things.

## Keys to Success

As our story illustrated, many teams struggle with their initial implementation of Scrum, not because they are reluctant or closed-minded, but because Scrum requires them to work in a way that feels uncomfortable and unfamiliar. The characters in our story tried to hold on to the elements that they were familiar with, not knowing that those elements were slowing them down, keeping them from success. To have a successful Scrum implementation, teams must adhere to the basics.

First, teams must understand the rules. Scrum is a simple framework for getting things done. Because of its simplicity, people tend to modify the rules without understanding the implications of their actions. This is dangerous. Just as you would not drive a car without knowing the rules of the road, you should not attempt to implement Scrum without a good deal of study. Learning the rules takes time. Use this time to understand how they apply to you, your team, and your company.

Next, team members must learn the base mechanics. Teams and their organizations need to understand how things work and feel with Scrum. It takes time for this to happen. As we saw with Satir's Stages of Change, moving from the known to the unknown is a difficult process that takes patience and practice. It is akin to learning to ride a bicycle. We cannot ride Le Tour de France when we are five years old; instead, we wobble and weave and often fall down. It's practice that makes us sure and steady. Give people time to learn the basics and help them along the way. Make sure you keep their feelings in mind and understand that as the base mechanics are being practiced, people may be fragile, skeptical, and anxious. These insecurities will be overcome with time, but only if people can practice.

Third, give it time. Learning a new way of working takes more than a weekend workshop. I've found that the majority of Scrum teams and companies implementing Scrum need at least three months to learn the basics and to start rolling. Some can do it in less and some take longer, but on average, plan for three to six months, depending on the group being transitioned, of change management.

Fourth, don't adopt Scrum midstream. I have seen countless "Scrum failures," where teams implemented Scrum in the middle of a development cycle, often as a result of management deciding that Scrum is the magic bullet that will solve all the company's problems. Management, seeing the potential benefits that come with a high-performing team, expects the team to become experts at using Scrum overnight. As you can imagine, this throws the team into a tailspin as they are forced to work in a new fashion while an immovable pending deadline looms. The ensuing chaos causes delay after delay and great sacrifices in quality. I recommend that you implement Scrum at the beginning of a new project. In the meantime, you can create a transition backlog of the things you need to have in place, and working, to ensure the best Scrum adoption possible.

Last, ensure time is allocated for continuous learning. Too often teams ignore retrospectives, considering them either a luxury or a waste of time. Teams who skip the retrospective, or go through the motions without applying any of the learning to future sprints, most often fall back into their old habits. Why? Because they are not setting aside time to learn. Learning is one of the key aspects of Scrum that cannot be sacrificed. The team cannot move toward a high-performing state without it.

Through all these technical and psychological challenges, just remember to stick with it. Learning Scrum is no different from learning anything new. There will be great satisfaction one moment and great frustration at another. Educate yourself and keep an open mind. Remember too that if NASA could put a man on the moon with a computer system inside the Apollo 11 that had somewhere between 36k and 72k of memory, we can implement Scrum.

# References

[SCHWABER 01]   Schwaber, Ken, and Jeff Sutherland. 2011. "The Scrum Guide." http://www.scrum.org/storage/scrumguides/Scrum%20Guide%20-%202011.pdf. Also available at http://www.scrum.org/scrumguides/ or download a copy at http://www.mitchlacey.com.

[SCHWABER 02]   Schwaber, Ken. 2004. *Agile Software Development with Scrum.* Redmond: Microsoft Press.

[STERLING]   Sterling, Chris. Sterling Barton website. http://www.gettingagile.com/2009/07/15/the-forgotten-scrum-elements/ (accessed on 3 July 2010).

[STACEY]   Stacey, Ralph. 1996. *Strategic Management and Organisational Dynamics, 2nd Edition.* Financial Times Management.

[SATIR]   Satir, Virginia, John Banmen, Jane Berber, and Maria Gomori. 1991. *The Satir Model: Family Therapy and Beyond.* Palo Alto: Science and Behavior Books. pp. 98–119.

# PART I
# GETTING PREPARED

# Chapter 2

# GETTING PEOPLE ON BOARD

M. Scott Peck wrote, "The truth is that our finest moments are most likely to occur when we are feeling deeply uncomfortable, unhappy, or unfulfilled. For it is only in such moments, propelled by our discomfort, that we are likely to step out of our ruts and start searching for different ways or truer answers."

As much as we might complain, we are often all-too-comfortable with our ruts and our unhappiness. After all, as bad as our current situation may be, at least we know the terrain and rules. Scrum offers a way out, but it brings with it a new, unknown, unfamiliar way of working. When faced with the choice between the known and the unknown, we are often hesitant or even downright reluctant to change. It is not until immense pressure is applied, until our current rut itself becomes too painful, that we escape to a better future.

Getting people to take a chance on a Scrum project requires more than just a "Scrum is Good" campaign. It takes a healthy dose of persuasion, a steady increase in pressure, and a whole lot of patience.

## The Story

Ryan was an enthusiastic project manager working in the corporate IT department. Historically, he had a good track record, but his last project required a significant architecture change that caused a delay of nearly six months. By the time it ended, Ryan was ready to find a new way to work. Like many of his peers in the group, he was frustrated with his team's inability to deliver on time and with the high quality expected by the business. The problem was that Ryan had no idea how to make things better.

Ryan and his family had a two-week vacation planned at their cabin in Montana. Ryan decided that the two weeks would be best spent finding some new tools for his project manager's tool belt. He packed a suitcase full of books on project management. As he was about to zip up the bag, he saw a book that his boss, Steve, had given him several months ago, *Agile Project Management with Scrum* by Ken Schwaber. "Might as well throw this in too," Ryan thought and tossed it in the bag with the rest.

Ryan burned through the traditional project management books. He picked up a few tips, mainly on communication plans and risk management, but found nothing that would have prevented the architectural issue on his last project or any of the other problems his teams had been having. Reluctantly, he picked up Schwaber's book, grabbed a drink, and went out to the deck to read it.

His initial skepticism soon gave way to excitement. He could visualize the patterns in his work that directly related to the ones in the book, patterns around complexity and value-driven work. He also recognized truths that he had ignored on his past teams, such as actually building a team of people instead of using a collection of resources. The more Ryan read, the more interested he became. He closed the book later that afternoon with a great desire to learn more. He went immediately inside and ordered two more books on agile development, with next day shipping.

Ryan was not a workaholic, but the reading he had done sparked a passion. While his wife read the latest summer novels and his kids played soccer in the yard, he spent his time poring over books on lean, agile, XP, Kanban, and Scrum. Upon returning from his vacation, Ryan ran into Steve, the division manager who gave him the Scrum book, and an old friend.

"Steve, I've got great news!" Ryan exclaimed. "While I was in Montana, I read all these books and I think I have a solution to not only the problems I've been having with my projects but with all the project issues we have been having in our division!"

"That's a lot to get out of a few books, Ryan," said Steve, smiling. "But come on in and tell me about it."

Ryan and Steve spent the next three hours talking about everything Ryan had read. Then Ryan asked the question that had been in his mind the whole way back from Montana:

"You know the Michaelson project we have coming up?"

"Yes…" said Steve, with a hint of curiosity in his voice.

"Would you let me try this Scrum stuff on that project?" Ryan asked. "Remember that objective you laid down for the group to find a way to increase overall operational efficiency by 50 percent without increasing the overall group size? I think this is one way to help achieve that goal. And I think it can be done within this year like you had hoped."

Steve sat quietly for a minute, thinking, and then replied, "Ryan, I think you are right. The Michaelson project will be a good trial for this, and yes, it will help achieve my desire to increase overall efficiency without growing the overall size of the group."

"Great!" exclaimed Ryan. "My hunch was correct! Now can I…"

"Wait," Steve interrupted. "Now, don't get too excited. You don't know this, but when I worked at Megaco, I actually ran several Scrum projects with great success. I have managed large organizations and teams that have been able to get more than 50 percent efficiency, so I know this can work. Your biggest challenge will be getting started, which is more work than you realize, especially getting people on board with Scrum."

"So I can have a team to try this out?" asked Ryan.

"No," said Steve. "You can have the project, but you need to build your own team. I'll let management know what we are doing, but you need to recruit and build a team that is willing to work this way before I approve anything. I will support you any way you need me to, and you have free reign to do what you see fit, within reason, to get the project off the ground and the people on board. I will be your sponsor and will let the other senior managers know what we are doing. Remember, not everyone will have the enthusiasm you have for this, so tread lightly."

"I'll work on recruiting my team. I do have one last question for you," said Ryan. "If you knew about Scrum, why haven't you already introduced it or extreme programming to the group?"

Steve paused. "When I was at Megaco, I was very much like you. Enthusiastic, outgoing, very in-your-face with this agile stuff. I pushed it from the top down on my people there, and they reacted by rebelling. I eventually won most of them over, but not without a lot of hardship and attrition. That experience made me realize that this needs to be a bottom-up approach. I put the goal out there in the beginning of the year hoping someone would grab onto it and suggest an agile solution like Scrum or XP, or both."

Both Ryan and Steve sat there, letting this sink in.

"That makes sense" said Ryan. "I'll keep you posted on my progress."

"Remember, I'm here to help," said Steve. "As your sponsor for this effort, it's my job to help clear bigger issues and provide guidance. Don't be afraid to come to me for advice."

Ryan left excited, but a little worried about the idea of recruiting his own team. He spent a few days considering his approach.

The first person Ryan met with was Daniel, a developer in his mid-forties who had been at the company for more than 12 years. Daniel was methodical in his approach and very good, but lately had become cynical and vocally critical of the way the group was run.

"Daniel, I'd like to talk to you about a project I am starting. It's the Michaelson project and…" Ryan began.

"Why are you talking to me about this?" Daniel interrupted. "You should talk to my manager. He handles my time and will tell me what to work on next."

Ryan felt a little perturbed that he was cut off mid sentence but forged on.

"I can do that, Daniel. I thought I would talk to you first to see if there was even an interest before talking to Alan about this. Steve said it would be a good idea for me to talk to people directly to build the team and you…"

Ryan was cut off again.

"Steve? Our big boss Steve?" asked Daniel.

"Yes," said Ryan. "You see, this Michaelson project, it's a real interesting project. My idea is to use this project management framework called Scrum to run it. We'll use extreme programming practices like test-driven development and pair programming," Ryan said with exuberance.

"Pair what? Extreme Scrum? I don't get it," stated Daniel bluntly.

"Pair programming, you know, where two people work on the same code at once. And Scrum is a project management framework that allows us to…" said Ryan, before being cut off yet again.

"Ryan, listen. I hear you're a nice guy and all, but this isn't for me. I have no interest in this Scrum stuff, and I most certainly will not try pair programming or test whatever. Sorry, but no," said Daniel.

"But, Daniel, if you'd just listen, you'd be amazed at how..." Ryan started.

"Look, Ryan, I don't know how to be clearer. The answer is no. I'm not interested!" exclaimed Daniel.

Ryan left discouraged. Still, he had another chance at the one o'clock meeting he had scheduled with Meghan.

At one o'clock Ryan went to Meghan's office, but Meghan wasn't there. *Where is she?* Ryan wondered. He sat and waited in her office. She finally came in 15 minutes later and seemed surprised to see him sitting there.

Ryan greeted her, "Hi Meghan, I was just about to give up on you. I'm here because I wanted to talk to you about this new project I'm doing. We're going to use Scrum and..."

Meghan cut him off.

"Ryan, I need to come clean with you. Daniel has already warned me about what you want to talk about. I can already tell you I'm not interested. Honestly, I was kind of hoping you wouldn't be here if I was late. I hate saying no, but I'm not saying yes."

Ryan hung his head and sighed. Meghan relented.

"OK. Fifteen minutes."

Ryan got right to the point. He enthusiastically described what the project was about, the revelation he had over his vacation, and how Steve said he could build a team to do this work and try something new. He was very clear to emphasize that he had Steve's full support. It was approaching half past one.

"That's some good stuff, Ryan. I can see how it might work on a web project or something small, but the Michaelson project is huge! It requires a lot of architecture and design, which we need to do in the beginning to plan out the work. I don't think what you are proposing will work. And, I'm with Daniel, I don't want to pair program or do testing," said Meghan.

"It's not exactly testing. It's test-driven development..." Ryan began. Meghan quickly cut him off.

"Let me put it another way. I'm not doing this. Ever. It's not for me. It's not for our division. And if you want to keep your job, it shouldn't be for you either. There's no win for any of us in trying something so extreme," Meghan explained. "I'm sorry. I've got to go to my next meeting," she finished, getting up and leaving Ryan sitting in her office.

Ryan sat there for 15 minutes with his head in his hands, wondering why Meghan and Daniel were so resistant. What was he doing wrong?

By Friday, he had two more meetings with two different people. No luck. He went to see Steve later that afternoon to discuss his lack of progress.

"Ryan," Steve began, "I had a quick talk with Meghan and Daniel yesterday after you left. I've got some advice for you, as a friend. You can't be in-your-face with people. Let them come around the way you did, slowly. They need to read about it. Understand it. Have time to make up their minds. Give them books or some of those papers you read over your vacation. When people try new things, we have to gradually bring them around and give them time to get comfortable," said Steve.

"You're right, you're right," said Ryan. "I've gone about this the wrong way. I'm going to take your advice and take a step back. Gradually. Logically. Got it."

Ryan spent the next two weeks slipping Meghan and Daniel copies of chapters from his favorite books and research papers. He highlighted key parts and made notes on the copies as to why he liked them and how he thought those sections could apply to the team he was trying to build.

One Monday morning, Meghan dropped by his office.

"OK, Ryan," she began. "I'm starting to see your point. I'm willing to help with one condition. I've got kids and I cannot afford to lose my job, not in this economy. I'm really going out on a ledge here, and I need to be sure that Steve will see this through," said Meghan.

Ryan assured her that he would have Steve give her a call. Later that day he once again dropped by Steve's office. He updated him on his progress so far, adding that Meghan was willing to join the team but needed some reassurances from Steve before committing.

"I'll talk to her," said Steve. "So that's one. How are you going to convince everyone else?"

"Well, I did some research and it turns out we have two experts in XP here at the company, Jim and Ward. I asked them if they would be willing to have a discussion with our division about what this agile stuff is all about," said a nervous Ryan.

"Good idea," said Steve. "What do you need me to do?"

Thrilled that Steve liked the idea, Ryan laid out his plan for the talk. "At the discussion, I'd like you to be the first one to talk. Reiterate your goals for the division and then about what I'm trying to do. Sound OK?"

"Oh, absolutely!" said Steve, smiling.

Over the course of the next week, Ryan put up flyers around the building, set up the logistics, and gave Jim and Ward some background on the group. Meghan helped get the engineering people to commit and suggested to Ryan that they order lunch to ensure a crowd. "Free food is a strong incentive," she said.

The day of the meeting arrived at last. Ryan looked out at the crowd and smiled. More than 90 percent of the division had shown up, much more than he had expected. Steve spoke first, explaining the goals he was trying to meet and Ryan's effort to find better ways to build software systems. Then it was Ward and Jim's turn.

Most of the people in the room knew who they were and what they had accomplished. Ward and Jim spent a couple hours describing the principles, values, and practices of Extreme Programming. The audience listened attentively and had plenty of questions. Even after the talk had officially ended, nearly 50 people stayed on after lunch to talk more; it was three o'clock before the last person left. Through it all, Ward and Jim happily answered everyone's questions and provided gentle reassurance that Scrum and XP were just another way to approach software development—modern engineering practices, if you will. The last person to leave? Daniel. He approached Steve and Ryan.

"Well, I've got to say, these guys were pretty persuasive. I'm still not completely sold, but if Steve thinks this is important, I'm willing to do it on one condition," said Daniel.

"What's that, Daniel?" asked Steve.

"That if things go wrong, I won't take the fall," said Daniel, looking Steve in the eye.

"First of all, it's not *if* things go wrong, Daniel, it's *when*. My first clue that Scrum and XP are working will be when you fail—how could I blame the team for doing the right thing?" said Steve.

"I'm not following. What do you mean, *when* we fail?" asked Daniel.

"I'm talking about one of the best thing agile processes give teams—the ability to fail early. I know the team will mess up; what's important is *when* they mess up. If the team waits until the end of the project to fail, as has happened on our other projects, we're going to have all the same problems we've had before. On the other hand, if this team fails in the first three months and learns from it, the project has a much better chance of success. Ask Ryan. He wishes he had failed early on his last project because if he had known about his architectural issues sooner, he could have quickly fixed the problems and avoided all the end-of-project pain. Failing isn't the problem; failing late is.

"As far as taking the fall goes, I know that there will be stumbling blocks, and I'm willing to give you some leeway to figure out how to work in a new way, but I expect everyone on the team to be fully committed. You succeed—and fail—as a team," cautioned Steve.

"So it's all of us or none of us, and you *want* us to fail, as long as we do it early. Wow. I actually think I'm going to say yes," said Daniel. "I just need another month to figure it all out in my head—really it scares the bejeezus out of me."

"Me too," said Ryan.

This caught Daniel off guard.

"But Ryan, you're the guy pushing this crap. What do you mean it scares you?" asked Daniel.

"Are you kidding? I think it's the right thing to do, but that doesn't mean I'm not scared. I have a vision of how this can work, of how we can help achieve the goal laid out by Steve. But once we make this leap, like Steve says, we are in this together, as a team—succeed or fail, it's all on us," said Ryan.

"Well said, Ryan," said Steve.

"Let me noodle on this," said Daniel as he turned to walk back to his office.

"Not a bad showing today, Ryan. How do you feel?" asked Steve.

"This is so hard," said Ryan. "Getting these people to change their minds is excruciatingly tedious. I wanted to be up and running by now, but here we are, nearly four weeks into it, and I still don't have a team. It's pretty frustrating," said Ryan.

"Hang in there. Today was a great meeting for our division. People wanted to hear about this, and I think you made a lot of progress. Still, don't be surprised if there are people who won't change their minds, no matter what you do or say or give them to read," said Steve.

Over the next three months, Ryan worked with Meghan and Daniel, calming their fears and winning them over. They, in turn, won over a few more people to fill out the team. They were all surprised at the resistance from middle management, who were unsure how they would do performance reviews and monitor who was working on what if their people were on a cross-functional team. Steve was a big help with the managers, reassuring them that he had done this before and that those problems would work themselves out. Finally, after four months, the team was ready to start the project.

"Phew!" said Ryan to Steve over beers on a Friday night. "I finally did it."

"Now comes the hard part," said Steve. "You have to figure it all out, experiment, and learn."

"Oh, that'll be easy after these past four months," said Ryan.

"Sure it will, Ryan," said Steve with a smile. "Sure it will…."

## The Model

In this story we saw poor Ryan come off a large project that required an architectural change late in the project. Failing late had been an emerging trend of his group. Desperate for answers, he bought and read several books on project management that didn't tell him much he hadn't already tried. As a last resort, he read a book on Scrum, given to him by Steve, the head of the group. His initial skepticism gave way to excitement. He read more books on other agile practices. The more he learned, the more convinced he became that this was the way forward.

Convincing others proved much more difficult for Ryan. Ryan's peers met his newfound enthusiasm with fear, anger, and suspicion. One problem was that Ryan's last project did not inspire trust with his colleagues. Another obstacle was Ryan's delivery style. By almost attacking people with his zeal for Scrum, Ryan was making people feel defensive before they'd even had a chance to hear what he had to say.

Steve, Ryan's sponsor of this change effort, helped him realize it was his emotional method of persuasion that was alienating people. He advised Ryan to adopt a much slower, fact-based approach. He explained that while Ryan had the luxury of reading and thinking about Scrum for weeks before coming to a decision, he was expecting others to jump on the bandwagon on no more than his say-so.

In response, Ryan stopped his active campaign and took a gentler, but more time-consuming, approach. He handed out papers and chapters to give people the facts. He involved Steve as a vocal sponsor to help soothe people's fears and also to help them understand the need to make changes. Finally, he reached out within the company network to find reputable people to advocate an agile approach, so that it wasn't just his advice that people were taking. Even after all that, it was still several months before he had a full team ready to begin a new project.

Bringing people on board with Scrum, especially in a bottom-up manner, often takes time, persuasion, and patience.

# Change Takes Time

Change is hard. The status quo, as bad as it may be, is at least known. Venturing into the unknown requires quite a leap of faith. Ryan was able to make this leap because it was clear to him that the path he was on would only lead to more failure. Steve was willing to change because he had seen it work before.

Steve provided a clear vision: his desire to increase operational efficiency by 50 percent. Ryan had his own sense of urgency: He wanted to have more successful projects and feel better about his own job performance. Neither of them was sure how to accomplish their goals, but both were open to the possibilities inherent in a change to Scrum.

In a 1995 article in the *Harvard Business Review*, John Kotter [KOTTER] outlined an eight-step model for addressing change. A summary of that model is shown in the following list:

1. Establish a sense of urgency.
2. Form a powerful guiding coalition.
3. Create a vision.
4. Communicate the vision.
5. Empower others to act on the vision.
6. Plan for and create short-term wins.
7. Consolidate improvements and produce still more change.
8. Institutionalize new approaches.

Both Ryan and Steve were following (albeit unknowingly) some of Kotter's approaches. Let's look at some concrete steps we can take to help ease people's fears of what life will be like with Scrum.

## Establish a Sense of Urgency

Steve's goal was to get fifty percent more efficient without increasing the overall group size (e.g., adding people), and he wanted it done within the year. Steve issued it as a challenge to the division, encouraging them to find ways to make it happen. This was one of the contributing factors that prompted Ryan to look for ways to add to not only his own project management techniques but to the performance and delivery of the entire division as well.

To convince people to try something new, you need to give them a reason to make the change. Issuing a challenge or establishing a sense of urgency helps people understand why a change is necessary. Keep in mind, however, that the challenge must be reachable and the sense of urgency real. People will rise to a real challenge but will shrug off one that they perceive as impossible or false.

## Form a Powerful Guiding Coalition

A sponsor is a person in an organization who ultimately has the responsibility for the success of the project and for breaking down barriers and dysfunction within the organization. In our story, Steve was the sponsor. Steve had hoped that the division would turn to agile principles and practices but had also realized that the division would be resistant to a top-down implementation of Scrum. As a result, he decided to wait for someone to take his challenge of increasing operational efficiency, which would result in a bottom-up, grassroots approach. Once the grassroots movement began, Steve's job was twofold: Clear the path for Ryan and also work with middle management to help them understand what their roles would be. While Ryan was building his team, Steve was working behind the scenes to build a coalition of supporters that would ultimately enable Ryan to be successful in achieving his goal.

A good sponsor is someone in the organization who believes in the change and has the authority to work with the leadership team and the middle managers to communicate a vision, explain why it is important, and establish a timeline for effecting the change. The sponsor should also be able to help explain to managers what their roles will be in the new process and solicit their help in making it happen. When necessary, a sponsor should also intervene with potential saboteurs to alleviate their fears and concerns.

## Create a Vision/Paint a Picture of the Future

Before trying something new, people first need to understand what the future will look like and how they will fit. In our story, Ryan expected people to jump on board based only on his enthusiasm. He was forced to take a step back and take a different approach. He reminded people of Steve's goal, that they had been asked to ratchet up the output, and started educating them about the mechanisms he had found to achieve their goals: Scrum and XP. He also mined the company network for people who had tried Scrum and XP and achieved success. He found Jim and Ward, two distinguished people in the agile field who happened to work at his company. After a brief introduction about what he wanted to do, Ryan got Ward and Jim to come to his division to give a talk about XP. People stayed around after to talk about what they heard and began to visualize how a new approach might work for them.

## Communicate the Vision

There are many approaches you can take when introducing people to agile principles and practices. First, provide literature for them to read—books, white papers, research papers, and the like. They are a great way to help people understand what has been tried, what the issues are, and the successes and failures that others have had. This also helps separate your emotions from the data, enabling people to reach their own conclusions.

Not everyone learns by reading, though, so also consider social learning mechanisms. Create a book club, have brown bag lunch sessions where people in the group talk about a topic passionate to them, participate in webcasts and local user groups, and, of course, if other teams you know of are doing Scrum or XP, ask if you can watch their reviews or planning meetings.

Next, use your network. There are often people, both inside and outside our companies, who are very familiar with Scrum. Reach out to those in your local area and become genuinely interested in them. Invite them to present to your group about their experiences, how they got started, and techniques for success. Even if there are no experts in your local area, it's still helpful to bring in outsiders to share their stories. After all, we will often listen to someone we don't know and trust the words, even while disregarding people we *do* know, who are saying the same thing.

## Empower Others to Act on the Vision

Steve, as the direct manager of the group and Ryan's project sponsor, was also the creator of the vision and the one building the supporting coalition. As such, he was able to empower Ryan to do what needed to be done. His backing in effect gave Ryan a badge and a gun. Ryan asked for and was given the authority to find a project on which he could try the new process. The challenge for Ryan was assembling a team of willing participants. Steve's backing gave Ryan both credibility and also a foot in the door. From there, however, it was up to him to use influence to build his team.

Even after people were convinced that Scrum might be a good idea, they were still hesitant to commit. Meghan gave a bunch of excuses, but her real fear was that she would fail and lose her job. She had a good reputation and didn't want to lose it. The decision for Daniel, too, came down to whether or not he'd be successful. As the sponsor, make sure you clear the way for team members to address any issues that surface on the team or in the project. Reassure them that they can do what they need to do to resolve their own issues with impunity.

If, even with strong backing, people are reluctant to commit, consider offering them a trial run. In a trial run, the team would have a designated period of time (perhaps three months) in which they would agree to put forth their best effort. At the end of the trial, they could either continue with Scrum or walk away clean. Running a trial helps to remove the fear of the unknown, creating a comfort zone where people can try new things without repercussion.

A trial run can also be a way to prove to the team, the skeptics, and the rest of the organization that the new methodology doesn't just work in theory, but it works in practice, in this company, and on a specific type of project. It can also provide insights into things that don't work initially and how these challenges can be overcome. The data from a trial run can be used to help build a coalition of supporters. Over time, fear will be replaced with confidence.

## Plan for and Create Short-Term Wins

Scrum is designed to provide short-term wins. When transitioning teams to Scrum, help them understand that the potentially shippable product increment is not intended to highlight what they have yet to finish; on the contrary, it is to highlight what the team has accomplished and to get customer feedback. It is always better to fail early when the investment is small than it is to fail late when the investment is large. When showing working software always remember to be transparent and honest—be up front about both the good and the bad of the project and embrace the changes that are being made.

Short-term wins also help build the trust between the team and the stakeholders. Trust is fragile in the beginning. Showing working software, even small bits of it, will help increase the confidence of the team members and the stakeholders.

## Consolidate Improvements

Help people realize that they will not see a 100 percent increase in anything out of the gate; it takes time. Just as a weight lifter cannot expect to start with a 300-pound weight but must build up to it, teams can't expect to suddenly be powerful and strong. That kind of change will take training, practice, and time.

As the project progresses, new practices will become ingrained habits, making the work itself easier. At the same time, improvements will get harder and smaller. New champions of Scrum will emerge as people find the way they are working now to be a significant improvement.

## Institutionalize New Approaches

I like to think of institutionalized new approaches like a change in diet or exercise. At first it's painful. As you progress, though, you achieve short-term wins and get better and better by finding what works for you. Eventually you wonder how you ever did what you used to do as the new way just feels right. Agile approaches are no different.

As the consolidated improvements become commonplace, you and your teams will begin to wonder what it was like to work in a non-agile environment where you only shipped once a year. When this happens, ask these champions to spawn off and create new teams, further institutionalizing the framework across the organization.

# Keys to Success

Even when you do all the right things, winning people over is challenging. It took Ryan four months to build a team; it might take you just as long to bring people on board. It all depends on the culture of the company, the management, and of course, the people themselves. Bottom-up efforts take a while to spread. The most important keys to success are patience and information.

## Be Patient

One of the hardest things to do is let others come to a realization you've already reached. But as Steve learned at his former company, pushing a solution down people's throats is equally challenging. Plant the seeds but be willing to let them grow. People learn at different paces and using different styles. What convinced you may not work for everyone. Ask yourself, "How would I feel if someone was asking me what I am asking of them?" Often, your answer to this question will cause you to change your approach.

Find out what other people's triggers are. Listen when others explain that they don't understand, are afraid, or are reluctant to change. Ask questions designed to elicit answers that will allow you to uncover and address underlying concerns. Try not to let what you perceive as a lack of progress frustrate you. Things of great value take a fair amount of time.

## Provide Information

Ryan gave people highlighted chapters, research papers, and case studies to help prove his case. Be prepared to give your own colleagues some hard data to overcome their initial reluctance. Ryan also arranged for people to talk to trusted individuals who had succeeded with an agile approach. You should do the same. Training is another great option for helping open people's minds to a new way of thinking.

Remember that though our current rut is painful, most of us are unwilling to move unless we truly believe there is a better path. Your job is to clearly explain the alternative you are proposing and to wait patiently while people make up their minds. In the end, the only person you can control is yourself. Throughout the challenging process of getting people on board, keep your head up. You may hear no more often than yes. Stay focused. Stay positive. Stay strong. This is challenging stuff.

# References

[KOTTER]   Kotter, John P. "Leading Change: Why Transformation Efforts Fail." *Harvard Business Review.* 1995-03-01. Vol. 73, Iss. 2; p. 59.

# Chapter 3

# USING TEAM CONSULTANTS TO OPTIMIZE TEAM PERFORMANCE

In *The Fifth Discipline*, Peter Senge defined learning organizations as "organizations where people continually expand their capacity to create the results they truly desire, where new and expansive patterns of thinking are nurtured, where collective aspiration is set free, and where people are continually learning to learn together" [SENGE]. Creating a team structure where people can grow their skills while accomplishing business goals is a challenge.

Data tells us that the best team sizes are between five and nine people, all of whom are fully dedicated to a project for the duration of the project, and who work together in a cross-functional way to deliver working software at the end of every sprint. What many companies find, however, is that there aren't enough good people to go around. Creating one or two teams? Sure. Creating a whole company of fully cross-functional, dedicated teams? Much more difficult.

Some people have great skills but don't necessarily make good team members. Others are in such high demand that it's hard to hold them on one team for the length of the project. In light of these realities, how can you structure a team that is dedicated to the project, contains all the skills you need to get the job done, and provides opportunities for personal growth?

This was the problem facing Rebecca, a project manager at a large company. Her solution is one that has worked at many companies and in many situations. Implementing it, however, requires an open mind and a new way of looking at teams.

## The Story

Rebecca is a manager in a medium-sized (300+) software company. Today, like she does every single Friday, she is sitting in the resource planning meeting. And today, like they do every single Friday, the management team is reviewing what everyone is working on, which projects are coming up, and how to juggle key subject matter experts among competing projects. We join Rebecca in the middle of this meeting. She's bored and is passing the time doodling on her notepad. Through the haze of her doodling and the buzz that accompanies the business of shuffling people from project to project, it suddenly hits her. She will *never* have enough skilled people to create a dedicated team for her upcoming Cougar project. She stops doodling and begins to tune in. Just as she suspected, none of the people she wants are available for a dedicated team. What does that mean? It means she's either going to have to share a team with other projects or create a second-rate team that she can have all to herself.

"I just need to choose the lesser of the two evils," she decides. "That's probably a shared team. So what if the team is split across multiple projects? If I time it right, I can cherry-pick the skill players. I'd have an all-star team."

Rebecca starts to get excited about this option. Glancing at the schedule, she sees that the star developers and testers are each available for 20 hours per week during her project—and they can be all hers if she locks them in now. Just as she leans forward to speak up, she hears someone shuffling yet another person off one project to help save another. Rebecca sits back in her seat, recalling her Poodle project. On that project, she had Mark and Bill, who were supposedly fully dedicated to her project. Yet when push came to shove, they were *the only people* who could do certain work, so they got called off her team to help others. Eventually, their split time caused her project to slip. "That won't work, either," she concludes. "Even if I get my all-stars, in the end they will just be pulled off my project to help save others. That will leave me over budget, understaffed, and struggling to maintain quality."

"What other options do I have?" she wonders. She picks up her pen and begins doodling again. She begins to list the people she can get full time.

- Larry: great at databases but really bad at UI and not a great team player
- Joel: wonderful all around tester with some development background
- John and Randy: C# aficionados but lacking SQL skills
- Scott and Michelle: great data warehousing skills, but they tend to work best *together* and not as well with others

Those people would make a decent team, but they can't do everything the project needs. "Who else could I choose?" Rebecca wonders, looking up at the resource chart. "Nobody I'd want. The people who have the skills I need *and* are available full-time are not team players. They'd do more harm than good.[1] Rebecca tosses her pen on the table. No matter how she slices it, a dedicated team can't cover all the project needs.

Suddenly an idea comes to mind. "What if I can have both?" Rebecca's idea is simple, yet outside the mainstream for most companies. She picks up her pen and draws a big circle around her key players. "A core team," she muses. "I could have a core, dedicated team, supplemented with a pool of 'team consultants,'" she realizes. These team consultants would be company employees who don't work for any team full-time but instead are on call to supply the right skills at the right time. This could work. The only problem is that the company currently doesn't have that pool of team consultants. That's a problem she can solve. She speaks up in the meeting.

---

1. See Chapter 21, "When Cultures Collide," for an example of a team member who does more harm than good.

"Everyone, I apologize for interrupting, but I'm noticing a recurring trend. During the last 30 minutes, we've had to move seven people from their currently assigned project to another project in distress. Why? Because they are the *only* people that we believe are capable of doing a particular task. I agree that they have special skills, but where does moving them leave their original projects? It leaves those projects in the lurch and in danger of needing saving a week or two from now. That's where. And will moving them work to save the troubled projects? The truth is, we don't know, but the game we've been playing has likely been creating the troubled projects more than fixing them." A heavy silence follows Rebecca's words as every head turns to look at her.

"What other solutions do we have?" asked Rebecca's boss, Dave. "Shifting people around is the only way to manage the work we have."

Rebecca looked down at her half-baked idea, sketched among a bunch of doodles. She forged on, unable to pass up the opportunity Dave's question presented.

"Well, I was thinking. The most successful projects I have ever run have had a dedicated team..."

"That's impossible here," interrupted Dave.

"I know. Hear me out," said Rebecca. "Traditionally, dedicated teams have all the personnel they need to be successful, from developers and testers to designers and architects. I'm not asking for that. I'm suggesting that what I need is a dedicated *core* team. They can do most of the day-to-day work. For those special times when we need a SQL expert or an architect or a UI designer, I'd pull from a pool of specialists who aren't assigned to any one team. A pool of internal consultants that we could *all*..." she gestured around the room, "utilize as needed. They'd act as consultants to the core team. In the short term, they would do, or help the team do, the specialized tasks that the core team isn't comfortable doing. Over the long term, if we use pairing and coaching correctly, the core team members can pick up new skills and take on more work themselves. We accomplish our business goals while working toward our cultural goal of being a learning organization."

Dave shook his head. "Rebecca, I appreciate your effort in trying to solve this problem, but I really don't think it will work. We have a very complex organizational structure. We need to keep our organization matrixed so we can solve issues like that when they come up on our projects. This 'team consultant' role you are talking about just seems like it is not going to work. How will I manage their time? What guarantee can you make that these problems won't keep happening?"

Rebecca thought for a moment. Dave didn't seem averse to the idea as much as unsure of why it would work and how he would manage it. She thought of an analogy that she knew would speak to everyone.

"OK, everyone—question—have you ever had your house remodeled or had a new house built?" she asked. Over half of the 40 people in the room raised their hands. "Now, how many of you were completely satisfied with your general contractor? How many of you had contractors who showed up on time and delivered what they promised?"

Everyone laughed, but no one raised their hand.

"Yep. That's what I thought. Sad, right? OK. Now how many of you have used that same contractor again after your initial experience?" Rebecca asked, eyebrows raised.

Again, no hands.

"Nobody? Why not?" she asked.

A barrage of answers came out.

"They broke our trust." "They would show up late or not at all." "They didn't return our calls in a timely fashion." "I felt like I had to hound them to get our work done." "They were constantly full of excuses like 'the person to do the tiling is on another job today.'" The list went on and on.

"Right. I hear you. Now, how many of you have since hired specialists (maybe people you met through your general contractor) to do a job?" Rebecca continued.

"I have," said Ian. "The tile guy. He's great. He shows up when he says, always calls me back, and is very good at his craft. In fact, he just went out on his own as an independent."

Rebecca asked, "Do you think that being on his own makes him more accountable to you?"

"Absolutely," said Ian. "His reputation is at stake. All his business is by referral. I have sent him to all my neighbors for work and they love him, too."

"Does he manage his own time?" asked Rebecca.

"Well, he sure better. He's the one making the commitments to his customers, and he's the one doing the work. I trust him to manage his time," said Ian.

"That is a key point, Ian," said Rebecca. "For people to be able to follow through on their work, to be fully committed, they have to make the commitment for themselves. In this meeting, this resource planning meeting, what are we doing? We are making commitments for *resources*, people other than ourselves. We are juggling them around like pawns, not considering their time, their previous commitments, or their interests. We are simply looking at their skills and applying them to projects that are in urgent need of those skills. Worse, we don't trust them enough to allow them to do it themselves."

She glanced around the room again, "Everyone, we're acting like general contractors, and we're surprised when it doesn't work. Our customers trust us to deliver on time, on budget, and with the quality they expect. What's going to happen if we don't meet their expectations?"

"We lose our customers," said a voice from the back.

"Right, we lose our customers!" exclaimed Rebecca. "To please our customers, we need to have employees that are vested in the projects. The best way for us to do this is to have them sign up for work and manage their own schedules. We've said we want to be a learning organization, a company filled with empowered employees who are cross-trained and satisfied with their work. This model seems like a way to please our customers by delivering what they need when they need it. At the same time, it gives us a way to foster happy employees who want to stay with the company long term."

Dave was becoming visibly flustered. "Rebecca, you can't be serious. Our delivery teams are not capable of managing their own schedules. That's why we have resource managers."

"No, Dave, we have resource managers because we are, how did you say it, a highly matrixed organization and don't push accountability or commitment to the people doing the work. The structure we have in place makes it too much of a challenge and far too bureaucratic for our people to try to manage their own time; that's why we created the resource manager role. Ian's tile guy went out on his own because he was able to manage his time and bring in work for himself. He made commitments based on his schedule and his skill set. We don't see Ian committing his tile guy to install windows. Sure, he might be able to install a window if he really needed to, but what he does best is tile, so that's the service he sells. We have people in our company who are great generalists—they love doing a little bit of everything—and we have people in our company who are very specialized—great at database design and object-oriented design patterns or fantastic at system and network design. They like their specializations and want to focus on them. Our problem is we are managing everyone's time for them. When we do that, if teams fail to deliver, they can blame us because we are the ones telling them what to do. They are not accountable to their projects; they are just executing work—and we don't enable them to do their best work because we hold them back," said Rebecca.

Dave seemed at a loss for words.

Rebecca went in for the kill, "Dave, tell you what, let me run an experiment on the Cougar project. Give me license to approach a few people about being part of a core team that is fully dedicated to the project. If they agree to work together and with me, we'll then sit down and identify some candidates to be our team consultants. I want to be able to tell everyone that we have your support in creating a hybrid team of core members and a few people who will float between projects. In return, we'll keep you and the rest of management well informed of how this trial is going."

Before Dave could object, Jim, the director of the group, spoke up.

"Rebecca," said Jim, "I'm going to let you try this. Two caveats: You will work in our customers' best interests, and you will be a test bed for the rest of the company." He looked at Dave. "She's right. Too many hours are wasted in this meeting and too many people are shuffled from project to project. This problem has to stop, and this is the best solution I've heard to date. Rebecca, let me know what you need to make this a success."

With that, Rebecca had what she needed to implement the model that started out as a doodle born of boredom and desperation. Let's explore it below.

## The Model

In the story we saw Rebecca dealing with frustration inside her company. She was able to implement a solution for her team that eventually spread through the entire company: the use of team consultants.

A team consultant is someone in your organization who is available for some amount of work and directly fills a skill gap between the team and the project. Team consultants are not core team members. They have no team, per se. They choose instead to offer up their services as internal "guns for hire," providing specific expertise as needed. Team consultants often work for multiple teams and are typically very specialized, so specialized in fact that they might not make good core team members. That doesn't mean the team consultants hoard their knowledge, though. As part of a learning organization, team consultants help others by teaching, giving advice, coaching—whatever the team needs during a sprint. And the team consultants grow, too, learning how to work as part of a cross-functional team and how to share their expertise with others.

Though team consultants occasionally may be booked for the length of the project, they typically will not work full-time on that project. They are hired specifically to solve an immediate problem or to contribute a limited number of hours per sprint. The core team, on the other hand, is made up of team members whose time is fully dedicated to the project. Collectively, they are responsible for delivery of the work. They are a cross-functional team who work on only one project, eliminating context switching and multitasking.

Just as a Scrum team doesn't have to take on all the work proposed by the product owner, a team consultant does not have to work for every team that asks. However, team consultants should make these go/no-go decisions within the context of business priorities, personal availability, and technical expertise.

Implementing the team consultant model is a two-part process: establishing a team consultant pool and building your team. If you are limiting your implementation to a one-team trial, however, you can skip the first part until you decide to scale the model throughout your organization.

## Establishing a Team Consultant Pool

Establishing a pool of available team consultants is easier than it may seem. It involves these two steps:

Step 1.    Develop and communicate a transition plan.

Step 2.    Give people the choice between being team consultants and core team members.

### Step 1: Develop and Communicate a Transition Plan

The first thing you need to do is develop a transition plan that includes the reason for the change, the vision of the future, and the path to achieving your goals.

- Detail the common problems that you are experiencing within your organization.
- Communicate a shared vision as to why it is important to create a learning organization.

- Help people understand that their roles are not going away; on the contrary, they are being enhanced.
- Reinforce the fact that now, more than ever, individual and team commitments drive customer satisfaction and, ultimately, business success.

The next thing you need to do is ask people to sign up as either team consultants or core team members by a certain date, which brings us to *Step 2: Let People Choose*.

## Step 2. Let People Choose

The person in the best position to determine whether he or she should be a core team member or a team consultant is the person doing the work. Communicate the differences in the two roles, perhaps even posting a table like Table 3-1 that lists the benefits and downsides of each role.

Team consultants will work on multiple projects and will need to manage their time accordingly. Team consultants often choose this role because they are passionately dedicated to their crafts. These people have been working in their subject matter for so long that they are the "go-to" people for certain types of work.

Signing up to be a team consultant, however, does not mean that you get to practice your craft without helping others. On the contrary, whenever possible, team consultants should work to bring up the skills of the entire organization. This is easier in some areas than others. For instance, we would not expect to see a graphic designer teaching design elements to a ten-year veteran of infrastructure projects, but we would expect to see a SQL expert helping out a core team member who has some SQL skills but needs to learn more to be most effective in her current project. Team

**TABLE 3-1    Roles, Benefits, and Downsides**

|  | NATURAL FIT | BENEFITS | DOWNSIDES |
|---|---|---|---|
| TEAM CONSULTANT | • SOFTWARE ARCHITECTS<br>• DESIGNERS AND UI<br>• TECHNICAL WRITERS<br>• DEEP TECHNICAL EXPERTS<br>• DEVELOPMENT MANAGERS<br>• SOFTWARE LEADS | • FOCUS ON ONE CRAFT<br>• REMAIN LONE WOLF<br>• ACHIEVE SATISFACTION OF HELPING OTHERS LEARN YOUR SPECIALITY<br>• BECOME A LEADER IN ONE SPECIALTY<br>• MANAGE ONE'S OWN COMMITMENTS | • MAY NEVER SEE THE FRUITS OF LABOR IN FINISHED PROJECT<br>• NOT MUCH OPPORTUNITY TO LEARN NEW SKILLS<br>• MUST PROVIDE GOOD SERVICE OR MAY QUICKLY BECOME OVERHEAD |
| CORE TEAM MEMBER | • MULTI-TALENTED PROGRAMMERS OR TESTERS<br>• INDIVIDUALS WHO WANT TO GROW THEIR SKILLS<br>• PEOPLE WHO LIKE WORKING ON ONE PROJECT AT A TIME | • CAN FOCUS ON ONE PROJECT THROUGHOUT LIFECYCLE<br>• LEARN NEW SKILLS AS PART OF CROSS-FUNCTIONAL TEAM<br>• HELP MAKE OTHERS BETTER BY TEACHING THEM A NEW APPROACH<br>• ALLOWS A PERSON TO GROW PROFESSIONALLY AND TECHNICALLY | • MUST BE ABLE TO WORK WELL AS A TEAM MEMBER<br>• NOT A GOOD FIT FOR PRIMA DONNAS |

consultants also are not there to tell the team how to do the work. Instead, they advise and influence the team as to which direction to take. Consultants work alongside the team but provide leadership as well.

A typical week for a team consultant with a technical background includes coding, code reviews, documenting, solving technical problems the team is stuck on, providing architectural guidance, or doing anything else that the team asks. For creative services like graphic design and technical writers, the time will likely be spent with the team and/or product owner, reviewing the items needed. Technical writers especially need to be aware of the "done" criteria for the team and help the team deliver all required documentation each sprint.

It is up to the team to schedule the time directly with the team consultant and to make sure the work is queued when the consultant arrives. If a team consultant overbooks herself on too many projects, it's up to that person to fix the situation. The benefit the team consultants see is that they can stay focused on their core skills and that they can be instrumental in teaching others, thereby growing and building the company while raising the bar across the board.

The people that make up the core team, on the other hand, are skilled in multiple areas. They are not expected to be experts; in fact the team is designed to provide cross-functional balance of expertise. Like a team consultant, a core team member is responsible for his or her own time, but all this time is dedicated to one team and one project. Core team members can stay focused on a single project throughout its life cycle and can learn new skills by working hand-in-hand with other core team members and team consultants.

The ability to stay with one team and project yet learn new skills is an advantage that should not be downplayed. Two of the biggest complaints I hear at companies around the world are

- I have to split my time.
- I never learn new things.

As a result, people look elsewhere for better opportunities.

On a cross-functional Scrum team, core team members continually learn new skills and are able to stay focused on a single project. As such, the business profits by having a stable workforce that is continually learning, enabling the business to remain competitive and responsive to change.

## Building Your Team

Whether you choose to first build a companywide pool of consultants or are just trying out the model on a small scale, the first thing to consider when building a team are the skill sets you need for the project. If you are not technical enough to do this, ask for help from a colleague familiar with the project. After you've identified the technical skills, you should also consider softer competencies, such as communication skills, open-mindedness, and the ability to be a team player. These are often much harder to determine but are vital to success. The list looks something like the one shown in Figure 3-1.

Once you have listed the skills and competencies you are looking for, begin identifying the people you have to choose from and map them to your wish list. Include their availability as well. Rank each individual on a scale of one to five stars. Remember, there is nothing absolutely quantitative about this; it is purely subjective. You might want to ask for help with this, just for the added perspective a second opinion can add to the process. The resulting chart, as shown in Figure 3-2, will be customized to your own people and requirements; it's a more formalized version of the analysis Rebecca, from the story, did on the fly.

| COMPETENCIES | SKILLS | AVAILABILITY |
|---|---|---|
| TEAM PLAYER | C# | |
| GOOD COMMUNICATOR | SQL | |
| CUSTOMER FACING | AJAX | |
| COMFORT WITH CONFLICT | | |
| OPEN MINDED (WILLING TO LEARN) | | |

**FIGURE 3-1** Sample list of competencies, skills, and availability

| | LARRY | JOHN | RANDY | SCOTT | MICHELLE | DAVID | MICHAEL | STEFAN |
|---|---|---|---|---|---|---|---|---|
| ROLE IN COMPANY | DEV | DEV | TEST | TEST | DEV | DEV | ARCH | ARCH |
| **COMPETENCIES** | | | | | | | | |
| TEAM PLAYER | *** | ***** | *** | ***** | ***** | * | * | ***** |
| GOOD COMMUNICATOR | ** | ***** | * | *** | ** | ** | **** | ***** |
| CUSTOMER FACING | | ** | * | | | ***** | ** | ***** |
| COMFORT WITH CONFLICT | *** | ** | * | ** | ** | ** | ***** | ** |
| OPEN MINDED (WILLING TO LEARN) | ***** | | * | ***** | ***** | ** | *** | ** |
| **SKILLS** | | | | | | | | |
| C# | ** | **** | ***** | | ** | ** | ***** | ** |
| SQL | ***** | ** | | ***** | ***** | ***** | ** | ***** |
| AJAX | | *** | | | | | | **** |
| USER INTERFACE DESIGN | | | *** | ** | *** | ***** | * | *** |
| ARCHITECTURE | * | ***** | | * | ** | *** | ***** | ***** |
| DATA MODELING & ETL | | | | ** | ***** | *** | * | *** |
| AVAILABILITY | *** | ***** | * | *** | ***** | ** | *** | ** |

**FIGURE 3-2** A subjective analysis of potential team members

## Core Team

Let's say Figure 3-2 is the chart that Rebecca creates following her meeting. Looking at Figure 3-2, you can see right away that both John and Michelle are very available and together they bring three key skills to the table: architecture, SQL, and data modeling. In addition, they are both considered good team players. As it happened, Rebecca's project is heavy in SQL work, so though Michelle has SQL skills, Rebecca decides she will need even more help in that area. Looking at her other SQL people, Rebecca circles Larry and Scott; they are both marginally available but can probably become full-time members. Her prospects for the dedicated team are John, Michelle, Larry, and Scott, as shown in Figure 3-3.

## Team Consultants

As you can see by looking at Figure 3-3, Rebecca's core team does not cover the entire set of skills needed for this project. Once you have formed your core team, meet as a group to determine your own strengths, weaknesses, and gaps in project coverage. If you find you have gaps in skill coverage, it's time to consider which team consultants you might be able to utilize.

Have the team reach out to individuals in the team consultant group (or in the organization as a whole if you do not yet have a dedicated pool of team consultants) who meet those needs and who they feel would work well with the team on a limited basis. Let's say that Rebecca's team gets a commitment from Michael to be available for C# code reviews and some pairing help on APIs the team was not sure about. The team also asks David and Stefan to be consultants for user interface and Ajax, respectively. The final team chart looks like the one in Figure 3-4. Notice how the team consultants close the core team's coverage gaps.

## Size Matters

We all have this inherent understanding that teams that are smaller in size tend to produce faster. Adding people comes with the additional cost of ramp-up time. In the *Mythical Man Month*, Fred Brooks put out the principle known as Brooks' Law: "Adding manpower to a late software project makes it later" [BROOKS]. But is this always the case?

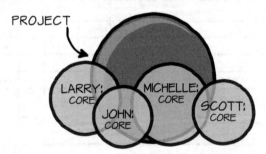

**FIGURE 3-3**   The core team can't cover the entire project

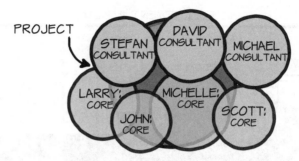

**FIGURE 3-4**   The team consultants fill the voids on the project

In a 1999 article, Steve McConnell suggests that "controlled projects are less susceptible to Brooks' Law than chaotic projects," because people can be safely added due to better tracking, documentation, and design [MCCONNELL]. However, even McConnell acknowledges that every project reaches a point when adding people becomes counterproductive. This then begs the question—how big should a core team be and how many consultants should it have?

A study done by Lawrence H. Putnam and Ware Myers in 1998 investigated team size [PUTNAM]. Their findings were published in the Cutter Consortium in 1998. Putnam and Myers looked at 491 medium-sized projects, those with between 35,000 and 95,000 "new or modified" source lines of code. All were information systems and were completed between 1995 and 1998 (the last three years prior to publishing).

What they confirmed was that smaller teams of five to seven not only delivered in less time (see Figure 3-5), but that there was a significant increase in effort when team sizes reached nine or more (see Figure 3-6).

When working with team consultants, the right team size should be four-to-six core team members, allowing you to add between one and three consultants while

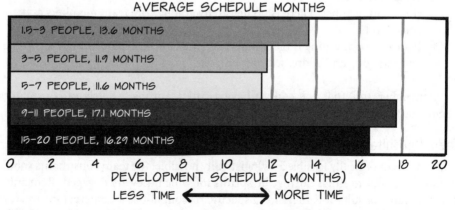

**FIGURE 3-5**   Average schedule months—smaller takes less time

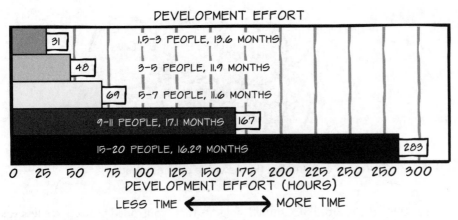

DEVELOPMENT EFFORT

| | |
|---|---|
| 31 | 1.5–3 PEOPLE, 13.6 MONTHS |
| 48 | 3–5 PEOPLE, 11.9 MONTHS |
| 69 | 5–7 PEOPLE, 11.6 MONTHS |
| 9–11 PEOPLE, 17.1 MONTHS | 167 |
| 15–20 PEOPLE, 16.29 MONTHS | 283 |

0   25   50   75  100  125  150  175  200  225  250  250  300
DEVELOPMENT EFFORT (HOURS)
LESS TIME ⟵⟶ MORE TIME

**FIGURE 3-6**   Exponential development effort growth when team size increases beyond eight

still keeping the team sized correctly. Remember, consultants will come and go, but the core team should remain the same.

## Core Teams Working with Team Consultants

Once you've built a team of core members and consultants, you need to establish guidelines to encourage teamwork. The specific guidelines vary from organization to organization but should include the following:

- During the course of the sprint, the team and team consultants are jointly and equally responsible for delivering on their commitments.
- Team consultants should show up on time, be part of daily meetings whenever possible, and conduct themselves as team members for the length of the sprint.
- Team consultants are experts in one area but otherwise no different than a core team member. There is no hierarchy among core team members and consultants.
- If anyone or anything is blocking a task, the task should be brought up at the daily standup and addressed immediately.

Remember, too, that you cannot have a core team made solely of consultants. The majority of the team should be dedicated to the project from beginning to end.

## Team Consultants and Meetings

Whenever economically feasible and logistically possible, the team consultants should attend all Scrum meetings during the sprints for which they are engaged. Remember that the team consultant is there for a specific reason, not as an emergency overflow person. Consultants have specific tasks for the sprint, whether that is to do the work directly, help the other team members do the work themselves, or both. As such, they should be able to report on progress in a daily meeting and should have input into planning and reviews.

- **Planning meetings**—Having the consultants at the planning meetings can add a new level of expertise. If the team is estimating and comes across a story that it is not as familiar with as the team consultant, the consultant's input would be beneficial.
- **Daily Scrum meetings**—Having consultants in the room helps drive awareness and keeps them up to speed on how the project is progressing.
- **Sprint review meetings and retrospectives**—Having the consultants in the room in the review meeting shows the customer everyone who is working on the project, both full time and as a consultant. Having them in the retrospective is beneficial because they get a better understanding of team dynamics, but remember that the time they spend in the retrospective comes out of the total availability pool they have.

If budgetary or time constraints make sprint meeting attendance impossible, the team should work with the product owner to decide how best to spend the consultant's time. If a consultant is only available for eight hours during a sprint and the tasks he is being asked to commit to will take the full eight hours, it might be more valuable to the team and product owner to get more work done than to have the consultant in the sprint meetings. On the other hand, the team and product owner might choose to dial back a consultant's tasks to have him be a part of the day-to-day sprint activities. Whatever you decide to do with regard to meetings, the core team, Scrum-Master, consultants, and product owner all need to be aware of the commitments and arrangements made between the team consultants and the core team.

# Keys to Success

Using team consultants can be a good idea not only because it fills skill gaps, but also because it creates an environment where one's job stability is directly related to the work done with and for others. In our story, Rebecca compared the team's ability to hire (and fire) consultants to a homeowner's ability to hire an independent contractor to make repairs to a house. Homeowners hire specialized people, who they know or suspect are good at their job. The contractors work hard to please those homeowners so that they get referrals and repeat business. Having team consultants enables teams to follow a similar model.

## Accountability

Accountability is a strange thing. While it is not something that can be mandated or managed, we still try. Take Dave from our story. His matrixed solution assumed that people could not self-organize. Rebecca's, on the other hand, pushed the responsibility for managing one's time down to the individual. In Scrum, the people who estimate the work do the work. The same philosophy applies here—the people who do the work commit to the work, whether they are team consultants or core team members. Team consultants are accountable to the people they sign up to do work for. Core team members are accountable to each other and to the team consultants as well.

One of the keys to making this model work is the self-monitoring and balance of accountability. As you can imagine, this model quickly identifies low or nonperformers. For instance, let's imagine that Larry is a team consultant. Larry frequently commits to teams but either fails to deliver on time or turns in low-quality work. The end result is that Larry does not have many teams willing to work with him, either because his reputation precedes him or because they have worked with him before. If someone like Larry is allowed to continue at the company despite his poor track record, it would be demotivating for the other team consultants and for the core team members who would be forced to work with him. The better course of action is to treat him like the unnecessary overhead he has become and remove him from the payroll.

Identifying people who are underperforming, though painful, enables corrective action—underutilized consultants will either choose on their own to improve their performance or leave the company or they will be forced by management to make changes or make tracks. To ensure that they remain relevant and employed, team consultants should seek out feedback on how they are doing, their contributions to their teams, and the value they are adding. In the end, with companies constantly striving to become more efficient and productive, reducing overhead and trimming fat is a good thing.

## Experiment

For this model to succeed it must have management support. By management support I mean that the middle and senior managers not only realize they want an effective organization but that they have the courage to actually do something about it. To get management and individual contributors to get a feel for this model, try it out on a small scale, like Rebecca did in our story. Choose your core team and determine which experts will be needed. Gain their commitment and let them know approximately when their expertise will be needed. If, when the time comes for them to work with the team, they are unable to because a manager has committed the experts (consultants) to work with another team, you will need management to be willing to step in and solve the conflict. These types of blocking issues will be common as an organization moves toward adopting team consultants. Eventually the team's ScrumMaster will be able to remove that sort of impediment, but during a test run, the ScrumMaster might not have enough authority or influence to make things happen.

## Be Cautious of Overloading

When I first help companies implement this model, we notice that the team consultants have a tendency to overcommit—after all, optimism is on their side. The threshold for overloading seems to be crossed when a consultant takes on the fourth project. Three is OK. Four is usually too many. If you see consultants sign up for more than three projects, warn them that they need to leave some availability and flexibility for the teams they are servicing. There is nothing worse for a team than being stuck or needing guidance on a project and having a consultant who does not have time to address it until next sprint. This is a blocking issue that a ScrumMaster will need to address.

## Plan for Potential Downtime

There will be times in the ebb and flow of projects when team consultants and core teams both go idle. Since we have been trained to be at 100 percent utilization, and suddenly we are not, management might push to break up a team, forcing its members into potential team consultancy, or worse, to go back to the way things were and have specialists do specific jobs on projects and then move on to the next specific job. Don't let them do it. Take a cue from contractors: Keep a few small projects in reserve for slow times—projects that never seem to get done because something else is more important. When downtime happens, feed teams and team consultants those projects to work on until the timing is right to take on another large job.

## Team Consultants Are Not a Replacement for Dedicated Teams

Some might look at this model and think that it circumvents Scrum's call for dedicated, cross-functional teams. It does not. What it does do is provide teams and companies the flexibility to stay within the boundaries of Scrum by having a dedicated, cross-functional team while enabling that team to call on experts, team consultants, to help out as identified and needed *by the team*. It is not the job of a resource manager or an executive to randomly assign people to the team; that will not work. It is the job of the team members to determine and manage their schedules. If you start to see "teams" of consultants, ones in which there are only one or two core team members, the dedicated, cross-functional team has been lost. Remind the business of the importance of an actual core team supplemented by consultants and reboot.

Having a dedicated team with all the skills necessary to get the project completed is ideal. But most teams will, at some point in the project, find themselves wishing for a particular expertise. If you have internal people who can fill this gap on a temporary basis, bring them in to the project. If your organization does not have team consultants who can fill the gaps, you may want to bring in external consultants for limited engagements. A team consultant can sometimes score a lot of points for a project that might otherwise struggle with a skill gap.

# References

[BROOKS]    Brooks, F. P., Jr. 1995. *The Mythical Man-Month*, anniversary ed. Reading, MA: Addison-Wesley.

[MCCONNELL]    McConnell, Steve. Personal website. http://www.stevemcconnell.com/ieeesoftware/eic08.htm (accessed on 2 January 2011).

[PUTNAM]    Putnam, L., and W. Myers. 1998. "Familiar Metric Management: Small Is Beautiful-Once Again." http://www.qsm.com/sites/www.qsm.com/themes/diamond/docs/fmm_28.pdf.

[SENGE]    Senge, P. M. 1990. *The Fifth Discipline*. New York: Doubleday/Currency.

# Works Consulted

Pedler, M., Burgogyne, J., and Boydell, T. 1997. *The Learning Company: A Strategy for Sustainable Development, 2nd Ed.* London: McGraw-Hill.

O'Keeffe, T. 2002. "Organizational Learning: A New Perspective." *Journal of European Industrial Training*, 26 (2), pp. 130–141.

## Chapter 4

# DETERMINING TEAM VELOCITY

Software teams are a bit like cars in that you can measure their economy in terms of efficiency. Cars measure efficiency in terms of fuel economy, how far a car can travel per unit of gasoline. Teams, on the other hand, measure their efficiency in terms of how much work they can complete over a certain period of time. This measure is commonly known as velocity and is typically expressed in terms of story points. Simply put, velocity is the average number of story points a team completes per sprint, as defined by the team's done criteria. (Read more about done criteria in Chapter 7, "How Do We Know When We Are Done?")

I say that teams are a *bit* like cars because they are mostly *unlike* cars. Teams do not come packaged with a manufacturer's estimate of velocity. Teams, therefore, must predict with some degree of confidence what their future velocities might be. And, while we can easily compare two cars' fuel efficiencies, we cannot (and should not) compare the efficiency of two teams based on their relative velocities. That's because while miles per gallon (or kilometers per liter) is an objective, standardized measure, velocity depends on each team's own subjective estimates. So while we can sometimes use another team's velocity to give us a starting point for what our future velocity might be, we cannot say that one team in a company is somehow more efficient because it has a higher velocity than another team. The teams might just estimate differently.

As you have likely experienced, predicting velocity is a difficult task, especially for teams that are new to each other and new to an agile framework. Let's visit one Scrum team and see how it dealt with this complex issue.

## The Story

Wendi was the ScrumMaster for a new team. The team was excited to start its first Scrum project, but was stymied by how to give management even a ballpark figure for how much work they could accomplish and by when.

Wendi asked the team for suggestions. One team member, Paul, who was visibly frustrated, started the discussion, "How are we supposed to give them velocity estimates before we've even started our first sprint? What are we supposed to do? Just point at a random spot on the product backlog and say here's how far we'll get? That seems irresponsible. Making wild 'guess-timates' is what has gotten us into so much trouble in the past. Scrum was supposed to be different."

"I agree, Paul, but can you image what would happen if we tell them we have no idea? That we'll just let them know when we figure it out?" asked his teammate

Freddie. "The reality is, if we don't give them some kind of number, they will do it for us—'Here's your goal. Hit it.' We've all been down that road before."

"I wish we had some historical data," mused Ignacio. "I talked to a friend of mine who is running a Scrum project. His team looked at their past velocities on other projects and used those numbers as a starting point for a new project. I thought about using his data to help predict our velocity, but dismissed the idea because even though our team is somewhat similar to his, we're also very different. Our team is new, we've never used Scrum before, and our project has some complicating factors. I don't know how to account for all the variances."

They all looked at Wendi.

Paul asked, "So what are we going to do?"

Wendi went up to the whiteboard and wrote down the three ideas that had been proposed and rejected:

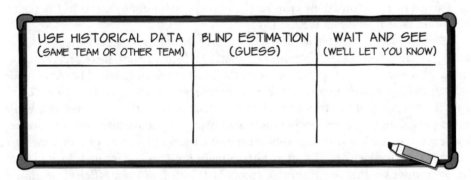

| USE HISTORICAL DATA (SAME TEAM OR OTHER TEAM) | BLIND ESTIMATION (GUESS) | WAIT AND SEE (WE'LL LET YOU KNOW) |
|---|---|---|
| | | |

"I know, Freddie, that your suggestion to tell them, 'we'll let you know when we figure it out,' was more tongue in cheek than anything. But I'd like us to consider it as a viable option," Wendi explained. "So that leaves us with three options. All are problematic, but it looks like we've got to choose one of them. So, let's spend some time looking at them," suggested Wendi. "Maybe if we brainstorm some positives and negatives, we can figure out what the best solution will be. Let's start with historical data. Call out some positives and negatives."

As the team brainstormed answers, Wendi filled in the chart she had begun on the whiteboard.

| USE HISTORICAL DATA<br>(SAME TEAM OR OTHER TEAM) | |
| --- | --- |
| POSITIVES | NEGATIVES |
| • GIVES US A DATA POINT WE CAN START WITH<br><br>• IS USED BY OTHER TEAMS | • WE ARE A NEW TEAM<br><br>• WE DON'T HAVE DATA OF OUR OWN<br><br>• WE ARE DEALING WITH SOMEWHAT NEW TECHNOLOGY<br><br>• DATA MAY NOT MAP TO OUR ACTUAL VELOCITY ONCE WE START |

"Good," said Wendy. "Let's discuss this a bit before we move on to the next section."

"I'll go first," said Ignacio. "We are a new team so we don't have data of our own. Ideally, we'd pull data from a similar team in the company, but I don't know of any."

"Yep," agreed Paul. "I can't think of any teams that we can use as an example either. Most aren't doing Scrum at all. Those that are using Scrum are either just getting started like us or their project is too different from ours."

"We could look at my friend's team," suggested Ignacio. "But with him being at a different company, it feels like a stretch."

Freddie nodded. "I just don't think this one will work for us. If we had been working together for a long time, and could use our own historical data, I think it'd be OK, but to grab some random team's numbers and use them as our estimate really scares me."

Everyone nodded in agreement.

"I think we all agree that historical data has far more negatives than positives. Let's move onto the next one, blind estimation," said Wendi, reaching for her marker.

| BLIND ESTIMATION (GUESS) | |
| --- | --- |
| POSITIVES | NEGATIVES |
| • WE CAN PROVIDE AN IDEA OF WHAT WE CAN DO UP FRONT<br><br>• MANAGEMENT LIKES IT<br><br>• GIVES US A REFERENCE POINT TO START FROM | • ESTIMATES ARE COMMITMENTS<br><br>• FALSE SENSE OF SECURITY<br><br>• LIMITS/EXAGGERATES WHAT WE BELIEVE WE CAN DO<br><br>• CREATES A FALSE BASELINE |

The team quickly came up with the pros and cons of blind estimation.

"This is a good list," said Wendi. "Let's talk about a couple of these. Who came up with the phrase, *estimates are commitments*?" asked Wendi.

"I did," said Paul. "My concern is that once we estimate our velocity, we'll be held accountable to it throughout the project. What if our initial estimate is too optimistic? We need to build in a safety cushion. Take our estimate and subtract five, or something."

The team grumbled in agreement.

"Let me make sure I understand. You're saying that if our initial velocity estimate is too high, we will burn out trying to hit that higher number each sprint?" asked Wendi.

"Exactly!" said Paul.

"I hear you, Paul," Freddie interjected. "But it's no better if our estimate is too low. They'll say, 'With all that talent on your team, you're saying you can only do this much work per sprint? What will you do with the rest of your time?' People will panic before we even get started; management might even say we need to add more people to get the velocity up. Then, we'll have to start over."

"It wouldn't be the first time," agreed Ignacio.

"If I hear you correctly, Freddie, you're concerned that management will either tell us to do more—to have a higher velocity—or that they'll add people to the project because they will assume that we must need more people to get the job done, right?" asked Wendi.

"Yes," said the whole team.

"Fair enough," said Wendi. "Even if we don't go with this option, I'll make a note to talk to management about velocity in general because this might be a concern no matter how we arrive at an estimate. I want to make sure that they understand exactly what a velocity estimate means, and what it doesn't mean."

Wendi wrote an action item, Wendi to educate management about velocity, on the side of the whiteboard.

"OK," Wendi continued. "Let's look at another of the negative points. What does *creates a false baseline* mean?"

"I wrote that one," said Freddie. "If we start with a wild guess as our baseline, and then do better than we expect, people will talk about how much we must have improved. If we do worse than the so-called baseline, people will wonder why. We can tell them it's a guess all we want, but once there is a real number written down somewhere, we're compared against it."

"I know exactly what you mean. I'll make a point to include that tendency in my talk with management," Wendi said.

"Even with education, though, when it comes down to it, it's a wild guess, a stab in the dark," exclaimed Paul. "If we're going to be agile, I want us to follow the principles. Plucking a number out of the air and promising to deliver it might make everyone feel better, but not for long. It's an empty promise and will create a bad environment to try to make Scrum work."

"I hear you, Paul," said Ignacio. "But the fact is, that might be what we have to do, at least this time. On our next project, we'll have some historical data of our own to work with."

The rest of the team nodded in reluctant agreement.

"Well, I do know some ways to make blind estimation a little less of a shot in the dark," said Wendi. "But before we give up and start guessing, let's take a look at my personal favorite, *wait and see*. By that I mean we politely but firmly refuse to give management an estimate now. Instead, we promise a much more accurate number after we've run three sprints and have some real data. I can tell you my ideas on the positives."

Wendi wrote three positives on the board. "So, you guys tell me why it won't work."

The team quickly pointed out the flaws.

| WAIT AND SEE | |
|---|---|
| **POSITIVES** | **NEGATIVES** |
| • REAL DATA WILL GIVE A BETTER RELEASE PLAN | • MANAGEMENT WON'T LET US (TOO MUCH PRESSURE TO KNOW UP FRONT WHEN WE'LL BE DONE) |
| • EXPECTATIONS WILL BE MADE ON FACT, NOT GUESSING | • IT WILL TAKE AT LEAST THREE SPRINTS TO GET ENOUGH DATA TO BUILD A RELEASE PLAN |
| • WILL SHOW US WHAT WE CAN ACTUALLY DO | • DATA IS ONLY GOOD AS LONG AS WE KEEP IT UP TO DATE |
| | • WE ARE A NEW TEAM, SO OUR INITIAL VELOCITY WILL BE LOW |

"Thoughts?" asked Wendi

"I'd love to go with *wait and see*," said Ignacio, "but I don't think it's realistic. There is *no way* management will let us wait three sprints to give them an estimate."

"And," Freddie added, "even though having real data would allow us to have an accurate and reliable release plan, we're a new team. It will take some time for us to get up to speed. I'm nervous about what our actual velocity will be during the first few sprints. What if it's really low?"

"It is a risk," said Wendi. "But I think it's our best option if we want to succeed. We just have the one tiny obstacle of getting management buy-in," said Wendi, smiling at how clearly facetious her last statement was.

"We'll never get this by them!" Paul exclaimed. "They will *require* us to provide data up front. There has to be another option."

"If someone has something better than the three we've already discussed, I'd love to hear it," said Wendi, looking around the room.

The team was quiet.

Wendi continued, "We've walked through our options. The truth is, we just don't have enough information at this time to be able, with any confidence, to determine our likely velocity. We could give management a number, but it would be a wild guess. Let's try something as bold as we are. Let's show them the options, walk them through the pros and cons, and explain that we want to *start* this project like we intend to complete this project: transparently and honestly.

The team looked at her with hesitation.

"But," Wendi went on. "And this a big but. We will promise them that we'll post our observed velocity and as soon as we have enough historical data of our own—three sprints worth, let's say—we'll give them an estimated velocity range so that they can make a release plan."

Wendi went on to explain in detail how the wait and see approach would work. The team agreed to give it a try. They were even able to convince a very reluctant group of managers to wait for real data.

Beginning with sprint one, the team posted its tracking charts in public places and updated them at each daily standup. At the end of three sprints, the team gave management an estimated velocity range and explained what that meant in terms of likely functionality. The product owner planned a release based on the pessimistic and optimistic ranges provided by the team.

Though the team ultimately delivered toward the low end of its predicted velocity range, its estimates proved accurate. As a result, no one was surprised by the released product. The product owner had all the must-have features he expected. The customers had all the features they had been promised (and had not been teased with any of the features that were questionable for the initial release). In the end, everyone agreed that combining real data with patience, education, and transparency had been the best solution.

# The Model

Wendi and the team struggled with how to give their product owner an idea of how much they could accomplish each sprint. After a brief brainstorm, they came up with three solutions: historical data, blind estimation, and wait and see. Wendi's team ultimately elected to wait and see. Why did they eliminate historical data and blind estimation?

## The Problem with Historical Data

Historical data is a viable option when your team has worked together before. In our story, Wendi's team dismissed this because they were new to working together, so the only historical data available to them would have been data from another team, likely one at a different company. While it's possible to derive a number based on another team's performance, it's not an option I would recommend because of all the different variables involved:

- The newness of the team and its composition
- The political environment
- Project size and complexity
- The product owner and customer

The first variable to consider is the relative newness of the team. The newness of a team will affect its velocity as compared to an existing team, if only because a new team takes time to gel. Team members must learn each other's strengths and weaknesses and determine how best to work together. Further, a new team may not be ideally composed. It might still be clinging to some traditional approaches, like having two separate teams—one made up only of developers and one dedicated to testing. This mono-functional team approach will not see a big performance improvement out of the gate like a truly cross-functional team will.

The next variable that can affect velocity is the political environment. Over time, companies restructure or change direction. What may have been the company goal a year ago may be obsolete now. Key managers may have shifted roles, changing the dynamics of the environment. Sometimes political changes are obvious; other times, the changes are pervasive but much more subtle. Teams using historical data must allow for these nuances, which can be very difficult to do.

The third variable to consider is project size and complexity. Teams, new or well established, that take on a project that has different technology or a change in complexity cannot rely on historical data. When Jeff Sutherland was CTO at Patientkeeper, he often told me that his teams could snuff out the competition because they were able to respond to change quickly. One of the reasons they were able to do this was because the work was similar and the teams remained consistent; they were not switching from a legacy C++ application to a Java web platform. They weren't slowed down by a learning curve.

The last variable has to do with the product owner and customer. While these may not seem like likely variables to consider, they can be huge factors. Say the team remains the same but the product owner is new. The velocity that the team saw in the past is sure to change because not all product owners are created equal. The relationship between the team and the product owner, much like the one among new team members, needs to develop over time. By the same token, working with a new customer requires adjustments that could affect velocity as well.

If you find yourself in the situation where you are considering using historical data, take these factors into account and *be careful*. Using other teams' velocities as a data-point is fine. Using it as your team's predicted velocity, however, is fraught with peril. Proceed at your own risk.

## Shedding Light on Blind Estimation

If you are forced to provide some sort of estimate before you've done any work together, blind estimation is probably your best bet. Rather than just actually guessing blindly at a number, however, you can do some background work to shed as much light on your guess as you possibly can before predicting your velocity.

The steps in this "not-quite-blind" estimation technique are as follows:

- Estimate the product backlog.
- Decompose a reference story.
- Determine a point-to-hours approximation.
- Identify the team capacity.
- Estimate the team velocity.
- Communicate the velocity as a range.

Once you've got some numbers to help you make a more educated guess, throw them away. They're artificial, a crutch to help you get started. And, worst of all, they're based on a big agile no-no, mapping story points to hours. Please don't think I'm advocating this as a general practice. I only suggest it for those situations when you absolutely have to take a guess. Every number you provide in a blind estimate should be replaced with real data as soon as you've had time to do a sprint or two. And every point-to-hours approximation you make to arrive at that number should be discarded, no exceptions.

### Estimate the Product Backlog

The first step in this admittedly less-than-ideal technique is to estimate the product backlog. If the product backlog has already been estimated in points, skip to the next step. If not, you need to provide point estimates for the product backlog items. To do this, browse the product backlog with the team. You are looking for a two-point reference story. (I use a two-point story as a reference so that if the team comes across a story that is smaller, it has room to assign it a smaller point value.) Once the reference story has been identified and has been given a point estimate, work with the team to compare that story with every other story in the product backlog, assigning point values until each story in the backlog has a point value associated with it. I like to use planning poker [GRENNING] for this, but you can use any method you choose as long as the entire backlog is estimated in points when you are done. (For more on estimating raw product backlogs, see Chapter 29, "Prioritizing and Estimating Large Backlogs.")

## Decompose the Reference Story

Once the product backlog is estimated in points, it's time to identify a rough hour-to-point mapping. To do this, you must first decompose a reference story. With the team, choose a two-point story (this may or may not be the same story as you used in step one). For that story, identify the tasks necessary to complete it. I use the brainstorming technique identified in Chapter 7 to identify the tasks. This is a highly interactive process and is most effective if everyone participates.

Once the team has identified the tasks for the reference story, it needs to estimate how many hours those tasks will take to complete. You can use planning poker to arrive at these estimates; just have the numbers on the cards represent *hours* instead of *points*. Because I advocate that teams limit estimates of any task to no more than 13 hours (if a task will take longer than 13 hours, break it into multiple tasks), remove all the higher cards for your deck—you might even consider removing the 13. Further, stick to the numbers on the cards. If you are using the Fibonacci sequence, that means you will have six values to choose from: 1, 2, 3, 5, 8, 13. What if a person estimates the task at four hours? The person must choose—three or five. This is done to maintain a level of accuracy that is good enough without being too precise.

## Points-to-Hours Approximation

Let's say that when the hours for each task are added together, the total for our reference story is 14 hours. We now extrapolate: All two-point stories in the product backlog will take the team *roughly* 14 hours to complete. Of course, in actuality the team might complete this, or any other two-point story, in 2 hours, 8 hours, or 16 hours. It's a rough estimate—and for the purposes of blind estimation, that's OK. Now that we have a points-to-hours approximation, we can calculate a loose approximation of how many hours the entire project will take. If there are 200 points in the backlog, and we believe a typical two-point story will take approximately 14 hours to complete, we can extrapolate that the project will take roughly 1,400 hours to complete.

*14 hours/2 points = 7 hours per point*
*7 hours \* 200 points = 1,400 hours*

Let me emphasize one more time that you shouldn't believe (or communicate!) for one minute that the project will actually take 1,400 hours to complete. You don't know nearly enough about your team, your project, or the realities of the development to have a number that specific in mind. Use the points-to-hours approximation to help build your initial estimate and then throw it away.

## Team Capacity

Next, we need to determine the team's capacity. To calculate this, decide how many hours per sprint *the team* (not individuals) will contribute to the project. To get this number you have to collect data at the individual level; however, remember to report back what the *team* commitment is, not what the individual commitments are.

Have each team member write the number of hours he or she has available per week to contribute to the project. Remember, this number should not be 40. Everyone has unrelated project activities that often interfere with dedicated project time. This overhead ultimately takes away from the time each person has available to do actual task-related work. Ask people to communicate their availability as two numbers: best case (high) and worst case (low).

Add the worst-case estimates together and multiply by the number of weeks in a sprint. This is your low-range team capacity. Add the best-case estimates together and multiply that by the number of weeks in a sprint. This is your high-range team capacity. Table 4-1 presents an example.

In Table 4-1 we took the sum of our low-range weekly capacity and multiplied it by the number of weeks in a sprint (2) to get a total of 176 hours. We then took the sum of our team members' high-range capacities per week and multiplied it by sprint length in weeks (2) to get a total of 236 available hours. It is likely that the actual team capacity will not be either the absolute high or the absolute low; the team should feel confident, though, that its capacity will fall somewhere in between the two extremes.

## Estimate Team Velocity

At this point we have calculated the following:

- The product backlog has 200 points.
- A two-point story is estimated to take roughly 14 hours, or 7 hours per point.
- Finishing the product backlog will take roughly 1,400 hours (7 hours *200 points).
- The team believes it can deliver between 176 and 236 hours of work per sprint.

**TABLE 4-1**   Team Capacity Estimates

| NAME | WORST CASE PER WEEK | BEST CASE PER WEEK |
|---|---|---|
| JOHN | 25 | 32 |
| JANE | 15 | 25 |
| MIKAEL | 28 | 36 |
| FREDDIE | 20 | 25 |
| TOTAL TEAM CAPACITY PER WEEK | 88 | 118 |
|  | LOW | HIGH |
| TOTAL PER TWO WEEK SPRINT | 176 | 236 |

We now have enough data to estimate the velocity for the team. We determine a low velocity and a high velocity by dividing the low- and high-capacity ranges for the team by the estimated hours per point, and *rounding down*, as shown in Table 4-2.

We can now communicate our estimated velocity as being between 25 and 33 points per sprint. We look at how to use that information to devise an initial release plan in Chapter 11, "Release Planning."

### Increasing Confidence in the Technique

Extrapolating the number of hours it will take to complete a backlog from one reference story is very rough and very quick. If you'd like, you can refine your estimate further by estimating a few different reference stories of varying sizes. Select three stories—a small one (2 points), one that is about midsized (5 points), and one that is larger (13 points)—and break them into tasks. Let's say that the 5-point story was estimated at 90 hours and the 13-point story at 225. Instead of multiplying the number of points times a set number of hours, you can assign each 2-point story 14 hours, each 5-point story 90 hours, and each 13-point story 225 hours. Any stories in between can be estimated based on the closest story (3-point story ~ 1.5*14; 8-point story ~ 1.5*90; and so on). Adding more reference points may help you more closely estimate the number of hours the project might take, but it does take significantly more work and relies on a relatively well-estimated product backlog. It might also give you a false sense of security in your estimate.

Remember that no matter how many data points you use, at the time in which you are estimating these stories, your team has yet to do any work. You really don't know for certain at this point how long it will take you to accomplish any task. Whether you choose to extrapolate from one data point or from three, remind your team and your stakeholders that the estimated range is very rough and will certainly change as the team begins to get a better picture of how much work they can accomplish per sprint.

## Wait and See (Use Real Data)

Wendi and the team ultimately decided to wait and see what their average velocity is for the first few sprints before providing an initial estimate. The team planned to run three sprints, capturing the observed velocity data at the end of each one. I prefer this option because the team is making its calculations based on real data, data that does not exist until the project is running.

**TABLE 4-2**    Estimating Velocity

|                | LOW HOURS | HOURS PER POINT | ESTIMATED VELOCITY |
|----------------|-----------|-----------------|--------------------|
| LOW VELOCITY   | 176       | 7               | 25                 |
| HIGH VELOCITY  | 236       | 7               | 33                 |

Even if you have to communicate an estimate using historical data or blind estimation, you should still collect your own data and revise your estimate based on that
data as soon as you can. In fact, you should track your velocity and refine your estimates throughout the life of your project, no matter which initial method you choose.
(For details on how to maintain a release plan, see Chapter 11.)

The benefit of waiting and seeing, of using real data, is that the team is using its
own data on its current project. Basing an estimate on reality enables a release plan to
reflect fact, not fiction. The main hurdle to this approach is that management is going
to want a number before you are ready to give them one. To overcome this obstacle,
communicate the benefits of waiting to the management team and lay out a plan as to
when the team will provide numbers and why real data is worth waiting for.

When using real data, you should follow these steps:

1. Collect and chart your actual velocity for at least three sprints.
2. Calculate average velocity, but communicate a range.
3. Map your velocity range to the product backlog.
4. Update your velocity and likely velocity range after each sprint.

## Collect and Chart Real Data

The first step is to collect your team's data. Track your velocity for three sprints, mapping the data on a public chart posted in the team area. At the end of three sprints,
your chart will look something like the one in Figure 4-1.

## Calculate Average Velocity but Communicate a Range

Once you have three sprints worth of data, calculate your average velocity. Do not,
however, communicate this average. Why? First, because yours is a new team, this
initial data might not be stable enough to use for an extended period of time. Second,
you want to avoid misunderstandings that arise from fixating on a set number. For
example, as I was writing this chapter, my wife asked me what time I would be done
and ready for dinner. I told her, in about 30 minutes. What I meant when I said *about*
was somewhere between 20 and 40 minutes. What she heard was *30 minutes*—not 29,
not 31—30. She fixated on a number and held me to it.

When the 30-minute mark came, therefore, she said, "OK. It's been 30 minutes.
You should be done—come and eat or the food will be cold." My response, which was
less than stellar, was, "But I'm not done. I said *about* 30 minutes; I need another 10
to 15." This frustrated her beyond belief. I was 95 percent confident that I would be
done in 20 to 40 minutes, but I did not communicate it that way; I communicated 30.
My wife heard this as a commitment. I meant it as an approximation.

If I had given my wife a range ("I am 95 percent sure I'll be done in 20 to 40
minutes), she would have known to have dinner ready in 40 minutes (my worst-case
estimate) but would have had some hope that I would be there to help set the table

and open the wine if I finished earlier. By saying 30 straight up, I communicated a high degree of confidence in a number that was merely the middle of a likely range.

You don't want frustrated management and disappointed customers. If you give them a set velocity, they are likely to make plans around that one number. If you give them a range, on the other hand, they are more likely to plan for a best-case and worst-case scenario. If you tell them you have a range but are not very confident in it yet, they are likely to make those plans a little more flexible. It's all about communication. Avoiding misunderstandings goes a long way toward having a satisfied customer.

So, even though you'll *capture* your average velocity, you will not *communicate* your average velocity. Instead, talk in terms of a likely velocity range and your confidence in that range. Let's imagine that the numbers in the chart in Figure 4-1 reflect your actual velocity during your team's first three sprints. Your average velocity would be 12 ((10 + 14 + 12)/3). Your likely velocity range, however, would be 10–14 (low velocity to high velocity). And because you are a new team that is still forming and storming (for more information, see Chapter 20, "Adding New Team Members"), your degree of confidence that future velocities will fall in this range might be 75 percent.

It is important to remember that the degree of confidence is subjective and qualitative. While there are ways to measure subjective confidence, I don't recommend that you try to measure it in any absolute sense. I find the effort too high compared to the small amount of value gained.

To determine the team's degree of confidence, have each team member write down his or her confidence rating on a piece of paper—when everyone has a number written down, flip over all the written pages at once. (Skip this if your team is comfortable doing this verbally and all at the same time.) What you want to prevent is having people influence others' confidence ratings. If there are specific reasons why you are less confident (e.g., we think we'll go faster in future sprints because it will take us some time to understand the technology; we think we might slow down for

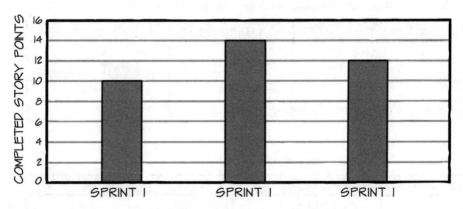

**FIGURE 4-1**  Sample velocities captured during three sprints

a few sprints because we're going to learn how to work in pairs), communicate those as well.

## Truncated Data Collection

Too often teams who initially get permission to collect data for three sprints before communicating a range are coerced into providing data after only one or two sprints together so that the product owner can communicate the release plan to management, customers, and stakeholders. The limited amount of data makes it difficult to communicate a realistic range.

If you find yourself in this situation, consider two approaches. The first is to use Mike Cohn's multipliers. This table of multipliers gives teams a way to communicate a probable velocity range until they have enough meaningful data to calculate their own. In *Agile Estimation and Planning*, Cohn explains how to use multipliers to estimate future velocity [COHN] based on observed team velocity, as seen in Table 4-3. You can see that Cohn recommends that if you have only completed one iteration, you should multiply your velocity by the high and low multipliers to arrive at a range you can communicate.

In my early projects I started with Cohn's values listed in Table 4-3. They were extremely helpful. As I encountered different teams with different backgrounds working on different technologies, however, I found that I started modifying Cohn's matrix into something that was not driven by the number of iterations a team has under its belt, as illustrated in Table 4-4. Why? I didn't always have experienced teams, and often after the fourth sprint, we'd still be stuck with the same multiplier as we were in sprint one.

For example, let's say Team SuperBunny is a newly formed team for a project and its team members are working together for the first time. The team runs its first

**TABLE 4-3**   Mike Cohn's Observed Team Velocity Matrix

| ITERATIONS COMPLETED | LOW MULTIPLIER | HIGH MULTIPLIER |
|---|---|---|
| 1 | 0.6 | 1.6 |
| 2 | 0.8 | 1.25 |
| 3 | 0.85 | 1.15 |
| 4 OR MORE | 0.9 | 1.1 |

**TABLE 4-4**   Modified Velocity Matrix

| CATEGORY | TEAM/PROJECT MAKEUP | LOW MULTIPLIER | HIGH MULTIPLIER |
|---|---|---|---|
| 1 | ESTABLISHED TEAM | 0.85 | 1.20 |
| 2 | NEW TEAM | 0.60 | 1.60 |

sprint and, like the team in Figure 4-1, achieves a velocity of 10. If after that sprint, the team is pressed to communicate a range, it should use the low and high multipliers for Category 2, new team.

As I progressed with this modified matrix, I realized another factor that continually surfaced: the technology or project type the teams were working on. I started asking myself "is the project technology completely new to the people (unknown technology) or is it something that the majority or all of the team has experience with (known technology)?" This is important to consider as unknown technologies create a level of uncertainty and risk that would not otherwise be present for a team that is just doing "the same old type of work."

Because of this, the next filter I pass a team and a project through expands on my original modified velocity matrix in Table 4-4 and includes project/technology familiarity, illustrated in Table 4-5. Of course, how familiar a team is with a technology is subjective, but it is an important factor when a team is in the early stages of a project and working to communicate its velocity.

The volatility of the team's velocity varies based on its makeup and project type. I find that more stable teams can stop using this table after one or two months (two to four sprints depending on sprint length). Newer teams have a harder time and should continue to factor in high and low multipliers for about three months (three to six sprints depending on sprint length). Once three months have passed, teams should not use this table and should instead rely solely on their realized velocity ranges.

## Keys to Success

Determining your team's velocity does not have to be a challenge. Three techniques listed in this chapter can help you get started and keep your velocity on track.

I often get asked which approach I recommend. Each approach has its right time and place and its own merits and issues. Table 4-6 summarizes my recommendations.

Waiting for the observed velocity produces the best result, as it is based on actual team data. It can, however, make management or customers (especially those new to Scrum) feel uncomfortable, as there will be no initial release plan generated by the team. This may negatively affect the trust the team has with its stakeholders, resulting

**TABLE 4-5**   Modified Velocity Matrix with Project/Technology Familiarity

| | | UNKNOWN TECHNOLOGY | | | |
| | | KNOWN TECHNOLOGY | | | |
| CATEGORY | TEAM/PROJECT MAKEUP | LOW MULTIPLIER | LOW MULTIPLIER | HIGH MULTIPLIER | HIGH MULTIPLIER |
|---|---|---|---|---|---|
| 1 | ESTABLISHED TEAM | 0.85 | 0.9 | 1.1 | 1.2 |
| 2 | NEW TEAM | 0.6 | 0.8 | 1.4 | 1.6 |

**TABLE 4-6**   When to Use Each Approach to Estimating Velocity

| | HISTORICAL DATA* | WAIT AND SEE* | BLIND ESTIMATION* |
|---|---|---|---|
| EXISTING TEAM, KNOWN TECHNOLOGY | 1ST | 2ND | 3RD |
| EXISTING TEAM, UNKNOWN TECHNOLOGY | 2ND | 1ST | 3RD |
| NEW TEAM, KNOWN TECHNOLOGY | 3RD | 1ST | 2ND |
| EXISTING TEAM, UNKNOWN TECHNOLOGY | 3RD | 1ST | 2ND |

*CHOICE

in increased pressure for the team to deliver. Compound this with an initial velocity that is not what management or the customers were expecting, and the team will find itself in a hole that it must dig itself out of before it even starts. To make waiting a viable option, the ScrumMaster must work especially closely with the product owner to help manage expectations and communicate progress. Some suggestions for ways to keep stakeholders in the loop are to invite them to the sprint review meetings, to allow them to watch the daily standup meeting, and, if needed, to host small informal midsprint reviews for people concerned about how much progress is being made.

Using historical data can be an excellent option with an existing team working in an environment similar to those it has encountered in the past. As the list of varying environmental conditions increases, however, the viability of this option decreases. Factors such as changes to team composition and technology or a new customer or product owner will impact a team's ability to rely on historical data elements.

Blindly estimating the team's velocity using reference stories will, at least at first, give the team, customers, and management the comfort they are looking for. Doing so, however, sets a trap: Too often the team's initial release plan, which was based solely on its calculated velocity, is turned into a commitment. The ScrumMaster must work with the product owner and customer to correctly manage their expectations. The ScrumMaster must be sure that everyone involved understands that the velocity calculation the team derived is a calculated guess intended solely to help build a release plan. All stakeholders must understand that once observed data is in place, the calculated estimates will disappear and be replaced with real data.

Whatever technique you use to arrive at your velocity, remember that this number is the epitome of a ball-park estimate. As soon as you have run a sprint, any estimates derived from historical data or blind estimation should be thrown out and replaced with a predictive range based on whatever velocity was attained in your first sprint. As the project progresses, your confidence in your velocity range will increase. Continue to throw out previous estimates and replace them with new ones as you gather more data. Most importantly, communicate with and be transparent to your customers and stakeholders so that they too understand how much confidence they should place in your initial, interim, and later estimates. In all cases, remember to use ranges and to express your answer with a degree of confidence that will help people understand how much trust to put into each estimate.

## References

[COHN]    Cohn, Mike. 2006. *Agile Estimating and Planning.* Upper Saddle River, NJ: Prentice Hall.

[GRENNING]    Grenning,    James.    http://renaissancesoftware.net/files/articles/ PlanningPoker-v1.1.pdf (accessed on 11 June 2009).

# Chapter 5

# IMPLEMENTING THE SCRUM ROLES

Traditional teams who shift to Scrum encounter new roles and different ways of thinking. They have to find a ScrumMaster, whose job is to keep the process running smoothly without dictating solutions. They have to have a product owner, who is tasked with steering the team in the best direction based on business value. Then, they have to learn to be good team members, which involves cultivating a cross-functional attitude, learning new skills, and working on tasks that might be new to them.

Fitting existing team members into the Scrum roles can be challenging. After all, sometimes people don't fit neatly into just one category—a jack-of-all-trades developer might also have great leadership skills. A former team leader might also have crucial coding skills and a deep knowledge of the product market. When that happens, should these multifaceted individuals take on more than one role for the good of the team? What are the potential benefits and the anticipated, and unanticipated, negative impacts that can come from allowing one person to wear multiple hats on a Scrum team?

## The Story

Marcus was asked to build a new Scrum team to release a mission-critical application for the company. Marcus and his newly formed team did not have any experience with Scrum, but they did have the sponsorship and support of management to learn to use the Scrum framework.

The first thing the team members did was get together to figure out how they would structure themselves. On former teams, Miguel and Jose had been developers and Hugo and Dominic had been testers. Their roles on the Scrum team were clear: They would be team members responsible for executing the vision of the business as communicated and managed by the product owner through the product backlog.

Marcus, on the other hand, was more difficult to position. On his former team, he had been the project manager. He also had a development background. The team went back and forth on how to best use Marcus. Should he be a member of the core team, doing work on the sprint backlog? Or should he serve as the ScrumMaster, formalizing his current leadership role? Or, should he perhaps be the product owner, helping steer the project in the right direction? And if Marcus didn't fill these roles, who would? No one else on the team had his understanding of Scrum and the market.

Because the team members did not have the authority to bring in any consultants to help fill any gaps in their skills,[1] they came up with what they thought was the best

---

1. See Chapter 3, "Using Team Consultants to Optimize Team Performance."

possible solution: Marcus should split his time between all three roles. Most likely, they imagined, the tasks of the ScrumMaster and product owner wouldn't require someone full time. Marcus could do both. Then, they reasoned, when Marcus wasn't busy doing "managerial" things, he could fill his time with team tasks. After all, it wasn't that unusual in their company to have managers also take on hands-on work. So they forged ahead.

Things went well at first. Each day during the daily scrum, Marcus reported his status like the rest of the team, highlighting that he did not have any impediments and that the tasks he signed up for were on track across the board.

By the end of the first week of the one-month sprint, he had met with the known stakeholders to further build the product backlog, facilitated all the necessary meetings, and signed up for several tasks (40 hours' worth). His plan was to accomplish ten hours of work on the sprint backlog per week. This first week, however, he had not spent even one hour on those tasks. He and the team weren't worried, though. His ScrumMaster and product owner duties would probably scale back now, they reasoned, and there were still three weeks left in the sprint for him to complete his tasks.

The second week yielded both the first Scrum-related improvement and the first hint of trouble brewing. Marcus spent the first few days of the week reviewing the sprint backlog looking for trends, one of the ScrumMaster duties he hadn't gotten to during the first week. While reviewing the backlog, he noticed that every work item that Hugo worked on was taking about 50 percent longer than the team had estimated. The pattern was unique to Hugo; every other team member was within 20 percent of the estimates. Marcus raised this pattern in the daily scrum meeting that Friday. Hugo confirmed that he was struggling with the work. The team decided that Hugo would pair with Jose, a senior developer, and that they would work tasks down together. Marcus was ecstatic. After only two weeks using Scrum, they already had identified an issue that would have gone unaddressed otherwise.

The team, while happy about the improvement, was a bit concerned about the fact that Marcus hadn't found time to work on any of his tasks. His fellow team members pointedly asked Marcus about the work that he signed up for—could he do it or did they need to find another solution. Marcus agreed that it was time for him to put on his team member hat. Next week, he promised the team, he would begin his team member tasks.

Week three quickly passed. Despite his best efforts, Marcus could not focus on the sprint tasks he had on his plate. His time was consumed by a crisis with the stakeholders (15 showed up out of the blue, claiming they had been left out of the original meetings and demanding better placement on the backlog for their stories), the resulting reprioritization of the backlog, negotiations with stakeholders, and all-around firefighting. Marcus and the team had no idea how time consuming the job of product owner could be, not to mention the tasks required of a ScrumMaster.

Marcus was stuck. He was a committed core team member and knew his teammates were relying on him to do work, he was the product owner and had to ensure the stakeholder interests were being addressed by the team, and he was the Scrum-Master and was supposed to be focusing on team health. Something had to give.

At the start of the fourth week, Marcus dedicated himself to his sprint backlog items in solitary confinement. He shut off his email, retreated to his office, locked his door, and shut the blinds; however, the work that he signed up to do was in fact much larger than he or anyone else had anticipated.

By Wednesday evening of the fourth week, Marcus accepted that he was not going to be able to deliver his tasks this sprint. He buried his face in his hands and began to search for ways to tell the team that he had failed. Suddenly, Marcus had what he considered a brilliant idea. He wasn't just a team member, he was the Scrum-Master and the product owner, too, wasn't he?

Delusional from burning himself out, he decided it was time for Marcus the product owner to meet with Marcus the ScrumMaster and Marcus the team member. How convenient that they could all get together in one person! Together they decided it would be best to postpone the tasks that Marcus had signed up for and put them back on the product backlog to be reprioritized and addressed in a future sprint. Marcus the team member updated the sprint backlog, reviewed it with Marcus the product owner (all with Marcus the ScrumMaster watching), and it was done. No harm. No foul. Marcus took off his many hats, wiped his brow, and sighed with relief: problem solved.

The next morning at the daily scrum meeting, Marcus handed copies of the burndowns to everyone to review, just as he had done every day. Today, though, something smelled a bit rotten on these suddenly-on-target burndowns. Miguel spoke up.

"Marcus, what is this drop in the work remaining?" he said, referring to the burndown shown in Figure 5-1.

"Oh that," he replied. "I removed some tasks that I had signed up for. No big deal. As product owner, I decided we can do that stuff next sprint."

The room went silent and all eyes turned to Marcus.

"You did what?" exclaimed Dominic. "You cut your own work?"

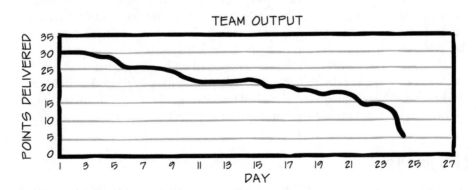

**FIGURE 5-1**   Burndown chart

"Marcus, you can't do this. What were you thinking?" demanded Hugo, without allowing Marcus time to respond to Dominic's question.

The team continued to dig into Marcus, demanding an explanation. Marcus realized he was in a deep hole.

"Guys, I'm sorry. I'm sorry!" pleaded Marcus, trying to get a word in. "I didn't think it would matter!"

"Well it does!" said Jose.

Marcus felt his heart sink into his shoes. He felt awful for letting the team down and understood, too late, that what he did was wrong.

"Marcus, if this is going to work, you can't do that again," said Hugo.

"You need to decide what you're going to do on this project because it is clear that you splitting your time between ScrumMaster and product owner *and* signing up for work on the sprint backlog does not work," added Dominic. "We've got team issues that are going unaddressed. We need you to see what we are missing on the team dynamics! All of your time has been spent with the customers and you're letting us down."

Marcus acknowledged his mistake.

"Guys, I'm sorry. I did not think the roles of ScrumMaster or product owner would be so demanding. My job as product owner has taken almost all of my time this sprint, and I don't see it getting any better. I don't want to let you guys down as a team, but I know my job as ScrumMaster is not working out either. And my team member role! Man! I blew that one," admitted Marcus.

"Look Marcus," said Hugo. "I know this is tough on you most of all, but we need you to focus on one thing and do it well. What do you want to do?"

Marcus contemplated his options. He'd done a decent job as ScrumMaster. He really liked the product owner role and could see himself doing that job. Still, he hated to give up development work altogether.

"C'mon Marcus, it's been five minutes," said Hugo. "Time to decide."

"I'll be the product owner—I've got the most invested in that now. What are we going to do for a ScrumMaster?"

"We were all pretty sure you'd pick that," said Hugo, with the team nodding. "We've talked to Filipa about becoming our ScrumMaster, and she tentatively accepted. She's going to want to turn to you for some answers at first, but the work of ScrumMaster will be her priority, not yours," said Hugo.

Marcus felt the weight of the world being lifted off his shoulders.

"Thanks, guys, I really appreciate this. I couldn't have kept up the circus act for another sprint!" exclaimed Marcus. "I had no idea what I was getting myself into. No one on a Scrum team should wear multiple hats; I don't care how small the team is!"

## The Model

In our story we saw Marcus and the team struggle with what Marcus' role should be. He had experience in development and had moved on to become a project manager, where he had been successful for several years. He struggled with how to narrow his diverse skill set to one of the roles in Scrum. Teams new to Scrum often struggle with the same issues. They try to map current company roles to the ones in Scrum, attempt to mix roles, or misinterpret what the time and skill requirements are for the various Scrum roles.

Let's take a look at each of the roles, starting with the **product owner**. The primary job of the product owner is to be the customer representative, turning the vision into a workable product backlog for the team to execute and managing the return on investment/business value of the product or service under development. The product owner helps bring clarity to the vision of the product to be delivered and then works with the customers and stakeholders to build a list of requirements called a *product backlog*. The product backlog contains anything that needs to be done to deliver the vision—everything that will contend for the team's time over the life of the project *and* that brings value to the end deliverable. Typical items in a product backlog include stories (or features), taxes, spikes, and preconditions (for more information on this, see Chapter 25, "Optimizing and Measuring Value"). The product owner should demand efficiency and excellence from the team and, if possible, should let the team work itself as hard as possible to get maximum value.

The role of the **ScrumMaster** is multifaceted. First, the ScrumMaster should work to build and maintain a high-performing team. On the surface, this appears to be simple: manage the daily standup meeting, collect status from the team, and coordinate the various meetings and tasks. The truth is, though, that nothing about a ScrumMaster's job is simple. The ScrumMaster is not the team manager or leader; on the contrary, the ScrumMaster is the fluid that ensures the team's gears are turning at optimum effectiveness. ScrumMasters keep the team focused and on track. To do this effectively, ScrumMasters need to be able to see the forest through the trees—to see the big picture and look for places where the team can make improvements.

Second, the ScrumMaster is expected to work with the product owner, helping as needed but also providing a key check and balance against the will of the product owner. The product owner will want a team to have a high velocity; it's the Scrum-Masters job to make that happen while protecting the team's health. Good Scrum-Masters increase velocity by removing impediments, monitoring team health, and helping the team know how it is tracking toward its delivery of the sprint goal.

The final job of the ScrumMaster is to be a change agent in the organization. Good ScrumMasters reach beyond transforming the team to help transform the company as well. ScrumMasters look for opportunities to create a learning organization, offering lunch and learn and other informal training on Scrum, advising new Scrum teams, and generally being a resource and advocate for Scrum throughout the organization. A ScrumMaster's subtle, servant leadership can have a tremendous impact on the rest of the company.

**Core team members** deliver the vision and build the work needed to implement features from the prioritized product backlog, as managed by the product owner. To do this most effectively, team members depend on the ScrumMaster and product owner to deal with the noise, enabling them to focus solely on the task at hand.

What makes Scrum unique is that each role has minimal overlap and is in intentional conflict with the other roles. The product owner is expected to drive the team to execute the vision of the business and deliver business value to the stakeholders and customers. The ScrumMaster, on the other hand, focuses his or her time on ensuring the team is healthy and able to execute the vision of the product owner as effectively and efficiently as possible. The team concentrates on delivering the work. Without a product owner, the team risks missing the mark. Without a ScrumMaster, the team risks burnout. Without committed team members, the project itself is at risk.

## Choosing Roles

Now that we have an understanding of what the roles are and why they exist, let's look at how to match people to those roles. The first thing to remember when picking your roles is to disregard any assigned titles that might exist in your company. Titles do not map to the roles in Scrum. Skills do. Consider the competencies you want to have in the roles and match people to them.

Table 5-1 summarizes some key competencies to look for when filling each of the three roles in Scrum.

You can flip this around the other way, too, if it's more helpful. List the key duties of a typical project manager in your organization, for instance. Then compare those to the responsibilities of each Scrum role. In Table 5-2, you can see examples of the types of work of a traditional project manager mapped to the roles in Scrum.

**TABLE 5-1**  Scrum Roles and Competencies

| ROLE | CHARACTERISTICS |
|---|---|
| SCRUMMASTER | • BUILDS TRUST<br>• HELPS OTHERS SEE ISSUES<br>• PROVIDES LEADERSHIP THROUGH INFLUENCE<br>• LIKES WORKING WITH PEOPLE<br>• IS CALM UNDER PRESSURE |
| PRODUCT OWNER | • CAN DETERMINE WHAT CUSTOMERS MEAN BY LISTENING TO WHAT THEY ASK FOR<br>• CAN BRING STAKEHOLDERS AND CUSTOMERS TO CONVERGENCE ON FEATURES AND FUNCTIONALITY<br>• HAS PRODUCT MANAGEMENT EXPERTISE<br>• HAS BASIC FINANCIAL EXPERIENCE<br>• HAS A BACKGROUND IN THE INDUSTRY OF THE APPLICATION UNDER DEVELOPMENT |
| TEAM MEMBER | • HAS AN OPEN MIND<br>• IS LOOKING TO IMPROVE AND TO HELP OTHERS BECOME BETTER<br>• HAS A TEAM ATTITUDE<br>• CAN BE RESPECTFUL<br>• IS HUMBLE |

**TABLE 5-2**   Mapping Project Manager Duties to Scrum Roles

| PMI ROLE WORK | SCRUMMASTER | PRODUCT OWNER | TEAM |
|---|---|---|---|
| COMMUNICATE WITH CUSTOMERS | | PRIMARY | SECONDARY |
| MANAGE REQUIREMENTS | | PRIMARY | SECONDARY |
| MANAGE BUDGET | | PRIMARY | |
| MOTIVATE THE TEAM | PRIMARY | | |
| PROJECT DOCUMENTATION | | | PRIMARY |
| FIX PROBLEMS AND ISSUES | PRIMARY | | PRIMARY |

Though these charts can help you stop thinking in terms of titles and start thinking in terms of skill sets, choosing people for a task is never that cut and dried. If a former project manager takes on the role of the ScrumMaster, she might find herself wishing she could be more "hands-on" with the tasks in the sprint backlog. A tester who is particularly gifted at facilitation, on the other hand, might desire to take on the ScrumMaster role. Give people freedom to choose the roles that best suit them. What people are called is so much less important in Scrum than what people do.

## Mixing Roles

Mixing roles in Scrum is when a single person takes on more than one Scrum role; for example, a person is a team member and the ScrumMaster, or a person is the ScrumMaster and the product owner, or the person is the product owner and a team member. The other option, of course, is what we saw with Marcus—a person who takes on each role simultaneously.

It is tempting to think that a single person can split time across roles effectively; after all, that is what we have been doing for years on our projects. I, too, have mixed all the roles in Scrum. Like Marcus, I thought that I could do everything, and, like Marcus, I failed miserably. I have also tried each of the possible combinations at least three times, some more. Each time they ended in failure. I can and will tell you not to do it; however, I also understand that you'll want to try it anyway, so consider this a disclaimer.

People often ask what's wrong with mixing roles. This comes from a fundamental misunderstanding of what each role entails and how that role interacts with the other members of the Scrum team.

A **combination product owner/ScrumMaster** is akin to a two-headed dragon. Eventually one head will eat the other. The product owner and ScrumMaster roles are in conflict with each other by design. One exists to drive the team; the other to protect the team. Let's say you are the product owner for a team and the customer is riding you hard to push the team. If you do not have a mechanism in place (the

ScrumMaster) to monitor this, it is likely the team will be pushed beyond the level of its endurance. Productivity will be realized in the short term due to the extra push, but the customer will come to expect this as a long-term thing. The issue here is that the team is not working at a sustainable pace. Eventually productivity will decrease and morale will suffer as team members burn out. The product owner might not care if the team is keeping its morale up and might not even care if quality suffers, as long as the dates are hit and the customer's needs are perceived to have been met.

It's equally ineffective to have a ScrumMaster but no product owner. Without the sense of urgency a product owner brings, it is likely that the team will move too slowly. Without a product owner to keep the team focused on delivering value, the team might include functionality that it thinks would be fun to build or would be something nice to have. The team soon ends up driving the product vision, and not the customer. In these cases, the customer will soon begin to question whether the product will ever be delivered, will wonder whether the team could be moving faster than it is, and will wonder why they are paying for features they did not ask for. Eventually, they will lose faith in the team altogether.

If one person is playing both roles, and there is a pushy customer, the person playing the roles will need to decide which job wins out: the ScrumMaster, whereby he will not satisfy the customer but protect the team, or the product owner, whereby he will satisfy the customer and likely hurt the team.

These conflicts come up in every project, which is why it is important to not mix roles.

The two-headed dragon that a combination ScrumMaster/product owner becomes is one thing. In contrast, a **combination team member and ScrumMaster** seems innocuous. Still, there are issues that make this less than ideal. Earlier in this chapter I said that the ScrumMaster's job is to build and maintain a high-performing team. Consider the team member's primary function: to build and execute on the vision as communicated by the product owner. This directly conflicts with the job of a ScrumMaster. If the ScrumMaster's job is to see the forest through the trees, the job of a team member is to be in the forest, staring at a single tree (e.g., user story) for the duration of the sprint. The problem with mixing these two roles is that if the Scrum-Master is doing work, she won't be as likely to see the bigger issues with the team and therefore cannot elevate the team to greatness.

A **combination product owner/team member** role is nearly impossible to do well. A product owner just has too much noise to contend with. Early in any project, the job of the product owner will be intense. The product owner will be working with customers and stakeholders, working to build a product backlog and to understand the vision in depth. The faster the team goes, the harder it will be for the product owner to keep up with the team's demand for stories, clarification, and verification.

The only benefit to this combination is that the team will have the product owner in the room most of the time. Even then, it is difficult for product owners to have a clear vision of what the team is working to execute when they are splitting time between development and product owner duties.

What about Extreme Programming's call for having the "customer in the room," which I am all for but rarely, if ever, see? Could having a **combination client/product owner** be the next best thing? Sometimes.

First consider that if the product owner is the actual client, he holds the money. This gives him the power to pull the "I have the money card, so do what I say" routine. Not a fun situation for the team or the ScrumMaster who is trying to protect them.

Second, consider that a customer has other work to do. For example, a colleague of mine was running a Scrum project at an organization we'll call ZDev. The client, let's say WiCo, had a representative acting as the product owner, but not by choice. She was elected product owner by her manager at WiCo because she had the most knowledge of the system that was under development. She served as the actual product owner for ZDev's Scrum team because WiCo didn't want to pay ZDev for a product owner's time.

Things were great in the beginning and the team got what they needed. As time went on, though, the client/product owner became more and more distant, eventually only showing up for the demo meetings and even then not being engaged. ZDev noticed this trend and stopped the project. The big wigs at WiCo flipped out and demanded an explanation. ZDev explained that the product owner was not engaged; under those circumstances, ZDev would rather build nothing than build the wrong thing.

WiCo did an investigation as to why the product owner had checked out of the project. The client/product owner explained that she had to keep doing her primary job in addition to the extra work of product owner, which had been handed to her simply because she was a subject matter expert. When she looked at what she would be judged on for her performance review, she elected to sacrifice the ZDev project because it was tiny compared to her other goals for the year. WiCo realized that it would have been cheaper and more effective to have hired a PO from ZDev in the first place, so they restarted the project with a product owner from ZDev.

**Combining all three roles**, a situation I affectionately refer to as the trifecta of death, is an exceedingly bad idea. I can't think of an upside. Still, I've been where you are and know many of you will try it anyway. If you have a one- or two-person team, this *might* work—even then, don't bet on it. This dysfunction is a symptom of larger issues, including the possibility that you should not have taken on the project in the first place.

## When, Not If, You Decide to Mix Roles Anyway

Hopefully by this point I have made a clear case for not mixing the roles. I realize, though, that you're probably going to try it anyway. When you do, I suggest you mix only the team member and ScrumMaster roles. Why? It's the least damaging combination, puts the ScrumMaster in the room with the team, and will likely be the easiest to sell to management, especially if they are saying you "cannot do Scrum" because of the perceived additional overhead in the roles. Be careful when you do it, and make sure everyone on the team is on the same page from the beginning. Read more about how to justify having a full-time ScrumMaster in Chapter 8, "The Case for a Full-Time ScrumMaster."

## Keys to Success

Marcus' story illustrates an extreme case of mixing roles in Scrum, but the more I work with teams the more I find mixing to be an option that teams propose. It is all too common to see a ScrumMaster also act as a team member and is not unusual to see one person acting as both ScrumMaster and product owner. Neither mix results in the best solution for your customers or your team.

Even on a small team, resist the temptation to deviate from the Scrum "recipe," especially at first. You will find that you will ultimately perform much better if you take the extra effort to build the intentional tension that having three distinct roles on your team provides. If you're strapped for cash or personnel, share a ScrumMaster or product owner with another team. Having a part-time ScrumMaster is much better, and so much more in keeping with the checks and balances inherent in having three distinct roles, than having one team member trying to play multiple roles. If you do this, keep in mind that it's far easier to share a ScrumMaster than a product owner, because once a team gets cranking, a part-time product owner likely will have trouble keeping up.

If you are in a core team member role and miss your leadership duties, look for ways to lead from within the team. Head up an improvement community. Start or grow a local user's group. Become a Scrum advocate inside your organization by being a mentor or offering lunch-and-learn opportunities. You might even consider volunteering as the part-time ScrumMaster for another team, where your duties won't directly conflict with your team member responsibilities.

Be creative. Be persistent. And be prepared to have to justify the importance of having three separate individuals serving as ScrumMaster, product owner, and team member.

Some teams have claimed success in rotating the role of ScrumMaster among the team members. I've never attempted this and have never seen this result in a good outcome for anyone. Without long-term focus, the ScrumMaster becomes a glorified administrator for the team. The skills required of a ScrumMaster are specialized and the role too important to be handed around the campfire like a bottle of moonshine.

I prefer to have one ScrumMaster for as long as the team is together, and see nothing wrong with having the team choose a new ScrumMaster if the team feels that person might have the right stuff to shepherd the team and stand up to the product owner.

I recognize that reality often gets in the way of what would be ideal. But in all your decisions, keep in mind that when push comes to shove, someone mixing roles ultimately will be forced to choose a role. Someone splitting the team member and ScrumMaster roles will be forced to choose which one to do and which one to sacrifice. This is inevitable. Recognize this cost if you establish a team in which people must act in multiple roles.

# Chapter 6

# DETERMINING SPRINT LENGTH

There is no one-size-fits-all, magic bullet for determining a sprint length that works well for every team. Originally, Scrum called for one-month sprints, but nowadays many teams have been successful with two-week or even one-week sprints.

With all these options, how do you choose the sprint length that works best for your team and project? Is there ever a time when it's OK to have a sprint length that is longer than one month? Why would a team ever want to implement one-week sprints? And what are the factors that influence what the right sprint length should be, especially on a new project?

Let's explore these questions and the concept of sprint length through a story. After that, we will look at ways you can determine which sprint length makes sense for your team.

## The Story

Jay and Rachel were tapped to deliver an order tracking system for their client, Tegla, an executive aircraft manufacturer. We find Jay and Rachel in the middle of a discussion about sprint length and requirements.

"Rachel, I've been going over these requirements documents for days and I'm stuck. We've got some difficult constraints to work with. Tegla needs us to build an order-tracking system. The problem is Tegla's budget cycle ends at the end of the year, which means we have to get the system built quickly and correctly, because after the first of the year we won't have a budget to fix it. From what I can tell, the stakeholders at Tegla are not yet very clear on their requirements. All they know is they don't want the next version of what they have today; they want something completely new."

"Wow," said Rachel. "That's vague."

"What's worse is the requirements are a bit dated. There is a visual design document that someone put together for them, complete with UI elements, behaviors, and system interactions. We can use this as a starting point. We also have the legacy system as a reference, along with the use cases that were built to support it. The rest of it will need to be developed over time," replied Jay.

"Hmmm," said Rachel. "Let's divide and conquer and see what we can figure out. If you can identify the essential people for the core of the team based on what you know, I'll talk with the customer and come up with a recommendation for how to structure this project."

After a few days, Rachel and Jay met again.

Jay described his efforts to build a core team. Rachel responded with her own conclusions and questions.

"I think using Scrum to manage this project would really help," said Rachel. "How much experience does the core team have with Scrum?"

"Actually, the team members have been on a few Scrum projects together and are experienced with technical skills like test-driven development and continuous integration. They're pretty strong," Jay replied.

"Good," said Rachel. "I spoke with the stakeholders at Tegla and gave them a high-level overview of our various project engagement styles and they liked Scrum the best. I gave them a bunch of information on how Scrum works and they were receptive. What I did not tell them is how long the sprints will be; we need to figure that out. Here's what we know so far."

Rachel wrote a bulleted list on the whiteboard (see Figure 6-1).

"Great summary, Rachel," said Jay. "The biggest issues I see are the 31 December deadline and the fuzzy requirements. We don't know exactly what it is they want, and neither do they. With our team, their deadlines, and the fuzzy nature of the requirements, I'm thinking short feedback cycles will work best. I'm thinking weekly sprints."

Rachel smiled. "Me too. The real variable is Tegla. I don't think the stakeholders have the time needed for one-week sprints. They would have to be very committed and available to the project for one-week sprints to work, and I just don't know if they'll be willing or able to do that. Logistically, it would be possible. All the customers are located in the one local office. Still, they're pretty busy with other duties. I can't think of any project with Tegla where we've asked for that level of commitment," said Rachel.

"Well, all of the other projects we have done with Tegla have been better defined," countered Jay. "We didn't need that level of commitment." He paused for a moment then continued. "Let's set up a meeting. We'll ask them a few questions and get an

- WE WON'T HAVE FAA REGULATORY COMPLIANCE ISSUES TO DEAL WITH
- CORE TEAM HAS STRONG SCRUM EXPERIENCE
- WE HAVE TO DELIVER BY DECEMBER 31 DUE TO END OF YEAR FISCAL CONSTRAINTS
- REQUIREMENTS ARE PRETTY FUZZY AND LOOSELY DEFINED
- TELGA HAS AN INHERENT WATERFALL CULTURE
- TELGA STAKEHOLDERS ARE WORKING ON MULTIPLE PROJECTS, WE MIGHT NOT GET A LOT OF THEIR TIME

**FIGURE 6-1**   The situation

idea of how much time they have to commit to the project. Then, we'll make our case for weekly sprints and see what they have to say. Never hurts to ask, right?"

The customer meeting came before Jay and Rachel knew it. They had a good turnout: All five customer representatives from Tegla were present. Jay decided to start by recapping why everyone was there and what the purpose of the meeting was. "Hi folks," he said. "We are here today to talk about how we are going to work together to build the system in the timeframe you want."

Jay continued. "We have a solution that we think will work for our team, but to make it work we need your commitment. Our approach will provide you frequent opportunities, we hope weekly, to review the system. We will work with you each week to determine what we build the following week. We will deliver code in a state that is potentially shippable so we can put it on your production systems and not have issues dealing with operations."

The customers' eyes got very wide upon hearing this. "Weekly releases and feedback? Sounds great. What's the catch?" one of them asked.

"Well, in order to ship every Friday, we are going to need you to spend a lot of your time guiding us in the right direction. We're talking 20-30 hours per week for one person, less for the rest of you. That time will be spent refining the product backlog, running through all the stories to ensure they work to your satisfaction, helping prioritize the upcoming sprints, reviewing and helping triage bugs—and writing bugs for that matter. Also, we'll need you to…"

Jay stopped in midsentence as he saw the eyes of the customers gloss over in disbelief. One of them spoke, "We have jobs to do. How are we going to be able to do this?"

"Well," said Jay. "It is a lot, I agree."

Rachel nodded her agreement.

Jay continued, "However, doing this each week will give us about 22 opportunities—one per week for six months—to adjust the direction of the project. It's the best way to make sure that what you have at the end of the year is what you want."

"It might be the best way," replied one of the customers. "But I know I can't commit to the amount of time and feedback you will need. Is there a way we can stretch it out a bit? What if we did this once a month instead of every week?"

Rachel chimed in this time, "Jay and I discussed this option before the meeting. Monthly feedback cycles do work for many projects. The issue we both identified is around the requirements; they are very soft. Combine that with the fixed end-of-year deadline and we run a high risk of building the wrong thing, which none of us want. Monthly sprints only give us five opportunities for feedback, because by the sixth sprint, we're delivering the system."

"It's all about stimulus-to-response time," agreed Jay. "If you were to cut your finger, how quickly would you want your brain to respond to the cut? Immediately, right? Well, when we build a piece of functionality, it's better for the overall health of the system if you respond to these changes almost as immediately. So, we want to build in several stimulus-to-response cycles; doing that requires an investment on your part. However, making that investment means we have a higher likelihood of getting it right."

Rachel nodded and said, "I know you'd rather have monthly sprints, but given the time duration of the project, I strongly feel we won't get enough response that way. What if we compromise and have two-week sprints? That's not as ideal (or intense) as the one-week sprints we proposed originally, but it still gives us an adequate stimulus-to-response time."

The customer team knew the math. A six-month release window with two-week sprints meant they would have between ten and twelve opportunities to impact the direction of the project. They also knew that getting the system in place by the end of the year—and having it be the right system—was critical. Otherwise, the budget would be gone and they would be stuck with half a system or one no one could use.

"We'll find a way to make two weeks work. We'll just have to juggle our schedules a bit for the next six months," said their decision maker. "We're going to need your help, though. We are new to this Scrum thing, so you will have to help guide us through. We are a little skeptical, but you make a good argument. Let's go with a two-week sprint length and get this thing out the door."

## The Model

Choosing the right sprint length is about determining an appropriate stimulus-to-response cycle. In the story above, the team and the customer were pressed with a tight deadline, something not uncommon in software projects. Rachel and Jay explained to the customers that, with their firm end date and fuzzy requirements, the stimulus-to-response time for the project needed to be as short as they could handle.

In a sprint, the initial stimulus is the customer setting the priority of the stories. The response is the team building working software. The building of the working software is in turn a stimulus to the customer. The customer's response is feedback. The more instantaneous that feedback, the higher the likelihood that what is delivered in the end is what the customers really wanted, which is not necessarily what the customer originally asked for. This stimulus-response cycle continues until the project ends.

Rachel and Jay recommended one-week sprints. They arrived at this conclusion by taking into account the following criteria:

- The expected duration of the project
- Customers/stakeholders
    - How often can they provide feedback and guidance
    - Scrum familiarity
    - The cultural barriers existing in the company or with the stakeholder/customer group
    - Environmental factors

- The Scrum team
  - Scrum experience
  - Technical capabilities (such as automated acceptance testing, TDD, automated releases, etc.)
  - Ability to decompose work

These elements play a critical part when any team is trying to determine whether its sprints should be one, two, three, or four weeks. Let's look at each element in more detail.

## Project Duration

Sprint lengths should be chosen in relation to project duration; however, they should *never* be longer than four weeks. Consider a three-month project. If it has four-week sprints, the stakeholders will only get to participate in two demos before the project is released. This is not enough feedback to mitigate the risks. Shorter sprint lengths are a necessity.

What about a year-long project? Assuming four-week sprints break approximately monthly, that project would offer 11 opportunities (plus the final release) for stakeholders to see the developing product. Four-week sprints are a realistic option, depending on the other factors involved.

The area between three months and one year is less clear. The project in our story was a six-month project. If a six-month project is run on a four-week sprint model, the team has a scant five opportunities for feedback; the last sprint will end the project. Is that enough feedback to produce the right product? It depends. My advice for projects of greater than three months and less than one year would be to choose a sprint length that mirrors the project length—meaning a project that is short should have many *short* (one- to two-week) sprints. A project that is long should have many sprints between two and four weeks. Again, and I can't stress this enough, sprint length should never be longer than four weeks/one month. In fact, I recommend two weeks for nearly *all* of my projects as I find it gives the right amount of stimulus to response.

If a project is expected to last more than one year, rethink the project. Multiyear projects are too big. Find a way to divide it into shorter releases. Just as you wouldn't want a two-month sprint, you don't want a two-year project—divide it into four, six-month projects instead. If you find you can't come up with a way to break the project into smaller components, then you likely have larger cultural issues in your company that should be addressed before you try to use Scrum.

Figure 6-2 shows another way to view it: The lighter the sprint length bar is, the more likely you are to build the right thing as you will have more clarity. As you move to the right, to a darker shade, you have less clarity, less customer involvement, and you increase the risk of building the wrong thing.

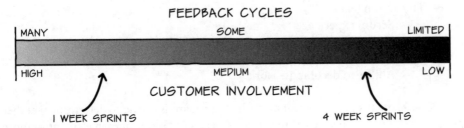

**FIGURE 6-2**   Amount of feedback and customer involvement

## Customer/Stakeholder Group

When working to determine sprint length with your customer, it is important to factor in three things.

- Customer group
- Company culture
- Customer environment

Look at the customer group first. It's crucial to balance the team's needs with the needs of your customer. Having a one-week sprint might solve some team problems but could put too much stress on the team's relationship with the customer. Talk with your customers, just as Rachel and Jay did. Explain why their time commitment is so important to the project's success and tell them what they will get out of the added expense of their time. Remember, in most cases, customers who are new to Scrum are not used to Scrum's demand for interaction. They are used to dropping the requirements off at the beginning of the project and picking up their product at the end. Regardless of the sprint length you choose, you will want to spend time educating your customers about the value of frequent feedback and the necessity of their involvement in the development process.

Next, examine the customer's company culture. Is working with a Scrum team new to the company and its culture? Is it perhaps being tested in a pilot group? If so, consider that short sprints may give a false impression that Scrum teams put undue pressure on the customer. Find ways to align the values of the company with those of the stakeholders and Scrum team. If the stakeholders and Scrum team value the idea of having working software every two to four weeks but the company values an all-encompassing project plan, the project will struggle regardless of sprint length. Again, education is key. Having a corporate sponsor on the customer side can help protect the team from distractions. Meanwhile, the more results the team produces, the more willing a reluctant company will be to accept the value of frequent iterations over a comprehensive plan.

The environment in which the customer conducts business can also affect the project. Environmental factors (such as regulatory issues) are often overlooked but, from my experience, often affect what the team can deliver and when. If your team has a large number of regulatory issues to contend with, you will probably want to choose sprint lengths of at least two weeks (three or four may be ideal), because of the amount of compliance assessment and auditing that will need to occur before any software can truly be considered shippable.

## Scrum Team

The Scrum team itself is a factor in determining sprint length. Considerations include the following:

- Team experience with Scrum
- Team engineering capabilities (e.g., test-driven development, continuous integration, pair programming, etc.)
- Team ability to decompose work

In our story, the team members had some experience with Scrum and XP. They knew each other well, would not have to start from scratch, and felt comfortable working within the Scrum framework. None of them had the "I own this part of the code" mindset. Jay and Rachel knew this, so they felt confident with one-week sprints. As a rule, an inexperienced Scrum team should stick with two- or four-week sprints as a one-week sprint is much more advanced and better suited for established teams that have a good working relationship.

If you do choose a one-week sprint length, you need to have the engineering capabilities in place (or learn them awfully quickly) to execute work in that compressed time frame. Good engineering practices are just as important with longer sprint lengths, but their absence is not as painful or glaringly obvious on a four week-sprint as it is on a one-week sprint. To efficiently execute a one-week sprint, the team must be able to establish and maintain a continuous integration server and should follow engineering practices like test-driven development and pair programming. Utilizing an automated acceptance testing framework such as the tool *Framework for Integrated Tests*, or FIT, is also a requirement as the testing debt growth will be fast and furious. If learning these mechanisms is your goal, then a one-week sprint might make sense. Otherwise, don't even think about a one-week sprint until you have these capabilities in place.

The ability of the team to decompose its tasks is critical on short sprints and still important on longer sprints. Decomposing tasks is in and of itself an art form, one that requires critical thinking, a clear mind, and the ability to see beyond the surface of a problem. If your team is good at decomposing tasks (or wants to get good in a hurry), shorter sprints (one-to-two weeks) can work. If your team is still learning how to decompose tasks, you might want to start with longer sprints (two-to-four weeks). Read more about task decomposition, and ways to improve, in Chapter 12, "Decomposing Stories and Tasks."

## Determining Your Sprint Length

"So this is all fine and dandy" you say, "but at the end of the day I need to figure out how long *my* team's sprints should be!"

I find myself asking a series of base questions each time I set up a project, just like Jay and Rachel did above. These questions help determine sprint length, but are not conclusive and should be considered guidelines rather than hard and fast rules. What I've ended up with is a quiz like you'd see in a magazine, where you answer a series of multiple choice questions, give a certain value to each answer, and then tabulate those answers to arrive at your ideal sprint length. Like any tool, use it wisely—if the answer it gives you does not feel right, then choose a different sprint length.

First, answer the following multiple choice quiz. Choose the answer that most closely matches your situation.

| | | |
|---|---|---|
| **1. PROJECT DURATION** | WHAT IS MY PROJECT DURATION? | A. PROJECT DURATION 0–3 MONTHS<br>B. PROJECT DURATION 3–6 MONTHS<br>C. PROJECT DURATION 6–9 MONTHS<br>D. PROJECT DURATION 9–12 MONTHS<br>E. PROJECT DURATION 12+ MONTHS |
| **2, 3, 4, 5 CUSTOMER** | HOW AVAILABLE IS MY CUSTOMER/STAKEHOLDER GROUP FOR FEEDBACK AND GUIDANCE? | A. HIGHLY AVAILABLE FOR FEEDBACK AND GUIDANCE<br>B. LESS AVAILABLE FOR FEEDBACK AND GUIDANCE<br>C. NOT AVAILABLE FOR FEEDBACK AND GUIDANCE |
| | HOW FAMILIAR IS MY CUSTOMER/STAKEHOLDER GROUP WITH SCRUM | A. HIGHLY FAMILIAR WITH SCRUM<br>B. SOMEWHAT FAMILIAR WITH SCRUM<br>C. NOT FAMILIAR WITH SCRUM |
| | HOW WOULD I RATE THE CULTURAL BARRIERS? | A. NONE OR LIMITED CULTURAL BARRIERS TO ENTRY<br>B. SOME CULTURAL BARRIERS TO ENTRY<br>C. MANY CULTURAL BARRIERS TO ENTRY |
| | HOW WOULD I RATE THE REGULATORY ISSUES? | A. NONE OR LIMITED REGULATORY ISSUES<br>B. SOME REGULATORY ISSUES<br>C. MANY REGULATORY ISSUES |
| **6, 7, 8 TEAM** | HOW WOULD I GAUGE THE SCRUM TEAMS' EXPERIENCE? | A. YEARS OF SCRUM EXPERIENCE WITH TEN+ PROJECTS<br>B. SOME SCRUM EXPERIENCE WITH FOUR TO NINE PROJECTS<br>C. LIMITED OR NO SCRUM EXPERIENCE WITH THREE OR FEWER PROJECTS |
| | WHAT IS THE SCRUM TEAM'S TECHNICAL CAPACITY? | A. EXCELLENT TECHNICAL CAPACITY<br>B. AVERAGE TECHNICAL CAPACITY<br>C. POOR TECHNICAL CAPACITY |
| | HOW CAPABLE IS THE SCRUM TEAM IN TERMS OF DECOMPOSING STORIES/TASKS? | A. EXCELLENT TASK DECOMPOSITION ABILITY<br>B. AVERAGE TASK DECOMPOSITION ABILITY<br>C. POOR TASK DECOMPOSITION ABILITY |

Once you've answered the multiple choice questions, use the scoring key in Table 6-1 to assign a number for each question based on your answer. You'll notice that there are three numbers in the key: 1, 3, and 5, where 1 = Bad Choice; 3 = Workable; 5 = Ideal. You'll carry all four numbers that match your answer into the sprint length model.

As an example, recall that in the story Jay and Rachel had a timeline of six months. Let's use this as the data point to answer the first question: What is my project duration? Their answer would be c. 6–9 months. If you had a project duration that matched Jay and Rachel's, you too would go to the 6–9 months row in the scoring key and copy the numbers into the Sprint Length Model as shown in Table 6-2.

**TABLE 6-1** Scoring Key

| | | SPRINT LENGTH | | | |
| --- | --- | :---: | :---: | :---: | :---: |
| | | 1 WEEK | 2 WEEKS | 3 WEEKS | 4 WEEKS |
| **1. PROJECT DURATION** | A. PROJECT DURATION 0–3 MONTHS | 5 | 5 | 1 | 1 |
| | B. PROJECT DURATION 3–6 MONTHS | 5 | 5 | 5 | 1 |
| | C. PROJECT DURATION 6–9 MONTHS | 3 | 5 | 5 | 3 |
| | D. PROJECT DURATION 9–12 MONTHS | 3 | 5 | 5 | 3 |
| | E. PROJECT DURATION 12+ MONTHS* | 1 | 5 | 5 | 3 |
| **2, 3, 4, 5 CUSTOMER** | A. HIGHLY AVAILABLE FOR FEEDBACK AND GUIDANCE | 5 | 5 | 3 | 1 |
| | B. LESS AVAILABLE FOR FEEDBACK AND GUIDANCE | 3 | 5 | 5 | 5 |
| | C. NOT AVAILABLE FOR FEEDBACK AND GUIDANCE* | 1 | 1 | 1 | 1 |
| | A. HIGHLY FAMILIAR WITH SCRUM | 5 | 5 | 5 | 5 |
| | B. SOMEWHAT FAMILIAR WITH SCRUM | 1 | 5 | 5 | 5 |
| | C. NOT FAMILIAR WITH SCRUM* | 1 | 1 | 3 | 3 |
| | A. NONE OR LIMITED CULTURAL BARRIERS TO ENTRY | 5 | 5 | 5 | 5 |
| | B. SOME CULTURAL BARRIERS TO ENTRY | 1 | 3 | 3 | 3 |
| | C. MANY CULTURAL BARRIERS TO ENTRY* | 1 | 1 | 1 | 1 |
| | A. NONE OR LIMITED REGULATORY ISSUES | 5 | 3 | 3 | 1 |
| | B. SOME REGULATORY ISSUES | 3 | 5 | 5 | 3 |
| | C. MANY REGULATORY ISSUES* | 1 | 3 | 3 | 5 |
| **6, 7, 8 TEAM** | A. YEARS OF SCRUM EXPERIENCE WITH TEN+ PROJECTS | 5 | 5 | 3 | 1 |
| | B. SOME SCRUM EXPERIENCE WITH FOUR TO NINE PROJECTS | 3 | 5 | 5 | 3 |
| | C. LIMITED OR NO SCRUM EXPERIENCE WITH THREE OR FEWER PROJECTS* | 1 | 3 | 1 | 5 |
| | A. EXCELLENT TECHNICAL CAPACITY | 5 | 5 | 3 | 1 |
| | B. AVERAGE TECHNICAL CAPACITY | 3 | 3 | 3 | 3 |
| | C. POOR TECHNICAL CAPACITY* | 1 | 3 | 5 | 5 |
| | A. EXCELLENT TASK DECOMPOSITION ABILITY | 5 | 5 | 1 | 1 |
| | B. AVERAGE TASK DECOMPOSITION ABILITY | 3 | 5 | 5 | 3 |
| | C. POOR TASK DECOMPOSITION ABILITY* | 1 | 1 | 3 | 5 |

*ANSWERS MARKED WITH AN ASTERISK ARE WARNING SIGNS. IF ONE OR MORE OF YOUR ANSWERS ARE MARKED WITH AN ASTERISK, YOU MAY NEED TO ADDRESS THOSE ISSUES BEFORE YOU START USING SCRUM

**TABLE 6-2**   Answers to the Project Duration Portion of the Sprint Length Model

|  | ONE WEEK | TWO WEEKS | THREE WEEKS | FOUR WEEKS |
|---|---|---|---|---|
| PROJECT DURATION OF SIX–NINE MONTHS | 3 | 5 | 5 | 3 |

You would then answer the next question, taking the numerical values from Table 6-1 and populating the Sprint Length Model. You should do this until you have answered all questions.

For example, let's assume that your answers for questions 2 through 5 (about the customer) were all "b" and your answers to questions 6 through 8 (about the team) were "b," "a," and "a." Your completed model would look like the one shown in Table 6-3.

In the last row, you will see we have some numbers (3, 4.75, 4, and 3). These are calculated averages (we added the numbers in each column and divided by eight, the number of questions). Based on this, your project should work best with a two-week sprint, with three weeks being a close contender and one- and four-week sprints coming in last.

## Be Warned

You should have noticed that some of the options in the model above run contrary to the recommendations I have made. You can select, for instance, a project duration greater than 12 months. These options have been highlighted as *warning sign* answers (denoted by an asterisk in the scoring key). If you find yourself with one or more warning sign answers, you likely have larger issues to deal with in your company than

**TABLE 6-3**   Example Sprint Length Model

|  | ONE WEEK | TWO WEEKS | THREE WEEKS | FOUR WEEKS |
|---|---|---|---|---|
| 1. PROJECT DURATION OF SIX–NINE MONTHS | 3 | 5 | 5 | 3 |
| 2. SOME CUSTOMER AVAILABILITY | 3 | 5 | 5 | 5 |
| 3. SOME CUSTOMER FAMILIARITY WITH SCRUM | 1 | 5 | 5 | 5 |
| 4. SOME CULTURAL BARRIERS EXIST | 1 | 3 | 3 | 3 |
| 5. SOME REGULATORY ISSUES | 3 | 5 | 5 | 3 |
| 6. SOME TEAM EXPERIENCE WITH SCRUM | 3 | 5 | 5 | 3 |
| 7. EXCELLENT TEAM TECHNICAL CAPABILITIES | 5 | 5 | 3 | 1 |
| 8. EXCELLENT TEAM TASK COMPOSITION ABILITY | 5 | 5 | 1 | 1 |
| AVERAGE RATING | 3 | 4.75 | 4 | 3 |

sprint length. These issues should be addressed *before* you try Scrum. Teams that start using Scrum with these issues in place usually end up failing and then blame the framework. Using Scrum for the first time is stressful enough. Trying to do it with too many preexisting warning signs is nearly impossible.

## Beyond the Quiz

After you get good at this, you will be able to gauge a good sprint length for your team in much the same way that Jay and Rachel did, by analysis, discussion, and feel.

When we do not have experience running sprints, we tend to experiment with various sprint lengths, which can be confusing for the customer and debilitating to the team. One company I worked with wanted to experiment with all the sprint lengths to see which one fit them best, even though two weeks was the obvious choice based on the sprint length model and just simple gut feel. They started out with three-week sprints, then two-week sprints, then a one-week sprint, then a four-week sprint, then back to a two-week sprint, and finally a three-week sprint. They ended up settling on two-week sprints, but by the time we finally landed on a sprint length, the team felt like they had just walked away from a car crash with no seatbelts.

If your team is new to Scrum, you should start with one of the two accepted standards (two weeks or four weeks) and do that consistently for several sprints. If you find that you are having difficulty at that point, it is much more likely that Scrum has uncovered a problem your team is having than that there is something wrong with your sprint length or with Scrum.

# Keys to Success

Determining sprint length does not need to be a daunting task, but it also is not something that should be taken lightly.

When determining sprint length it is essential to remember the following things:

- Project duration
- Amount of risk you are willing to take on
- The ability of the team
- The tolerance of the customer

For each of these, remember that the stimulus-to-response time should be the main driver in your decision. The more feedback you have, the better able you will be to tolerate risk. Shorter sprints enable you to identify potential risks sooner but come with a cost of increased customer interaction and more interruptions for the team. Longer sprints mean that it will take longer to find the risks but have the benefit of fewer interaction points and interruptions. Balancing feedback with interaction and interruptions is a challenge that your team and customer will perfect over time.

The questions and corresponding scoring key I provided in this chapter may not work for everyone; when you're adjusting sprint length, consider it a starting point. Don't stress as much about following the model's exact questions and answer weightings; focus instead on whether you are considering both your customer and your team when determining your sprint length. Finally, don't forget that the reason we are doing our work in short one-to-four-week cycles is to gather customer feedback, show project progress through working software, and to frequently deliver a project that is potentially shippable. The right sprint length balances our craving for customer feedback and input with our ability to deliver and their ability to respond.

## Sprints Longer Than Four Weeks

In *Agile Project Management with Scrum,* Ken Schwaber writes, "The Sprint is time-boxed to 30 consecutive calendar days.… This is also the maximum time that can be allocated without the Team doing so much work that it requires artifacts and documentation to support its thought processes. It is also the maximum time that most stakeholders will wait without losing interest in the Team's progress and without losing their belief that the Team is doing something meaningful for them" [SCHWABER, p. 136].

This is important because the whole purpose behind the 30 or less day sprint length is the feedback loop—validating that the path the team is on is the correct one. Another way to put it is that in the beginning of the sprint, the team heard what the product owner (and the stakeholders) asked for. At the end of the sprint, they are presenting what they think they heard—essentially trying to prevent what I call the What I Meant syndrome, in that customers and stakeholders say after a sprint or release, "You built what I asked for but not what I meant." This plagues so many of us, why would we not want shorter feedback loops?

## Extending Sprint Length

"If we can't finish our work, should we extend the length of our sprint to finish the work we have in the backlog?" I get this question all the time. This is dangerous. Ron Jeffries told me once, "If you can't get your work done in three or four weeks, what makes you think you can get it done in five, six, seven, or eight?" His suggestion to me at the time? Switch to one-week sprints. Why? Simply because you can come in on a Monday and see what you need to do by the end of the week. It's clear and simple. Further, it forces stories and tasks to be smaller and provides the team more opportunities to reflect and correct issues. In other words, it greatly improves the stimulus-to-response time.

# References

[SCHWABER]   Schwaber, Ken. 2004. *Agile Software Development with Scrum.* Redmond, WA: Microsoft Press. p. 136.

# Chapter 7

# HOW DO WE KNOW WHEN WE ARE DONE?

"Are you done yet?" This seemingly harmless question is asked countless times on almost every software project. The way we answer, however, is anything but innocuous. If you respond with a "yes," you might be forced to take on additional work. If you say, "no," you could be branded as someone who can't get things done. If team members' answers vary, you could lose your stakeholders' trust.

Establishing an up-front, common understanding of "done" can save teams and businesses countless hours of process thrash, ambiguity, and hidden work. In this chapter, you learn what a definition of done is, how it adds value, and the value it communicates to stakeholders. You learn an exercise that helps you build your own definition of done and manage it over time.

We join our product owner, Mary Anne, who is hosting a story workshop with her customers and stakeholders.

## The Story

Mary Anne was hosting a story workshop to build the product backlog for a large back-office infrastructure project. She had gathered roughly 20 stakeholders in the room, including systems engineers, general managers, developers, marketing people, product managers, and salespeople. Each had varying degrees of interest in this project, and each thought that his thing was the most important and should be built first. Mary Anne knew from the beginning that such a diverse group would be a challenge and that she would need to focus the meeting to filter out the noise and get the real stories needed to start the work.

Mary Anne had her team's definition of done in her back pocket. Even so, she decided not to distribute it at the beginning of the meeting for two reasons: She wanted to ensure people felt open and unconstrained by a predetermined list, and she did not want them to get the impression that the definition of done was up for negotiation.

Two hours into the meeting, the group had authored approximately 200 stories. This was a huge success; however, people were starting to get hung up on the sequence in which the stories would be accomplished—their ordering. Naturally, the systems engineer wanted to see monitoring, security, and all hardware and network infrastructure built first. The marketing people just wanted a release date. The developers and testers wanted to drill into the weeds to figure out what each story meant.

It was at this point that Mary Anne revealed the definition of done identified by the team. The list covered what it meant to be done with a story, a sprint, a release to the integration environments, and, finally, to release to production environment.

A partial list of the definition of done that Mary Anne presented to her stakeholders in the meeting is shown in Figure 7-1.

The stakeholders were shocked. Never before had they seen such detail and commitment to a quality release before this. Bill was the first to speak up.

"Mary Anne, this looks pretty comprehensive. Are you saying that with each sprint, you will do performance testing?" Bill asked.

"Yes" said Mary Anne, "and more. We plan to do everything needed to ship our system as it's being built instead of waiting until the end."

Bill continued. "What about the environment build outs? Why aren't they on here?"

"Simple," stated Mary Anne. "Our definition of done covers the things that will be present throughout the life of the project. For example, the troubleshooting guides that we will write for your team will be expanded with each story, meaning we won't have a 'documentation phase' at the end of the project to do all the documentation. We will do everything needed to deliver our system every sprint."

"I think I get it," said Bill. "Your definition of done is all about things that are constant throughout the project—not one time things. Those would be more on the task level, or maybe story level?"

TEAM "DONE" LIST

| ...WITH A STORY | ...WITH A SPRINT |
|---|---|
| • ALL CODE (TEST AND MAINLINE) CHECKED IN | ALL STORY CRITERIA, PLUS... |
| • ALL UNIT TESTS PASSING | • PRODUCT BACKUP UPDATED |
| • ALL ACCEPTANCE TESTS IDENTIFIED, WRITTEN & PASSING | • PERFORMANCE TESTING |
| • HELP FILE AUTO GENERATED | • PACKAGE, CLASS & ARCHITECTURE DIAGRAMS UPDATED |
| • FUNCTIONAL TESTS PASS | • ALL BUGS CLOSED OR POSTPONED |
| | • CODE COVERAGE FOR ALL UNIT TESTS AT 80% |

| ...RELEASE TO INTEGRATION | ...RELEASE TO PRODUCTION |
|---|---|
| ALL SPRINT CRITERIA, PLUS... | ALL INTEGRATION CRITERIA, PLUS... |
| • INSTALLATION PACKAGES CREATED | • STRESS TESTING |
| • MOM PACKAGES CREATED | • PERFORMANCE TUNING |
| • OPERATIONS GUIDE UPDATED | • NETWORK DIAGRAM UPDATED |
| • TROUBLESHOOTING GUIDES UPDATED | • SECURITY PASS VALIDATED |
| • DISASTER RECOVERY PLAN UPDATED | • THREAT MODELING PASS VALIDATED |
| • ALL TEST SUITES PASSING | • DISASTER RECOVERY PLAN TESTED |

**FIGURE 7-1**    Sample done list

"That's right," said Mary Anne. "Our definition of done is about keeping our professionalism high. Like a Christmas present is done when it's under the tree and wrapped with a bow, our definition of done is when a task, a story, a sprint, or a release meets this criteria. We'll test for it each sprint and demo it in the review meeting as well."

After seeing the team's definition of done, the systems engineers were comfortable with the level of work Mary Anne's team was doing to address their needs on each story, sprint, and release. The security team was equally pleased to see the level of architecture, documentation, and threat modeling that the team was doing. Equally (if not more) satisfied were the sales, marketing, and general management stakeholders. Knowing that the team would complete the work to such a detailed level each and every sprint helped assure everyone that his own piece of the pie would be done correctly.

## The Model

Having a "definition of done" for your team helps all the stakeholders visualize the team's commitment to do the best possible work to meet the needs of the business and its customers. To teams that use it, the definition of done becomes a way of life—not a checklist to follow, but a commitment to excellence.

The definition of done also gives teams a way to communicate. When everyone can see what it means for this team to be done with its work, the team no longer hears, "Are you done with this or are you done with that?" Instead they are asked, "Is this story complete? Is the iteration complete? Have you released to your environments?" And everyone understands what an affirmative answer really means.

Each team should create a definition of done that is unique to its own particular company, product, or situation. The following exercise helps your team explore what it means when a story is done.

YOU NEED THE FOLLOWING TO PERFORM THIS EXERCISE:

1. YOUR TEAM (YOUR PRODUCT OWNER IS OPTIONAL BUT HELPFUL TO HAVE ASSIST

2. MANY PADS OF POST-IT NOTES IN MULTIPLE COLORS (STICKIES)

3. PENS (I FIND THAT SHARP, PERMANENT MARKERS WORK BEST)

4. A ROOM THAT THE TEAM CAN UTILIZE FOR 2–4 HOURS

5. AN OPEN MIND

6. NO INTERRUPTIONS

The Definition of Done Exercise is constructed from these components:

1. Brainstorming Session
2. Categorization Session
3. Sorting Session
4. Definition of Done Creation and Publishing

This exercise helps you create your initial definition of done. Notice I said "initial." Definitions are not created once, buried in a drawer, and never seen again. Teams should schedule time during retrospectives to periodically review their definitions of done and determine whether there are opportunities for improvement or modification. Feel free to revise the list to meet the needs of the team and its stakeholders, but be careful. Too many revisions too frequently may create doubt about the validity of the definition of done in the eyes of the stakeholders. Invest the time to create a solid baseline and modify the list based on the experience and findings of the team.

## Introduction

People often ask me who from the team should participate in this exercise. This question always catches me off guard.

We have been conditioned to work in our functional silos for so long that people often look perplexed when I answer this question. I believe that everyone on the team, no matter his or her expertise or background, can add value and should be involved.

If the team's project is a backend database system or a three-tier web application, some people on the team will have less experience and knowledge of the technology than others. That is just a fact. Keeping team members out of this exercise, though, only deprives the team of the valuable contributions of other team members. It also keeps them from having a valuable team building exercise.

Therefore, I recommend having the entire team do this exercise, regardless of skills, background, or role on the team. Consider including your product owner, who has insight and information that the team may find valuable. If the product owner becomes too overbearing, gently remind him to be respectful.

## Brainstorming Session

Alex F. Osborn is widely known as the father of brainstorming. In his books, *Your Creative Power* [OSBORN01] and *Applied Imagination* [OSBORN02], Osborn outlines the brainstorming technique, a system that uses the brain to "storm" creative solutions to a problem. This creative approach is designed to generate a free flow of ideas. In the brainstorming session, there are no right or wrong answers. There is no criticism, there are only ideas. The rules of brainstorming, outlined by Osborn, are simple:

- No criticism of ideas.
- Go for large quantities of ideas.
- Build on each other's ideas.
- Encourage wild and exaggerated ideas.

At the beginning of the brainstorming session, set the proper tone. The reason the team is together in the room is to identify everything that it needs to do to ship software, the truest measure of project progress I have encountered to date.

It is important to set the direction of the brainstorming session in the beginning. Start by writing on a whiteboard the question the team's definition of done will answer. What question is that? It depends. The most common question is this: "What do we need to do, as a team, to ship software to our customers/stakeholders?"

Your question may vary, depending on your own team's unique circumstances; however, the purpose is the same. Make sure the question is on a whiteboard, or any other viewable place in the room, before you continue.

Hand everyone a pen and a sticky pad. I have found that individuals like having different colors; this ultimately depends on your team members' preferences.

You are now ready to begin brainstorming. Kick it off by repeating the question you are answering (see the previous one for an example). Have each team member write an answer on a sticky, call out the answer, put that sticky in a pile in the middle of the table, and repeat. Team members can write only one answer per sticky and must call out after each answer is written. As team members start to share their answers, inevitably some will say, "I've already written that." Do not worry about creating duplicate items at the moment. This will be addressed later.

Why the callout? I have found that the callout puts the *storm* in brainstorm. I have personally identified multiple additional items when fellow team members have called out a definition of done item. I have also witnessed team members building on each other's ideas when coaching teams through this exercise. I have run this exercise without the team members calling out what they wrote on the stickies, but it resulted in a stale, unproductive meeting. Calling out might feel weird and uncomfortable at first; however, the feeling subsides very quickly once the team becomes engaged and the meeting begins to flow.

Run the brainstorming part of the session until people run out of ideas. It is generally easy to identify when people are done because the flow of sticky notes begins to dwindle. People begin looking around the room and at each other, searching for something new.

## Categorization Session

There should now be a large lump of sticky notes on the table, waiting to be categorized.

Start by asking the team members how they each think the sticky notes should be categorized.

The most common responses I see look like this:

- Development
- Test
- Project Management
- Other

All of these typical responses are decomposed by functional work area. This makes sense. After all, we have been conditioned to work in functional silos, not in cross-functional multidiscipline teams. Unfortunately, categorizing this way reinforces our functional roles within a team and does not promote cross-functional interaction. Additionally, customers and stakeholders generally do not care about what it means to be done with development or test. They care about what it means to be done with a release to production or a release to manufacturing.

If you get those responses, challenge the team to focus on customer value: delivering stories at the end of an iteration and releasing to an integration environment where customers can use and interact with the software provides value. Even more value is provided if a system is released to a production environment and officially done.

After introducing this line of thinking, the responses I typically see change dramatically:

- Done with a story
- Done with an iteration
- Release to integration
- Release to production

Once the categories are identified, clear, and understood by the team, create areas on the walls in the room to post sticky notes under each category.

This is a team exercise. Each person grabs some sticky notes (preferably others' notes) from the table and begins placing each note under the appropriate category. Team members should not spend a great deal of time wrestling with whether categories are right or wrong—at this point, they should just get the notes on the wall. Sorting the notes should take between 10 and 20 minutes, depending on the quantity of sticky notes generated.

Once all sticky notes are on the wall, have everyone take a few steps back and look at the wall.

That is a lot of stuff.

## Sorting and Consolidation Session

Once everything is on the wall and categorized, it's time to begin consolidation, using an approach similar to that advocated by Mike Cohn [COHN].

This is a team exercise. Each person reviews the sticky notes on the wall and looks for duplicate items. Types of duplicates include exact matches, similar matches, and "we don't know what the heck these are."

For exact matches, simply take the two matching sticky notes and stick them to each other so that the top one fully covers the one underneath as illustrated in Figure 7-2. Do this only when it is clear that the items are exact matches and that the decision to marry them will require little discussion later in the session.

For similar matches, have the top sticky note offset the one underneath as illustrated in Figure 7-3. This helps everyone easily identify items that are similar, but not exact, matches. These items require further team discussion to determine a clear meaning for the definition of done candidate item.

For stickies that make no sense at all, as illustrated in Figure 7-4, create a new category off to the side and name it "other" or something similar. The team will revisit these items last.

Again, have the team step back and look at the wall. They probably still are overwhelmed but starting to feel that things are a bit more manageable.

**FIGURE 7-2**   Exact matches

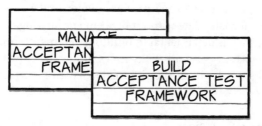

**FIGURE 7-3**   Similar matches

**FIGURE 7-4**   Initially makes no sense

Once all notes are consolidated, the team is ready to discuss what the comments written on each sticky note mean.

The process I use for this is relatively simple. As facilitator, start with a set of stickies (I like to start with the exact matches, as they are the easiest), take them off the wall, read them to the team and ask, "What does this mean?" Once the team answers, move on. If certain team members do not answer, query them directly and ask for confirmation that they understand what a specific sticky set means before moving on. It is important to time box this activity. If the team cannot come to consensus, or even agreement, shelve the item for later or take a mental break by going for a walk.

After the exact matches are finished, move on to the similar match sets. These are managed slightly differently. Take the set off the wall, read them to the team, and ask, "What does this mean?" When the team answers, pick the card from the set that most closely matches the team's answer or create a new sticky to reflect what was discussed.

After a set of similar items has been discussed, the team should be left with only one card that represents what will be committed to and communicated by the team. Throw out duplicates or consolidate them like their "exact match" counterparts. Throughout the process, new stickies may be created and old ones discarded. This is key.

Lastly, move on to the stickies that are anomalies or make no sense. Use the same process of pulling a sticky off the wall, reading it, and asking what it means. Follow this by asking, "Does the team need to include this item in its definition of done?" If the team responds with a resounding "yes," move the sticky to its proper category. If the team is unsure or hesitant, facilitate a discussion that results in either a resounding yes or the item being tossed. If the team responds with a plain no, toss it.

If your product owner is in the room at this time, she may have questions as to why items are being tossed. Help the product owner understand that while things can always be added at a later date without breaking or hurting trust, removing items once the list is published is detrimental to building and maintaining trust.

Once the team has reviewed all sticky notes, understands what each one means, and agrees that all stickies are in the right category, this portion of the exercise is complete.

## Definition of Done Creation

Teams are generally tired at this point. The entire exercise is a draining experience but very rewarding. Creating and publishing the definition of done is the easiest part.

Take a digital picture of what is on the wall and put it in electronic format. Publish the list on the internal team website and create a poster that can be hung for all to see. It serves as a reminder of what it means for the team to be done and acts as a powerful communication tool. When stakeholders ask, "Are you done yet?," the team can point to the definition of done and answer, "We are done with our stories and working on our release"—and the person asking will understand exactly what the team means.

### What About "Undone" Work?

Let's say the team gets to the end of a sprint and some items don't meet the definition of done criteria. What happens? Should they get partial credit (whatever that means) for work completed or should the work not count toward their velocity?

For me it's simple, and I suggest you follow the simple model as well: If a story meets the definition of done, it's done. If it does not, then it is not done. It's pretty black and white. Factoring in complexity, "almost or nearly done," or any other excuse to say a certain story should be included in the velocity should be discounted. Undone work goes back to the product backlog for prioritization by the product owner and may be re-added to the sprint backlog in the following sprint.

## Keys to Success

Creating and publishing a definition of done accomplishes three things.

First, it helps build a bond between team members. It gives them the feeling that they are "all in this together" and that it is more important to deliver on their joint commitments than to focus on specific individual tasks.

Second, it provides clear communication to stakeholders, and by implication, drives down the risk of technical (or other) debt being deferred to later in the cycle. If a stakeholder asks the team if the software works, and the response by the team is, "Sure it works, but we don't have an installer," the team has racked up technical debt because the component is not truly done. Through the done list, and through the communication of that list, stakeholders gain a clear understanding that if the team says they will be releasing to production, they will have met a series of requirements that are needed for such a release. No more will done simply mean that something is coded. On the contrary, done will mean exactly what is published in the done list. Stakeholders will come to expect this level of quality and commitment.

Third, it keeps the team on track and focused. When planning an iteration, the team has a reference point as to what it means to be done. The guesswork is removed, enabling the team to focus on delivery instead of speculating about what could be "if only this or that happened." The commitment is made, published, and adhered to. The list should be revised as needed and re-published. When used correctly, it provides the team with a common vision on how to achieve the iteration, release, and project goals.

## References

[COHN]    Cohn, Mike. 2004. *User Stories Applied*. Boston: Addison-Wesley.

[OSBORN01]    Osborn, Alex F. 1948. *Your Creative Power*. New York: C. Scribner's Sons.

[OSBORN02]    Osborn, Alex F. 1957. *Applied Imagination*. New York: Scribner.

# Chapter 8

# THE CASE FOR A FULL-TIME SCRUMMASTER

Organizations often have difficulty transitioning to an agile process such as Scrum or XP. Even after they get past the "it's a fad" or "we can't work like that" excuses, some in the organization still have trouble letting go of old ideas and habits. One of the most common arguments teams face is that the organization can't justify or afford a full-time ScrumMaster. Organizations are used to having people wear multiple hats; having a team leader that doesn't also contribute to the work of the iteration is hard for many to understand.

In Chapter 5, "Implementing the Scrum Roles," we talked about how ScrumMasters do their jobs most effectively when they are fully dedicated to that role and do not also serve as team members or product owners. But did you know having a full-time ScrumMaster can actually save the organization money in the long run? Let's follow Stein as he explains this notion to his boss, David.

## The Story

"I just don't get it," said David. "You are one of the best developers I have. Why should I sacrifice all your coding ability and make you a dedicated ScrumMaster? Can't you do the coaching bit on the side? From what I can see, it's just a glorified reporting job."

Stein sighed quietly. David was his immediate manager, and while they had been doing Scrum in the company for some time, David had always fought it.

"I've taken the training, talked to teams who have done several different agile processes, and read several books and articles on this, David," explained Stein. "They all say the same thing: A full-time ScrumMaster is essential to making the most of Scrum."

David sneered. "Yours isn't the only team around here doing Scrum, you know. Take the Colletti project, for instance. I've seen what that ScrumMaster, Teresa, does—she just schedules the meetings and collects data. Big deal. I need you in the trenches, Stein. You can do your reporting in four hours a week."

Stein was ready for this. "I hear you and I agree. I could do reporting in four hours a week. Let's talk about the Colletti project for a second, though. What kinds of improvements have you seen from that team?"

"Well, at first the team got better—about 20–30 percent faster than they were before—but then it stalled out. I haven't seen any of those huge gains the consultants promised me."

"I agree with you, David. The Colletti project hasn't made much progress after the initial improvements. But one of the reasons is because Teresa hasn't been allowed to let go of her team member role. She doesn't have time to do any of the things ScrumMasters are supposed to do."

Stein went to the whiteboard and began writing some of the key functions of a ScrumMaster (see Figure 8-1).

"Reporting is a tool good ScrumMasters use, but it's only a contributing activity to the real things ScrumMasters are supposed to do every day," explained Stein, as he continued to write. "These are just a few of the others," he explained (see Figure 8-2).

"I agree those things are important, but I'm not convinced they're worth removing you from your hands-on work. I've got to be able to justify the cost," said David.

"I'm working up to that. Indulge me for a minute while I walk through this with you. You remember what velocity is right?" asked Stein.

"Yes, the amount of work, or story points, or something, that a team gets done in a sprint," stated David.

"Close enough. So my job as the ScrumMaster is to help the team get their velocity up, which essentially drives the cost per point down," said Stein.

"Cost per point?" asked David.

"Yes, you see the velocity is calculated on the number of story points a team delivers in each sprint. Every team has a cost, the loaded team cost. Let's say that my

- INCREASE OVERALL TEAM PERFORMANCE
- GET BLOCKERS REMOVED QUICKLY
- BUILD A COHESIVE, TIGHT TEAM

**FIGURE 8-1** Key functions of a ScrumMaster

- FACILITATE TEAM ACTIVITIES
- KEEP THINGS FLOWING SMOOTHLY

**FIGURE 8-2** Other key functions of a ScrumMaster

team costs ten grand per sprint, just to keep our math simple. Every sprint, my team delivers ten story points. What is the cost per point?" asked Stein.

"A thousand bucks per point. So what?" asked David.

"Well, if you give me time to do all the things on this whiteboard," said Stein pointing back to his list, "I can get that cost per point down to \$500–\$650."

"\$500, huh? Cut it in half? What magic are you going to perform to do that?" asked David.

"That's what makes this a full-time job. I look up from the noise of everyday work to see trends, patterns, problems that are blocking the team from going faster. If you have a kink in a hose and the water is on—how much water comes out? Not much. If you unkink the hose, the water flows again. One of my jobs is to look for kinks and then work with you or other teams or HR or senior management to get those kinks out as quickly as possible."

"I'm with you so far," said David. "Keep going."

"So my other big responsibility is to build a cohesive team. Like a coach on a football team, right? He's not out there passing the ball or running plays, is he? But does that mean he has nothing to do but record the stats? No. He's leading the team, watching film, working out strategies, helping them see where they need to improve. He lifts them up when they're down and keeps them grounded when they start to stray from their goals. He focuses them on fundamentals and discipline and just plain functioning as a unit.

"The ScrumMaster job is like that. I'm still hands-on; my hands are just busy doing other things. I lead and guide the team through the process all the while keeping a higher level view of what needs to be done. I remove impediments, keep them focused, find ways to improve, all in the name of increasing velocity. Now, unlike a football coach, I can help out and write code from time to time. But I would only do that as part of helping the team when they are stuck; it's not really part of my job. Making sense?" asked Stein.

"Good points," said David. "But you haven't explained how this costs me less, yet."

"Well, if I do my job well the team will go faster, get more done, right? Because there will be fewer impediments, more teamwork, improved performance. With me as a part-time ScrumMaster, we'd perform about like Teresa's team. So my 10 grand team would go from a velocity of 10 story points to 12 or 13, and your cost would go from 1,000 per point to 750–800 per point. With me on full-time, we'll start out with those improvements but then quickly move to 17–20 story points per sprint. So points that used to cost a grand are now costing you…"

"\$500–\$600 per sprint. Is that realistic, though? Can having a dedicated Scrum-Master really double team performance?" asked David.

"The research I've done and the people I've talked to suggest that it's possible, but I'm hesitant to make those kinds of promises without having done it before," said Stein. "However, the research does lead me to believe that we can't reach our true potential unless I'm working on this full time. You're paying me to work on the team anyway. So, if having me work as a ScrumMaster instead of 'in the trenches' means we do even a little better than Teresa's team, wouldn't you grant me that the cost savings make having a full-time ScrumMaster worthwhile?"

"Yes. If you can show me that this works and get some good gains and improvements, and help drive the change back into the organization, I'll grant you anything you want," David said, smiling. "Show me what you can do."

# The Model

One of the jobs of the ScrumMaster is to remove impediments. Another is educating the Scrum team (including the product owner), stakeholders, and others in the organization so that the team is eventually able to resolve its own impediments. This ultimately results in more efficient teams that can get more done. Good ScrumMasters function as the oil in the engine—they reduce or remove friction, enabling teams to move to a high-performing state.

I am often asked how I measure the impact a ScrumMaster has on a team or organization, and how I convince management to "allow" a person to take on the ScrumMaster role full time. My answer: Start with rates of improvement and relate that to dollars and cents.

Though each team will have different velocities, run a different number of iterations, and have different overall results, the rate of improvement on an agile team follows the same general pattern. I want to walk you through an example with fictitious numbers so that you can see how that pattern forms. I don't want you to get caught up in the exact numbers, though. It's the pattern that matters—and it is evident in the trend line in each chart that follows. Once we've established what the pattern is, I show you some real charts from real teams so that you can see the pattern repeat itself again and again.

Our fictitious team is running two-week sprints and is about two months into the project. After four sprints, the team is averaging around 10 points per sprint (see Figure 8-3). During sprint 3, they come to the realization that they want to add a full-time ScrumMaster to the team.

After adding a full-time ScrumMaster, the team begins to see some initial improvements. The team learns to work together in an agile way and the ScrumMaster starts to remove impediments. The average from sprints 5 through 8 goes up to about 12 points per sprint (see Figure 8-4).

To recap, sprint block 1 (sprints 1-4) had an average of 10 points. The team did not have a full-time ScrumMaster until sprint 4. Sprint block 2 (sprints 5-8) had an average of about 12, a 20 percent improvement with a full-time ScrumMaster.

Let's roll back the clock and work on the premise that the team never adds a full-time ScrumMaster (let's assume the team has one, but that person is splitting time between team tasks and ScrumMaster responsibilities). After the first six sprints, the team would begin to plateau, as illustrated in Figure 8-5, which shows a downward trend. The team has likely achieved its maximum output.

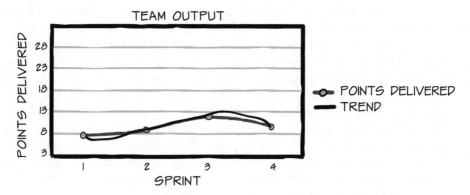

**FIGURE 8-3**    Output pattern for the first four sprints

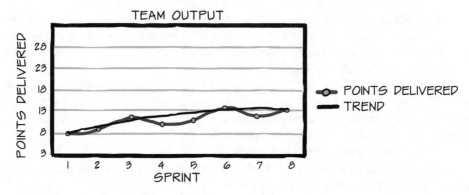

**FIGURE 8-4**    Output pattern for sprints 1 through 8

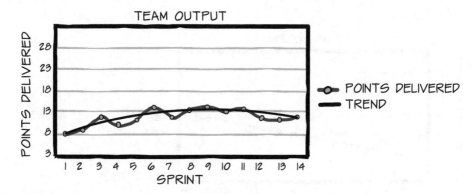

**FIGURE 8-5**    Output without a ScrumMaster

Notice that the team sputtered out, for whatever reason. It could be that the ScrumMaster was doing too much sprint task-related work, it could be that the impediments facing the team could not be resolved, it could be that there was no cohesive core team, only a variety of people working on various parts of the code. Regardless, this is where most teams end up. They start Scrum, get some small gains (10 percent to 25 percent), and then sputter out. They become frustrated because they know they can do more; some even end up reverting back to traditional development approaches.

Let's go back to the original premise, where the team added the ScrumMaster in sprint 3. The team is well coached and is in a reasonably supportive organization. This team also stumbles a bit but then rights the ship—after the first six sprints, the team takes one step back and then begins to show marked improvement in sprints 11-14, as identified by the trend line shown in Figure 8-6.

Now what we see is that the average from sprint 8 to sprint 14 is more like 15 to 17 points per sprint. So far this team has moved from a 10-point average, through a 12-point average, to a 16-point average, a 60 percent improvement so far.

This team isn't done yet, though. The team continues to improve, clearing blocking issues and obtaining training in many engineering practices. The team begins to perform at high levels, finding their sweet spot and hovering at a sustainable pace (see Chapter 23, "Sustainable Pace," for more on this topic).

The final chart in Figure 8-7 shows an average of 24 points per sprint from sprint 15 to 23. The team then tops out at an average velocity of 28 for the next five sprints, sprints 24 through 28. The trend line flattens eventually, but at a much higher level than the team without a full-time ScrumMaster.

Table 8-1 summarizes the improvements.

Improved velocity is great. But to help bring the point home to your manager, we need to put it in terms of cost per story point.

Teams generally have a flat cost that can be easily identified by the employee loaded cost. Let's look at a model where the numbers are rounded but are based on an actual company (see Table 8-2).

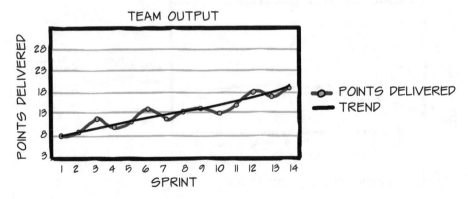

**FIGURE 8-6**   Output with a ScrumMaster

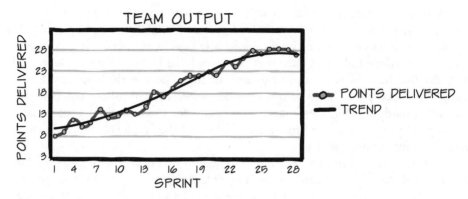

**FIGURE 8-7**    Output peak

**TABLE 8-1**    Summary of the Improvements

| SPRINT BLOCK | SPRINT NUMBERS | AVERAGE VELOCITY | IMPROVEMENT FROM THE START |
|---|---|---|---|
| 1 | 1-4 | 10 | |
| 2 | 5-8 | 12 | 20% |
| 3 | 9-14 | 16 | 60% |
| 4 | 15-23 | 24 | 140% |
| 5 | 24-28 | 28 | 180% |

**TABLE 8-2**    Employee Loaded Costs

| EMPLOYEE LOADED COST | DOLLARS |
|---|---|
| BASE SALARY | $100,000 |
| PAID TIME OFF (3 WEEK, 15 DAYS) | $5,500 |
| COMPANY CONTRIBUTION TO BENEFITS (E.G. 401K MATCH) | $4,000 |
| EMPLOYEE TRAINING | $3,000 |
| HR OVERHEAD | $1,000 |
| EMPLOYER TAXES ON BEHALF OF EMPLOYEE: (FUTA, FICA, MEDICARE, ETC.) | $7,000 |
| OPERATIONS AND GENERAL EXPENSE (OFFICE SPACE, PHONE, ETC.) | $10,000 |
| COMPANY BENEFITS | $25,000 |
| PAYROLL RELATED EXPENSES | $10,000 |
| SELLING, GENERAL & ADMINISTRATIVE EXPENSE PER EMPLOYEE | $35,000 |
| TOTAL COST TO THE COMPANY PER EMPLOYEE | $200,500 |

ASSUMPTIONS: 100 EMPLOYEES, 4 VPS, 8 DIRECTORS, 5 SALES

What we see here is that an employee's cost adds up to about double his or her salary. So if we have an employee loaded cost of $200,000 (rounding), and that employee has about 47 working weeks available (52 weeks available minus 3 for PTO, minus 2 for federal holidays), then that employee has 1,880 hours available to work. At $200,000, that comes out to just under $107/hr in cost to the company. (Funny thing is that companies need to make money, especially consulting companies, so they often mark up what they charge their clients for their employees' time, say to $150 or $225 an hour depending on the skill set of the employee. But let's use the actual cost for our analysis.)

Now, we were talking about cost per point, and we know what it costs per hour for one employee. If a team can bust out 10 points per sprint and the loaded team cost is about $440 an hour (team of four people at $110 an hour loaded cost), the team costs, per sprint, $35,200 ($440 times 80 hours for a two-week sprint). This assumes a dedicated team working on one project and that the time spent on non-project-related tasks is still a loaded cost on the project.

A team costs $35,200 per sprint. Let's see how that maps to Table 8-1 (see Table 8-3). What we see here is that our fictional well-coached team, with a full-time Scrum-Master, over the course of 8 sprints (4 months) reduced its cost per point by 17 percent. Over the course of 14 sprints (7 months), the same team was able to reduce the cost per point by 38 percent from the start and increase velocity by 60 percent. Over the course of 28 sprints (14 months), the team's cost per point was reduced by 64 percent, a result of the team's 180 percent improvement from the beginning.

Now I just made these numbers up to show you the overall pattern. Can real teams expect this same kind of improvement? Yes. Real teams, with full-time Scrum-Masters who are engaged in coaching the team, management, the stakeholders, and are actively removing impediments, can and do exhibit a strikingly similar pattern. Let's look at some real teams and real data. I typically capture ten sprints' worth of data because after about ten sprints, there is enough to see if the team is going to succeed or do poorly.

Example one is shown in Figure 8-8.

Notice that though the numbers are different, the pattern is the same as in the charts presented earlier in the chapter.

Figure 8-9 presents another example.

**TABLE 8-3**   Summary of the Improvements

| SPRINT BLOCK | SPRINT NUMBERS | AVERAGE VELOCITY | IMPROVEMENT ON LAST | IMPROVEMENT FROM SPRINT 1 | COST PER POINT | REDUCTION FROM 1 | PERCENT SAVINGS |
|---|---|---|---|---|---|---|---|
| 1 | 1-4 | 10 | | | $3,520 | | |
| 2 | 5-8 | 12 | 20% | 20% | $2,933 | $587 | 17% |
| 3 | 9-14 | 16 | 33% | 60% | $2,220 | $1,320 | 38% |
| 4 | 15-23 | 24 | 50% | 140% | $1,467 | $2,053 | 58% |
| 5 | 24-28 | 28 | 17% | 180% | $1,257 | $2,263 | 64% |

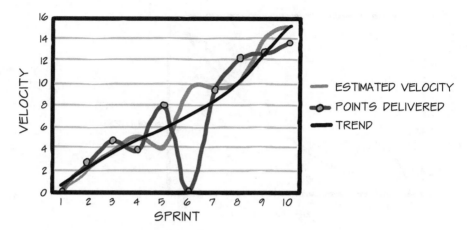

**FIGURE 8-8**    Output from a real team

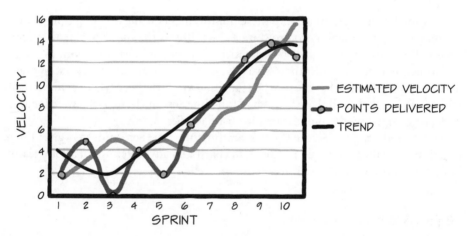

**FIGURE 8-9**    Output from another real team

Notice that though this chart reflects the performance of a different team, the pattern is almost identical to the previous chart. Note that in both examples, the team failed a sprint.

Figure 8-10 shows a chart for a team that failed its first sprint and struggled all the way through six sprints before improving dramatically.

The real teams you see in these examples all had varying starting points and sustained velocities, but in each case you can see a quick rise, followed by a shallow dip (where the team was in danger of stagnating), followed again by a sharp rise and a gradual increase to high sustainable pace.

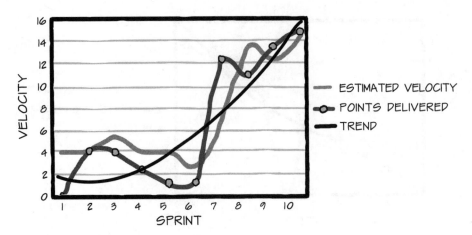

**FIGURE 8-10** A team that struggled

So why did these teams achieve these improvements while others sputtered out? The reasons for the inability to grow are as plentiful as the number of agile teams. Some fail to implement engineering practices, others don't learn to work as a true cross-functional team, still others struggle with organizational blockers. While I cannot say for certain what caused the teams shown in these charts to achieve their results, I do know that all these teams had full-time ScrumMasters who were focused on clearing impediments and maximizing team efficiency.

Don't handicap your ScrumMasters. Staffing full-time ScrumMasters gives them the ability to realize their true role of team coach and advocate. And it allows teams the opportunity to reach their full potential as well.

## Keys to Success

The job of ScrumMaster is real. It can have a big impact on costs as illustrated previously, saving the company money—period. But what does a ScrumMaster do all day to justify a full-time role? The following list encompasses most, but not all, of the day-to-day tasks.

- Remove impediments/resolve problems
- Break up fights/quarrels
- Act as a team mom
- Report team data
- Facilitate
- Help out where needed
- Educate the organization
- Drive organizational change

In 2007, Michael James published a great checklist at the URL in the references section [JAMES]. If the link is broken by the time you read this, search for "Scrum-Master Checklist Michael James" in your favorite search engine.

## Removing Impediments/Resolve Problems

Removing impediments and dealing with problems are always at the top of the list because, especially early in a project, there are many issues to deal with, both external and internal. Many chapters in this book are about removing impediments—running a good daily standup, having people show up on time, and so on—but there are more than just team-centric impediments. Impediments or problems found by teams in large companies could be that another team does not respond in a timely fashion, your team needs to understand how an interface works and the people who wrote it are not available, or you have someone out sick for a few days. You also have to interface with management, doing everything from convincing them that an agile process is worthwhile, to reminding them of the fact that your job is full time, to paving the way for bonuses based on team, rather than individual, performance. Finally, you work to help the team solve its own problems and remove its own impediments. A good ScrumMaster should strive to work himself out of a job by creating a high-performing team. For some, this may be impossible to achieve, but it should always be the goal.

## Breaking Up Fights/Acting as Team Mom

People are human. Sometimes we get in weird moods, don't get enough coffee, have a bad night's sleep, or just see something that sets us off in a bad way. Just the other day my youngest daughter, Emma, who is six, could not decide what shirt to wear and thought everything she picked out looked terrible—she lost it. My wife and I had to bring her back to reality.

I've had perfectly rational team members who come to work one day and lose it over a challenge to their ideas. Talking them off the ledge takes patience and people skills. Good ScrumMasters need to have the soft skills to intervene when necessary and the emotional intelligence to know when it's better to stay out of it altogether.

## Reporting Team Performance

The ScrumMaster needs to help the team improve. One of the ways this is done is through reporting. A good ScrumMaster tracks the team's historic velocities, burndown rates, and many other project-related metrics. This is done not only to assist the ScrumMaster's own team in improving its estimation and smoothing the rate at which stories are completed during a sprint, but also to help other teams (especially new ones) in the organization as well.

The important thing to remember is that *reporting team data,* either internally to the team or externally to management, does not mean you are collecting data to hold against the team. Instead, you are providing visibility into data that the team needs to see and understand to improve.

## Facilitate and Help Out Where Needed

To facilitate is to make things easier. Facilitate has its roots in the French word *facile,* which is to make things easy. The job of the ScrumMaster is to make it easier for the team to achieve its sprint goal.

Many ScrumMasters wrongly assume that the best way to facilitate is to just do the work, which is not the case. Facilitation is not solving other people's problems or doing it for them; it's making things run more smoothly. The goal of facilitation should be to help the team analyze and get a better understanding of the system and the problems at hand.

The job of the ScrumMaster is not to provide answers or to do everything for the team, but rather it is to help people get to the answers that they may already know. It's like teaching a man to fish so he can sustain himself versus just giving him a fish every time he's hungry. Good ScrumMasters practice a facilitative form of coaching called *servant leadership.* Jean Tabaka in *Collaboration Explained* summed this up nicely.

> *Simply stated, the servant leader as leader drives to serve the group first. Leadership evidences itself in servant leaders through their use of power; that is, in a position of strength, they determine that the greatest power they can wield is in service to their teams as leader. For technical leads, team leads, and project managers who have used power to control versus serve teams, this paradigm shift can seem antithetical to their role. Ultimately, however, as evidenced in the agile software development context, a shift to this altered style of leadership reaps the greatest rewards [TABAKA, p. 18].*

Now there may come a time when you need to help out to complete a task. Helping out is OK on occasion as long as you don't forget that it can hinder you in your role as ScrumMaster. As I've mentioned in previous chapters, as the ScrumMaster you need to see the forest, not just the trees. Team members are looking at the tree in front of them. If you start to help out with tasks and stories, you will only see the trees as well, potentially missing larger things or impediments that are negatively impacting the team.

When you do help out (and I know you will), remember that doing so must be the exception rather than the rule. While the team members might kick and scream when you refuse to help more often, remind them (and yourself) that you are *not helping* for their own good. If they start relying on you for too much and you impact the velocity, you have just done them a disservice by artificially inflating it. The line between helping a team and hurting it is a fine one. One example of this could be that the team has overcommitted. If the ScrumMaster is able to "help out" by doing some work items on the sprint backlog, thereby enabling the team to call the story complete and meet all or most of its commitments to the product owner, the damage is done. The team will not learn *why* it ended up in this situation and will likely repeat it again. The goal here is for the team to learn, not for the ScrumMaster to bail out the team.

## Educate the Organization and Drive Organizational Change

"If you want to make enemies, try to change something." That quote, commonly attributed to former United States President Woodrow Wilson, definitely applies to these two ScrumMaster tasks. It's tough to convince people to try something new because change is frightening. I find that when introducing new concepts, policies, or methodologies inside an organization, people's first response is to wonder how it will affect them. Will their jobs be safe? Will they be able to provide for their families? Others openly rebel, refusing to consider the new way because the status quo, as bad as it might be, is better than the unknown.

A good ScrumMaster finds a way to introduce new ideas and initiate change without shocking people's systems. For example, a friend of mine is running for the local school board. He's not going to just wait and show up on election day and ask people to vote for him. Instead, he's recruiting people, like me, to help with his campaign. That campaign will introduce the voters to him and to his ideas, and eventually attempt to convince people that he is the best choice for the post.

As a ScrumMaster, you should have a strategic campaign for educating the organization. Consider your timeline for rolling it out, where you want to be and when and who you can recruit to help bring in your message. Once the message is sent, hopefully in multiple formats, you will be able to bring people over to your way of thinking. As a result, they will be open to how you are working and what you are building. In the end, the job of the ScrumMaster is twofold: to help build teams and to help the organization become successful. To read more about getting people, and organizations, on board with Scrum, see Chapter 2, "Getting People On Board."

## In Summary

It's tough to justify your job, especially when it might not be a job you've done before. When approaching your manager about making the ScrumMaster role a full-time one, be sure to have a cool head and a good deal of ammunition.

Come armed with as many facts as you can get your hands on. Bring data showing the improvement realized by teams in your organization. If you don't have any from your own company, bring data showing improvements in other organizations. Relate those improvements to the cost per point.

Be prepared to remind management of the reasons we use agile processes in the first place: lower costs, reduced risk, happier employees, more satisfied customers, and an increased ability to respond to change.

# References

[JAMES]    James, Michael. 2007. "ScrumMaster Checklist." http://www.scrummasterchecklist.org/pdf/scrummaster_checklist09.pdf (pulled on 15 November 2009).

[TABAKA]    Tabaka, Jean. 2006. *Collaboration Explained*. Upper Saddle River, NJ: Addison-Wesley. p. 18.

# Work Consulted

Benefield, Gabrielle. 2008. "Rolling Out Agile in a Large Enterprise." Proceedings of the Annual Hawaii International Conference on System Sciences (1530-1605). p. 461.

# PART II
# FIELD BASICS

# Chapter 9

# WHY ENGINEERING PRACTICES ARE IMPORTANT IN SCRUM

Scrum does not talk about engineering practices. As such, you might assume that, like a Jedi master, you are expected to *use the force* to start the sprint, commit to the work, and then magically make it appear. You're not. But Scrum does expect that as the team begins to work in an agile manner, it will soon realize that good engineering practices are essential to becoming a high-performing Scrum team. Engineering practices are the magic, the force, the pixie dust needed to get things out the door. I do not attempt to define all the engineering practices that you need to implement on your Scrum projects—there are other books for that. What I do try to convey in this chapter, however, is *why* you need engineering practices and how they can help development teams overcome some typical obstacles. To illustrate, we join Patrick, a developer by trade who moved into project management at a new company and got a little *less* than he bargained for.

## The Story

When Patrick accepted his new job at Helix, he was excited. Helix had a great reputation, a fabulous product history, and had long been Patrick's dream company. Patrick could hardly wait to get started in his new role as ScrumMaster. True, he'd be inheriting a team, but he had been told the team was using Scrum, a framework Patrick was very familiar with, having used Scrum and XP from both the manager and developer perspective. And he was sure, since the team members had been together for some time, that they'd evolved into a fairly high-performing team.

Patrick was in for a rude awakening.

On his first full day on the job, Patrick sat down with the team members individually to get to know them and see how their processes worked. His first stop was Niall, reputed to be one of the best coders on the team.

"So, Niall," said Patrick. "I've been watching you work for a while. You're as good a coder as everyone says. I'm surprised, though, that you don't seem to use test-driven development. Why not?"

"Too much up-front work and too much throwaway code," Niall responded off-handedly. "It's kind of a waste of time. We've only got six months to get all this out the door," he said pointing to the wall full of index cards.

"Sure. TDD might take some extra time. And there is usually extra code, but the design that emerges is much cleaner, and when you encounter issues and errors…" said Patrick before Niall interrupted him.

"We've got a debugger and a cross-functional team that includes testers," said Niall. "We add any bugs we find to the next sprint and solve them as we find them. As for design, we had a lot of design meetings up front, so that's a nonissue for us."

"So your issue with TDD is extra time, correct, Niall?" asked Patrick.

"Yes, I don't have enough time to do it. We need to crank on the code!" exclaimed Niall.

"What about when you are dealing with bugs? How do you know where to look?" asked Patrick.

"I use the debugger to find the issues," stated Niall.

"What do you consider all the time you spend in the debugger? Isn't that extra time, too?" challenged Patrick.

"Well, I guess. I've never thought about it that way," Niall admitted.

Patrick nodded. "One more question. I noticed that here you wrote some code to create drop-down boxes. What's the acceptance criteria you're trying to fulfill with that?"

Niall smiled conspiratorially. "No one has asked for it *yet*. But once they see how cool it works, I think they're really going to like it. I like to give the customers a little something extra. It gets them excited about the final product."

"Your heart's in the right place, but it's the wrong thing to do," said Patrick. "We have to write just enough code to satisfy the story. Nothing more. Nothing less. We've got too much to do to spend time gold-plating the software. And just think of the time it would free up to do that TDD we were talking about. Think about it. We'll talk more later."

Patrick moved on to Claire, an experienced team member with a reputation for finishing her work quickly.

"This morning in standup, you mentioned that Story 1822 was done, right?"

"Right," Claire replied.

"So what if I asked you to prove it to me? What would you do?" asked Patrick.

"Well, it works. See?" answered Claire, giving Patrick a quick demo.

"Right. But what about all the things I can't see? Is it checked in yet?"

"No. I'm planning to do that later. I'm demoing it on my own machine."

"How often do you check in, Claire?"

"I try to check in once a day, but it's more like two to three times per week."

"If you check in that infrequently, how do you know that your code isn't breaking anything else?"

"Ummm. I guess I'll find out at check-in and deal with it then. It usually isn't a problem."

"Do other team members check in two or three times per week also?"

"Yes," said Claire.

"So right now, and maybe even when we check in (if all the others' code isn't checked in yet), we don't really know if a story is done, do we?" asked Patrick.

"We know it's written. We know it's working," responded Claire.

"I've also noticed there is no continuous integration server, and it appears that the team members don't share a lot of code with each other," said Patrick.

"We keep meaning to set up a CI server, but we don't have time or funding for it," said Claire. "I know we need to set it up, and we need to follow more rigorous engineering practices, but we're under so much time pressure. With management breathing down our necks, doing the right thing is almost impossible!"

A bit worried by the attitude of the senior team members toward what he considered basic engineering practices like TDD, static code analysis, shared code ownership, and continuous integration, Patrick spent the next three days looking at the backlog and burndown charts and digging around in the code to see what other trends he could find. He looked at the acceptance test framework that the team had implemented and saw that it had not been updated at all during the sprint. He looked at the size of the check-ins, often 1,000 lines of code or more. He noticed that the team tended to leave one or two stories unfinished almost every sprint. He also saw from the burndown that they often had a lot of work in progress until quite late in the sprint. What's worse, he found nothing related to good coding practices—various parts of the code were written in different styles, there were few comments in the code, and overall it just had a poor structure.

Patrick was shocked with how few basic engineering practices the team had implemented and the number of bugs that continued to pop up in every sprint. His big concern was how they would release a quality product, on time, without making some serious changes. He thought back to a couple of projects some colleagues had worked on at his last company—projects that had slipped by months because of large architectural issues that were identified late. He needed the team to understand why these practices were worth the effort. After thinking for some time, he came up with a plan.

The sprint ended, and after the demo the team gathered in the conference room for the sprint retrospective. While they were filtering in, Patrick quietly taped two big sheets of paper up around the room. The retrospective started. Patrick noticed that the accepted format seemed to be for everyone to take turns talking about what had gone well and what could go better. Perfect, he thought. He got up as they began talking and began writing down a few of the things the team was saying on one of the sheets, which he labeled "Stuff Going Wrong" (see Figure 9-1).

When the team had finished talking, Patrick moved to the next sheet of paper. He labeled it. "Stuff We Can Do to Fix It."

"So, team. I've talked to each of you individually. I've looked through the code. I imagine you have problems like these every sprint, right?"

"Sure," said Niall. "But we're going to have problems. There's no blame here."

"Not blaming," said Patrick. "Just wondering. Is there anything we can do about it?"

> ### STUFF GOING WRONG
>
> • BUGS IN STORIES 1823, 1842, AND 1832 — FIX THEM NEXT SPRINT
>
> • FOUND BUG BUT DIDN'T HAVE TIME TO TRACK IT DOWN
>
> • BROKE THE BUILD BUT ONLY BECAUSE SOMEONE CHECKED IN GARBAGE CODE
>
> • SPENT TWO DAYS IN DEBUGGER GOING THROUGH THE API LINE BY LINE
>
> • SAW SOME CODE THAT LOOKED WRONG BUT IT WAS SARAH'S, SO I DROPPED HER A NOTE TO FIX IT
>
> • COULDN'T FINISH STORY 1833 BECAUSE OF LAST-MINUTE INTEGRATION BUGS. PUT IT IN NEXT SPRINT
>
> • DIDN'T QUITE GET STORY 1825 DONE BECAUSE THE DROP-DOWN BOXES WERE BUGGY

**FIGURE 9-1**    Patrick's list

"Not if we want to keep up this pace," said Claire.

"That's interesting. Let's talk about pace. To me, all these problems," Patrick paused to point to the sheet full of issues then continued, "these issues that keep recurring… they are slowing you down the most: bugs, gold-plating, finding poor code but leaving it to fester until 'someone, someday' fixes it. We have a deadline to meet and right now, let me tell you, we're not going to get there. We've got to invest some time in getting better so that we can go faster."

He let the team soak that in for a few seconds.

"So what are we going to invest in?" asked Patrick. Then he sat down and let the silence grow uncomfortable, waiting for the team to respond.

"I see stuff every day I wish I had time to fix," said one of the team members. "So one thing we could do would be to include some refactoring tasks in each sprint."

"Good," said Patrick, standing up to write it on the paper. "What else?"

"Test-driven development," said Niall, in a low, resigned voice. "I realize it's the right thing to do, but it'll slow me down."

Patrick nodded but wrote it anyway. "Maybe at first. But we'll more than make up for that by creating fewer bugs and spending less time finding and tracking the ones that do slip through."

"Continuous integration," said Claire. "And more frequent check-ins will both really help. That doesn't take that much time once it's set up. It's just not a habit, and we don't have the tools right now."

Patrick wrote it. "Yep. Tools are easy when compared to habits. It's changing the habit that'll be hard."

The team went on to mention pair programming.

"And pair programming and TDD will help ensure that we build only what is necessary, which will ultimately increase our velocity as well," said Patrick. "Clearly, you know what you should be doing. So why aren't you doing it?"

The team went on to list several obstacles to adopting engineering practices, including lack of knowledge and fear of the unknown. They discussed each objection, with Patrick providing the rationale for at least giving it a try. In the end, they agreed to a new definition of done, which would necessitate immediately implementing certain engineering practices.

The team decided to implement other new practices one at a time in subsequent sprints. In turn, Patrick agreed to discuss their plan with management and explain to them why the team's velocity might drop for a sprint or two while they invest in practices that would ultimately help them go faster.

"We've got a long way to go to get from here to there," finished Patrick. "But I promise once we start working this way, you won't want to go back. The first thing I want us all to do is start challenging each other, every day, to prove it. Prove it's tested, prove it's not going to break the build, prove it's done. That'll get us a long way toward where we want to go."

## The Practices

What we saw in the story is not uncommon with teams new to Scrum. It's easy to get focused on doing Scrum right and never get around to implementing the engineering practices necessary to become a truly high-performing Scrum team. Patrick's solution was to work with the team members to make visible where they were falling short, to show them how it was slowing them down, and to convince them that investing in better practices would both solve their issues and increase their velocity as well. Patrick and the team agreed to implement five key engineering practices:

- Test-driven development
- Refactoring
- Continuous integration and more frequent check-ins
- Pair programming
- Integration and automated acceptance tests

All these engineering practices mean more work up front. You will recover the time later through efficiency, improved quality, and code stability. What is often forgotten, however, is that these are not silver bullets. Doing one or doing them all will not guarantee you success, but they will get you farther away from failure if they are done with diligence and discipline.

## Implementing Test-Driven Development

Contrary to what the name implies, TDD is not a testing process. It's a software design technique where code is developed in short cycles. You can think of the TDD process as Red, Green, Refactor. The first step is to write a new unit test without writing the necessary code to make it pass. Obviously, when you run that test, it will fail: We call this the red state. The next step is to write new code, just enough to make the unit test pass, or turn green. When the test passes, the code is working. The final step, which can occur multiple times, is to refactor. We talk about refactoring more in the next section, but in TDD it specifically refers to removing any "code smells," elements that might not be optimized, well-designed, or easy to maintain. Design changes can occur during this phase as well (also called test-driven design). During refactoring, the code is changed, but all the while, the tests must stay green, or continue to pass. The process then begins again from the beginning, writing new tests and new code until the story is complete.

I'm not going to attempt to teach you TDD; other books do a good job of that, and I've listed them in the references with this chapter. What I want you to know is why TDD helps a Scrum team and how you can help your own team reach the conclusion that TDD is the best choice for meeting sprint goals at a high velocity.

Implementing test-driven development is akin to weaving a net. Each automated test builds on the next, forming a safety net of automated unit tests. Consider the high wire act at the circus. The person hundreds of feet above the ground, trying to balance on a thin wire, can take the risks he does because he knows that if he falls, the net will save him. A team might choose to walk the high wire without a safety net, but if the team falls, it will take days, maybe weeks, to recover. Yes, more code is written with automated unit tests, and, yes, sometimes there is more throwaway code. In many cases, though, the reduced debugging time means that the total implementation time is actually shorter.

In 2008, researchers from Microsoft, IBM, and North Carolina State University published a paper [NAGGAPAN], looking at the benefit of TDD in teams. They looked at three teams from Microsoft (one of which I happened to be working on at the time) and one team from IBM. They found that all teams showed "significant" drops in defect density[1]: 40 percent for the IBM team and between 60 percent and 90 percent for the Microsoft teams. The increased time taken to follow TDD on these projects ranged from 15 percent to 35 percent. This initial decrease in velocity is compensated for by the increased stability and maintainability of the code.

---

1. Defined in the published [NAGGAPAN] paper as "When software is being developed, a person makes an error that results in a physical fault (or defect) in a software element. When this element is executed, traversal of the fault or defect may put the element (or system) into an erroneous state. When this erroneous state results in an externally visible anomaly, we say that a failure has occurred."

By following TDD, you will be less reluctant to implement some change that is required by a key stakeholder or customer, even late in the project. Often, these kinds of eleventh-hour changes are considered too risky because the team can't predict the ramifications of the change (coupled code), and there isn't time to test all the possible side effects. With a TDD safety net in place, the risk is substantially lessened, so teams feel confident that they can make required changes, no matter when they occur in the project. Good version control practices also help to increase confidence. If the refactoring goes horribly awry or breaks too many tests, you can easily roll back to a known good point.

Anecdotally, in the projects that I've run and on teams that I've coached, I have found that TDD significantly streamlines the writing of code, helps prevent analysis paralysis, minimizes impediments (like spending lots of time in the debugger), and gives teams the priceless gift of peace of mind. For these reasons, TDD is essential for teams that want to grow to be high-performing Scrum teams. And, remember, the compiler only tells you if your code obeys the rules of the language; your tests prove that your code executes correctly.

## Refactoring

Refactoring is the act of enhancing or improving the design of existing code without changing its intent or behavior. The external behavior remains the same, while under the hood, things are more streamlined.

How do you know when you need to refactor your code? When it begins to smell. It's best to follow the rules of Grandma Beck, "If it stinks, change it" [FOWLER 01]. Her comment was in relation to diapers, but it applies equally as well to code. A code smell is a seemingly small problem that is symptomatic of a deeper issue. Jeff Atwood lists some common smells in a 2006 blog post, breaking them out into smells within classes and smells between classes [ATWOOD].

Table 9-1 presents a few of my favorites from Atwood's list.

**TABLE 9-1**    Sample of Code Smells from Jeff Atwood

| SYMPTOM | PROBLEM |
|---|---|
| COMMENTS | THERE'S A FINE LINE BETWEEN COMMENTS THAT ILLUMINATE AND COMMENTS THAT OBSCURE. ARE THE COMMENTS NECCESSARY? DO THEY EXPLAIN "WHY" AND NOT "WHAT"? CAN YOU REFACTOR THE CODE SO THE COMMENTS AREN'T REQUIRED? AND REMEMBER, YOU'RE WRITING COMMENTS FOR PEOPLE, NOT MACHINES. |
| LONG METHOD | ALL OTHER THINGS BEING EQUAL, A SHORTER METHOD IS EASIER TO READ, EASIER TO UNDERSTAND, AND EASIER TO TROUBLE-SHOOT. REFACTOR LONG METHODS INTO SMALLER METHODS IF YOU CAN. |
| INCONSISTENT NAMES | PICK A SET OF STANDARD TERMINOLOGY AND STICK TO IT THROUGHOUT YOUR METHODS. FOR EXAMPLE, IF YOU HAVE OPEN(), YOU SHOULD PROBABLY HAVE CLOSE(). |

These might seem like basic coding standards, yet they are too often left undone.

When should you refactor? Refactoring can be performed at any time during a system's life cycle, whenever someone is working on legacy code, sees a piece of code that could be improved, notices the system acting sluggish, or if bugs start popping up in a particular section of the code—basically whenever someone notices a smell.

Remember that refactoring code does not mean rewriting the code. Instead, to refactor is to optimize the code without changing the intent of the code. Bob Martin [MARTIN] has a set of principles with the acronym SOLID, in which he talks about the first five principles of class design (see Table 9-2).

Why should you refactor? Simply put, it's an investment in your code. An analogy might be doing little things every day to help keep your house clean. If you walk in the house with dirty shoes on your feet on a regular basis, your house will get dirtier faster. If you throw your discarded wrappers on the counter rather than the garbage can because you're in a hurry, in a few days you're going to look up and find a counter full of wrappers that you'll have to clean. Refactoring is like cleaning up after yourself a little bit each day—sometimes you'll clean more, sometimes less, but the important thing is that you're cleaning on a regular basis and not waiting for it to pile up or for someone else to do it.

## Continuous Integration to Know the Status of the System at All Times

With discipline, continuous integration can take a Scrum team from somewhat good to just plain awesome. Martin Fowler defines CI best [FOWLER 02]:

> *Continuous Integration is a software development practice where members of a team integrate their work frequently, usually each person integrates at least daily—leading to multiple integrations per day. Each integration is verified by an automated build (including test) to detect integration errors as quickly as possible.*

**TABLE 9-2**   Robert Martin's SOLID OOD Class Design Principles

| PRINCIPALS | DESCRIPTION |
|---|---|
| SRP: SINGLE RESPONSIBILITY PRINCIPLE | A CLASS SHOULD HAVE ONE, AND ONLY ONE, REASON TO CHANGE. |
| OCP: THE OPEN CLOSED PRINCIPLE | YOU SHOULD BE ABLE TO EXTEND A CLASS'S BEHAVIOR, WITHOUT MODIFYING IT. |
| LSP: THE LISKOV SUBSTITUTION PRINCIPLE | DERIVED CLASSES MUST BE SUBSTITUTABLE FOR THEIR BASE CLASSES. |
| ISP: INTERFACE SEGREGATION PRINCIPLE | MAKE FINE GRAINED INTERFACES THAT ARE CLIENT SPECIFIC. |
| DIP: THE DEPENDENCY INVERSION PRINCIPLE | DEPEND ON ABSTRACTIONS, NOT ON CONCRETIONS. |

Continuous integration enables us to have quicker feedback loops on the code. Instead of checking in a thousand or more lines at one time, each person or pair might check in a hundred or so lines of code at once. They also create a local build before committing changes to the larger branch. Both the local builds and the main build should be fully automated, meaning the person submitting the code can "click and forget," while the build machine runs a suite of automated acceptance and unit tests. These builds might also run static analysis checks, check for desired unit test coverage, and so forth. Once the code is run and in the branch, a continuous integration server pulls everything into the branch and runs a larger suite of tests. Because the check-in is small, the feedback loop is short. Therefore, it is much easier to see what broke the build and why.

Why should you care about any of this? Let's associate it with real life.

- **Headlights**—Why do we drive at night with headlights on? Because we can see where we're going and others can see us, it reduces the risk of an accident. Continuous integration provides the same benefit—it shines a light down the path of code development so that you can see whether you're going to hit something. A CI build warns you almost instantly if something is blocking your way.
- **Washing machines**—What makes them great? They eliminate the repetitive, labor-intensive process of washing clothes by hand. Similarly, continuous integration reduces all (or most) manual processes. Not only does this free up time and resources, it also helps improve quality. When we do things manually, there is an increased chance for variation. Automating helps ensure that the same test runs the exact same way, every time. Having automation in place allows team members to focus on what matters, the system under development.
- **GPS**—Having a GPS in our vehicle allows us to know where we are going all the time. Following continuous integration does the same thing. It provides visibility into where the system under development is currently and where it is going next. This enables the team and the product owner to react in real time. Further, if teams add quality gates or checks such as unit test coverage, teams are able to identify patterns or trends with the code and make necessary course corrections in time to alter the system's course.

Scrum maintains that at the end of the sprint, all code should be potentially shippable, yet many teams struggle with what that really means. Continuous integration enables teams to build and release at any time. What does this look like in the real world? It means going into a customer review meeting and pulling the latest bits off the build server and installing them. No manual testing, no human validation, just pure trust in the system. And where does this trust come from? As teams develop good engineering practices, the confidence in their system grows. TDD gives them a safety net and shows them where their errors are while their continuous integration strategy allows them to fully understand the impacts of code changes. It is important to keep the build in a green state and not go home with a broken build. When breaks do occur, it is better to roll back any changes at the end of the day, go home in a green state, and fix any issues in the morning.

One of my favorite books on continuous integration is titled *Continuous Integration: Improving Software Quality and Reducing Risk* by Paul M. Duvall. As stated before, this is not a book on software design or hardcore engineering; buy Paul's book and learn just about everything you need to know about how to start doing continuous integration. Alternatively, a paper presented at Agile 2008 by Ade Miller titled *One Hundred Days of Continuous Integration* is also a great read.

## Pair Programming

Too often as people shift in and out of projects, the information shifts in and out with them—information ranging from how stories were implemented to why one design path was chosen over another. There is one technique that ensures that everyone on the team knows what the code *actually* does: pair programming.

Pair programming drives collective code ownership and increases knowledge sharing among team members. At its core, pair programming is two team members working together to accomplish a single task. One person is the driver and the other is the navigator (for more advanced pairing techniques, see Chapter 19, "Keeping People Engaged with Pair Programming"). When the pairs switch on a frequent basis, information passes among all team members, ensuring that everyone is familiar with the entire code base. Pair programming uses conversation to produce code, causing each person in the pair to question what the other is doing, continually. Pairs reinforce the team's coding standards on how to get the system built.

It is important to understand that practicing pair programming does not necessarily mean work takes twice as long. While at the University of Utah, Laurie Williams found that pair programming was 15 percent slower than two independent developers but produced 15 percent fewer bugs [WILLIAMS]. One thing that was missing from her study was "noise" such as interruptions, email, IM conversations, reading the news on the Web, etc. Each of these are huge time sinks, and they're completely gone with pair programming. This again shows us that teams making the investment in more disciplined engineering practices up front go a little slower at first but have a better payback down the road through reduced risk, better visibility, and lower defect rates.

Another benefit of pair programming is the reduction of noise. I define noise to mean phone calls, email, instant messages, unnecessary meetings, and other distractions. It would be rude to be working on a project with someone and check your email or be on a phone call, right? When you're pairing with someone, you focus on what you are working on with the other person, just because it's good manners. The side benefit of that focus is that you get more done.

I like to think of pair programming as "real-time code reviews," meaning the code is being reviewed and updated and managed in real time. A good pair is constantly reflecting on the work at hand. As a result there is no need for separate pre-check-in meetings to review what individual team members did. And because fewer bugs are created, fewer bug triage meetings are needed. All this noise reduction optimizes the team's time.

Pairing in a distributed environment is challenging but possible. Sharing a screen, using webcams, and having a direct line to the person you are pairing with are all requirements. It is obviously easier to pair when you are in the same time zone, so if you distribute, go north/south instead of east/west.

To do pair programming well, you've got to start with education and ground rules. Let people know that, as with trying anything new, pairing will be uncomfortable and a bit awkward at first—remind them to keep an open mind and to have courage, knowing that the entire team is going through this together. Encourage them to have a willingness to try—to really give it a good effort and be able to move forward objectively. If needed, invest in training and always be sure to implement coding standards.

There are some great papers and books on pair programming. Start with an older book, titled *Pair Programming Illuminated* by Laurie Williams and Robert Kessler. Another good reference is *The Art of Agile Development* by James Shore. To understand the cost benefits of pairing, read *The Economics of Software Development by Pair Programmers* by Hakan Erdogmus and Laurie Williams.

## Automated Integration and Acceptance Tests

Like unit tests, integration and acceptance tests are a form of automated tests. They fill out the top of the test automation pyramid, with unit tests making up the base layer (see Figure 9-2).

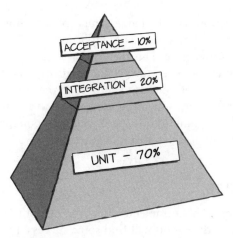

**FIGURE 9-2**  Test automation pyramid

Integration tests are designed to test various integration points in your system. They are designed to ensure that APIs, data formats, and interfaces are all working as expected while the team is developing the code. While it is generally easier to build automated integration tests than it would be to build automated acceptance tests, automated integration tests still have a high maintenance cost, especially in systems with hundreds or thousands of people working together in a single code base.

Acceptance tests are designed to emulate the behavior of the user. If you are building a system with a UI, these tests will be scripted to click and emulate the behavior of the user. These tests are often easily broken, as interfaces and customers' minds change. They are also prone to providing false positive readings, which makes their maintenance cost high—but not as high as a dedicated team member. A variety of tools are designed to let stakeholders and customers write tests and easily interface with the system to ensure the system is working from an end user perspective.

Even with the added work and maintenance cost, though, automated integration and acceptance tests are one of the best ways to ensure that a Scrum team is building the right thing. First, each allows the team to have a continuous feedback loop, similar to that provided by continuous integration and unit tests, which helps prevent long testing phases at the end of each sprint and each release.

Next, it's cheaper to fix issues when they occur than it is to fix them a few sprints down the road. Plus, fixing bugs early helps keep the overall codebase clean. While it might initially slow the team down with what can seem to be constant bug fixing, the end result will be a cleaner, more refined codebase over time.

Third, having automated integration tests helps ensure that the external integration points the system interfaces with are working, and continue working, as expected. I often ask teams, "What are your computers doing after you go home at night?" They should be working for the team, identifying weaknesses in the system so that they can be corrected the next morning.

Finally, having automated acceptance tests helps ensure that the UI/interface behaviors of the system work as expected. Acceptance tests should be fired off at every build if possible and should be continually built out over time, just as the unit test "safety net" is built out over time. This means that acceptance tests need to be written before the sprint starts so when the product owner goes into the sprint planning meeting, the team knows what it needs to "prove" to the customers and stakeholders from an interface point of view. When you don't invest in automation, each sprint the test debt builds and the amount of time spent each sprint on manual testing rises to a nearly unmanageable state as illustrated in Figure 9-3.

## Keys to Success

Yes, you can do Scrum without implementing even one of the engineering practices listed in this chapter. And yes, you will find some success. Eventually, however, you will find yourself asking, "Why are we not getting *significantly* better?" The answer

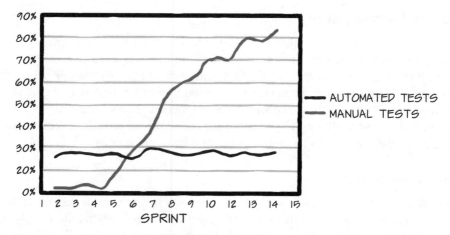

**FIGURE 9-3**   Time spent with automation versus manual testing

lies in how you actually build your software. If you do Scrum but refuse to change your engineering practices and your mindset, you'll struggle.

All I am asking you to do is think about things differently; understand the *why* when you do things. In the end, however, you have to do some additional initial work (TDD, pairing, setting up CI, creating an automated testing framework) and make a calculated bet that it will pay off in the end by having less rework to do—simply because you will have fewer bugs and integration issues.

## Not a Silver Bullet

I cannot stress this enough: Using Scrum or any of the practices listed in this chapter will not magically grant you the ability to more frequently deliver software of higher quality or guarantee that what you build will be what your customers really want. I can, however, predict that choosing *not* to use these techniques will likely result in failure. In the same way, riding a high-quality road bike won't guarantee a win at the Tour de France; riding a tricycle, however, will virtually guarantee a loss.

The practices in this chapter are not silver bullets. Instead they are meant as signposts that help guide you to your final destination, which is a high-performing team able to react quickly *and with high quality* to customer requests.

## Starting Out

Getting started with engineering practices can seem overwhelming, but it doesn't have to be. I have seen teams take two different approaches: They start slowly, gradually adding one new practice at a time, or they go full throttle and embrace everything. Either way you do it, it's important to realize that you are going to stumble as you work your way through revamping your engineering practices. This is OK—just remember to stay disciplined and focused, and seek help when you need it.

## Get the Team to Buy In

In the story we saw Patrick take the team to the *why* right out of the gate. Sure, he could have said, "Do it my way or the highway," but in my experience it works much better if the team understands why they are being asked to change. Patrick helped the team see his point of view, helped them understand what he wanted, and gave them guidance on how to get there and why it was important. This is essential, because if you have someone on the team who is not supporting the effort, there will be sabotage. Avoid the command and control aspect and focus on the why.

## Definition of Done

In Chapter 7, "How Do We Know When We Are Done?," you find an exercise on how to build a done list and how to work with your team to define what done is. At the end of this chapter's story, Patrick did a similar exercise with his team. Knowing what it means to be done is like having a set of blueprints; the practices in this chapter are the tools that allow teams to build. Without understanding what done is, you will be lost.

## Build Engineering into Product Backlog

For the team to get traction on the practices listed in this chapter, the product owner must understand and be willing to make the long-term investment in the team. One way to do this and to highlight the visibility of the team's effort to improve its engineering practices is to include related stories or tasks in the product backlog.

## Get Training/Coaching

Don't expect people to "just do it." Teach them how. You can do this by hiring a coach, finding someone in your company who has this experience, buying books, or sending them to training classes. If money is an issue, realize that the benefit that modern engineering practices will bring back to the company will be far greater than the financial investment being made up front.

## Putting It Together

Good engineering practices break things into small pieces, from unit tests to check-ins, so that the time between issue and fix is minimal. Further, the ability to change direction with small batches increases customer confidence. As a result, risk is reduced across the board. The automated unit test framework that the team has built over the length of the project alerts team members when there is a problem and tells them where the problem is—no more spending "days in the debugger." They also have better visibility into the code through pairing, as the "I own the code" mentality is replaced with collective code ownership. This cocktail results in lower defect rates and overall increases in quality—giving customers more trust in the team and the team more confidence in its ability to deliver working software every sprint.

Please understand that these practices are not easy to do. They require dedication, focus, and perseverance. You will be pulled away from them, naturally, due to the time investment needed to do each of them. With TDD, you will likely need to get trained (or some help) on how to do it and initially you will slow down. The same with setting up a CI server—though you can have it up and running in under an hour, getting it set up to suit your needs and the needs of the business takes time. Refactoring and pair programming also take time to become accustomed to. Overall, I find it takes from three to six months to go from a traditional way of building software to fully understanding and implementing the engineering practices listed in this chapter.

At the end of the day, the investment you make now will pay huge dividends in the future, giving you stability, quality, and the consistent releases your customers desire.

## References

[FOWLER 01]   Fowler, Martin, and Kent Beck. 1999. *Refactoring: Improving the Design of Existing Code.* Boston: Addison-Wesley Professional. p. 75.

[NAGGAPAN]   Nagappan, Nachiappan, E. Michael Maximilien, Thirumalesh Bhat, and Laurie Williams. "Realizing Quality Improvement through Test Driven Development: Results and Experiences of Four Industrial Teams." Microsoft Research. http://research.microsoft.com/en-us/groups/ese/nagappan_tdd.pdf (accessed 07/11/2011).

[MARTIN]   Martin, Robert C. "The Principles of OOD" http://butunclebob.com/ArticleS.UncleBob.PrinciplesOfOod (accessed 07/11/2011).

[ATWOOD]   Atwood, Jeff. "Code Smells." Coding Horror. http://www.codinghorror.com/blog/2006/05/code-smells.html (accessed 01/11/2009).

[FOWLER 02]   Fowler, Martin. "Continuous Integration." martinfowler.com. http://martinfowler.com/articles/continuousIntegration.html (accessed 03/15/2010).

[WILLIAMS]   Williams, Laurie. "The Collaborative Software Process." The University of Utah. http://www.cs.utah.edu/~lwilliam/Papers/dissertation.pdf (accessed 01/11/2011).

## Works Consulted

Astels, David. 2004. *Test-Driven Development: A Practical Guide.* Upper Saddle River, NJ: Prentice Hall.

# Chapter 10

# CORE HOURS

Scrum teams should work together as much as possible, ideally in a co-located space. This drives communication efficiencies, collaboration, and collective code ownership. But what do we do when some team members like to arrive at 7 a.m. and others like to arrive at 11 a.m.? What about end-of-day scenarios and lunch time?

While these may seem like trivial things, for many teams, they are not. In fact, a seemingly harmless and small impediment like core hours can sink an entire team. That's what nearly happened in the story that follows, when a more senior developer had an issue with a young developer's perceived lack of dedication to the team and the company nearly tore the team apart.

## The Story

Russ was a young developer, five years out of university. He loved gaming, riding his bicycle, and working on his classic car. He had spent the last few years working in a startup in Seattle where there was little process; careers were made not by teamwork but by pure raw talent. Though new to his current company, Russ was already known as one of the go-to guys, someone who got things done. Russ prided himself on keeping a good work-life balance, which drove him toward having some of the best code in the company. He frequently rode his bike back and forth to work, especially in the summer, often taking the long route from the eastside to Seattle by going around Lake Washington. He loved spending his nights playing online games with friends from work.

Jacob was the company's authority on CRM. He had been working on CRM solutions for more than 20 years and was familiar with every system both inside and outside the company. Jacob was not much of a social creature—he preferred to focus on his work. In his spare time, he built Lego robots with his young son. The solutions that Jacob delivered were always high in quality—customers raved about how stable and easy to maintain his solutions were. Jacob was happy in his routine and enjoyed the rhythm of his own regular schedule.

Both Russ and Jacob were about to experience the stress that often accompanies change. They were tapped to work on a new CRM tool for a client. It was a complex project that would require all of Jacob's experience and all of Russ's creative coding.

At first, things went well. Russ and Jacob assembled a core team and hired their team consultants (see Chapter 3, "Using Team Consultants to Optimize Team Performance," for more on team consultants). They set a start date, July 15, a mere two

weeks away. The product owner, Sally, worked feverishly to get the backlog established while Russ and Jacob worked with the team to establish engineering practices,
get the lab and machines set up, and create general team rules of engagement. Letitia,
the ScrumMaster, worked to schedule the meetings: the first sprint planning meetings, the daily standup meetings, and the customer review meetings. Everyone felt
confident going into the first sprint.

On July 15, the team assembled for their sprint planning meetings. There was the
normal ambiguity going on in the planning meetings, but nothing alarming. This
was, after all, a fairly experienced team on all levels.

The next day the team assembled in the team area to begin work on their chosen tasks; everyone except Russ, that is. Jacob, who had arrived early so he would
have time to go over some things with Russ, was visibly frustrated. He looked at the
clock—8:30—then at everyone else busy at work. "Russ is supposed to be one of the
leaders," he thought. "How can he set such a poor example?" Jacob started doing
some project work with one other team member and lost track of time. Just before
10:00, Jacob heard the stirring of the other team members. "Time for the scheduled
daily standup," he thought. As Jacob looked up, Russ popped in, fresh out of the
shower after a long bike ride.

"Hey guys! It's daily standup time!" exclaimed Russ.

"Glad you could join us. I thought you were taking the day off," said Jacob, with
a hint of sarcasm in his voice.

"Nope, just starting the day with a morning bike ride," responded Russ, not picking up on Jacob's sarcasm.

Letitia did pick up on the sarcasm, but chose to ignore it. The meeting went off
without a hitch. It ran just a hair over 15 minutes, not bad for the first time.

Over the next couple of weeks, the same pattern occurred. Jacob got to work at 7:30
and worked with another early-rising team member. Russ, on the other hand, popped
in right before the standup. One morning, as Russ bounced in, Jacob finally snapped.

"The day is almost half over Russ," quipped Jacob.

"Or half begun, my friend! I feel like I could climb mountains. I got up at five
this morning, went to the gym, and then logged 65 miles on the bike. What a great
day!" said Russ. He turned his attention to the other team members who had gathered for the standup. "I'm ready to rock. I'll go first!" and off went Russ, sharing his
accomplishments and plans.

Jacob went next. "Yesterday I completed task 18, 'Create the stored procedure.'
Today I'd like to work with Russ on the assembler, provided he *is* actually working
today and not leaving early or something."

"Sure," said Russ, laughing at what he considered Jacob's quirky sense of humor.
"We can work on that together; that'd be great!" he said energetically.

Letitia began to observe Russ and Jacob as they worked together. It was obvious
to her that Russ coming into work just before the standup bothered Jacob. In fact, it
seemed to bother him that the entire team was not there at 7:30 a.m. when he arrived.
As the most senior member on the team, both from an age standpoint and from an

experience standpoint, he seemed to feel that he was the one who should lead the team and set boundaries, such as who arrives when. Letitia knew there was bound to be a blow-up soon. Sure enough, as Russ and Jacob were coding, Jacob began to get irritated.

"Russ! Why are you calling the interface like this? You're not an idiot; why are you coding like one? Now we need to rewrite everything!" said Jacob, throwing his pencil at the screen in disgust.

Russ was astounded at the sudden outburst. "Jacob, calm down. What's the problem? Yelling at me won't help."

"This is just laziness, pure and simple. Though, what else could I expect from someone like you. How have you lasted here so long?" Jacob roared, as he rolled his chair back and threw up his arms in disgust.

Letitia quickly stepped in.

"Jacob, I'm hearing some very personal attacks. What is going on?"

"Russ is lazy and sloppy. Just look at this code!" said Jacob. "I can't work like this."

"OK, Jacob. Let's go for a walk and talk about it." Letitia took Jacob down to the local coffee shop. She had an idea of what was causing Jacob's discontent but needed to hear it from him, alone.

"Jacob, what is really bothering you?" Letitia asked him directly. "When we started, you were excited about this project, but now you seem so agitated and distressed," she added, gesturing to Jacob's shaking hands.

"It's Russ. I can't work with him. He's clearly not committed to this project. I can't do all the work on my own, and I don't know what to do about it," admitted Jacob.

"What makes you think that he is not committed?" asked Letitia.

"First of all, he comes in at 10! I get here at 7:30 and he gets here at 10? What's that about? It's not long after he saunters in that he leaves for lunch—'Gotta fill up, man'—such a bad example," quipped Jacob. "That code today shows that he's obviously rushing through, ready to leave early so he can get to the next party. When does he work?"

Letitia was happy to hear Jacob spell out the problem she had been noticing.

"I think you've got the wrong idea, Jacob. True, Russ comes in at 10. But he doesn't leave until after 7, well after you and the other team members have called it quits. He's on a different schedule than you, but he *is* working. Still, I can see that this is a problem, not only for you but for the rest of the team as well."

"So you'll have him come in earlier, then?" asked Jacob, still hoping to keep things on his terms.

"I have a different idea," Letitia replied. "On my last project we had a similar issue, and we solved it by setting core team hours."

"Core team hours?" asked Jacob.

"Yes, core team hours—these are the hours when everyone can commit to being in the team space. That way if we need to schedule pairing or if we need to talk to someone, we can." explained Letitia. "If you're willing, we can go propose it to the team now. I think it will help ease any concerns that might be lingering about people's availability and dedication."

Jacob thought about it. "We can try it. But do me a favor. Keep your eye on Russ. I'm still not convinced he's fully committed to this project" said Jacob.

Letitia smiled. "I'll do that, Jacob. But do *me* a favor. Give him a chance. And give the idea that people can have different schedules and still work together a chance, too. I think you'll be pleasantly surprised."

# The Model

Letitia was a very in-tune ScrumMaster. She quickly noticed the frustration that Jacob was having but did the right thing by keeping quiet until it was obvious that the team was ready for her to do something about it.

## Co-located Teams

If your team is struggling with different schedules, or if you are at all distributed, a core schedule helps to restore a sense of balance and cohesiveness. To get started, write everyone's name across the top of the whiteboard (we'll use the names from our story as an example). Down the left side, write "start of day," "lunch start," "lunch end," and "end of day." In the end, you'll have a chart that looks something like the one in Table 10-1.

From there, the team members need to indicate when they like to start, take lunch, and leave for the day. You can collect this information in one of two ways. Option one is to have the team members fill in the chart directly on the whiteboard. The only drawback to that option is that people might be influenced by others' answers and be tempted to adjust their schedule to more closely match the other team members. Option two is to have each team member write down his or her schedule privately and give it to you. Then, once all the schedules have been submitted, you can populate the chart with their answers. The resulting chart will look much like the one in Table 10-2.

**TABLE 10-1**   A Blank Core Hours Chart

|               | RUSS | JACOB | MIKAELA | SAM | ROCKY |
|---------------|------|-------|---------|-----|-------|
| START OF DAY  |      |       |         |     |       |
| LUNCH START   |      |       |         |     |       |
| LUNCH END     |      |       |         |     |       |
| END OF DAY    |      |       |         |     |       |

**TABLE 10-2   The Populated Chart**

|                | RUSS  | JACOB | MIKAELA | SAM   | ROCKY |
|----------------|-------|-------|---------|-------|-------|
| START OF DAY   | 10:00 | 7:30  | 8:30    | 7:30  | 9:30  |
| LUNCH START    | 11:30 | 12:00 | 12:00   | 11:30 | 12:00 |
| LUNCH END      | 12:30 | 12:30 | 1:00    | 12:30 | 1:00  |
| END OF DAY     | 7:30  | 4:30  | 6:00    | 5:00  | 6:30  |

Once the chart is filled in, you can extrapolate the core team hours, the hours that all team members are available, on the board. If we were to do that using the information in Table 10-2, we'd come up with the following core hours.

- Morning: 10:00–11:30 (1.5 hours of shared time)
- Lunch: 11:30–1:00
- Afternoon: 1:00–4:30 (3.5 hours of shared time)

The chart shows that the team has five hours when they are all available for work together. The next thing to do is ask the team whether there are small ways in which this chart could be optimized. For instance, the lunch hour is currently an hour and a half. If Russ and Sam, however, were to delay their lunch start times by 30 minutes, it would give the team more core hours. The new model would look like what is shown in Table 10-3.

The resulting core hours would be as follows:

- Morning: 10:00–12:00 (2 hours of shared time)
- Lunch: 12:00–1:00
- Afternoon: 1:00–4:30 (3.5 hours of shared time)

This small tweak would give the team 5.5 hours of working time *together*.

Once you have established your core team hours, it is best to publish them by posting them on a wall, making small index cards for team members to post on their

**TABLE 10-3   The Revised Core Hours**

|                | RUSS  | JACOB | MIKAELA | SAM   | ROCKY |
|----------------|-------|-------|---------|-------|-------|
| START OF DAY   | 10:00 | 7:30  | 8:30    | 7:30  | 9:30  |
| LUNCH START    | 12:00 | 12:00 | 12:00   | 12:00 | 12:00 |
| LUNCH END      | 1:00  | 12:30 | 1:00    | 1:00  | 1:00  |
| END OF DAY     | 7:30  | 4:30  | 6:00    | 5:00  | 6:30  |

monitors, or by putting them into the group calendar. Any solo work can be done outside core team hours; the work that requires pairing or collaboration should be done during core team hours.

## Distributed and Part-Time Teams

Not all teams have the luxury of having a fully dedicated team working together in a team workspace. While we strive for this, sometimes it just does not work out that way. The approach listed above can be applied to teams that are either distributed or have part-time people—or both.

### Distributed

If you have a distributed team, do the same exercise as above, but do it remotely. As ScrumMaster, host a virtual online conferencing session. Have people email their preferred start, lunch, and end times before the scheduled meeting start time. Then insert the data into a spreadsheet to share with the team during the online conference. Pick a common time zone reference. In Table 10-4, we chose central. Then map out the times, listing start and end times in both the common time zone and the primary time zone for that individual.

Based on this information, the sample distributed to the team shown in Table 10-4 has some big time gaps to discuss. Rocky likes to start his morning at 11:30 a.m. Central time, though it's only 9:30 in his time zone. Sam also gets a late start in Central time (10:30 a.m.), though again, for him it's only 8:30. The rest of the team starts within an hour and a half of each other. The end of the day is no better. Let's analyze the core hours.

- Morning: There are actually no morning hours when the whole team is available. Russ, Jacob, and Mikaela have shared morning hours between 9:00 and 10:30 a.m., central time. Sam and Rocky are both available while most of the team is at lunch, between 11:30 and 1:30 central.
- Lunch: 10:30–3:00
- Afternoon: 3:00–4:30

**TABLE 10-4**  Time Map

| | RUSS (EST) | | JACOB (CST) | | MIKAELA (CST) | | SAM (PST) | | ROCKY (PST) | |
|---|---|---|---|---|---|---|---|---|---|---|
| | CST | EST | CST | CST | CST | CST | CST | PST | CST | PST |
| START OF DAY | 9:00 | 10:00 | | 7:30 | | 8:30 | 10:30 | 8:30 | 11:30 | 9:30 |
| LUNCH START | 10:30 | 11:30 | | 12:00 | | 12:00 | 1:30 | 11:30 | 2:00 | 12:00 |
| LUNCH END | 11:30 | 12:30 | | 12:30 | | 1:00 | 2:00 | 12:00 | 3:00 | 1:00 |
| END OF DAY | 6:30 | 7:30 | | 4:30 | | 6:00 | 7:00 | 5:00 | 8:30 | 6:30 |

This only gives the team 1.5 total hours of shared time. Not good. Some of the problems could be mitigated by having Sam and Rocky pair and collaborate together in the morning separately from the rest of the team, who in turn are available for each other in the morning hours. The afternoon hours could be designated for whole team activities.

Imagine, though, if the team had team members around the globe! This model makes the challenges facing distributed teams very visible, especially when the team has a strong desire to work together. In instances like this, where people are many time zones apart, one viable option is to create small working teams locally, even if they are still distributed. This ensures that some team members, at least, are sharing common work hours.

## Part-Time Team Members

In the case of part-time team members, rather than list the start and end times down the left side, list the days of the week (see Table 10-5). Unless a team changes its hours from sprint to sprint, you'll only have to do this once at the beginning of the project, updating it only if someone's hours change. Once the table is populated, you can determine core hours for each day of the week. In this example, on Monday, the team has no true core team hours as Jacob can only work in the afternoon and Sam can only work in the morning.

**TABLE 10-5    Time Map for Part-Time Team Members**

|       | RUSS | | JACOB | | MIKAELA | | SAM | | ROCKY | |
|-------|-------|-------|-------|------|---------|------|-------|------|-------|------|
|       | HOURS | WHEN | HOURS | WHEN | HOURS | WHEN | HOURS | WHEN | HOURS | WHEN |
| MON | 6 | 10-12 1-5 | 3 | 2-5 | 8 | 9-5 | 4 | 9-1 | 3 | 2-5 |
| TUE | 6 | 10-12 1-5 | 3 | 2-5 | 0 | 9-5 | 4 | | 3 | 2-5 |
| WED | 0 | | 3 | 2-5 | 8 | 9-5 | 4 | 1-5 | 3 | 2-5 |
| THU | 4 | 10-12 1-3 | 3 | 2-5 | 0 | 9-5 | 4 | | 5 | 9-2 |
| FRI | 3 | 1-4 | 3 | 2-5 | 8 | 9-5 | 4 | 9-1 | 5 | 9-2 |
| MON | 6 | 10-12 1-5 | 4 | 1-5 | 8 | 9-5 | 4 | 1-5 | 3 | 2-5 |
| THU | 6 | 10-12 1-5 | 4 | 9-1 | 0 | 9-5 | 4 | | 3 | 2-5 |
| WED | 0 | | 4 | 1-5 | 8 | 9-5 | 4 | 9-1 | 3 | 2-5 |
| THU | 4 | 10-12 1-3 | 4 | 9-1 | 0 | 9-5 | 4 | | 5 | 12-5 |
| FRI | 3 | 1-4 | 4 | 1-5 | 8 | 9-5 | 4 | 1-5 | 5 | 12-5 |

# Keys to Success

We saw in our story that Jacob was very unhappy with what he perceived as Russ's slacker attitude. If Letitia had let this problem continue, the team could have split apart, just over a simple thing like when to start the day. Paying attention to little details like this can help prevent big team issues down the road. When determining the team's core hours, it's important to keep a few things in mind.

First, make sure the team understands why having core hours is important and that they are a collective agreement of preferred work hours and work habits. Whether the team is co-located or distributed, working with each other daily helps keep things in check and communication flowing. People who work together have the ability to learn each other's behaviors, skills, and patterns. As they get to know each other personally and professionally, they begin to gel as a team. Working together also provides people the opportunity to learn more about the project, as they spend more time working on parts of the system they may not ordinarily touch.

Second, establish core hours at the beginning of each project and regularly throughout the project as needed. Jacob would not have been as upset if he had known Russ's work patterns; though he comes in late (at least in the summer), he also stays late. These patterns may change throughout the course of the project—school, work, weather, and holidays can all impact availability—so it is important for the team members to communicate when their hours change dramatically. If the team is distributed or is part-time, and core hours vary dramatically from sprint to sprint, this activity may need to be done as often as at the beginning of every sprint.

Last, encourage the team to remain open and willing to bend. Everyone may not be able to work exactly the schedule they would prefer. Remind them that the benefits of working together far outweigh the personal habits of one person.

Establishing core hours is a small detail that can have a big impact on team performance. Calculate how many hours you are spending as a co-located team and work together to maximize those core hours while maintaining individual team members' flexibility. Charting core hours is a small but powerful tool that can help you build a high-performing team.

# Chapter 11

# RELEASE PLANNING

The most frequently asked question on any project might be, "When will you be done?" or "Will you have it all done by a certain date?" We all have experienced times when our projections have been way off and we've suffered as a result. Scrum promises a more adaptable planning scenario, one that allows for and indeed expects change. But does that promise mean that we don't have to—or can't—do release planning any more?

Let's follow Brian and Stephen, both relatively new to Scrum and approaching it from different points of view, as they explore release planning with Scrum.

## The Story

Brian was an experienced project manager and new ScrumMaster about to start his first Scrum project. He and his team members had been to an introductory workshop on Scrum and were well-versed in the by-the-book answers on how to get started and what to do. Brian was excited about the possibilities.

Until, that is, he got a visit from his corporate vice president, Stephen.

"By the way, Brian," Stephen said as he passed by his workspace. "I'm going to need a release plan as soon as possible."

Brian frowned. "Release plan?" he thought to himself. "Isn't that a relic from the waterfall days? I thought that when I switched to Scrum I could leave Gantt charts back there with broken promises and half-formed handoffs."

Out loud, however, he said only, "But Stephen, we're using Scrum. I can't tell you exactly when we'll be done. That's the whole point."

That answer stopped Stephen in his tracks. He came in and planted himself in the chair by Brian's desk. "Buddy, we need to talk. What makes you think that with Scrum you don't need a release plan?"

Brian leaned forward excitedly. He was ready for this one. "Simple. The problem with all the projects I've been on in the past is you think you're on track and then realize at the very end that you're not going to make it. That makes everyone anxious and causes us to rush to meet deadlines, which as we both know just means poor quality and burned out teams. With Scrum, if you don't get to something, it just doesn't get done. That's the beauty of priority order."

"I'm not sure that's exactly right," said Stephen.

"Well, remember that last disastrous project I was on?" countered Brian. "The team and I worked so hard and so well, and then at the end everything just kind of caught up to us. Suddenly we realized we were too far behind to catch up. I finally got it after that project. We can't trust our plans. They are just milestones, dates, and soft things that we make up to give everyone a sense of security, but in the end they are just a bunch of lies."

"I can't disagree with you about that, Brian," said Stephen. "But Scrum doesn't give you a free pass on release planning. I still have to know and be able to communicate to my bosses when we'll be done. I need a release plan."

"Well, Stephen, I could tell you a date when the entire product backlog will be done, but we both know it won't be accurate," started Brian. "I'm trying to think how to explain it to you. How much do you know about Scrum?"

"I went to the same course you did," answered Stephen. "In fact, I'm the one who brought the trainer in and suggested we use it," replied Stephen.

"Great," said Brian with a sigh of relief. "Then you know that we deliver working software every sprint and how the framework is structured. So you understand why it would be irresponsible of me to give you an exact date when we'll be done."

"No, I think it would be irresponsible of you to think that Scrum gives you free reign to just do what you want to do when you want to do it," challenged Stephen. "I've got to answer to our executive VP and then the CEO. We have plans that we need to make in advance as to when things will be in the market."

"Stephen's right, you know," came a voice from their right. It was Carol, a Scrum consultant they had hired to help them in their transition. "Sorry. I didn't mean to eavesdrop but I was fascinated by the conversation," she added as she walked closer to them.

"You can—and should—still do release planning with Scrum. But Brian's right, too, Stephen. Scrum does treat release planning differently."

Carol walked over to the whiteboard that hung near Brian's desk.

"You've both heard of velocity, right?" she began, writing it on the board. They both nodded.

"It's the measure of how much work a team can get done over time, usually expressed in story points," said Brian confidently.

"Exactly," said Carol. "So, let's liken it to the odometer in your car. Velocity is like a sprint odometer: It tracks how much ground you cover in terms of story points, per day or per sprint. So, if in three sprints you traveled 1,000 miles, 900 miles, and 1,100 miles, you'd have averaged 1,000 miles a sprint. Put a different way, you can travel about 100 miles per day and you'll cover 1,000 miles in a sprint, since we're doing two-week sprints. With me so far?"

"Yep," said Brian and Stephen in unison.

"But how does that get us closer to knowing what day you'll be done?" asked Stephen.

"Bear with me. There's a method to my madness," Carol said smiling. "So we have a velocity measure. How else can we tell where we are on our little trip? Well, back to my car metaphor, we'd look out the window and see what we see. In a sprint, we do that every day in our daily standup meeting. We pull ourselves up from our work—our driving, if you will—and look around to see how we're doing."

Brian and Stephen nodded.

"So. We can travel 1,000 miles every two weeks, and we make sure those miles are taking us in the right direction with our daily standups—and at a higher-level view, with our reviews and retrospectives. But our final measure is a burndown chart. The speedometer is the slope of the burndown," said Carol as she continued to sketch on the board.

"The burndown chart tells us if our average speed is such that we can expect to cover our 1,000 miles. We might not go exactly 100 miles every day, right? But as long as our speed is such that we average 100 miles a day, we're going to reach our 1,000-mile goal," Carol finished.

She held up a hand at the expression on their faces. "So where's the release plan, right? The release plan is our roadmap, marked with stopping points—waypoints—along the way.

Figure 11-1 summarizes the metaphor.

"So, Brian," said Carol. "Sticking with our car trip metaphor, let's say we want to go from San Diego, California, to Jacksonville, Florida. You're sitting at a computer. Pull up a map. How far is that?"

"Well, it depends on which way we go. But the shortest is 2,339 miles. That includes a stop in Juarez, though, and I don't want to drive that close to the border of Mexico," Brian mused out loud. "So, I'll just drag the route and go through Albuquerque instead, giving us 2,413 miles, but putting us in much more populated areas along the way: Phoenix, Albuquerque, Dallas, Amarillo, then Houston."

Stephen nodded, "So, if we travel 1,000 miles every two weeks, we're looking at about 2.5 sprints or five weeks to Jacksonville. That's all a release plan has to be. It answers the question, 'At our current rate and route, how long will it take to get there safely?' If it's the reverse—and I needed you to be in Jacksonville by a certain date, you'd need to do the math to see if it's possible—you might need to drive more hours

| MILES TRAVELED | VISUAL INDICATORS OF DIRECTION | ODOMETER | SPEEDOMETER | ROADMAP |
|---|---|---|---|---|
| 1,000 EVERY TWO WEEKS<br><br>100 PER DAY | STANDUPS<br><br>REVIEWS<br><br>RETROSPECTIVES | ODOMETER<br><br>BURNDOWN CHART | SLOPE OF BURNDOWN IN THE BURNDOWN CHART | RELEASE PLAN |

**FIGURE 11-1**   Indicators using the traveling car metaphor

each day, but you could determine if it is feasible to do that or discuss what you would need to make it possible. I told you release planning was possible with Scrum."

Brian frowned. "But wait. That sounds great if you're actually driving from Point A to Point B, but on our project, we don't always know exactly where we're going or how far it is from here to there. And even if we did, this perfect little roadmap doesn't take into account road work, which might slow us down. Or allow for foul weather that causes us to deviate from our route. Or factor in a great opportunity that requires we include an out-of-the-way stop, St. Louis, for instance, to our original plan."

Carol intervened. "Well, that's where you're both right. Release plans are good to have and worthwhile because they give us a preliminary roadmap—we can't just set out with no direction and no idea of when we'll likely arrive. But Brian's right that it's important for the stakeholders to understand that a plan is just that, a plan. And the plan *will* change. Despite our best efforts to estimate the product backlog, we might find out that the actual distance we have to travel to complete the project is much more or less than we anticipated. And despite our best efforts to track and estimate our expected velocity, we might run into problems that slow us down. And maybe we include a worst-case scenario for things like that. And if they discover gold in St. Louis, which is the equivalent of adding some new, undiscovered stories to the product backlog, we can include it in our trip, but it's going to cost in terms of either time or money, right?

"Remember our visual indicators?" Carol continued. "Our daily standups, reviews, and retrospectives? That's how we determine if the team is on the right track. We don't want to go all the way to Jacksonville only to realize that it's the wrong place to be. If we want to go to St. Louis or Louisville, so be it, but we need to communicate to the customers what the risks are and that, should they decide to include a detour, we just can't magically reappear in Jacksonville as originally scheduled as if we never took a left turn. The time will have been lost and the schedule adjusted accordingly."

"Understood," said Stephen. "I think we've got an idea of what to do. Thanks for stopping by and ending our stalemate."

Brian and Stephen continued their conversation well past lunch. Brian acknowledged that Stephen needed a plan. He then explained to Stephen how he should expect varying levels of functionality along the way, and why giving a hard date *and* a complete list of functionality this early in the project would be irresponsible because there wasn't enough known about the project to be able to nail down both things. In the end, Brian was able to give Stephen enough information for him to do his strategic work while the team executed the day-to-day tactical work.

Let's take a detailed look at the process that Brian proposed to Stephen.

## The Model

In our story, both Stephen and Brian sat through the same Scrum training but heard two very different things. Stephen didn't believe that using Scrum to run the project should affect his release planning, while Brian felt that Scrum's very flexibility meant he would no longer be tied to an unrealistic date. In a way, they were both right.

Historically, the release plan is one of the deliverables that comes out of a traditional project initiation phase [PMI] and often manifests itself in a Gantt chart. Its level of precision is very high. In a Scrum project, however, release planning is quite different. There is no Gantt chart that tells you exactly when a certain task will be done. Instead, an agile release plan tells us on a higher, more strategic level, what range of functionality will likely be done by a certain date. Your release plan should be built before the first sprint and should be revised continually throughout the project to reflect changing priorities and project realities.

An agile release plan only has to include the best- and worst-case final release dates, but many plans also include smaller releases along the way, including end-of-sprint releases and quarterly releases. I have even scheduled daily releases when working on a sustained engineering team supporting a production system. What makes sense for your release plan depends on the specifics of your project and the reality of your situation.

I approach release planning in a very systematic way.

1. Sketch a preliminary roadmap.
2. Add a degree of confidence.
3. Include dates and adjust as needed.
4. Update the plan every sprint.

## Sketch a Preliminary Roadmap

To build an agile release plan, you need three inputs:

1. An estimated, ordered, and prioritized product backlog
2. The team velocity
3. A sprint timeline

The product backlog is a detailed accounting of what it will take to get from Point A to Point B. The product backlog is updated throughout the project to reflect what needs to be accomplished, the relative priority of each item, and approximately how much effort it will take to complete each product backlog element. Don't attempt a release plan until the team and the product owner have estimated, ordered, and prioritized the initial product backlog. That doesn't mean all the stories should be broken down into small pieces at this stage or that your estimates or priorities won't change as you learn more about the project. But a rough story point estimate and priority ordering are essential for planning, even at this early stage.

Once you have a prioritized and estimated product backlog, you need to know your team velocity, how much work a team can do over time. This number can either be pulled from historical data or estimated. (See Chapter 4, "Determining Team Velocity," for more information.)

The last thing you need to know is your sprint timeline—the intervals at which your sprints start and end. This could be one week, two weeks, three weeks, or four weeks. Regardless of the interval, once you determine your sprint length (see Chapter 6, "Determining Sprint Length," to help figure out your sprint length), keep it consistent. From your sprint length, you can easily calculate all your end-of-sprint dates.

As an example, let's suppose that we estimate our total product backlog size to be 200 points. Through some method, we have calculated our expected team velocity to be between 15 and 22 points per sprint. We also know we are using two-week sprints. We first draw a roadmap at the low velocity. To do this, we start at the top of the product backlog (where the highest priority stories live), count down 15 points, and draw a line. We then repeat that for four to five sprints, or until we reach a point in the product backlog where the story estimates are as large or larger than our low-range sprint velocity.

Next, we draw a roadmap of how the project will fare at the higher velocity. Again, we start at the top of the product backlog, but this time we count down 22 points, and draw a line. We repeat this until we reach a point where our story estimates are too large for the roadmap to be meaningful. Figure 11-2 shows us our approximate release roadmap at the team's high and low velocities. You can see that with a velocity of 22, the team will complete more product backlog items per sprint, and as a result, deliver more features overall.

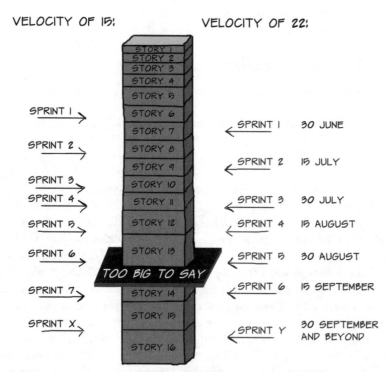

**FIGURE 11-2** Mapping estimated velocity to the product backlog

Keep in mind that the actual velocity, and how much of the product backlog is completed by a certain date or within a certain budget, will likely fall somewhere between the two ranges. In some cases, the actual velocity might even fall below the low-range estimates, especially at first. This roadmap is just a preliminary sketch of how things would look given probable conditions. We talk more about how the velocity estimate ranges relate to the overall release plan later in the chapter. First, let's decide how confident we are in our predictions, given the stories in the backlog and the accuracy of our velocity estimate.

## Add a Degree of Confidence

Let's assume that our team has worked together on similar Scrum projects before, so its members are fairly confident in the velocity ranges they have put forth. We next have to consider the stories themselves. How clear are they? How accurately can they be estimated? Using the roadmap and detailed product backlog, we decide that we have a high degree of confidence that the stories in the early sprints, because they are clear and appropriately sized (small), will be done in, at worst, four sprints and, at best, three sprints. The remaining stories, however, are large and unclear, so their estimates are correspondingly fuzzy. Because we are much less confident in the later story estimates, we are also less confident in how much of the product backlog we can accomplish after the first three to four sprints.

When sharing the initial release plan, then, we need to make two things clear. First, we are confident in its predicted velocity range. Second, there is a clear distinction between the first three to four sprints, where the stories are high priority, small, and relatively clear, and future sprints. Because the stories are better understood in the first few sprints, our confidence in completing them is high (80 percent to 100 percent). As the stories get bigger, fuzzier, and lower in priority, our confidence in the estimates drops. By the time we reach the bottom of the initial release plan, we really have no idea how much is involved in implementing the stories, so we can't say with any confidence how long they will take. Our confidence in completing them, therefore, is very low, 10 percent to 25 percent.

A preliminary release plan is an educated guess, one that the team will refine as it learns more about the product, the project, and itself.

## Include Dates and Adjust as Needed

Now that we have a rough picture of the initial roadmap and an idea of how confident we are in those breakdowns, we can extrapolate some preliminary release dates for our highest priority stories. Keep in mind, though, that these dates will likely change as we obtain real velocity data and learn more about the product we are building.

As previously mentioned, we believe with a high degree of confidence that we'll finish approximately 60 points' worth of stories in the first three-to-four sprints. We can confidently communicate that in one to two months, we will have completed about

60 points' worth of work, though there might be changes based on priority, emerging requirements, and sprint review meetings. We add those dates to the product backlog.

That's a good start, but we also need some idea of how long the rest of the product backlog will take. So we make an educated guess. After the first four sprints, at our low-range velocity, we calculate that we will be done with the remaining backlog in about nine more sprints. At our high-range velocity, on the other hand, we'll only need a total of two more sprints to complete the remaining work in the product backlog. Let's look at the math. Take a look at Figure 11-3.

As the figure shows, with the knowledge we have on hand, we think we can complete the entire product backlog in somewhere between 9 sprints (4.5 months) and 13 sprints (6.5 months).

We now have two sets of dates for completing the entire product backlog, a worst-case scenario and a best-case scenario. In reality, though, these estimates are bounded by either time (a deadline) or budget. When the budget runs out, or the deadline arrives, we'll likely deliver a portion of the product backlog that is somewhere between our best- and worst-case scenario. To help communicate this fact, we include one last element on the preliminary roadmap: a high and low watermark.

Let's assume our project is bounded by budget. We have a 200-point product backlog and a set amount of money, say $200,000. When the money is gone, the project will end. The team burns about $20,000 per sprint. We know, then, that we can run approximately ten two-week sprints of work before we run out of budget.

The high watermark, then, reflects how far down the product backlog the team will get at its low-range velocity, at the worst-case scenario, before the project runs out of money. In our case, that line would be drawn at 150 points down the backlog (10 sprints × 15 points per sprint).

```
LOW-RANGE VELOCITY = 15
TOTAL ESTIMATED BACKLOG = 200 POINTS
TIME TO COMPLETE FIRST 60 POINTS = 4 SPRINTS
                          (VELOCITY OF 15 X 4 SPRINTS)
TOTAL REMAINING POINTS = 200 - 60 = 140
140 / 15 = 9 SPRINTS (ROUNDED DOWN FROM 9.3)

HIGH-RANGE VELOCITY = 22
TOTAL ESTIMATED BACKLOG = 200 POINTS
TIME TO COMPLETE FIRST 60 POINTS = 3 SPRINTS, 66
POINTS
                          (VELOCITY OF 22 X 3 SPRINTS)

TOTAL REMAINING POINTS = 200 - 66 = 134
134 / HIGH-RANGE VELOCITY (22) = 6 SPRINTS (ROUNDED
DOWN FROM 6.09)
```

**FIGURE 11-3**   Calculating future sprints using a velocity range

The low watermark, reflects how much of the product backlog could be accomplished with the same budget but at the high-range velocity. In our case, that line would be drawn at 220 points (10 sprints times 22 points). In other words, if things go perfectly and all the estimates are spot on, the team could complete the entire current product backlog before it runs out of funding.

Note, however, that the confidence meter applies to the watermarks as well. The team's confidence in delivering the stories near the high watermark is much higher than those near the low watermark. The likelihood that we will finish everything is actually fairly low at this stage.

These marks help the stakeholders and groups like marketing visualize what stories they will probably get (those above the high watermark), what they might get (those between the high and low watermarks), and what they probably won't get (those below the low watermark).

Figure 11-4 shows a preliminary release plan that includes the end dates for each sprint and the high and low watermarks. Though it might look neat and complete, remember that this release plan is fluid. The sprints are not preplanned and this is not set in stone. It's simply a sketch of how the release would look at a certain velocity and

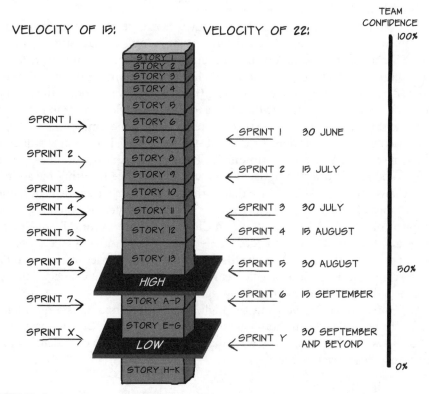

**FIGURE 11-4**  Release roadmap as it relates to time

with no substantive changes (that's where the degree of confidence comes in). Like an actual roadmap, the release plan's primary purpose is to give management some idea of how long it will take to go from Point A to Point B. Additionally, stakeholders can see at-a-glance how a story's priority affects the date it will be completed. They also have a tool to help them consider date-sensitive market conditions and events such as tradeshows or competitive releases.

Using the initial release plan, if a story or set of stories absolutely needs to be done by a certain date, the product owner and team can work together before the project begins to ensure that the story is ready for the earlier sprints and prioritized accordingly. Juggling stories and priorities will necessitate changes to the initial release plan, but that's OK. Even after it's published, the release plan is designed to adapt to project realities throughout the project life cycle.

## Maintaining the Release Plan Throughout the Project

In Scrum, we know that most projects don't move from Point A to Point B at a constant rate of speed with no detours or mishaps. As such, we update the release plan to reflect reality at the end of every sprint. We adjust our projections to include the actual *average* team velocity to date and the knowledge we have gained from creating working software and receiving feedback.

For example, let's imagine that ours is a new Scrum team. In our initial release roadmap, we assumed/guessed/calculated a velocity of 15 to 22 story points per sprint (refer to Figure 11-4). We also communicated that our velocity estimates were very uncertain. In the first sprint, we accomplish 11 story points rather than the 15 to 22 we had estimated. Though no one is surprised by the lower velocity, the team and product owner do need to update the release roadmap to reflect the drop in velocity.

At the same time, let's assume that our team spent some time in the first sprint grooming the product backlog. As a result, the team added some new stories and broke some of the bigger stories into smaller, more manageable pieces. These changes must also be reflected in the updated release roadmap. The resulting release roadmap is shown in Figure 11-5. Notice that in the revised plan, we are using a rounded velocity range of 10 and 15 points per sprint. This is calculated based on the velocity multipliers of .8 and 1.4 from Table 4-5 in Chapter 4, "Determining Team Velocity." Notice, too, that because we've added new stories and are moving at a slower pace than our original estimate, the team will accomplish fewer stories in each sprint and over the course of the project based on current data. (This might change as the team improves and moves into a high-performing state.)

As before, everything between the high and low watermarks is a questionable area for the team. The team should get everything done above the high watermark, is 50/50 between the high and low watermarks, and has very low confidence for anything below the low watermark.

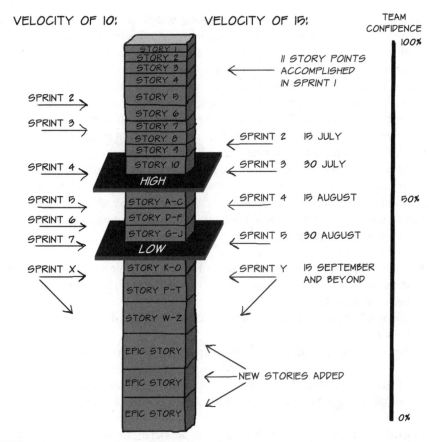

**FIGURE 11-5**    Release plans updated to reflect current reality

After we run the next sprint, we again modify the release plan to reflect our average velocity from sprints one and two (expressed as a range) plus any additions or subtractions to the product backlog or any refined story estimates. We update it again after the third sprint, and so on. Eventually our velocity and product backlog becomes more stable and the release plan much clearer.

## Determining the End Game

All agile practices focus on delivering value to customers early. Sometimes this means that the project ends early and sometimes it means delivering essentially as planned. Other times, it's clear after the first few sprints that the project will run out of money before you run out of stories. Each of these scenarios is manageable within the Scrum framework and with an agile release plan.

Releasing a project that meets everyone's expectations under budget and earlier than expected is a good goal. The key to doing so is to build only what is needed to accomplish the business objectives, without all the extra gold plating and unnecessary functionality that is rarely or never used. Chapter 30, "Writing Contracts," offers two methods that you can use to release your system early and under budget.

Typically, however, even high-performing teams release somewhere between their low and high watermarks. They deliver enough functionality to meet the needs of the business, as planned, by the time the project runs out of money. They hit the arrow dead-center on the target. Everyone is happy.

The third outcome, and the one I see most frequently, is a release plan that predicts that the budget will run out long before the stories do. The stakeholders look at the plan and decide that there is a large gap between the low watermark and the true business value the customers are asking for. When that happens, you have several options for solving the problem.

- You might be able to increase velocity by building a higher performing team. Perhaps there are impediments in the way or the team needs to implement better technical practices.
- You might be able to increase your budget, resulting in more of the product backlog being executed.
- You might have to decide to drop desired functionality. Re-evaluate what is truly essential and what is desirable. Some items are lower in priority than others for a reason. Though a certain feature might not make it into *this* release, it might be acceptable to include it in future releases.

Regardless of whether you deliver early, as predicted, or even fall a little short of your initial worst-case scenario, the good news is, with Scrum, the customers are in the loop from the first day. As the project progresses, and the larger stories become clearer and receive more accurate estimates, the product owner and stakeholders might need to consider whether certain things can be left undone, what tradeoffs need to be made, or whether the schedule should be pushed to accommodate more functionality. The advantage to making these tradeoffs in Scrum is that they are being made based on software that is working and, ideally, has customer and stakeholder feedback. Additionally, having working software means that last-minute glitches and integration issues are much less likely to impact the release late in the schedule.

The initial tradeoff of having less clarity in the release plan actually provides an opportunity to give people a better product or service. Stakeholders see working software at the end of each sprint and can make adjustments based on what they see. They are given an updated release plan after every sprint, so they know where the project stands in real time. They have understood and been a part of the tradeoffs and have helped guide you and the team along the path of optimal delivery. By the time the project ends, there should be no surprises.

# Keys to Success

Release planning is meant to provide answers as to when certain functionality and the entire project will be done. Though these are often moving targets, with agile release planning we acknowledge this fact up front and revise our plans accordingly. To make agile release plans work most effectively, you need to do five things: communicate up front and often, update the release plan after every sprint, try to do the highest priority items first, refine estimates on bigger items, and create working software every sprint.

## Communicate Up Front and Often

I learned the hard way that no manager or leader in the company likes surprises, no matter how well intentioned. Your release plan should be a topic for discussion on a regular basis. People should ask questions about it, and you should not get defensive. It is a good idea to post your release plan on the wall for everyone to see and to repost it every time there is a change.

## Update the Release Plan after Every Sprint

Scrum is all about change. Your plan will change frequently, perhaps as often as every sprint, as backlog items shift in priority and estimates get more refined. It is important to update the release plan every sprint. This helps stakeholders know what to expect and when to expect it based on the feedback they provide at each sprint review.

## Try to Do the Highest Priority Items First

While doing the highest priority items first may sound like a no-brainer, it's often forgotten. Whenever possible, teams should be working on the highest priority items from the product backlog in each sprint. Sometimes the highest priority item might not be the item the team is dying to sink its teeth into, but unless there is a compelling reason (dependencies, size, lack of understanding), it's the one that should be completed first.

## Refine Estimates on Bigger Items

As items move up the product backlog in priority, they require more attention. They need to get smaller so they can be brought into a sprint. As such, remember to have a grooming meeting with the product owner and the team to review the product backlog every sprint. This is a forward-looking meeting, where the team and the product owner work together to refine and break stories down into small chunks and estimate them, and to re-estimate other stories that might have more clarity.

## Deliver Working Software

No release plan or Gantt chart gives the true status like working software. Working software is your best insurance against last minute problems derailing your release. No matter what your release plan, Gantt chart, or task board says, working software is the true measure of project progress. Never forget that.

## Scrum and Release Planning

On Scrum projects, release planning does not disappear; it's just approached differently. By couching estimates in ranges and confidence levels, agile release plans actually provide more information than more traditional release plans. And, by creating an adaptable release plan that is not only designed for but actually expects changes, your stakeholders and managers have a transparent look into how the project is doing, where it's going, and what they can expect every step of the way.

# References

[PMI]   Project Management Institute. 2008. *Guide to the Project Management Body of Knowledge, 4th Edition*. Upper Darby, PA: Project Management Institute.

# Chapter 12

# DECOMPOSING STORIES AND TASKS

Writing stories and tasks that are right-sized can mean the difference between succeeding with Scrum and failing miserably. It's that important. What's worse is that the symptoms of wrong-sized work elements (not finishing, poor estimation, painful standups) don't at first seem related to story and task size at all.

During one of my first projects, we found we were having problems completing our work by the end of the sprint. Our first inclination was to blame the sprint length—we assumed a longer sprint would solve our problems. Through a serendipitous encounter we discovered that it was actually our tasks and stories that needed to be resized, rather than our sprints.

## The Story

In 2005, the team and I were killing ourselves trying to figure out why we were not able to finish every item on the sprint backlog. For the past three sprints, there had been a handful of items that had to be put *back* on the product backlog. We discussed the problem at length, but were no closer to an answer. Because it always felt like we needed one more week to tie up all the loose ends, extending the length of our sprints to five weeks seemed to us to be the perfect solution. At the same time, though, we'd never heard of sprints longer than four weeks, so we were unsure about what to do.

Luckily for us, the Agile Alliance Agile Development conference was just around the corner. We had problems we needed to solve and, with enough begging, were pretty sure we could get management to send our team. A few weeks later, with plane tickets and sprint backlogs in hand, we were off to the conference. Of all the answers we had set out to find, determining the length of our sprint was at the top of our list.

On the first day of the conference I found myself in line for coffee with Ron Jeffries. I introduced myself and asked him if he'd be willing to get lunch with the team, our treat. He agreed. I tracked down the team and told them the good news. Everyone was very excited. Later that day we found ourselves sitting with Ron discussing, among other things, how long our sprints should be.

After our initial introduction and a good serving of food, I started off by telling Ron about our team, our project, and the hurdles we were facing. I then pulled out a prioritized list of items we wanted to discuss and started with number one: the length of our sprints, the trouble we were having trying to accomplish our work in 30 days, and how we thought we should extend our sprint length.

"Ron, we cannot get our work done in 30 days. There are always stories left undone. We've decided we need to extend the length of our sprints to finish these stories, but the books say not to go longer than four weeks. What do you think?" I asked.

"I think you need to shorten the length of your sprints," said Ron, bluntly.

I'm sure Ron could see the team's collective jaw dropping. Of all the answers we were expecting, this was not one of them. Mike chimed in.

"Uh, Ron, I don't think I heard you correctly—did you say to *shorten* our sprints?"

"Yup," said Ron.

"I must have explained it wrong," I said. "You see, the problem is our sprints are too short already. We can't get our work done in the time we have."

"No, I get it. But what makes you think that you'll be able to get anything done in 45 days or 60 days?" asked Ron.

"Simple. We just need more time," answered John.

At this point Ron asked to see our most recent sprint backlog. We showed him our backlog, a portion of which you can see in Figure 12-1.

Ron pointed to the estimate for *Create a Configuration Settings Singleton class*.

"John, why is this task eight hours?" asked Ron.

"That's how long it will take me," stated John.

"I can do that in five minutes. Why does it take you eight hours?" inquired Ron.

John sat there for a minute, thinking about his answer and of all the work needed to accomplish the task. There was just too much to list out.

"It takes me eight hours because that's how long it takes. Why are you peppering me on this?" stated John, abruptly.

"I just wonder why a five-minute task takes you eight hours. How many other five-minute tasks are in there that you are all masking in huge numbers of hours?"

| EXTENSION DLL | NAME | EST |
|---|---|---|
| IDENTIFY CUSTOMERS ACCEPTANCE TESTS | MITCH | 12 |
| IMPLEMENT END-TO-END AUTOMATED CUSTOMER ACCEPTANCE TESTS | MITCH | 12 |
| EXECUTE AUTOMATED CUSTOMER ACCEPTANCE TESTS | MIKE | 6 |
| CONFIGURATION FILE | | |
| CREATE A CONFIGURATIONSETTINGS SINGLETON CLASS | JOHN | 8 |
| EXTRACT SETTINGS FROM CONFIGURATION FILE | JOHN | 24 |
| EXPOSE SETTINGS FOR GET_ METHODS | JOHN | 20 |
| REFACTOR EXTENSION AND TEST DLL TO USE | MIKE | 20 |
| TEST CONFIGURATION FILE AND CLASSES IN UNIT TESTS | BART | 8 |

**FIGURE 12-1**   The backlog shown to Ron Jeffries

asked Ron. "It's no wonder you guys think you need to extend your sprints; you have easy tasks that take forever!"

It was easy to see the frustration quickly building in John's face.

"Ron, I'll have you know that I've been working in software for more than 20 years. If I say that's how long it will take, that's how long it will take!" exclaimed John.

Ron smiled. He had John just where he wanted him.

"OK, John. You're right. Tell me, what does this task entail? What will you do to complete it?" asked Ron.

At this point John started listing off not only work related to this task, like writing the class and meeting the done list criteria, but also many additional work items that were not captured on the sprint backlog at all. By the time he had finished, John had listed about a dozen tasks, only one of which was captured on the sprint backlog.

"OK, John, do you see the problem? You have just listed off a dozen tasks, each one of which should be listed on the sprint backlog and have an estimate. Instead, you've buried them all into this single, seemingly simple eight-hour task," stated Ron.

The light bulb went on for all of us.

"I am thinking of all the stuff we'd have to list for this DLL task," I said. "How many of our tasks have other work items buried in them?"

"Lots," whispered Mike under his breath. "Lots."

"You see, guys," explained Ron. "Your problem isn't your sprint length. You need to improve your task decomposition."

As we were settling into this truth, Ron shocked us even more.

"So, like I suspected, to fix your problems, you need to shorten your sprints. Doing that will force you to think critically about your work and decompose your tasks into small units. I suggest you try one-week sprints," said Ron.

"A one... What?" said John, verbalizing our amazement that this would even be proposed.

Ron smiled and nodded, "One week. Trust me."

By the end of the lunch, we were convinced. We left the conference and took Ron's advice, using one-week sprints to force us to learn to decompose work. In the beginning, we found one-week sprints to be a challenge. After a while, though, working in short sprints not only forced us to decompose our tasks and our stories, it also made us look at them in a new light. As time went on, we found ourselves accomplishing more, in less time, than we ever imagined possible.

# The Model

It happens all the time. Scrum teams feel pain and immediately start second-guessing Scrum. In the story above, we couldn't finish our stories so we thought we needed longer sprints. In reality, we couldn't finish our stories because we were hiding all sorts of work inside seemingly straightforward tasks. This caused our estimates to be off, our standups to be painful, our sprints to feel too short, and an immense amount of pressure. Our sprint length wasn't the problem. Our ability to decompose work was.

## Setting the Stage

To better understand decomposition, let's first examine the different elements of work that might need to be broken down. In the product backlog, we have user stories. These stories typically come in three flavors: epics, themes, and stories. At each sprint planning meeting, stories are broken down into tasks, which are stored in the sprint backlog.

- Like the *Lord of the Rings*, an epic is vast in scope. "Redesign the user interface for the document editor" would be an epic.
- A theme is a central idea of the larger epic. "Redesign the menu bar for the document editor," might be a theme inside the larger epic, "Redesign the user interface...."
- A story is one event in a theme. "Redesign the edit menu" might be a story in the "Redesign the menu bar" theme of the epic "Redesign the user interface" [DICTIONARY.COM].
- Tasks are the specific actions needed to accomplish a story. They are the elements that together make a story complete and potentially shippable.

Figure 12-2 shows the relationship between stories and tasks and how they fit into sprints and releases.

A story will have multiple tasks. A sprint will have multiple stories. A release *might* have multiple sprints. I say *might* because while many teams don't release every sprint, some teams actually do. That's why we use the words *potentially shippable* to describe completed stories; the stories theoretically could be released at the end of the sprint, but it might not be economically practical to do.

A theme, on the other hand, is typically too big to be completed in one sprint and must instead be done over a couple of sprints. An epic is often the subject of several sprints or a single release.

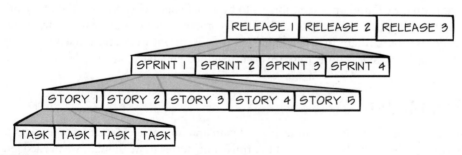

**FIGURE 12-2**  Task, story, sprint, and release model

In the story, our team had *tasks* that had not been broken down enough and were hiding smaller associated tasks. In many cases, though, the problem is that the *stories* are too big and hide large amounts of work. Problems with decomposing work typically begin at the story level and can continue through to the task level. It's tough to find the right balance between too much and not enough decomposition. There is no one-size-fits-all model out there; every team must find its own balance.

## Story Decomposition

Let's walk through some work decomposition together. We'll pretend that we are writing the stories to create an account management page for an online retailer, Big 'n Huge (see Figure 12-3). What are the things we can do on this page?

First, we can manage several factors of our account. So, let's turn that into a story: "As a BnH customer, I can manage my account." This is a good story, but by

| ORDER HISTORY | MORE ORDER ACTIONS |
|---|---|
| View Open Orders | Return Items or Gifts |
| View Your Digital Orders | Manage Magazine Subscriptions |
| Download Order Reports | Leave Seller Feedback |
| | Leave Packaging Feedback |

| PAYMENT METHODS | GIFT CARDS |
|---|---|
| Manage Payment Options | Manage Payment Options |
| Add a Credit or Debit Card | Add a Credit or Debit Card |
| Your Rewards Cards | Your Rewards Cards |

| ACCOUNT SETTINGS | ADDRESS BOOK |
|---|---|
| Change Account Settings | Manage Address Book |
| Forgot Your Password? | Add New Address |
| Manage Text Tracking Alerts | |

| DIGITAL MANAGEMENT | YOUR MEDIA |
|---|---|
| Your MP3 Settings | MP3 Download |
| Your Games and Software | eBooks |
| Your Apps and Devices | Your Collection |

FIGURE 12-3    Big 'n Huge's "Your Account" page

simply looking at the screen shown in Figure 12-3 we can see that it is too high level to mean anything; it's an epic. In fact, it will likely bring more questions to your mind than answers:

- What can I do to manage my account?
- Can I update credit cards?
- Can I manage my address book?

Given that we still have all these questions (and more), we need to break the story down to something more meaningful (see Figure 12-4), based again on the screen shot shown in Figure 12-3.

We now have three stories that roll into the large epic, "I can manage my account." Still, the stories are quite large. I still have more questions than answers. Let's decompose some more (see Figure 12-5).

What have we done? We decomposed "manage payment options" into its four primary stories, all of which roll up into the "manage payment options" story, which in turn rolls into the "manage my account" story.

- I can manage existing payment options
- I can edit or delete an existing credit card
- I can add a credit card
- I can manage gift cards

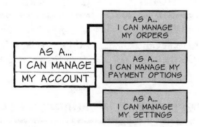

**FIGURE 12-4**   Initial story breakdown

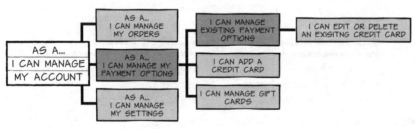

**FIGURE 12-5**   Further story breakdown

Each of the three larger stories (I can manage my orders, I can manage my payment options, and I can manage my settings) can be considered a theme. A theme is a group of pieces of functionality that tie together. They are typically visible on product roadmaps that show when each theme will be released. A theme may be its own release or may be part of a larger release that occurs several sprints later.

Let's continue decomposing the theme "I can manage my payment options." We've come a long way, but we are still at the wrong level of decomposition. The story "I can edit or delete an existing credit card" should be decomposed. Why? Because it is really two different stories, albeit closely related, in one (see Figure 12-6).

Let's also decompose "manage my settings" (see Figure 12-7).

In this example, we probably want to further decompose both "change my name" and "manage my address book." For the sake of brevity, we'll just decompose "manage my address book." On our fictional website Big 'n Huge, I can edit existing addresses or I can delete existing addresses. So, we write a story: "As a BnH customer, I can edit existing addresses saved in my address book." This is a good level of decomposition because it is testable and small. Could we decompose that further? Sure. The question is do we want to? Look at the decomposition shown in Figure 12-8.

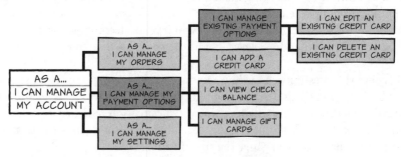

**FIGURE 12-6**   Decomposing the story "I can edit or delete an existing credit card"

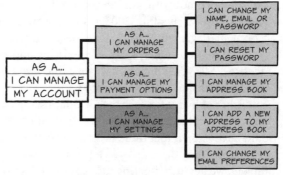

**FIGURE 12-7**   Decomposing "manage my settings"

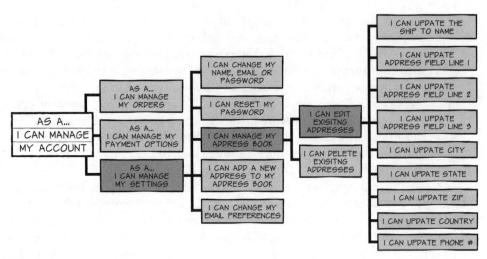

**FIGURE 12-8**    Decomposing can go too far

At this point, we've probably gone too far for a story at the product backlog level. Users do not often update only the address field or the state; most of the time, they update the entire address. As a result, the right level of decomposition for this story would be at the overall address level, not at the specifics that comprise the address itself.

This begs the question—how do we know when the story is the right size on the product backlog? I use this general rule of thumb: *A story is at the right size when it describes the smallest action that a user would typically want to do, or it is the smallest piece of functionality with business value.* Now, this is not a steadfast rule, but it's a good guideline that helps you gauge the size of your story.

## Task Decomposition

In our story, the team struggled not with story decomposition but with task decomposition. Let's pretend that my struggling 2005 team is working on the interface for Big 'n Huge's account management screen. They decide during sprint planning to estimate the story "As a BnH customer, I can edit existing addresses in my saved address book" (see Figure 12-9). They break that story into two tasks: Update configuration file and Update extension DLL (see Figure 12-10).

We estimate the number of hours for each task. Updating the extension DLL will take 50 hours. Updating the configuration file will take 80 hours. Even when we first started, my team would have known that these tasks are way too large.

So, we continue to break down these tasks (see Figure 12-11).

Once that is complete, we begin estimating task sizes (see Figure 12-12).

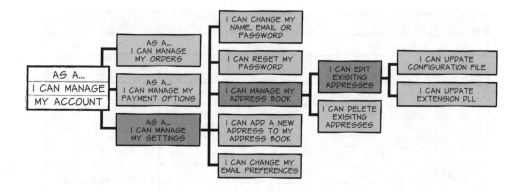

**FIGURE 12-9**    Decomposing "Edit existing addresses in my saved address book"

| TASK | NAME | EST |
|------|------|-----|
| UPDATE EXTENSION DLL | JOHN | 50 |
| UPDATE CONFIGURATION FILE FOR DLL | MIKE | 80 |

**FIGURE 12-10**    The story "Edit existing addresses in my saved address book" decomposes into two tasks

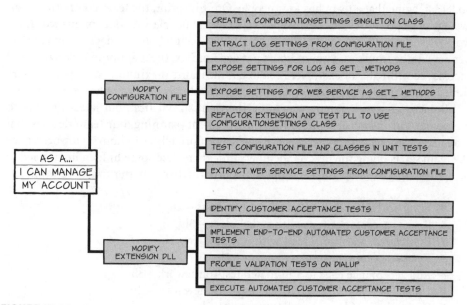

**FIGURE 12-11**    Sample task breakdown from a user story

| EXTENSION DLL | NAME | EST |
|---|---|---|
| IDENTIFY CUSTOMERS ACCEPTANCE TESTS | MITCH | 12 |
| IMPLEMENT END-TO-END AUTOMATED CUSTOMER ACCEPTANCE TESTS | MITCH | 12 |
| PROFILE VALIDATION TESTS ON DIALUP | JOHN | 12 |
| EXECUTE AUTOMATED CUSTOMER ACCEPTANCE TESTS | MIKE | 6 |
| **CONFIGURATION FILE** | | |
| CREATE A CONFIGURATIONSETTINGS SINGLETON CLASS | JOHN | 8 |
| EXTRACT LOG SETTINGS FROM CONFIGURATION FILE | JOHN | 12 |
| EXTRACT WEB SERVICE SETTINGS FROM CONFIGURATION FILE | JOHN | 20 |
| EXPOSE SETTINGS FOR LOG AS GET_ METHODS | JOHN | 20 |
| EXPOSE SETTINGS FOR WEBSERVICE AS GET_ METHODS | JOHN | 8 |
| REFACTOR EXTENSION AND TEST DLL TO USE CONFIGURATIONSETTINGS CLASS | MIKE | 20 |
| TEST CONFIGURATION FILE AND CLASSES IN UNIT TESTS | BART | 8 |

**FIGURE 12-12**   Estimating task sizes

These numbers look much better. Are they still too large? That depends on the team. First, follow the rule that tasks should be completed in no more than two days. So let's imagine that a team has four people. On this sprint, the team committed to an average of 16 hours of work burned down per day (4 people × 4 hours of burned-down work). The team's maximum task size should be about 8 hours (2 days × 4 max hours per day). If the team's maximum hours per day were six, the maximum task size would increase accordingly, for example, 12 hours. If the team's maximum hours per day were three, the maximum task size would decrease accordingly, for example, six hours.

Sometimes a task can appear to be the right size at first, but later turn out to be too big. For instance, suppose that during sprint planning, our team decides that "Identify customer acceptance tests" is sized appropriately at 12 hours. However, once the team starts doing the task its members quickly realize some hidden items need to be addressed. They stop and decompose the task further to better track the work:

- Brainstorm and document acceptance tests – 2h
- Review acceptance tests with stakeholder – 3h
- Brainstorm additional tests with stakeholder – 2h
- Review acceptance tests with team – 1h
- Add acceptance tests to automated test framework – 3h
- Update acceptance test data elements for new tests – 2h
- Set up the profiler to handle new tests – 2h
- Add new tests to build machine – 1h

These tasks may feel too small at first, but for many teams, especially those just starting with Scrum or having trouble finishing their sprints, these are the right size because they are small, easily manageable and understood, and precise.

The best advice I can give is to question everything. Look back at similar past tasks to see how close your current estimate is to the actual time you spent on the task. The goal is not to have 100 percent precision, because that is not achievable, but rather a degree of accuracy that the team is comfortable with while providing the product owner with enough information to maintain a release roadmap.

## Keys to Success

Decomposing stories and tasks is challenging but is essential to creating realistic estimates and becoming a high-performing team. The best way to figure out if a story or task is too large or small is to ask a series of questions to help determine the level of decomposition. While this is not an exact science and no two teams are alike, understanding these basic elements helps in determining what level of decomposition is right for you.

- Can the team estimate the product backlog in story points? (If this is answered with a question like "What are story points?" then your answer will likely be no.) Putting that aside, if you can estimate your product backlog in story points you are off to a good start.
- Is there clarity on the stories in the product backlog? Some teams have their product backlogs estimated but have factored in dozens if not hundreds of assumptions into their estimates. They do this because they have more questions than answers but have "mitigated" that by adding the assumptions. A lack of understanding is a big red flag that the stories are likely too large and need further decomposition.
- How precise are your stories? And what is the right level of precision? While I cannot recommend an answer that would apply to all stories, you can ask yourself the following simple questions:
  - Is it testable?
  - Is it small?
- Do I understand this story well enough to do it myself? This relates to both clarity and precision. If you don't understand it personally, it's likely that the story lacks either clarity or precision.

Sometimes we find our stories or tasks have become too granular. We suspected this earlier, when we took one BnH story down to the managing address line fields. It is important to remember, though, that some teams may not find this level of detail too granular. My advice is, at first, to go past the point of where you feel comfortable, to experiment with what level of granularity works for your team. What might at first seem like too much detail can sometimes be the right granularity level for you. You can always go back a level during the next sprint.

One indicator that a group of stories might be too granular is if the estimate for the stories is zero or half a point. If lumping all the stories together makes a one point story, but individually they are all a half point, the stories are likely too granular. Similarly, if each task takes 15 minutes but the group of tasks would take 2 hours, you've perhaps gone a step too far in decomposing the work.

Another indicator that stories or tasks are the correct size is that independent estimates during planning are roughly equal. When stories/tasks are hiding additional work, estimates will vary wildly. This can be weeded out (identified) using planning poker [GRENNING].

As we saw in the introductory story, everyone on our team was good at masking work. We hid tasks inside tasks without even realizing it. To prevent this from happening on your team, challenge estimates. Do not challenge them in a negative way; strive to seek knowledge on how the team came up with the task estimates. Estimate collectively. Look for assumptions. Ensure that you understand the story or task well enough to do it yourself. Above all, don't be afraid to go a bit outside your comfort zone in decomposing work. You might be surprised with the results.

# References

[GRENNING]  Grenning,  James.  http://renaissancesoftware.net/files/articles/ PlanningPoker-v1.1.pdf (accessed on 11 June 2009).

[DICTIONARY.COM]  epic and theme. Dictionary.com. *The American Heritage® New Dictionary of Cultural Literacy, Third Edition*. Houghton Mifflin Company, 2005. http://dictionary.reference.com/browse/epic and http://dictionary.reference. com/browse/theme (accessed 23 July 2011).

story. Dictionary.com. *Collins English Dictionary - Complete & Unabridged 10th Edition*. HarperCollins Publishers. http://dictionary.reference.com/browse/story (accessed: 23 July 2011).

# Works Consulted

Beck, Kent. 1999. *Extreme Programming Explained, 2nd Edition*. Reading, MA: Addison-Wesley.

Cohn, Mike. 2004. *User Stories Applied*. Reading, MA: Addison-Wesley.

# Chapter 13

# KEEPING DEFECTS IN CHECK

Potentially shippable. You've heard this before and you'll hear it again. So what about defects then? Is a story potentially shippable if at the end of the sprint it has some defects that were left unaddressed? This then leads us to thinking, should each project have a sprint (or two) dedicated to fixing defects? How about a stabilization phase? After all, we need to reach the mythical *code complete* phase, right?

Defect management is one of the easiest things to forego on any agile project. After all, we have been conditioned to address our defects at the end of our projects. Failing to deal with these defects on an ongoing basis, though, results only in low-quality software and the need to "build quality into the system" during a defect-fixing phase or sprint.

So how should a team manage its defects? Dozens of books and techniques explain how to manage defects, but I have found a strategy that I particularly like and have successfully applied to a large majority of my projects, both big and small, new code and legacy systems. Before we take a look at it, let's start with the story that led to this pattern.

## The Story

Miguel and his team were new to Scrum. Miguel was excited about his new role as product owner and had been reading books and practicing what he had learned. Unfortunately, because the project started about one week after the team was formed, he hadn't had much time to pick up all the learning he wanted.

About halfway through its first sprint, the team asked Miguel how he wanted to handle defects.

"Miguel, right now we're two weeks into this four-week sprint and we've got about 20 defects," said a team member. "Should we hold off and have a dedicated sprint or plan some time between sprints to fix defects?"

Miguel was a bit perplexed. Everything he had read led him to believe that a dedicated defect-fixing sprint was the wrong way to go, but he really wasn't sure what to suggest as an alternative. As far as he knew, the only way defects were ever fixed at the company was in a dedicated defect-fixing phase.

"Just hold off and let's see how it goes," said Miguel. By the end of the sprint, the team had found even more defects, so many, in fact, that the customer review meeting was cancelled.

The team went into the retrospective and asked Miguel to join. As they all started writing things on the wall, the one that emerged was the most obvious, *we have too many defects.*

Raul was the ScrumMaster and he saw this as a big impediment, so he asked, "How should we handle the defects?"

The team sat there for a while, and then the ideas started coming.

"Have a defect-fixing sprint," said one team member. Raul wrote it on the whiteboard.

"How about we just have a fixed amount of time each sprint to fix defects at the end, say a day or two?" said another. Raul again added it on the whiteboard.

"I read somewhere that teams put defects on the product backlog. I guess we can just do that," added another team member.

Then the room was silent, until finally Miguel spoke up.

"Why don't we just fix them in real time?" he asked.

The team looked at him like he was crazy.

"Real time? As in we just fix them as we find them?"

"Yes," said Miguel. "That way we keep our costs low. All the other ideas we've identified so far all have the same pattern—pushing off the defects until some later date. The problem is if we do that, then we'll be writing code on buggy software. How will we know if the code we write days later, on top of a buggy API let's say, won't have defects in it, too?"

The team sat there a bit stunned.

"What if we just do the second option, setting some time aside at the end?" someone asked.

"I was thinking about that," said Miguel. "Since we never know how many defects we'll have during a sprint, it'll be nearly impossible to set time aside. What if we have too many defects and not enough time? Then we're back to where we are today. I'm willing to try it as a last resort, but I'd rather try the real-time thing first."

The team sat there, thinking.

"Yes, I think you're right" said a team member, "I'm willing to try real-time bug fixing, but are we going to fix every bug in real time? Even the low priority stuff?"

"I think the most critical defects need to be fixed in real time. Any items that are lower priority can go back on the product backlog and I'll prioritize them," said Miguel.

"That's a fair compromise. I'm willing to try this, too," said another team member.

Raul took some notes, "Great! Then it's settled. We'll do real-time bug fixing. Now, let's figure out what that really means."

## The Model

I am a strong advocate for prioritizing quality above all else, *when it makes sense.* I also understand that even code that lives up to the highest quality standards will never be perfect—will never be forever free from defects and maintenance. As such, I accept that defects are a part of life. That doesn't mean, however, that we don't need a technique for managing them, preferably in real time.

The first step in defect management is to realize what is important to the customers, the product owner, and the team. Customers want the team to deliver features that, at least in theory, can be released to production; they don't want to pay for defects. Product owners want to meet the requests of their customers; they know that customers want defect-free code. Teams want the freedom to mitigate against defects when they realize a piece of their code is in bad shape.

The second step in defect management is to understand that frequent testing reduces overall project costs and defects [BECK] and that it's just plain cheaper to fix defects sooner rather than later. How much cheaper? Industry standard numbers to fix a defect range from the familiar 1:10:100 rule, where things identified on the team member's desktop have a cost of one and as they move through the software life cycle, they get more expensive. We also have Barry Boehm's data from *Software Engineering Economics,* where he observed a 4:1 cost/fix ratio [BOEHM]. My favorite study, however, was done in in 2002. Johanna Rothman published an article on the StickyMinds website [ROTHMAN]. In her article, based on customers she works with, she concluded that a team that waits until the very end to fix defects will have a defect cost price 400 percent larger than a team that addresses defects in real time or near real time. What's worse is that the cost to fix a defect post-release is 300 percent higher and takes triple the amount of time to get out the door.

All this data was enough to convince me that it is just better to fix defects in real time. From this, I created a simple model that gives teams the freedom to fix critical defects in real time, while allowing the product owner to prioritize less critical defects using the product backlog. In essence, all defects are rated on a priority scale of 0-3, where priority 0 and priority 1 are critical defects and priority 2 and priority 3 are less critical. The team has full authority to fix p0 and p1 defects as they see fit. The p2 and p3 defects are put onto the product backlog to be reviewed and prioritized.

At this point you may be wondering how to differentiate between P0, P1, P2, and P3. Determining these values is essential in guiding the team members as to when they should use their full authority to fix a bug. Table 13-1 illustrates how I rate these values. Use my definitions as considerations and not the default standard for your projects. In other words, talk about this with your team and decide on a model that works for you or your company.

Once you and the team have determined a standardized way to prioritize defects, the team can begin ranking them during the sprints. When a new defect surfaces, the person or pair who discovered the defect must quickly triage the issue in real time and determine its priority using the scale in Table 13-1 (or the one you create). If the defect is a p2 or p3, the defect is immediately logged with as much detail and as many supporting files or logs as possible. The defect number is then put on the product backlog for review and prioritization by the product owner.

**TABLE 13-1**   Defect Rating System

| PRIORITY | |
|---|---|
| P0 | CATASTROPHIC: MAJOR FUNCTIONS OF THE SYSTEM ARE NON-OPERATIONAL; NO PRACTICAL WORKAROUNDS EXIST |
| P1 | HIGH: MAJOR FUNCTIONS OF THE SYSTEM ARE NON-OPERATIONAL; WORKAROUNDS EXIST |
| P2 | MODERATE: SYSTEM USABILITY IMPAIRED |
| P3 | LOW: MINIMAL IMPACT; COSMETIC ISSUE OR INCONVENIENCE, CAN WAIT UNTIL AFTER PRODUCT IS IN PRODUCTION TO BE ADDRESSED |

If, on the other hand, the defect is a p0 or p1, the person or pair has *one hour* to accomplish the following tasks:

- Stop the work they are doing.
- Identify the root cause of the defect.
- Fix the root cause.
- Update all tests (unit, integration, acceptance).
- Build or update any build verification tests (BVTs).
- Ensure that all tests (acceptance, unit, etc.) are passing.
- Check the code in.
- Push the bits to, at least, an integration environment.

If the person or pair can do this within one hour, they are not required to open the defect tracking software to log the defect. However, if this cannot be done within one hour, they must take the following steps:

1. Stop at the end of one hour.
2. Log the defect in the tracking system.
3. Continue driving the defect to completion with the criteria listed above.
4. Once this is complete, log the defect, writing all steps taken to get it to completion, and then close the defect.
5. Create a new line item in the sprint backlog for the defect that was fixed, along with the hours spent on driving the defect to completion.

This is a simple, yet effective approach. With the team focused on quality throughout, and building automated tests to fix issues when defects surface, you can release on a regular basis with extreme confidence.

## Keys to Success

Managing defects in any software project is a challenge. We have years of learned brain muscle memory that tells us we should fix defects at the end, after development. As a result, as we transition to agile, we naturally feel we should fix our defects at the end of the sprint, or have a bug-fixing sprint. We have to retrain our brains.

The number one key to a successful agile project is to deliver a potentially shippable product increment, where the code is tested and the technical debt is low, at the end of each sprint. Doing this requires a shift in mindset that is difficult for people, teams, and companies alike. Changing such ingrained habits requires discipline and effort.

Those of you working on a legacy system might believe that this approach could never work for you. Reconsider. You're probably concerned about the sheer volume of issues you will find. I hear you. A friend of mine at a large software company spent two years fixing defects before he was able to write mainline code. This approach allows you to move forward with new code while logging noncritical defects and fixing critical ones in real time. I realize that it could be days, weeks, or even months before you find a good rhythm and get out of defect-fixing mode. That's OK. The important thing is that you start paying down all the technical debt that the legacy system has accrued while also demonstrating new functionality.

Whether you are doing this on a new project or with legacy code, this approach exposes technical debt and defects quickly. Before you begin, you need to explain to the customer, management, and stakeholders what you are doing and why it is important. Start by building a common understanding on what a defect means for the team and ideally the group or company. Next, educate your customers and stakeholders. Give them examples of what makes a good defect report and teach them how to write defect reports that give the team the information they need to duplicate and fix defects. Once you have a system in place, communicate the priority of the defects in your backlog and make it visible and available.

By establishing a well-understood process and making defects visible, you and your company can break free of your waterfall attitude toward defects once and for all.

## References

[BECK]    Beck, Kent. 2005. *XP Explained, 2nd Edition*. Boston, MA: Addison-Wesley.

[BOEHM]    Boehm, Barry. 1981. *Software Engineering Economics*. Englewood Cliffs, NJ: Prentice-Hall.

[ROTHMAN]    Rothman, Johanna. StickyMinds Website. http://www.stickyminds.com/sitewide.asp?Function=edetail&ObjectType=COL&ObjectId=3223    (accessed 30 June 2011).

## Work Consulted

Ward, William T. 1991. The CBS Interactive Business Website. "Calculating the Real Cost of Software Defects." http://findarticles.com/p/articles/mi_m0HPJ/is_n4_v42/ai_11400873/ (accessed 30 June 2011).

# Chapter 14

# SUSTAINED ENGINEERING AND SCRUM

"Quick, we have a service outage and we need you to fix it, ASAP!" This is, unfortunately, quite common in software development today. After decades of development and billions of lines of code having been written, often without a strategy to manage them, we find ourselves in a situation where legacy systems must be maintained even as new systems are being developed to replace them. How can this issue be tackled? Does sustained engineering have a place in Scrum? One team struggled to find a way to make it work.

## The Story

Rohit was the product owner for a flight price-tracking system. The project goal was to replace an existing system used only by travel agents with a new one that would be used by both agents and consumers. The legacy system was quite old, with integration components that tied back to an IBM S/390 mainframe. Very few people were left who knew how to manage the mainframe tie-ins, and maintaining the codebase had become an ever growing challenge for the entire business. The new system would be a win for everyone. In the meantime, though, Rohit's company still had to keep the existing system going until its replacement was online.

Things ran smoothly at first. Rohit enjoyed attending daily standup meetings as a fly on the wall and hearing first-hand about the work the team was doing. The system was working beautifully, and he could tell that he and the team were going to be very pleased with the product they ultimately delivered. He was concerned, though, about how often work on the legacy system seemed to interfere with progress on the project. Just yesterday, he had created an alarming graph that showed the release plan nearly spiraling out of control, not because of bad estimates, new stories, or changes to the system they were rebuilding, but because of the constant, yet still unpredictable, demands of the legacy system on the team's time. He had emailed the graph to the team's ScrumMaster, Kent, with a note that said, "Let's discuss."

With these concerns fresh on his mind, Rohit joined the next morning's daily standup just as Tim began talking.

"Yesterday the legacy system had an outage, and the operations team called me for an immediate fix. I initially thought it would be about an hour, but it ended up taking me all day and half of last night, so I accomplished nothing on the story I had said I would work on."

"Your story was 'allow an external customer to see prices for the three days before and after their planned travel dates,' right?" asked George.

"Yes," said Tim, "and I think it's at huge risk right now. I was here until just after midnight and my brain is fried. I don't know how useful I'll be today guys. Sorry."

"I'll help you out," said George, "but I don't really understand that story. If we work together, though, we can get through it."

"Do you have time, George?" asked Kent.

"Tim's story is a higher priority than mine so I'll make time. But it's going to mean the story I had planned to finish today and the one I had planned to pick up will have to go back to the sprint backlog. If we don't bring in someone else to help us, we're likely going to have to drop at least one story from the sprint," explained George.

Rohit caught Kent's eye. Kent understood that Rohit wanted to talk about the system outage issue. After the meeting, the two went to get a coffee. Rohit and Kent had a good relationship. They had worked together at a company in the past and knew each other's styles well. So when they sat, Rohit got right to the point.

"Kent, you saw the graph I sent you yesterday. The team is consistently failing to complete all the stories for the sprint. And, just like Tim this morning, people always give the same reason: 'We got called away suddenly for an urgent fix in the legacy mainframe code.'"

"Yes," said Kent, "unfortunately, we seem to be the only ones left who know how to fix it. We have inherited the tribal knowledge of that system; we can't just hand the problem to another group because explaining it would take too long, and there is no real documentation to help get them up to speed. I have to believe that keeping the legacy system going is worth the loss in velocity on the new project. We have to balance keeping our current customers happy with the demands of the new product."

Rohit was all too familiar with the reality of tribal knowledge. Still, he had customer expectations to manage, and every day the legacy system was active was a day their competition was pulling farther and farther away. The company needed to get the new system up and running in production as soon as possible.

"Kent, I understand our team has unique expertise on the legacy system, but if we do not keep our focus, we will never get our current release out the door. We need to find a solution to these interruptions. Out of 14 sprints, 11 have been interrupted. That's unacceptable," said Rohit.

"I don't see a way around it. If the system goes down, we have to fix it right then," said Kent.

"Agreed—live legacy system outages must take precedence over the new version. Still, you and I both know that we cannot afford to be distracted every time there is a small system hiccup, right?" asked Rohit.

"Yes, but like Tim described this morning, some of these hiccups aren't so small. The system is down, and it can take anywhere from one hour to one day to bring back online. We never know until we start fixing it how long it's going to take," said Kent.

"I have an idea. In the last company I was with, we had a dedicated engineering team. Their primary job was to keep the existing system running. I think it would work here, too," said Rohit.

"Who would we get to run it?" asked Kent.

"That's the problem. We would need to take one or two people from each team or project to staff the team," explained Rohit.

"That's not likely to happen," said Kent.

"You're probably right," said Rohit. "Do you have another idea?"

"Well, when I was a team member on one of our past projects here, we had this same issue. What we did, while it was not ideal, was set aside a certain number of hours each sprint to work on the issues that came up," said Kent.

"What if there were no issues?" asked Rohit.

"Then we would take another item off the product backlog that we thought we could get done for the sprint or we would clean up the new code. There was always something to work on," said Kent.

"I'm not sure about this—you said you actually block out time in the sprint? Doesn't that take away from the total work the team can do? Right now they deliver 20 points per sprint. Won't this model take that number down?" asked Rohit.

"Yes. That's often what it comes down to," admitted Kent.

"I don't want to lose team velocity. Do we have any other alternatives?" asked Rohit.

"Well, we could talk about the loss in terms of story points, instead of hours, for example, but every solution I can think of will ultimately lower team velocity. Rohit, the thing is, team velocity is down anyway. Like you said, for 11 out of the past 14 sprints, we've failed to deliver on our commitment and always for the same reason: the legacy system. When there are no production issues, our velocity is great. The team is working hard and wants to get into a dependable rhythm. Each time they have to come to a sprint review with their heads hung low because they haven't finished, morale drops a little further," said Kent.

"Yes. I can see how that would happen. We don't want that. Lowering velocity isn't ideal, but it is certainly better than lowering morale. And, part of the problem now is I can't make any plans because I have no idea what the velocity is going to be from sprint to sprint. I'm at the mercy of the legacy code. If we could find a way to stabilize the velocity, I could predict releases," Rohit mused. "Let's sit down and see if we can work something out."

Kent and Rohit spent the next couple of hours looking at the historical sprint data the team had accumulated. They found that the team missed about 50 hours' worth of work on average from sprint to sprint. Some sprints were higher, some were lower, but this gave them the number they were looking for. They used this data to build a sustained engineering plan that was adequate for the business and the team.

# The Model

There are many approaches to sustained engineering (SE), two of which were discussed by Kent and Rohit. The models, having a dedicated team or allocating a certain amount of time for unforeseen issues (dedicated time), are ones I have used with great success. Let's explore each option.

## Dedicated Time Model

In this model, a single Scrum team is responsible both for working through the product backlog on its project and also for dedicating time to work on issues that might surface from an existing product or service. These teams treat legacy system work just as they would vacation time or other commitments: They subtract it from the time available for sprint backlog items. Once they've done that, the team continues with sprint planning and breaks down and estimates the work accordingly. An example of this is shown in Figure 14-1.

Determining how many hours to deduct from the team's sprint is a challenge if you have not been capturing the data. If the team does not know how many hours it has spent in the past on outages and sustained engineering, take a guess. After all, your team will have experience so the guess will be somewhat accurate. Then, as each sprint progresses, gather real data each time an event requires the team's attention. This data allows future guesses to be more accurate, as shown in Figure 14-2.

|  | HOURS |
|---|---|
| TOTAL TEAM HOURS FOR SPRINT | 300 |
| TIME DEDICATED TO LEGAL SYSTEM | 50 |
| TIME AVAILABLE FOR STORIES | 250 |

FIGURE 14-1    Work on legacy system subtracted from time available for sprint backlog items

|  | SPRINT 1 | | SPRINT 2 | | SPRINT 3 | | SPRINT 4 | | SPRINT 5 | |
|---|---|---|---|---|---|---|---|---|---|---|
|  | EST | ACTUAL | EST | ACTUAL | EST | ACTUAL | EST | ACTUAL | EST | ACTUAL |
| TOTAL TEAM HOURS FOR SPRINT | 300 | 310 | 300 | 290 | 300 | 300 | 300 | 300 | 300 | 300 |
| TOTAL TEAM HOURS FOR SPRINT | 50 | 90 | 80 | 80 | 80 | 60 | 60 | 55 | 50 | 50 |
| TOTAL TEAM HOURS FOR SPRINT | 250 | 220 | 220 | 210 | 220 | 240 | 240 | 245 | 250 | 250 |

FIGURE 14-2    Data to make estimates better

## Data Gathered Over Time

In Figure 14-2, we can see the team has five sprints' worth of data. It has spent between 50 and 90 hours per sprint on sustained engineering tasks and 210 to 250 hours on stories from the sprint backlog. The product owner now has enough information to see that he can have high confidence in the team being able to complete up to 210 hours of story-centered work and some potential for the team to complete up to 250 hours of story tasks per sprint. The product owner also knows that any hours above 250 will likely be dedicated to sustained engineering work.

The advantages of **dedicating time**:

- The people working on the new version feel the pain of the legacy system, helping to ensure the same shortcomings are not repeated.
- It may be cheaper.
- Fixes to the legacy system can be (nearly) immediately incorporated into the new system.
- No one feels exiled to the dedicated SE team.

The disadvantages of **dedicating time**:

- Personnel- and team-switching costs are higher, especially if issues surface in small pieces each day. Multitasking and context switching can dramatically hurt productivity.
- The constant shift from the new system to addressing live system problems can cause frustration over time.
- Some issues may take longer than the allocated time.
- Fluctuations in outage issues may cause team velocity to vary widely, resulting in poor predictability.

## Dedicated Team Model

In the story, Rohit suggested creating a team dedicated solely to maintaining the legacy system. I used a similar approach many times at Microsoft and other companies. It is a pull-based system that borrows some elements from Scrum and Kanban/Lean.

Just like a Scrum team, a dedicated sustained engineering team should contain all the skills necessary to do the work. Also, just like a Scrum team, the team should work from a backlog that has been prioritized by the stakeholders; only in this case, the backlog is made up of issues rather than new features. The issues can be in a product backlog, or they can be on a board for the team to pull from. And, just like a Scrum team, the sustained engineering team should have a product owner to ensure that issues are being triaged such that the highest priority items are being worked on at all times.

The sprint length must be shorter than by-the-book Scrum, allowing the team to react more quickly to changing conditions and problems, as they arise in real time.

I advocate and prefer daily sprints but some issues may not be able to be fixed and released daily. In these instances, the issues are reported on daily, both to stakeholders and to the rest of the team.

When a team is releasing daily, team activities (planning, meetings, releases, and commitments) happen fast. In the morning there is a brief planning session, addressing any new issues that surfaced overnight and any legacy issues still being addressed. As team members address the issues and fix them, they release either throughout the day or at the end of the day in one batch—the timing is always dependent on the organization. At the beginning of the next day, the team briefly talks about its prior accomplishments before moving on to planning the current day.

For larger issues, however, dedicated SE teams should have weekly goal planning, daily standups, and a weekly stakeholder meeting.

## Goal Planning

On the first day of each week, the team meets to review the queue of large work issues and to plan a weekly goal, such as "move 50,000 orders through the system" or "reduce customer support response times by ten seconds." The team members review the current issues backlog, associate them with the goal, and determine the work they think they can accomplish that week, based on the information they have that day. They understand that the plan may change if there is a sudden outage or unforeseen issue.

## Daily Releases and Standups

At the end of the goal planning meeting, and then again at the start of each day, the team should perform its daily standup meeting, where the members determine which issues they believe they can address that day and then commit to completing them. They should also provide status on the same-day issues they are in the process of fixing and plan to release. Near the end of each day the team should also meet to share progress and impediments, check for new issues that need to be added to the backlog, and demo and release the work, if possible. The team should drive to release fixes as quickly as can be managed by the business. My teams released daily. Other teams in our organization released weekly. The urgency of a particular fix depends on many factors, including the pain the customers are experiencing. If a new issue surfaces during the week, it is the job of the dedicated team to react to it.

## Stakeholder Meetings

At least once a week (more often if an urgent issue arises), the team should meet with the stakeholders to demo fixes and prioritize new issues. Stakeholders should understand that some fixes may have already been released. Having this formal review helps the team feel a sense of accomplishment and allows the stakeholders an opportunity both to commend the team for its efforts and provide any feedback into ways the process could be improved.

Working on a dedicated team can be rewarding, but it can also be a chore. Still, it is one way to manage the problem of legacy systems.

The advantages of **dedicated teams:**

- Dedicated teams can be a training ground for new employees, who can cycle to new product teams after they've learned the existing systems.
- Dedicated teams can respond quickly.
- Team members are (or will become) experts on the legacy system.
- They are generally able to address issues more quickly than new product teams.
- They are able to release more often.

The disadvantages of **dedicated teams:**

- The work is often boring and repetitive.
- Team members may not have passion for their work.
- Morale suffers if quick wins are not shown, recognized, and acknowledged.
- Dedicated teams cost more because people with specialized skill sets will need to be replicated on the dedicated team and in the larger organization.
- Other teams may be less conscientious knowing someone else will do the cleanup work for them.

# Keys to Success

Jeff Sutherland once told me the best code is no code because *no code* is sustainable, maintainable, performs well, and costs nothing. Unfortunately, we must write some code to build our systems. And all code, once written, is legacy code. Legacy code that has supporting elements, such as unit tests and automated acceptance tests, and is well documented and clean is cheaper to maintain, but maintenance costs and responsibilities can never be eliminated.

Regardless of the model you choose to support legacy code, remember to treat your sustained engineering process as you do the process for teams building new features and functionality: Evolve it over time, making changes that allow the team to be more successful.

## Cycle Dedicated Maintenance Team Members

If your organization uses a dedicated maintenance team, its members can (and probably should) be cycled between a team that is developing new features and functionality and the maintenance team. This is important for several reasons. First, it helps prevent specialist skill problems. Specialist skills are those built up over time when people do the same repetitive tasks over and over again, especially if they are working on the same technology or functional area of a system. Switching people keeps them fresh. It also helps mitigate frustration and boredom. I often see people become envious of others who are on new feature teams because that is where the fun is—they are creating something new as compared to cleaning up someone else's mess that has been long since forgotten. Cycling people among teams helps alleviate that.

## Retrofit Legacy Code with Good Engineering Practices

I often see teams that follow the dedicated time model but only apply their engineering practices, such as TDD, to the new products or services that they are building. When a legacy system issue surfaces, they throw those practices aside. This is the wrong approach. The dedicated time model needs to factor in the effort to build into the legacy code unit tests, acceptance tests, and any other modern engineering practice the team has implemented. A great resource for managing legacy code is Michael Feathers' *Working Effectively with Legacy Code* [FEATHERS].

## In the End

Supporting a defunct system while trying to build its replacement is inherently difficult. Whatever approach you choose, the most important thing is to acknowledge that making it work requires a commitment of either time or personnel. Martin Fowler introduced the world to the term *strangler application* in 2004 [FOWLER]. His blog post illustrates a trip he took to Australia where he saw fig trees with strangler vines dropping down from the high branches. The vines wrap around a host tree; as the vines take root, the host dies. The same thing has to happen to your legacy system: The new strangler application will eventually choke it out. But until that happens, you need a viable approach that allows you to reduce risk and maintain functionality until the strangler application is live and the host is retired.

# References

[FEATHERS]   Feathers, Michael. 2004. *Working Effectively with Legacy Code*. Upper Saddle River, NJ: Prentice Hall PTR.

[FOWLER]   Fowler, Martin. Personal website. http://martinfowler.com/bliki/StranglerApplication.html (accessed 3 March 2011).

# Chapter 15

# THE SPRINT REVIEW

Ideally, the sprint review should be plug-and-play, meaning things should just "work." The team is supposed to be able to prepare for no more than an hour and, without a presentation or undue fuss, demo the work in an environment as close to production as possible. In reality, though, a sprint review is enough to make your teeth rattle. Sometimes the customer asks a question you aren't prepared to answer; occasionally a feature doesn't work as expected; and every now and then, something crashes unexpectedly. In some cases, one or two of these embarrassing moments occur in every meeting, degrading the trust between the team and its stakeholders and making every sprint review an unpleasant and uncomfortable experience for all concerned.

That was the case for the team in our story. Let's find out how a series of unfortunate meetings and a breakdown in trust caused the team to reconsider the way it prepped for and ran its sprint reviews.

## The Story

One by one, the team members slunk out of the sprint-three review with heads hung low.

"I can't take many more meetings like that," commented Mike, looking sideways at his teammates. "We looked like complete idiots, *again!*"

Mike and the team made their way to the team room for the retrospective. As soon as the door closed behind them, the floodgates opened. Groans, moans, and grumbles filled the room.

ScrumMaster Jim stood up and asked for quiet. "Write it down," he said, motioning to the whiteboard.

The team members grabbed markers and made their way to the "what went wrong" whiteboard. In a matter of minutes it was filled with problems, most of which centered around sprint reviews. "Every meeting is worse than the last," one said. Another read, "Reviews are painful and embarrassing." Mike's was written in large capital letters, "COULD WE PLEASE STOP SHOWING OUR BUTTS TO THE CUSTOMER!"

Once the whiteboard was filled to capacity the team members sat down, tossed their markers on the table, and looked at Jim expectantly.

Jim laughed. "OK. Let's clarify. Mike, want to start?"

Mike dove in, "I've read all the Scrum books, and they say that these things are supposed to be plug-and-play. No prep. Just show up, show the new features, and the customers accept it. But every time I'm in a sprint review meeting, I feel like I'm in a nightmare where I'm back in university, there is a test in every course, and I haven't studied for any of them!"

Michele followed up. "There has got to be a better way. I refuse to believe there are teams out there that just *show up* and everything works for them."

"Exactly," said Maria. "They asked so many questions that I just wasn't prepared to answer!"

Jim interjected with an idea he'd gotten from one of the other teams in the company. "You all know Sam's team, right? I talked to him last week, and he shared his team's review procedure with me," said Jim. He uncovered a pre-prepared flip chart and began to point out key elements. "The team uses these slide templates with spots to plug in information about each sprint that details what the team committed to, what it got done, project metrics, and more!"

"Doesn't that go against the 'no PowerPoint rule' though?" asked Mike.

"Sure it does," said Jim. "But it does not go against the 'use common sense' rule."

Michele and the rest of the team laughed.

"Reviews should be easy," Jim continued. "I think if we do a few things differently during the sprint, involve the product owner more, and do a better job of communicating, we'll feel much more prepared and much more comfortable."

Jim and the team decided to have a select group work on the sprint review problem immediately following the retrospective. The group spent two hours coming up with a plan for the next sprint review. The plan included midsprint activities meant to inform stakeholders and engage the product owner.

Sprint four passed quickly. The team could hardly sit still as the sprint review got underway. Each of them felt excited and ready. "Nice change, huh?" whispered Mike to Jim.

Jim nodded.

Dan, the product owner, kicked off the meeting. "Thanks, everyone, for coming. Normally I'd start the demo right now, but I've been working with the team on a new way to run the meeting. I think we can all agree the past three meetings have been, well, *special*."

Everyone burst out laughing, even the team.

"Without further delay, let me hand it over to Michele, one of the team members. Michele?" Dan motioned for her to take the floor.

A perplexed look came over the customers and stakeholders. Why was Michele, a team member, doing the demo? The product owner had always done the demo.

"Thanks, Dan" said Michele. The room did not move. "Let me start by showing you a presentation of the work we committed to. I'm going to follow that with a look at what we actually got done and what we didn't get done; then I'll show you some project metrics, recap the decisions we all made. When I'm through, Jim will walk us through the demo. I think the paperwork, all the stuff before the demo, should take about 10 to 15 minutes, leaving us plenty of hands-on demo time. How does that sound?"

Suddenly Michele had the attention of the room. She went through her slides, showing the customers and stakeholders what the team had committed to doing, what it had gotten done, what it had failed to get done and why, and the decisions made by both the team and Dan with the customer.

"Any questions?" asked Michele. "No? Then, I'll turn it over to Jim."

"Thanks Michele, excellent recap. Now, today, as we demo our features, we are going to do things a little differently. Dan is on board with this change as well, right, Dan?"

Dan nodded eagerly.

"OK." Jim continued, looking at the stakeholders in the room. "Who would like to validate the first story for us?"

"I'm sorry. I'm not sure what you're asking," said one of the stakeholders.

"Well," said Jim. "What we would like you to do is to pick an item that is listed as 'done' in the slides we handed out. Any one will do. Then we want you to work it, validate it, play with it… see if it does what you expect, or does something you don't expect."

A key stakeholder, Meher, walked hesitantly to the laptop and grabbed the mouse.

"Are you sure you want me to do this?" she asked with great hesitation in her voice. "I know how it should work, because it's my story, but I don't want to mess anything up."

"Don't worry," said Mike. "If something breaks, it's our fault, not yours. And the sooner we find the problems, the sooner we can fix them. Please give it a try like you normally would."

The team took a collective deep breath as she moved the mouse and started validating the user story "As an accountant I can pull up last month's sales report by region." She started with the southwest region. She clicked it. At first, nothing happened. Three long seconds passed, and then the report appeared onscreen.

"Huh," said Mike under his breath, but loud enough for everyone's eyes to gently shift up in his direction. Mike was expecting a much faster load time; this was one of the stories that he did not review during the sprint.

Meher continued clicking, selecting various drop-downs, shifting through different views, and clicking through the data to get expanded reports on the region.

"This report looks really good!" she said. "I would expect some different data here, but it's more or less my job to validate it. I have time next sprint to work with you. Hey! I've got a question, what happens when I click through here?"

The team had a good idea of what would happen, especially Michele.

"Click it and find out," she said firmly.

The customer clicked through one of the reports that had not been fully developed. The team watched the path she took to get to it, one that the team did not predict or think that a user would use. She clicked it and the application sat there. After 30 seconds or so it crashed with an alert box.

"I knew I'd mess it up," said the stakeholder apologetically.

"I'm glad you did," said Michele. "That's a workflow we hadn't considered. Mike, did you watch that flow and take notes?"

"Got it," said Mike. "I'll have it fixed before we go home today."

"Wait a minute, guys," said Dan. "I didn't specifically ask for that to be done this sprint. Should we really fix it?"

"Yeah, I can fix it. I know where the problem is, so it won't take me long," said Mike.

Jim nodded. "OK. Who would like to try the next story?"

"So, I'm a bit confused," another stakeholder admitted. "Why are you having us do this? It seems like it would be much quicker for you to just show us the feature. This seems like a waste of time. We're not even sure how you've designed these to work."

Jim, the ScrumMaster, spoke up. "We're having you do it because you are ultimately the ones who will be using the software. If it doesn't work the way you intuitively think it should, then we need to fix it. Watching you experiment with the feature teaches us quite a bit about how you think and what a typical workflow looks like, so I don't think it's a waste of time. And you're right. You don't know how we've designed these to work. So, it's important that you put your hands on it and make sure it works for you before you accept the work.

"We know that things haven't gone well. And we know that you're losing faith in our ability to deliver what you need. By communicating more and using this time to let you experience the system, we will get better and can adjust what we're doing based on what we see. Already in this demo we've learned that the reports load too slowly and our understanding of the workflow was inaccurate. And we've gotten buy-in from Meher to work with us on some data next sprint. It isn't perfect. But it's progress."

The stakeholder agreed and the meeting continued. After a few sprints, the team and the customer were much better aligned. The PowerPoint slides replaced former sprint status reports, Dan worked with the customers to help them understand that certain features weren't quite perfect yet did meet the stated acceptance criteria, and used their feedback to help refine the product backlog. As features began to match expectations, everyone—the team, the stakeholders, and Dan—began to feel more comfortable with the process, more at ease with each other, and more hopeful for the final product.

# The Model

It is common for new teams to struggle with sprint reviews. After all, for many, it's the first time they've had to stand in front of customers and stakeholders and show them what they have created, let alone demo items that are deliberately lacking full functionality and have only been alive for a few weeks. If the team failed to complete its stories, or if what has been done works poorly, the sprint review can be awfully embarrassing.

The purpose of the meeting is for the team to show the customers and stakeholders the work it has accomplished over the sprint. While ideally this meeting should be informal, many businesses treat it very formally. My advice: Treat it in a way that works for your company culture and does not cause the team undue stress.

The sprint review occurs on the last day of the sprint. The duration varies depending on sprint length. For a one-week sprint, the meeting should last about 30 minutes to an hour; a two-week sprint, an hour to an hour and a half. Teams running four-week sprints should allow two to four hours for this meeting. Besides acceptance of the sprint work, other intended outcomes of the meeting include additional customer interaction, increased feedback, and additions or changes to the backlog based on that interaction and feedback.

In the story, Jim and his team discovered that it is much more difficult to run a sprint review than it sounds. Thinking the review would just take care of itself, Jim's team tried to race all the way through the sprint with no thought toward the demo. The snafus, failures, and misunderstandings the team experienced as a result are all too common for new teams. In the story, the team's solution was to prepare more during the sprint, formalize the presentation to ensure all the right information was communicated, and encourage the stakeholders to participate in a hands-on way. The amount of preparation you do will vary depending on your company's culture and team's experience level. Let's walk through how I prepare for my sprint reviews.

## Preparing for the Meeting

First, I am a fan of using slides in the sprint review meeting. They help the team members organize their thoughts and provide something for the stakeholders to take with them when they leave. For every sprint review meeting, I use the following template; each bullet is an individual slide:

- The sprint goal
- The stories we committed to delivering
- The stories we completed
- The stories we failed to complete
- Key decisions made during the sprint, which may include technical, market-driven, requirements, etc., and can be decisions made by the team, the product owner, the customers, or anyone else
- Project metrics (code coverage, etc.)
- Demonstration of the completed work
- Priority review for the next sprint

Depending on the type of system you are building, you may also find you need to prepare technically, for instance, have a build ready or deployed to a pre-production or staging environment. In these cases, consider a mock run-through. Have a team member spend some time going through and reviewing some of the stories that will be shown to the customers. Is the data correct? Are the connection strings working? Did data get repopulated from one environment to the next? These small details can come back to bite you when you're in the meeting.

At first, all that preparation seems to be in direct violation of the rules, and if taken to the extreme, it is. Preparation should not get in the way of the work. Spending *some* time getting information together and planning the review meeting goes a long way toward making a team appear more informed and helping the stakeholders understand what they are supposed to be looking for. I don't live by a hard and fast rule that the team can spend only one hour preparing for the meeting, as this is extremely difficult for new Scrum teams to do. That being said, there's a limit to how much prep time is too much. I've seen teams take two days to get things ready, which, especially in a short sprint, is overkill, and points to larger issues. Therefore, although new teams will likely need more time to prep than an experienced team, all teams should be working toward the goal of prepping for an hour or less each sprint.

## Running the Meeting

In the story, the customers ended up executing the stories the team delivered in the meeting. This is different than the standard "the team demonstrates the work" approach in Scrum. On my teams, I ask the product owner to facilitate the meeting (just like a ScrumMaster would facilitate the retrospective), the team to do a high-level review of the stories, and the customers and stakeholders to execute/demonstrate the stories while the team observes the behavior.

Whenever possible, I also like to include the process of moving the installation off the build path and into the environment as part of every review. I always start with a fresh install, doing the actual install during the review, with the customer in the room. For example, on one Windows application project, where I was a product owner, a story in the first sprint review was to install the application from the latest build off the build box, an acceptance test that would recur in future sprints. The build was never more than five or ten minutes old. On one occasion, to save time, we had the application preinstalled on a computer we were using. The customers had grown so accustomed to seeing the installation at the demo that they complained. We uninstalled the application on the computer, went to the build machine, and installed fresh bits. Since then, I try to include installs (when appropriate) as part of every sprint review. It helps build customer confidence and exhibits a level of transparency that customers might have never witnessed before.

Once the demo is complete, teams should ask the customers to accept the work. After all, the customers have had the chance to demo the features themselves and the team should be confident that the work is potentially shippable at this point.

# Keys to Success

The sprint review is a time for the team to go on record and explain what it has accomplished. Like a child eagerly awaiting her parents' approval for taking out the trash on her own for the first time, new teams want and need positive feedback from the customers and stakeholders.

Don't cancel these meetings due to pressure or other excuses. They are critical and help the team:

- Build and maintain trust with the customers and stakeholders
- Make project course corrections in near real time
- Identify risks and issues
- Gather feedback

Positive sprint reviews increase customer confidence in the team and the team's confidence in itself. If the review goes badly, the trust will degrade, just as we saw in the story.

At the same time, don't forget that the main purpose of the sprint review is not a round of applause for a job well done. The real goal of a sprint review is to stop and ascertain whether the project is on the right track. The team and product owner need to know what they didn't know the last time they groomed the product backlog: How this incarnation of the product works in a customer's hands and what features need to be changed or added to make it more valuable. The best sprint reviews have an impact on what occurs in the following sprint. They increase both the team's tolerance for change and the customers' expectation that they have permission to break things, to find flaws, all in the name of making the end product better. Reviews, when done right, foster a spirit of continuous improvement that is truly contagious. Here are some things you can do to make sure your reviews are done the right way:

## Take Time to Plan

Because a positive review experience is so important to the project's success, take a little time to plan the review so that you feel prepared and confident, especially if you are a new team or a team new to Scrum. It's perfectly acceptable to use a script or follow the slide outline. In addition, the team should take the time to prepare the demo environment. Set it up so that the customers can put their hands on the new features and experience it first-hand. You'll find that the team also learns more about how the end user might interact with the product. Allow time not only for the meeting but for some casual chat-time between the customer and the team after the meeting. I allow 30 minutes between the sprint review and the retrospective so that the team and the customer feel free to interact informally.

## Document Decisions

We all forget things, but it seems we are especially good at forgetting the things that we *need* to remember, like a workflow, a color choice, a button location. When a decision is made during a review, write it down and keep it safe. I've been in too many reviews where a customer says, "I don't remember that decision. I'm not paying for this and that."

Having a written record of verbal agreements means that even if something happens four months after the original conversation, you are able to point to the documentation and say, "Yes, we discussed this and agreed to move in this direction on September 1 of last year."

## Ask for Acceptance

Asking the customer to accept the stories during the meeting allows you to release soon after the review. Often, however, customers want time to use the application before pushing it out, so some teams opt to give the customers up to a week to formally accept the work. It is important to get acceptance. Regardless of when you get acceptance, make sure you get it.

Acceptance is important because it puts pressure on the team to ensure the features meet the published definition of done. One way to help the customers feel comfortable accepting on the spot is to follow your done list faithfully, highlight it during each review, and update it as needed. If customers are still hesitant to give you the green light, be sure to ask what you can do to make them feel more comfortable in accepting work that you all agree meets the definition of done.

## Be Brave

Even with planning, sprint reviews can be intimidating. Help team members fight through the fear by reminding them that they are ready for this review. They have implemented each feature as described by the product owner. When they had questions about a feature, they reached out to the product owner for help—and received it. They have followed their definition of done, which everyone has agreed should result in potentially shippable working software. The demo environment has been prepared. Slides are there to guide them through all that talking and all those pesky questions.

Encourage them to remember that any changes and any new stories that arise from the review are not only natural but *desired*. Without changes, the product would be exactly as imagined on the first day the product backlog was written, which we all know is never precisely what the customer wants. By embracing reviews and the myriad changes that come from each encounter with the customer, the team moves one step closer to their goal: a final product that delights the end user. Now that's a change we can all live with!

# Works Consulted

Schwaber, Ken, and Jeff Sutherland. 2011. "The Scrum Guide." http://www.scrum. org/storage/scrumguides/Scrum%20Guide%20-%202011.pdf. Also available at http://www.scrum.org/scrumguides/ or download a copy at http://www.mitchlacey. com.

Schwaber, Ken. 2004. *Agile Project Management with Scrum*. Redmond, WA: Microsoft Press. p. 137.

## Chapter 16

# RETROSPECTIVES

Retrospectives are often one of the first Scrum elements to go by the wayside. As schedule pressures mount, teams feel they don't have time for what they consider the luxury of a retrospective. Once teams start skipping retrospectives, the downward spiral begins.

We visit one team that is coming out of its third sprint and struggling. Frustration is running high and discipline is running low. People are ready to abandon the retrospective—not atypical for a team getting started with Scrum.

## The Story

Jamie knew the team was in danger of falling apart. Stories were slipping, builds were breaking, unit tests were failing. It felt like the project was crashing around them. Everyone was frustrated. Several team members had come to Jamie individually and expressed disappointment with other team members and with Scrum. To make it worse, just about everyone wanted to skip this retrospective, citing that they had "real work to do" and "besides, these retrospectives are a complete waste of time." It was time for an intervention.

Jamie knew that the upcoming retrospective would be a perfect time to address all these issues but was unsure whether the team would step up to the plate without facilitation. The past two retrospectives had not been productive. Loosely run by the team, the retrospectives had mainly consisted of listening to one or two people soapbox, either their complaints or their ideas for improvement. At the end of the diatribes, everyone left exhausted, deflated, and, in the end, nothing changed.

Jamie decided it was time to take matters into his own hands. He spent a couple hours reading about well-run retrospects and came up with a plan. A few minutes before the scheduled retrospective, Jamie went into the meeting room and removed every chair. He also hung three whiteboards and labeled them, "What Went Well," "What Needs to Improve," and "Rants."

As the team filtered into the room, these changes caught them off guard, especially Ben and Todd.

"What gives, Jamie?" said Ben.

"Yeah, where are our chairs?" said Todd.

"I removed them. Every time we meet and there are chairs, we go off into la-la land on our discussions and nothing seems to get done. I took them out so we can stand, like in our daily standup meetings," stated Jamie matter-of-factly.

The team let out a collective moan.

"What's all this?" asked Todd, motioning to the whiteboards.

"Simple," said Jamie. "For this sprint's retrospective, we are going to talk about what we did well, what we need to fix, and rants."

"Rants?" asked Ben.

"Yeah, rants. These are things that we just plain don't like, and they don't really fit in the *things to improve* category. On my last team, our team space was really hot and one team member kept writing, in big letters *fix the air conditioning*. Most of us just thought he was making noise, but after seeing him write that for three sprints, we realized, 'Hey! It is pretty darn hot in here!' and we fixed it."

The team nodded.

"So what do we do now, Jamie?" asked Todd, shifting from one foot to another, anxious to get on with things. "Do we take turns going around the room telling you what we like and don't like, and you write it down?"

"Nope. *You* are going to write it down," said Jamie, looking at Todd.

Todd looked over his shoulder to see if Jamie was speaking to him.

"Uh, *me?*" said Todd.

"Everyone." And with that Jamie started the meeting. "What I want each of you to do is grab a marker and just write on the whiteboard whatever comes to mind, the good and the bad. Don't worry about things that overlap or are similar; the key here is to gather data so we can figure out what to do about it, or maybe what *not* to do about it in some cases. So, up and at 'em!"

The team members looked at each other and began to move slowly toward the board. They all stopped there and stared.

Todd stepped up and wrote under *things to improve,* "Test coverage sucks!!!"

The team looked at Todd as if he was a sheep among wolves.

"See, that's all there is to it!" said Jamie, who in turn wrote something under the *things that are going well* section, "Teamwork and trust are improving."

One by one each of the seven team members wrote various items on the whiteboard. After about 20 minutes, the team had written nearly 50 items. Now came the hard part, sorting the data.

The team spent the next 15 minutes clarifying what they perceived to be duplicates and clearing them from the list. Once the duplicates were removed, Jamie introduced a technique he had learned at his last company.

"Team, what we are going to do now is prioritize this list. To do that, we're all going to imagine that you each have one hundred dollars in your wallets. That one hundred dollars can only be spent on the items on the board. If something is really important to you, you may spend all your money on it—it's a $100 issue. Other issues might only be worth $5 or $50 to you. Divvy up your money anyway you want among the issues that matter to you or that you feel are most impacting the team. Once we have all spent our money, we will add up the payments for each item. The items that received the most money will be our higher priority items; those with the least money are our lower priority items," explained Jamie enthusiastically.

Todd held his hand out. "I'm broke. I'll take that $100 now," he said with a smile.

The room chuckled and everyone started spending the virtual money. After 15 minutes, the team had a prioritized list of issues that it needed to discuss. Jamie copied each of them onto a new whiteboard and put a plus sign, a minus sign, or an R next to them to symbolize whether it was an issue that went well, a suggestion for improvement, or a rant.

Jamie looked at the clock and saw they had about 45 minutes left in their 90-minute retrospective, nowhere near enough time to work through all the issues. Jamie realized that, given the items on the board, the retrospective would run over. Since the team was new and struggling, he decided to extend the meeting by 30 minutes.

"We have too many items in our 'high priority' group to cover in the time remaining," Jamie began. "Basic math says that we can only spend four minutes on each item, clearly that won't work. Let's do a gut check. Is this list correct? Is this where we want to start?" asked Jamie pointing to the top item.

The team nodded yes.

"Great, here's what I propose we do. Let's address the items in 10-minute blocks, which will allow us to get through most of them in the next 75 minutes. Let's spend the first couple minutes of each time box making sure we all understand what the issue is. Once we have clarified the issue, we'll make a decision to act on it or to skip it for this sprint—basically to mitigate or not. If we choose to mitigate, then we will decide on actions that we, as a team, will work toward to either ensure we continue doing it (if it's a good item) to alter our behavior (if it's an item we want to improve). Then, for each item we choose to act on, we'll determine who will volunteer to drive it," said Jamie.

"Drive it?" asked Ben.

"Yes. Each item we choose to work on or mitigate needs to have someone on the team looking after it, so if a behavior or a pattern crops up, it can be called out. It's a way to ensure none of us forget what we decided to do in this meeting—it keeps the discipline and the focus."

The team began working through the issues. They ranged from "pair programming sucks and is worthless" to "retrospectives are a waste of time—just more meetings!"

The team closed with a plan on how to handle some of their biggest issues for the next sprint. Everyone felt good coming out of the meeting. The team walked out feeling hopeful for the first time in a long time. They had not just complained; they had actually come up with a plan to fix things. As drivers, each person had some responsibility for ensuring that the actions the team had committed to take would continue throughout the sprint. It wasn't all right yet, but it felt like it might get better.

# The Practice

Retrospectives are not easy. They take time, they take commitment, and they take courage. When the pressure's on, they're often the first thing to go. In the rush to deliver a product, having a meeting to vent your frustration can seem like a waste of time. And if that's all your retrospectives have become, I agree. You are wasting your time.

That doesn't mean, however, that you should axe retrospectives. On the contrary, if your retrospectives have become meaningless, it's even more important that you do them, and do them right. Why are retrospectives so important, you ask? And what are some key components of an effective retrospective? Let's answer both of those questions.

## Give Retrospectives Their Due Diligence

Retrospectives are a key part of a team's inspect-and-adapt cycle. Every other part of the sprint (sprint planning, daily standups, the sprint review) focuses on delivering working software. The retrospective is the sole opportunity for team members to examine how they work and how they are working together. It's a time for them to learn how to improve, how to work more efficiently, and how to deliver at a higher velocity and with superior quality. Retrospectives are a constant reminder of the need to continuously improve, to always be moving forward. Because when a team stands still, it falls behind.

Retrospectives also remind teams of the importance of continuing new technical practices. On one of my first projects, we cut the retrospective because we had too much work to do. (Or so we thought. It turns out our real problem was in properly sizing our stories and tasks.) After a few skipped retrospectives, we had a sprint where a team member was out of the office sick for four days. No one on the team knew what he was doing with the code. Sure, we knew the tasks, but we did not know what he did, where he was at with the story, or the design approach he was taking. We lost four days of work. How did this happen? It happened because we failed to identify in a retrospective that we were falling into old habits and working on what we were specialized in. We were not distributing information and knowledge in the code through pairing. It was not until this event that we realized, "Wow, I guess the retrospective does help!"

Retrospectives have a more subtle benefit as well. They give teams the opportunity to change behavior and team culture. They are a safe place for team members to share, constructively, feedback with others on how their actions (or inactions) impact the quality, morale, and attitude of the team. Left alone, these small problems fester, like an unattended cut. Retrospectives, on the other hand, allow teams to attend to their small wounds quickly, reducing the chance of infection.

## Plan an Effective Retrospective

So, we can agree that retrospectives are valuable. But how do you run them effectively, so that they don't degenerate into an unproductive complain-and-moan session? Like any good meeting, retrospectives run much more smoothly if they are well planned and well executed. The team should not consider a retrospective done until it has a solid plan of action based on what was discussed and a way to hold each other accountable to the commitment.

Planning an effective retrospective is a tricky thing. Some teams are able to accomplish them with no planning, some teams need a day to plan. Whether you are the ScrumMaster or not, if you are the one facilitating the meeting, you are responsible for making sure a few components are in place before the meeting begins: communication, physical setup, and ground rules. Remember, doing Scrum does not mean you don't have to plan and get to do whatever you want, whenever you want.

## Communication

Good communication starts with setting expectations up front. At the beginning of any Scrum project, I publish all scheduled meetings and put them in everyone's calendar, from team to customer. Retrospectives should be on those calendars. In addition, prior to each retrospective, send a meeting invitation that includes an agenda. This agenda should remind everyone what the meeting is about, why it is important, the benefits to the team, and how to prepare. It should also include a rough outline of how the time will be spent and a sentence summarizing the end goal.

## Physical Setup

New teams often struggle with staying on schedule during the meetings. As such, I often remove the chairs from the room, as Jamie did in our story. I want to prevent people from sitting so that they focus on moving through the parts of the meeting without endless discussion. I have been in too many retrospectives where everyone is leaning back in a chair, debating with no real outcome. I have found that removing the sitting aspect of the meeting helps keep people on track. If you want to keep your seat and have a more subtle reminder of time marching on, you could also display a timer that counts down each time block, perhaps flashing yellow or red as each section of your meeting approaches its close.

Hang on the wall a copy of the sprint burndown, the team done list, the team's vision for the project and the sprint itself, and a copy of any notes from the last retrospective. Then clear new space to collect data. Pre-label whiteboards or flip charts with the items for discussion. In the story, Jamie used "what went well," "what do we need to improve," and "rants." Derby and Larsen's *Agile Retrospectives* describes a "mad, sad, glad" approach to data collection [DERBY]. Whatever approach you use, make sure it's clear what data the team needs to collect.

## Ground Rules

Many meetings are derailed simply because there are no ground rules. Basic ground rules that should be posted in the room and verbally shared at the beginning of each meeting include the following:

- Be respectful.
- Do not interrupt.
- Put away laptops and phones.
- Park long discussions in the designated lot.
- Recap what you hear to ensure understanding.
- What is said here stays here.

## Run the Retrospective

The ScrumMaster and all team members should attend each retrospective. I do not recommend inviting the product owner regularly, because I have seen too many times where the product owner hijacks the retrospective to tell the team members where they went wrong, took a bad approach, didn't listen correctly—you name it. Occasionally, it might make sense to include the product owner, but for most retrospectives, the attendees should be limited to the team and ScrumMaster.

Typically the ScrumMaster facilitates the meeting. Because the room has already been set up, the meeting can begin as soon as everyone arrives. However you choose to run the meeting, the first 15 minutes or so should be dedicated to data collection. This could be everyone writing on whiteboards (as in the story), open-space style sticky notes (with people calling out their issues), or a scribe being responsible for writing down ideas on whiteboards. I've used all these techniques; the right one depends on the group dynamics. The facilitator should watch for interactions between people. If people are writing on the boards or flipcharts, the room is usually very quiet at this point. Watch carefully and listen for the sounds of silent agreement or disagreement, perhaps loud highlighting of something someone else wrote, and make a mental note. Notice if someone is not participating, hanging back and not engaging. Don't say anything in the meeting! Just make a mental note to see how they interact once it comes time to discuss. If someone is silent throughout the retrospective, you should have a one-on-one discussion with that individual after the meeting to get to the root of the issue. Once all the data has been collected, take a picture of any artifacts in their raw state.

Once the ideas have been collected, they need to be prioritized. There are many prioritization techniques, but I find the "buy an issue" technique used in the story to be very effective. It works like this. Everyone has some virtual currency. It can be anything. I have seen people use ping-pong balls, play money, even just plain "units." The important thing is to make sure that everyone has the *same* amount and everyone has the *right* amount.

If there are many high priority items on the whiteboard and each person only has three units to distribute, important things will get lost. At the same time, if everyone has 1,000 units to distribute, too many items will be chosen. If you have a five-person team, start with $25 or $50. If you have a larger team, start with $75 or $100. You can always increase the amount if it looks like the high priority list is too small. You can further limit the action by having people spend in $5 increments. (Luke Hohmann describes a similar game called "Buy a Feature" in his book *Innovation Games* [HOHMANN]. It can also be used in this situation.)

Once everything has been allocated, sum up the totals. You now have your prioritized list. Again, take a picture at this point and do a gut check—does everyone think this is a good list? Is something so blatantly obvious that it should be reconsidered? Use common sense.

Now that things are prioritized, the team needs time to discuss the high priority issues and make decisions. Timebox this part of the meeting based on the amount of time you have left and the number of items you need to discuss. Bring an egg timer if people have a hard time getting to the point. Once everyone understands the issue, ask, "Is this something we are going to mitigate/fix or not?" If no, discuss why not. Then, move on to the next one. When I facilitate retrospectives and I encounter an issue that the team decides not to fix, I write it down in my notes to capture on the team wiki. That way, when the team comes back and says, "Why didn't we ever fix this?" I can tell them exactly why we decided not to do it. I find it just helps with dealing with noise later on.

For the things you do want to work on or mitigate, come up with a plan. For complex issues where solutions are not immediately apparent, name one or two people responsible for coming up with ideas and options that the team can act upon. Keep the activity timeboxed to a couple days, have a follow-up meeting, and decide on a course of action. You will answer questions such as *What are the things preventing X from happening? How can we work around it?* This is a team exercise so make sure everyone participates.

Like Jamie did in our story, once you have a plan in place, write it down and ask someone to help drive it. The driver is the person on the team who looks for that specific behavior or pattern and alerts the team when it occurs. Remember that the team shouldn't just work on items that need improvement; it should also continue doing things that are working well. On one of my projects, we were not swapping pairs enough, so someone chose to drive that. The next sprint, the driver spent a lot of time keeping us on track. We chose to continue emphasizing switching during our next sprint, even though it had improved. During the following sprint, our switching was better, but we still heard from our driver, "Hey! You switched! I guess you don't need me to tell you." It was a form of positive reinforcement that worked well.

Once you have a list of actionable items, or the time has expired, it's time to close down the retrospective. I like to end it with a one-to-five quick rating of "how was this sprint?" and "what do you think next sprint will be?" One is bad; five is good. People can answer any way they want, but I try to weed out any ill will in the team that may require some discussion. I care about the answer, sure, but I'm more interested in how people answer. What I look for is nonverbal clues that may indicate that what people are saying does not match what they are feeling. I don't call it out in the meeting; instead I approach the person one-on-one, tell him what I observed, and just ask if there is anything wrong. If the person says that everything is fine again, I'll let it go and just observe the team over the sprint.

After the meeting, the ScrumMaster or facilitator needs to stick around to document things. I take digital pictures and notes and put things into a wiki. I never associate names and only use the pictures for my reference. I don't share them because the notes might be misunderstood out of context or someone might recognize a particular individual's handwriting. Part of the facilitator's job is to ensure that what happens in the retrospective stays in the retrospective.

# Keys to Success

Derby and Larsen summarize it best in *Agile Retrospectives*: "Productive teams judge retrospectives by their results" [DERBY, p. 145]. I could not agree more. The retrospective is a crucial part of the inspect-and-adapt cycle in Scrum. It enables teams to identify where they are failing and where they are doing well. Though they are neither easy nor trivial, retrospectives should feel good.

Even with all the good reasons to do retrospectives, they are still the first thing most teams cut when they're feeling pressured to perform faster, deliver more, or increase quality. What's ironic is that they are cutting the one thing that could help them both increase their velocity and quality. If your team is making noise about cutting retrospectives, the following actions will help them reconsider.

## Show Them the Why

New Scrum teams sometimes drop retrospectives because they fail to understand the purpose of the meetings—the *why*. Dropping retrospectives can cause catastrophic problems—glitches that are relatively easy to solve when they are new can stagnate, fester, and grow into larger issues. Common issues that manifest themselves when the retrospective is cut include drops in quality, a variety of failing tests, lowering of team morale, and more. Dropping the retrospective removes the team's opportunity to reflect. Without reflection, the team gets lost and wakes up one day to look in the mirror at a very different picture. It's almost like grooming yourself—most of us shower or brush our teeth daily because, if we don't, problems start to manifest. Without learning and continuous improvement, teams will fall back to their old habits and wonder what happened—and they will usually blame Scrum for their failure.

## Build a Good Environment

Retrospectives drive people to change their behavior over time. To ensure that your retrospectives yield results, make sure that people understand some basic principles:

- The retrospective is for the team and no one else. This means don't go blabbing about what someone said.

- Build confidence through small changes. Taking on too much at one time can build frustration. Taking on small, calculated changes and accomplishing them builds confidence.
- Own the changes. The team is responsible for its changes, not just the ScrumMaster. Get people involved in driving the changes identified in the retrospective.

## Hold Them When You Need Them

Retrospectives are not limited just to sprints. In fact, it is common to see retrospectives after a release, a large unexpected issue, anything. Remember why we do them: so that we can stop, look at the situation, and then make adjustments. In a postmortem, everything has already happened, and our ability to effect change is gone. In a retrospective, we usually are still actively engaged in the project. Consider adding higher-level retrospectives for releases (say every three months) and in case of sudden environmental changes like unexpected outages, scaling up for larger teams with more people, and creating occasional retrospectives between the team and the customers. The customer retrospective can help you identify areas for improvement between the team, the customer, and the product owner.

## Treat Retrospectives Like the First-Class Citizens They Are

Retrospectives deserve more attention than I can give them in one chapter. They are similar to the daily standup meeting. Daily standup meetings are about the *what,* and the retrospective is more meta and is about the *how.* Both are forums for identifying and solving problems and issues, for keeping people apprised on what is working and not working and for building the team.

For maximum effectiveness, you should read *Project Retrospectives: A Handbook for Team Reviews* by Norman Kerth [KERTH] and *Agile Retrospectives:Making Good Teams Great* by Esther Derby and Diana Larsen [DERBY]. When I first read Kerth's book, it influenced how I ran project postmortems. It was not until I moved to Scrum and XP, however, that I fully realized the potential of a well-executed retrospective.

Don't wait to make retrospectives a vital part of your sprints. Do the work. Create the plans. Help the team get the results they want. And don't settle for once-a-sprint vent sessions. When the team members begin to understand how effective retrospectives can be, they won't ever consider cutting them.

# References

[DERBY]   Derby, Esther and Diana Larsen. 2006. *Agile Retrospectives: Making Good Teams Great.* Raleigh, NC: Pragmatic Bookshelf.

[KERTH]   Kerth, Norman. 2001. *Project Retrospectives: A Handbook for Team Reviews*. New York: Dorset House.

[HOHMANN]   Hohmann, Luke. 2007. *Innovation Games: Creating Breakthrough Products Through Collaborative Play*. Upper Saddle River, NJ: Addison-Wesley.

# PART III
# FIRST AID

## Chapter 17

# RUNNING A PRODUCTIVE DAILY STANDUP MEETING

The daily standup meeting, or daily scrum, often does not get the respect it deserves. Done correctly, daily standup meetings keep everyone on the same page for the daily deliverables and moving as one toward the sprint goal. Done poorly, the meeting devolves into a mere status meeting, or worse, a finger-pointing session where people feel they must defend their past actions. Many quickly find they're spending far too much time talking and not enough time doing. Common obstacles teams run into include the following:

- Should we do a deep dive in the meeting?
- What do we do when people show up late?
- What if one person constantly dominates the meeting?
- We can't get our meeting done in 15 minutes. What do we do?

Solving these all-too-common problems is essential to running a productive daily standup meeting. Let's take a look at a story about an ineffective daily standup, discuss what went wrong and how to fix it, and then find ways to ensure that your team's daily standup becomes and stays productive.

## The Story

Tiago was the ScrumMaster for a team. Though he had previously worked as a senior developer for the company, he was relatively new to the ScrumMaster role. On his team were Cesar, Pedro, Nuño, Marco, Ricardo, and Mariana. Like Tiago, the team was new to Scrum—by the third two-week sprint, the team was still figuring out "this Scrum stuff."

At the appointed hour, Tiago started the meeting, "Welcome everyone. Thank you for coming today." Tiago looked around at the faces in the circle. "Has anyone seen Cesar and Marco?"

"I think they are getting coffee," said Pedro.

"Yes, I just got back from the coffee shop, and they were in line. While we are waiting, I'd like to discuss an architectural issue we're having," Nuño added.

Nuño started to discuss his issue with Pedro, Ricardo, and Mariana. They all moved to the whiteboard to start hashing out the problem.

"Hold on team, we need to wait to start the meeting. Cesar and Marco are not here yet," said Tiago.

Nuño stopped writing, glanced over at Tiago, and replied, "When they get here, I'll stop." The four at the whiteboard then continued their architectural discussion.

Five minutes later, Cesar and Marco showed up.

"Hey guys! Sorry we're late. We had a crazy night last night. This band *Pivit* played near the university and man, what a great show!" said Cesar.

Tiago chimed in, "OK, guys, we are all here, so let's start the meeting. Who's first?"

Cesar said he would go. "Yesterday I worked on the xml web service. I got stuck on one of the data elements, but I think I've figured it out. I'm going to ask Pedro to help me with it today and I'll be done," he said.

"Thank you, Cesar. How much time do you have left on your task?" asked Tiago.

"Ummm... about six hours," said Cesar.

"Yesterday you said the same thing: six hours. So, now you're saying you have six more hours?" asked Tiago.

"Yup, it's just not working out the way I expected," said Cesar.

Pedro jumped in. "Cesar, I think I know why it's not working the way you expect. I was looking at the web interface yesterday and saw some unexpected features in there that I think we should address."

"Do you mean bugs?" asked Mariana.

"Yes, bugs, but look." Pedro went to the whiteboard. "If we implement the class in this fashion..." He trailed off as he started to sketch a solution.

Tiago quietly walked to the other end of the whiteboard and wrote a note on it: *Pedro to work with Cesar on web service issue.*

"OK, guys. I've marked a note to discuss this after the meeting. Let's move on." said Tiago.

"I'll go next!" said an enthusiastic Pedro. "Yesterday I was working on the performance tests with Mariana and I came across this issue that seems to be impacting the way the data is passed through the sequencing subclass. We started looking into it, and I think we have a larger architectural issue that needs our attention. Also, I think it might be impacting Cesar because the symptoms he described show that the way we are handling our class variables will result in bad or malformed data being passed. I think Mariana and I should keep working on these tests, but I also think we all need to get together to update the system architecture in these areas. I don't want to just refactor it; I think it needs to be redesigned. If we approach this like we do our other classes and modules, I think we'll be OK—here, let me show you my idea."

With marker still in hand from his last sketch, Pedro began to illustrate this issue on the whiteboard as well.

Because they were all impacted by this illustration, Cesar, Mariana, and Nuño all jumped into the impromptu session. Ricardo, on the other hand, was becoming visibly bored. He appeared to Tiago to be texting with his mobile phone. After a few minutes, Ricardo left the room. Ten minutes later, Ricardo returned. The whiteboard session was still in full swing. Ricardo glanced over at Tiago with a "please end this" look.

"OK, team. It sounds like there is a blocking issue here. I'll mark it down and we can move on," said Tiago.

Mariana turned from the whiteboard and began speaking, "Yesterday I worked on the performance tests with Pedro. I'd like to keep working on that. I also want to work on this architectural issue that surfaced, so I'll be spending time on that as well. Oh, and I have a dentist appointment today after lunch, I forgot about that, so I'll be out the rest of the day. My son has one tomorrow morning so I'll be in late, probably around noon."

"What will you work on *today*, Mariana?" asked Tiago.

"I'm not sure. I mean, I've got this architectural issue, so I'll probably just work on that. Oh, and the performance tests. After that, I don't have any work left to do" said Mariana.

Ricardo jumped in, "What do you mean? We have a backlog full of work."

"Yes, but none of the tasks are testing tasks, so *I've* got nothing to do," said Mariana.

Ricardo nodded his understanding.

"I'll go next," said Marco. "Yesterday I worked on this issue from my old project. It took longer than I thought to fix, but it's a production issue, and I'm the only one who can fix it. I think it will take me the rest of the week. I don't have any blocking issues."

"Fine, who's next?" said Tiago.

Pedro chimed in again. "Hey, Marco, I know that issue. I was one of the people who found it. I can work with you on it today if you want." Once again, he moved to the whiteboard to illustrate where he had found the issue.

Mariana's eyes lit up. "I'd like to help on that with you as well, Marco," she added.

The next thing Tiago knew half of the team had volunteered to work on a production issue for a completely different project. His daily standup had turned into a problem-solving session.

"Now, hold on," said Tiago. "We have committed to do work on our project. We need to stay focused. We can't all go off and work on this issue!"

"Well, I've got to work on it," said Marco. "There is no one else to do the work; it's got to be me."

"We'll see what we can do Marco, what I'd expect is…" said Tiago, but was interrupted by Marco.

"Tiago, one other thing. I think it's too much overhead for us to meet every day with these daily scrum meetings—they seem to be a waste. We should only have this meeting twice a week for an hour; that will be a much better use of our time."

"I agree," said Cesar, much to the shock of Tiago. "And I think we should be sitting; all this standing is a bit of a joke!"

"Hold on a minute. We can discuss this offline; we need to stay focused!" said Tiago.

With a sign of resignation, Tiago turned to Ricardo.

"Ricardo, you're next."

"Yesterday I accomplished the ETL from the CRM warehouse. Today I plan on running the data validation tests to ensure everything is coming over as expected. I'll have that finished today and will update all my tasks before I go home today. I have no blocking issues."

"*Thank you*, Ricardo, that was good," said Tiago. "I am a bit concerned on the rest of our tasks though. Have any of you looked at burndowns lately? It looks like we have flatlined."

"Sorry, that's my fault. I identified some new tasks over the last few days, and I forgot to update them, so the burndowns are a bit off," said Cesar. "I'll get on it."

The team started to disperse, some of them toward the whiteboard; others toward the coffee station. Ricardo made a beeline for his desk. Tiago glanced down at his watch. "A 45-minute daily standup," he thought. "Not good."

# The Model

The daily scrum/daily standup meeting is a short meeting that the team holds daily to share what each person has accomplished, is working on now or will accomplish, and any impediments or issues that have cropped up. For teams new and old this is often a struggle. Just look at the issues Tiago encountered with his team:

- People showing up late
- Requests to condense the meeting to twice a week for one hour
- Wanting to sit instead of stand
- Task sizes increasing without understanding
- Deep-dive problem solving
- Rambling updates and lack of clarity
- Lack of teamwork
- Legacy projects consuming time
- Lack of transparency

These are all common impediments that block productive daily standups, or meetings of any kind for that matter. It's the ScrumMaster's job to clear these impediments, which can seem daunting. The truth is any team can have effective meetings. It just takes some work.

## Time of Day

I get asked every week, "When should we hold the daily meeting?" Some people like the end of the day, some people like the beginning of the day, and, yes, some people like the middle of the day. I do mine about 15 to 30 minutes after the first person arrives in the morning. This means that if your team is an early bunch, arriving to work at 8:00, you should do the meeting around 8:15 or 8:30. If the last person comes in at 9:30, do the meeting at 9:45 or 10:00. I find that having the daily standup at the beginning of the work day is much more effective for coordinating a team's actions than ones held at other times. It helps the team start fresh, lay down the plan for the day, and go.

## Start and End on Time

An effective meeting begins by starting and ending on time. If six people spend an extra five minutes at a meeting (whether it was because it started or ended late), you've wasted 30 minutes (six people times five minutes). If you do that every working day, you've wasted two and a half hours talking when you could have been working. Tiago's team did not start on time, and there seemed to be no consequence for being late. As a result, his meeting started out on a chaotic note and only got worse as it went on. Luckily, beginning and ending as scheduled is something you and the team can make happen.

### Late Starts

As ScrumMaster, insist that people arrive on time. Don't accept excuses. Politely remind any latecomers that the rest of the team spent $x$ minutes waiting on them. If sheer peer pressure won't do it, try punishment. Seriously, a little pain goes a long way toward correcting bad habits. On past projects, we've had "the Friday fund," where latecomers make a *donation* to the Friday fund and the team goes out for a beer at the end of the week. Used correctly, this can be a great motivational tool. Still, you will have that one team member who says, "I'll just pay $20 right now and be late all the time." Another option that I like is the "pick your own medicine" approach; people will be more committed to arriving on time if they choose a punishment that motivates them. Once when our team did this, I chose to do 29 pushups if I was late, Mike paid a dollar to the Friday fund, and Bart chose to go without coffee for the day. The day Bart was late was not a good day. Two hours after the meeting, the entire team brought him a full a pot of coffee and begged him to drink it to make him a tolerable person. If peer pressure and punishments do not work, you need to have a talk with the regular offender. Bottom line: Everyone on the team *must* arrive on time.

### Agenda, Rhythm, and Layout

As ScrumMaster, make sure the meeting ends on time, every time. Some people will try to dominate the conversation. Others will do deep dives. Still others will start to ramble. Your job is to prevent and deflect so that your meeting is not derailed. Let's talk about prevention first. Until daily standups get to be a habit, rhythm is everything. To start everyone out on the same beat, as soon as everyone arrives (on time, see above), restate the purpose of the meeting by saying, "Thank you for coming today. We are here to answer our questions. These questions are what did you do since the last meeting, what will you do today, and what impediments do you have (some teams add a fourth question, see Chapter 18, "The Fourth Question in Scrum"). Who would like to start?" Repeat this mantra *every single day*. Repetition leads to muscle memory. And good meeting muscle memory is essential for having an effective meeting. Last, if everyone is standing in a line, have them form a circle and look at each other. Once you start going around, the order of who is next is obvious and tends to move meetings along faster. It also encourages team members to report to each other rather than the ScrumMaster.

## Interruptions

Let's say you've done your best to prevent a late meeting by getting everyone there on time and by reminding them each day of the meeting format and questions. You are by no means done. Your team members, especially at first, will deviate from this format, even though you've just told them what to say. Your first challenge will be interruptions. One way to keep everyone focused is to use a talking object. To the first person speaking toss an object to pass on when he is done speaking. The rules are simple: When you are holding the object, you get to talk; when you are not holding the object, you don't. If you break the rules by talking out of turn, then you once again get to pick your medicine. For my talking object, I like to use Nerf footballs because they are always fun to throw and usually don't break anything. If a team member (or members) interrupts another's turn, the person speaking (or the Scrum-Master) can gently cut them off by waving to or pointing to the object as a visual indicator that "it's my turn to talk."

## Deep Dives

Your next challenge will be to curtail those who deviate from the questions and begin to dive deep into the problems they are facing. Do you remember the first time this happened in our story? Pedro was at the board, describing the bugs he had found. Pedro was not trying to derail the meeting; he was trying to help solve the problem his teammate was having. Without interrupting, Tiago wrote a note on the whiteboard to remind everyone that more discussion was needed. He then signaled the team that it was time to move on. Tiago did the right thing. By using this virtual "parking lot" for ideas, he kept the meeting flowing but captured the fact that a conversation would need to take place outside the daily standup. The second time Pedro approached the board and began sketching, though, Tiago did nothing—not a good thing for the meeting, especially since Ricardo actually left while everyone else was problem solving. As the ScrumMaster, watch for long-winded answers on "what I did yesterday," where the deep dives usually start. Look for other symptoms as well, such as other people joining in the conversation.

As soon as the deep dive begins, wave your hand (or otherwise signal the team) as shown in Figure 17-1; then write a note about the conversation thread on the

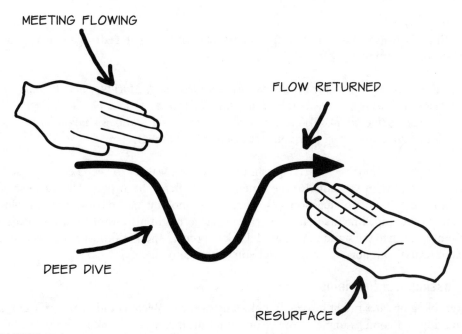

MEETING FLOWING

FLOW RETURNED

DEEP DIVE

RESURFACE

**FIGURE 17-1**   To signal a deep dive, move your hand following this pattern

whiteboard in an area called "discuss after the meeting" or "parking lot." This immediately puts you back on the path to resurface. If the speaker does not return to his three questions, remind him that you are focusing on updates and will explore his concerns in depth after the standup.

## Expose Hidden Impediments

If your only goal for a daily standup was to have people arrive on time, give an update as quickly as possible, and then leave, you'd be set. The daily standup, though, is intended to synchronize the team and expose any problems standing in the way. Your job as ScrumMaster, then, is to not only enforce the meeting timebox but to also make sure that the team members' answers move the team toward accomplishing these objectives. Look for signs that your team is not accomplishing these goals. Warning signs include team members who ramble, who gloss over problems, and who are overly vague. Each of these behaviors can stand in the way of a truly productive daily standup. Remind team members that they are synchronizing with each other, not the ScrumMaster, and the meeting is for them. Daily standups are prone to degenerate into daily project management status updates, whereas they should be about facilitating team collaboration.

## Rambling

Nothing is worse than a rambling update. The answer that Pedro gave is a good example of a ramble:

> *Yesterday I was working on the performance tests with Mariana, and I came across this issue that seems to be impacting the way the data is passed through the sequencing subclass. We started looking into it, and I think we have a larger architectural issue that needs our attention. Also, I think...*

He goes on and on. What Tiago should have done was try to keep Pedro focused, not only on his answer but also the time that he took *for* the answer. The purpose of limiting the number of questions is to keep things moving, not to come up with solutions to the impediments that are surfaced. Tiago might also want to talk to Pedro about coming to the standup prepared. Lack of preparedness is almost as bad as being late because you show up on time, but you're not really there.

## Glossing over Problems

Rambling updates might be bad, but glossing over a problem could be worse. Cesar's standup is a good example of the wrong kind of update. He stuck to the script but glossed over the fact that his task had grown in size since the day before. Tiago did the right thing by interrupting to point out the fact that the task that was six hours yesterday still had six hours left today. Sometimes our tasks grow in size, so the fact that it occurred in our story is not the problem. The dysfunction is that Cesar did not know why the size was increasing or how he was going to complete the task.

Tiago pointed out the problem but did not take the next step of noting the impediment on the team whiteboard for follow-up after the meeting. Clearly Cesar had an impediment—his work was growing—but neither Tiago nor the team stepped in to assist. The behavior we expect from our ScrumMaster is to highlight the issue, surface it, and address it. In this case, that did not happen.

## Being Vague

Giving answers that are overly vague, such as Mariana's "yesterday I did some testing and today I will do some more testing and I have no impediments" might technically answer the questions but does not help the team or provide valuable insight into what work is in progress. This results in a lack of transparency and increases the risk of having two tasks worked on simultaneously.

# End with the Beginning in Mind

You should now be set up to run a pretty good meeting. At the end of the meeting, review the items written on the whiteboard. Invite people to stay if they want to talk about them but announce the meeting is over so that those not impacted can leave.

The daily cycle begins at the end of the meeting, and there is often no better way to get started than to review the items on the whiteboard.

# Keys to Success

Running an effective daily standup meeting can seem daunting, but it is not. As a ScrumMaster, you will battle with these issues and more when it comes to the daily standup meeting. It's your job to help your team build muscle memory so that this all becomes part of the daily routine, like breathing. The keys to your success are to put and keep the *daily* and the *standup* in your daily standups, work as a team, and remain patient in the face of resistance and difficulty.

## Keep the Meeting Cadence

Daily standup meetings are most effective when they happen *daily*. In our story, Marco thought that meeting every day was too much overhead. He proposed that the meeting be condensed to two days per week at one hour per meeting. Marco's proposal has several flaws.

First, the meeting must happen in the same place and at the same time every day. *Every* day: not every other day, or every third day, but every day. It's nonnegotiable. We meet daily to maintain a pattern, a muscle memory. The team needs to get used to synchronizing work and moving as a team. Its members need to make public, daily commitments to each other, instead of working toward some distant goal. They need that 15 minutes every day (and they're less likely to complain if the meeting actually lasts 15 minutes or less).

Besides that, though, valuable information comes out of daily standups that can save time and money. Imagine if Tiago's team did meet only twice a week. Let's say Cesar starts working on his web service task on Thursday. He runs into trouble. He spends all day Friday and all day Monday working on it again. At standup Tuesday, he shares his problems. Pedro says, "Oh. I have a fix for that. Talk to me after the meeting." In essence, then, Cesar wasted two full days (Friday and Monday) working on a problem that Pedro could have helped him with at Friday's standup—if only the team had been meeting every day. Spending 15 minutes to prevent wasting two days of work? Worth it every time.

Extending the meeting time at all, but especially to one hour, is a bad idea. Longer meetings give us time to meander and ramble that short meetings do not. Short meetings keep us focused. Extending the time spent in the meeting only increases the team's dissatisfaction and feeling of too much overhead.

## Stand; Don't Sit

Like the *daily* in daily standup means every day, the *standup* part also means just what it says—it's a time to stand. Why do we stand? First, it keeps us engaged. When seated at a table or hiding behind a desk, we can fiddle with our phones, flip a pencil, or doodle. These behaviors go away when everyone stands and faces each other. Second, standing keeps the meeting short. When we're standing, we are acutely aware when the meeting is taking too long. If you're feeling the need to sit, the meeting has somehow derailed. Third, standing increases energy levels and awareness, making us much more focused. Some teams go so far as to not allow people to lean on walls or desks. Whether you choose to lean or not, the important thing is to stand, deliver, understand the day, and get to work.

## Work As a Team

When a Scrum team is really working, it is an integrated unit working toward a common goal, not a collection of individuals working on specialized tasks. On a true team, you should never hear, "My tasks are done and I have nothing to do" or "I'm the only one who can fix things on a legacy project." In our story, we heard Mariana say, "I've got nothing to do after I finish my tasks." We also saw evidence of specialization in the story of Marco, whose expertise on a legacy system was consuming his time. Both of these examples are clues that Tiago's team is still just a collection of individuals.

As ScrumMasters, we can gauge how well we are gelling as a team by thinking in terms of the team's "bus factor." The bus factor is the "number of people on your team who have to be hit with a bus before the project is in serious trouble." Consider anyone on your current project. If that person leaves, is the team able to step up and complete the work in the backlog or are you left unable to function, thereby missing your sprint commitment? If your answer is, "Yikes! We'd be dead in the water," your bus factor is one. (Prepare for a failed sprint in your near future.) Tiago's team's bus factor is definitely one.

If your team, like Tiago's, has a low bus factor, the first thing you need to do is alert the team members. Help them understand why specialization is a problem and how it will continue to hamper efforts unless it is addressed. Prepare them (and yourself) for the fact that there is no quick fix or simple solution. You can implement some practices, though, that will help:

- Work in a shared workspace.
- Practice pair programming and test-driven development.
- Have a dedicated team focused on one project at a time. (See Chapter 3, "Using Team Consultants to Optimize Team Performance," for how to structure the team to make this happen.)

Working in a shared space reduces multiple barriers to communication. For example, if the team from the story is scattered in offices throughout a building and Cesar wants to talk to Ricardo, Cesar must get up and find him. Ricardo might not even be in his office when Cesar arrives, or he might be busy, but at this point the distraction has already happened. Further, Cesar might get side-tracked along the way by someone else looking for answers (or conversation). In the end, what would have been a quick question can easily turn into a 45-minute answer safari. When you put everyone in a shared space, the answer safari goes away. The team learns how to manage the distractions on its own.

Pair programming, or a real-time code review, is a great way to get people up to speed on the *entire* codebase. You can take this a step further and practice pair programming patterns like ping-pong pair programming or promiscuous pairing, both of which take the extreme in XP to the super-extreme. (Read more about these techniques in Chapter 19, "Keeping People Engaged with Pair Programming.") Test-driven development builds further on pair programming in that it gives the team a loose set of guidelines and documentation on how the code works. If a team member gets stuck, she can always read the test to see what the intent of the code is.

Having a dedicated team removes distractions across the board. Instead of focusing on specific specializations such as "being the SQL guy," the team members focus on how they can work together to solve a specific set of stories each sprint.

## Be Patient

For teams new to Scrum, daily standups are going to be a challenge at first. That's a given. Like Tiago, new ScrumMasters find themselves faced with latecomers, ramblers, and deep divers. Correcting these behaviors takes time and patience. Remember that it can take two to three months to learn a new behavior or pattern. Don't despair if it doesn't go perfectly at first. Keep reminding yourself and your team why you're there. Keep your sense of humor. And invest in some Nerf footballs. One day you'll look up and realize that daily standups are just another routine part of your team's very productive day.

# Chapter 18

# THE FOURTH QUESTION IN SCRUM

You are on a team that is both newly formed and new to practicing agile. Your daily standup meetings appear to be going well and you are looking forward to your team's first demo. The big day comes, you get in front of the customer, and then the floor drops out. Your app starts acting in a way that is definitely not as intended—all because of a hidden blocking issue.

You wonder to yourself, "Didn't we do everything right? Didn't we ask all the right questions?" The team dusts itself off and gets ready to start the second sprint. How do you ensure that going forward the team drives out those blocking issues in the daily standup?

Add in the fourth question.

## The Story

The Hopping Mad Dolphins (HMD) were a new team, both to Scrum and to each other. Though the members of the HMD team had all been burned on projects in the past, they were all excited by the prospect of working on a Scrum team. They knew the basics but not much else. Still, they approached the framework with enthusiasm and dove in headfirst, following Scrum by the book as closely as possible.

Before they knew it, it was time for the first daily standup meeting. The Scrum-Master, Marc, was the first to arrive. His fellow teammates Jane, Maria, Cory, and Paco came in shortly thereafter.

"OK, guys. Daily standup time. We're supposed to answer three questions," answered Marc. He wrote them on the whiteboard.

- What did you do yesterday?
- What will you do today?
- What blocking issues do you have?

"So, who would like to start?" asked Marc. The team jumped right in. The blocking issues ran the gamut from stored procedures having timeout issues to things that never would have been brought up in the past, such as, "It's too hot in this little team space." After 15 minutes, the team members each had a turn and were feeling pretty pleased with themselves.

"This is kind of fun," said Cory on his way out of the room.

"We're communicating!" agreed Jane, half-jokingly. "Just like in the books!"

The daily standup meetings continued to run smoothly as the sprint went on. The team seemed to be holding itself accountable, and the blocking issues, even the heat issue, were being addressed. "This Scrum thing is pretty easy," remarked Jane at the end of one standup toward the end of the sprint. "We're going to knock their socks off at the sprint review."

Everyone laughed. Everyone, that is, except Paco, who simply shrugged his shoulders. Cory slapped him on the back and asked, "Paco, why the long face?"

Paco smiled and seemed about to answer, when Jane interrupted. "That's better, Paco. I knew you had a smile in you." Everyone laughed and Jane continued, "Hey, Marc, we've all had a turn, and it's been 15 minutes. My build should be done, and I'm anxious to get back to my desk. Can we adjourn this thing and get back to work?"

Marc nodded and the group quickly broke up, leaving Paco frowning, hands in his pockets, and eyes on the taskboard. Unfortunately, no one noticed.

For the rest of the team members, the first demo meeting could not come fast enough. They felt like kids on Christmas Eve. They had accomplished more work than they had imagined possible over the first 30-day sprint and wanted to show it off. The team worked hard to make everything perfect, including a slide deck (mandatory for all presentations at this company, no exceptions) that listed the accomplished work, the work that was not accomplished, and what it meant for the team to be done. The only team member who didn't seem to share in the excitement was Paco. Marc noticed him at the beginning of the sprint review, mainly because he was staring out the window instead of at the presentation. "I need to remember to ask Paco what's going on," Marc thought, turning his attention back to the screen.

The review went well at first, but when the team was demonstrating the last component, the system crashed with no warning. While the team scrambled to fix it on the spot, the stakeholders reassured them that it wasn't that big of a deal. One of the stakeholders said jokingly, "Well, since this is your first sprint we'll let you off with a warning."

Though the team members laughed, they were embarrassed and deflated. After the stakeholders left, the team sat trying to puzzle out the problem, and how it could have missed such a huge bug. Paco sat back in his chair and said under his breath, "I knew this was going to happen."

The room got quiet. Cory looked at Paco and asked, "What do you mean? How did you know this was going to happen?"

"Well," Paco began. "When I was reviewing one of the classes a couple weeks back, I noticed some irregularities. The way it was written wasn't exactly wrong, but I suspected that it might cause some bugs to pop up because I'd had something similar happen to me before. I thought I said something about it, but I guess I didn't say it directly enough. And it wasn't really blocking *me*; it was just more of a gut feeling. I didn't want to point out someone's mistake or redo someone else's work; it seemed presumptuous and rude. So, I decided I'd wait and see if there was a problem, and I guess there was."

The rest of the team sat there, letting it sink in.

"We don't know each other very well," said Jane. "But, please, if you ever see me doing something that is going to cause a problem, tell me. I won't be offended."

Everyone nodded.

"And part of being a team is working as a team," said Marc. "We need to get in the habit of fixing problems that we see, even if they aren't in 'our code' because we have collective code ownership. We're all responsible for every last line."

"I know and probably next time I will try to speak up or ask. The thing is, I wasn't really sure. Like I said, it was more of a gut thing," explained Paco. "But it ate at me and worried me for a couple of weeks."

"I wish you would have said something," said Marc. "I noticed something was wrong with you, but not until today."

"Yeah," said Cory. "I mean, we've all been busy, and we haven't been working together that long. I figured you were just a quiet guy."

"Well, I am a little quiet," said Paco. "And I'm not very comfortable just blurting things out. I really don't like conflict, and I didn't want to insult anyone."

"OK," said Marc. "I think we've been doing a good job at our daily standups of mentioning the more obvious blocking issues, but we're missing some of the sneaky, subtle ones that will jump out and bite us. Any suggestions?"

"We could trust each other more," offered Maria.

"We could ask each other's opinions more," said Cory.

"We could make sure that we're all feeling equally confident about things," said Paco.

"That's it," said Jane. "We need to add a question." She walked up to the whiteboard where the three questions were still printed in the upper right-hand corner and added a fourth question (see Figure 18-1).

"Are we allowed to do that?" asked Maria. "Can we just add a question?"

"I don't see why not. What do you think, team?" asked Marc. "If we'd had this question, would we have gone into a sprint review with a big, system-crashing bug?"

Everyone looked at Paco. He considered for a minute and then said, "Right around the middle of week two, my confidence level would have been much lower than anyone else's. And it probably would have given me the opportunity to air out my concerns without fear of looking like a know-it-all or being totally wrong. So, yeah, I think that would work."

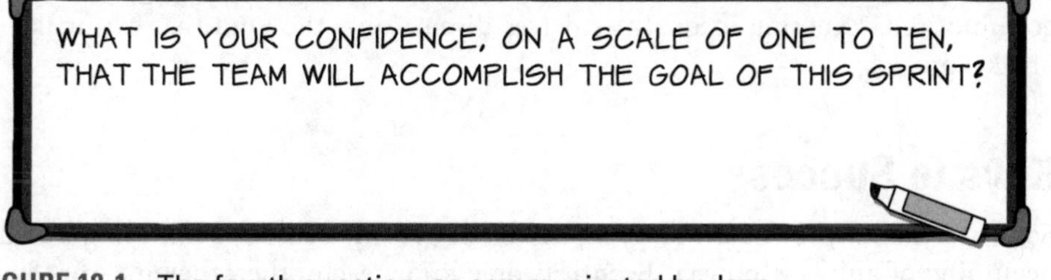

WHAT IS YOUR CONFIDENCE, ON A SCALE OF ONE TO TEN, THAT THE TEAM WILL ACCOMPLISH THE GOAL OF THIS SPRINT?

**FIGURE 18-1** The fourth question, as communicated by Jane

The team added the fourth question to the list and stuck to it throughout the project. And just about every sprint, someone would use the question as a way to raise a nagging concern. Some problems were real; others were just misunderstandings. But all of them were opportunities to follow up on a hunch that might have otherwise remained unspoken.

## The Model

The fourth question in Scrum might be simple, but it is a valuable tool to ensure that the team is on track—especially a new team. In the daily standup meeting, start with the three questions as you normally would:

- What did I do yesterday?
- What will I do today?
- What blocking issues do I have?

Then add the following:

- *What is your confidence, on a scale of one to ten, that the team will accomplish the goal of this sprint?*

So why does this question work so well? As we found in the story, not everyone is equally comfortable with conflict. And not everyone is used to airing an opinion, especially when trust has not been established. As such, those who are more outspoken and opinionated can dominate a conversation or a meeting without meaning to. In a daily standup or retrospective, the more introverted team members might agree with the stated opinion despite their misgivings because they feel they are alone in thinking differently, don't want to be wrong, or feel speaking up would cause an unnecessary stir.

Often, to get past the surface issues to the deeper issues, you need to ask a question intended to start conversations. Question four is that kind of question. It forces everyone to put a hard number on a soft feeling. It also focuses everyone on the overall project, rather than individual stories or tasks. And just as disagreements about estimates in Planning Poker can unearth hidden assumptions and misunderstandings, differences in project confidence can uncover core issues that might otherwise go unnoticed. Exposing inequalities drives discussion—the kind that can make or break a project.

## Keys to Success

So, when should you use the fourth question of Scrum? I recommend using it at the beginning of any new project. Even if people know each other, they may not have built the trust required to have the open and honest conversations that ensure project success. I've made it a required element for any team that is new to each other, to Scrum, or to both. Even if you're an established Scrum team, if you are going through your daily standup meeting without uncovering many impediments, yet during the sprint or the review, issues "keep cropping up," you need to add the fourth question of Scrum.

The fourth question is powerful on its own, but it's even more effective when the ScrumMaster is also on the lookout for the following:

- **Nonverbal communication**—Look for small signs that a team member might be unsure or uncomfortable. In the story, Paco's lack of enthusiasm was noticeable, but unexplained. If you see a behavior that seems out of place, ask about it. And stick around long enough to hear the answer.
- **People who are not comfortable with conflict**—A ScrumMaster doesn't have to be a psychologist, but the best ScrumMasters have probably done some research on how humans work and interact. Different personalities and cultures often respond to conflict in dissimilar ways. Get to know the people you are working with, ask those who have worked with them in the past about their natural tendencies, and spend some time chatting with them informally. Establishing trust goes a long way toward increasing communication.
- **Opportunities to practice continuous learning**—Two elements that have helped teams that I have worked on and coached are the Myers-Briggs assessment and workshop and the book *People Styles at Work* [BOLTON]. Providing team members with the tools needed to stretch themselves personally and to develop their competencies will have a lasting impact on the current project and all future projects.

As your project progresses and the team bond and trust becomes stronger, you might find that the fourth question is no longer needed. Most teams I work with use it for the first two to five months, or until the team reaches a performing state. The team will know when the question is no longer needed, so the team should decide if and when it should be dropped.

## References

[BOLTON]    Bolton, Robert, and Dorothy Grover Bolton. 1996. *People Styles at Work: Making Bad Relationships Good and Good Relationships Better.* New York: AMACOM.

Chapter 19

# KEEPING PEOPLE ENGAGED WITH PAIR PROGRAMMING

Pair programming is one of those things that people either love or hate. What no one can dispute, however, is that pairing produces high-quality software in a relatively short amount of time. Indeed, Alistair Cockburn and Laurie Williams [COCKBURN] have proven that while development time goes up when pairing, the number of defects injected will be fewer.

The problem with pair programming tends to be keeping people engaged when they are not the ones with their hands on the keyboard. This is exactly what was happening to the team we are about to visit. The team is pairing faithfully but having trouble staying focused on the task at hand.

## The Story

Lansing looked over at Colin and saw him yawn.

"C'mon man, snap out of it! I know I type slowly, but we've only been at this an hour!" said Lansing.

"Sorry, Lansing. It's not you. I'm trying to stay focused on what you're doing, but it's hard for me to stay awake today. I was up most of the night with a sick kid. I know that's not an excuse. Let's go get another cup of coffee" said Colin.

The rest of the team looked over at the pair, "We'll go with you. Sitting here is like watching paint dry," said Sean, who was pairing with Devon. They both rose to join Colin and Lansing in the break room.

As the team sat having a coffee, Lansing addressed the problem of pairing.

"Guys, we just don't seem engaged. Every time one of us gets too into the code, the other person falls asleep!"

"I know, I know," said Colin. "I'm sorry, guys."

"It's not just about today," said Lansing. "I mean all the time. I do it, you do it, everyone does it. We all get drowsy or check out when we pair for too long, even just 30 minutes! What are we going to do about it?"

Devon chimed in. "I was browsing the web on how to increase the performance of our build server, and I stumbled across this paper from the Agile conference titled 'Promiscuous Pairing and Beginner's Mind,' by a guy named Arlo Belshee [BELSHEE]. It is pretty interesting. He and his team increased their velocity significantly by having one person from each pair switch pairs *and tasks* every 90 minutes. No one stays on one task longer than 180 minutes."

"So let me get this straight," said Colin. "You're saying that if we were pairing like we were this morning—I'm with Lansing and you're with Sean. After 90 minutes, I would switch places with Sean so that you and I are pairing together on *your* task, and Sean and Lansing are pairing together on *our* task. Then after another hour and a half, you and Lansing would switch places so that we'd be back to our original pairs but not our original tasks?"

"Yep," said Devon. "Weird, huh?"

"Sounds confusing," said Colin.

"So who keeps the task going?" asked Lansing.

"The person who has been sitting at that computer the longest has to get his new mate up to speed, and quickly, because 90 minutes later that same person will be leaving to join a new pair," said Devon.

"That's a lot to absorb in 90 minutes. Do you get any coding done or are you always getting up to speed."

"That's the weirdest part," said Devon. "The team in the paper found that the velocity was highest when the pairs switched every 90 minutes, even with the learning curve. Something about beginner's mind. You should read the paper."

"Yep. I'd like to do that," Lansing answered. "I'd be willing to give it a go today, though, just to see if it helps. We can't go much slower than we are with Colin asleep in the passenger seat!"

Colin laughed. "That's true. It will definitely help keep me awake."

"I'm willing to give it a go, too," said Sean. "Switching things up might jump-start my creativity, too. I haven't contributed much today."

Devon continued. "Well, as long as we're feeling daring, I also came across this other web page by a guy named Peter Provost called *micro-pairing* [PROVOST 01]. His method was more extreme but would certainly keep us engaged. It looks like this." Devon pulled out a napkin and drew up a quick version of Peter's micro-pairing idea (see Figure 19-1).

"Devon, I'm all for shaking things up, but that looks insane!" exclaimed Lansing.

Devon nodded. "I agree that it's a lot of work, and I don't think we could do this all day but…"

"I'm willing to try it, Lansing," said Colin. "A routine like that would keep us laser-focused."

"I'm game, too," said Sean.

"OK, OK. You guys win. I'll give it a go. What do we have to lose?" said Lansing.

The team went back to their offices feeling both invigorated and wary. They had two new techniques to try, which would be sure to keep them awake but that might prove too hard to sustain in the long term.

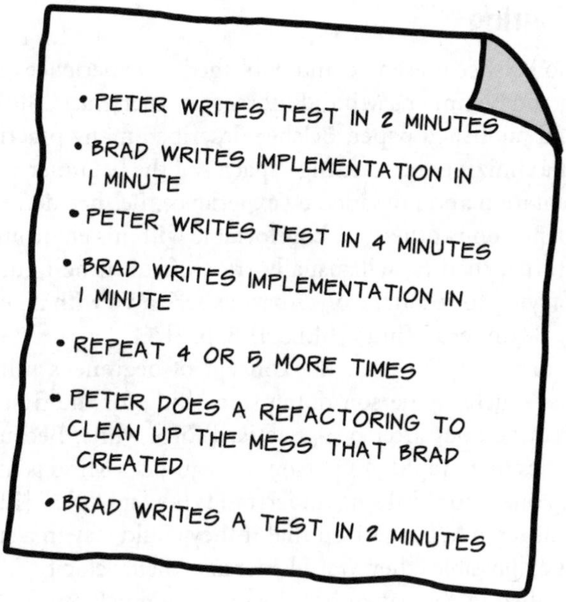

- PETER WRITES TEST IN 2 MINUTES
- BRAD WRITES IMPLEMENTATION IN 1 MINUTE
- PETER WRITES TEST IN 4 MINUTES
- BRAD WRITES IMPLEMENTATION IN 1 MINUTE
- REPEAT 4 OR 5 MORE TIMES
- PETER DOES A REFACTORING TO CLEAN UP THE MESS THAT BRAD CREATED
- BRAD WRITES A TEST IN 2 MINUTES

**FIGURE 19-1**    Devon's example of micro-pairing

## The Model

Keeping our heads in the game is a challenge. We're just so easily distracted. In "The Ebb and Flow of Attention in the Human Brain," Trey Hedden and John Gabrieli of MIT explore what happens when people are distracted by internal thoughts when doing complex work [HEDDEN]. They tell the story of Dan Jansen, an Olympic speed skater who, in the 1988 Winter Olympics, slipped and fell in both the 500m and the 1000m events [WEINBERG]. Jansen had trained for years and was normally a focused champion. Just seven hours before his race, however, Jansen's sister passed away from leukemia. Hedden and Gabrieli hypothesize that while Jansen's focus, his *external* focus, was on skating, he had small gaps when thoughts of his sister would intrude. These *internal* focus issues took Jansen's attention away from the external tasks at hand and resulted in his uncharacteristic falls.

In traditional pair programming, you usually have one person at the keyboard (a tactician) and one who is observing (the strategist). The tactician is usually better able to maintain external focus because he has the activity of typing to keep his mind focused on the task at hand. The strategist, on the other hand, is less active and there-fore more distracted by internal focus issues, which cause gaps in his attention that ultimately make the pair less productive than it could be.

Each of the models discussed in this chapter help keep both members of the pair engaged and focused, despite the numerous distractions that crowd our minds.

## Promiscuous Pairing

At Agile 2005, Arlo Belshee presented and published an experience report titled "Promiscuous Pairing and Beginner's Mind: Embrace Inexperience" [BELSHEE].

In the talk and published paper, Belshee described many practices, all of which have to do with maximizing the learning capacity of the beginner's mind, one that is open to experimentation and not jaded by experience. Belshee defines the beginner's mind as this: "If a person is otherwise comfortable with his environment but doesn't understand one thing, then he will usually try stuff until he figures that one part out. This state of trying to reconcile one's past experiences with an environment that doesn't quite fit is Beginner's Mind" [BELSHEE, p. 2].

Belshee goes on to explain that the concept of beginner's mind is behind the notion of beginner's luck: "A person doing something for the first time often does it much better than he does after he's practiced for a while. Because he tries more approaches, and tries them rapidly, a person in Beginner's Mind is more likely to succeed at a task than one who thinks he understands how it works" [BELSHEE, p. 2].

Belshee and his team hypothesized that if they could stay in a state of beginner's mind for as long as possible, they would increase their velocity. They tried several practices, all described in the paper, but the one that stuck out for me (and the one Devon describes in our story) combines team-owned tasks with a shortened pair-cycle time. His team has one person from each pair switch pairs and tasks every 90 minutes, thereby keeping an "expert" and a "beginner" on each task at all times.

Team-owned tasks are best explained in contrast to individually-owned tasks. Individually-owned tasks are those where one person stays with a task through to completion. So if Devon pulls a task from the backlog, he would work on it with any number of different pair partners until that task is complete. Team-owned tasks have no designated owner—if anything, the workstation owns the task. Any number of pairs might work on a task at various times until it is complete. There is no one person accountable for it from beginning to end.

Pair cycle time, or *pair churn* as Belshee calls it, is a predefined amount of time that a pair can stay together. Belshee's team experimented with many different lengths but found that for optimal velocity, pairs should stay together no longer than 90 minutes. My team experimented with this as well and found our optimal time to be two hours. Whether your optimal time is 90 minutes, two hours, or somewhere in between, moving pairs and tasks that often takes some getting used to. Let's look at how this works for a typical team.

### Promiscuous Pairing in Practice

Switch Team is a six-person team (not including the product owner or the ScrumMaster). Switch Team has established its core team hours (see Chapter 10, "Core Hours," for more on this topic) and has agreed that everyone will start work as a team at 10:30 a.m. and will stop working as a team at 4:00 p.m., with a one-hour break for lunch between noon and 1:00 p.m. Switch's daily standup meeting is at 10:00 a.m. (see Figure 19-2).

| | PAIR BLOCK 1 10:30 – 12:00 | | PAIR BLOCK 2 13:00 – 14:30 | | PAIR BLOCK 3 14:30 – 16:00 | |
|---|---|---|---|---|---|---|
| | PRIMARY | SECONDARY | PRIMARY | SECONDARY | PRIMARY | SECONDARY |
| **WORKSTATION 1** | A | B | B | C | C | D |
| **WORKSTATION 2** | C | D | D | E | E | F |
| **WORKSTATION 3** | E | F | F | A | A | B |

**FIGURE 19-2**   Switch Team pair block hours and swaps

Notice in this example that there are three pairing blocks. Each block has a primary person and a secondary person (I've named these people A, B, C, D, E, and F). Each pair block lasts for 90 minutes, as recommended in Belshee's experiment. The people rotate one spot to the left in an upwardly serpentine fashion, dropping to the bottom right from the top left. The tasks, on the other hand, stay with the workstations until they are complete. Depending on your task size, the people who start the task on Workstation 1 may never see that task again.

### The Challenge with Promiscuous Pairing

When my team first implemented these techniques, we were not ready. We captured our results and I published an experience report at Agile 2006, "Adventures in Promiscuous Pairing: Seeking Beginner's Mind" [LACEY]. In this paper I concluded that promiscuous pairing is an advanced skill, best suited for seasoned, well-practiced teams. New teams working in an unfamiliar framework will likely find this high-level practice too much to handle, at least at first.

When you are ready to try promiscuous pairing, consider using design concept cards. At the beginning of each task, have your pair write the design on a 3x5 card, with the larger assumptions and constraints. The purpose of the card is to allow new pairs to reference the brief notes rather than ask questions of the original pair who started the task. Otherwise, what I've experienced is that too much time is spent rehashing design decisions at each pair swap. By having design concept cards, the new pair can easily see why decisions were made and either accept or change the design, without wasting time trying to understand or justify particular decisions.

Even though they are best suited for advanced teams, I believe in the ideas communicated by Belshee. I have had success with them in past projects both as a way to keep pairs engaged and also as a tool for bringing new people up to speed on the system. Try it out and make a good faith effort when you do.

### Micro-Pairing

Micro-pairing, coined by Peter Provost in 2006, has its roots in a game invented by Peter and Brad Wilson, *The Pair Programming TDD Game* [PROVOST 02]. It is similar to the Pair Programming Ping Pong Pattern on Ward Cunningham's C2 Wiki site [CUNNINGHAM]. The ping-pong pattern, as written by Cunningham, is as follows:

> *A writes a new test and sees that it fails.*
>
> *B implements the code needed to pass the test.*
>
> *B writes the next test.*
>
> *A implements it.*
>
> *And so on. Refactoring is done whenever the need arises by whomever is driving.*

Micro-pairing was born out of frustration with traditional pairing, specifically with the strategist's tendency to drift in and out of focus while the tactician completes tasks. It differs from the ping-pong pattern in that every transition of state in the diagram causes a keyboard shift, where keyboard shifts in Cunningham's pattern happen only after a new failing test has been introduced. Micro-pairing forces pairs to make frequent transitions both in who has the keyboard and also in what that person is doing with the keyboard. The rules of the original game are simple (adapted from the description by Peter Provost [PROVOST 02]):

- One person writes a test and then passes the keyboard to his partner.
  - If the test fails (if the light turns red), the partner implements the required code to make it pass.
  - If the test passes (if the light turns green), the partner writes an additional test or refactors the passing implementation.
- The keyboard then passes back to the original person to write another test or to refactor the code that was written.
- The pattern continues until the task is complete.

Let's consider why we would want to write a passing test rather than a failing test. One reason is to codify or document behavior that already exists through another test but is not adequately documented. Doing this locks in some functionality or confirms some suspicion about the behavior of the code. Another, perhaps more entertaining, reason is when you set out to write a failing test and you end up writing a passing test. Whoops! This should raise a bunch of questions. Is the test that was just written bad? Was the previous test bad? Does the code do more than you expected it to do?

More often than not, you will write failing tests in this pattern, but don't forget about writing passing ones to confirm your suspicions. Remember that you still pass the keyboard even after writing a passing test, which means your partner will probably be the one writing failing tests, and so will be driving the design, at least temporarily.

In playing the game, the pattern looks something like this:

1. Lansing starts in a green state and writes a failing test, which takes about two to three minutes.
2. Lansing passes the keyboard to Colin, who is in a red state. He implements the code to make the test pass, which takes about a minute.
3. Colin passes the keyboard back to Lansing, who is now in a green state.
4. Lansing writes another failing test and passes the keyboard back to Colin, again taking about three to four minutes.
5. Colin implements the code to make the test pass, which takes another minute or two, then passes the keyboard back.
6. This cycle goes on for four or five more cycles, and it ends up with Lansing, who decides to clean up the code that Colin has written.
7. After cleaning up the code, Lansing hands the keyboard to Colin who now takes a turn at writing tests.

In traditional pair programming, the tactician would do all these steps herself while the strategist watched the design and the code evolve. This could go on for an hour or two without interruption. By using micro-pairing to switch control of the keyboard at every state transition, the pairs are more likely to have a conversation about the bit of code that was just written, regardless of whether it is production code or test code. Without these forced transitions, people are less likely to interrupt someone who is in the flow, resulting in degraded code quality.

As you can see from this example, however, the pairing aspect of the session can become fairly intense due to the transition of the keyboard at every state change. The person in the green state is ultimately the one driving the design because that person can choose to write a passing test, refactor, or write a failing test. The person in the red state has only one choice: to make the test pass (unless he chooses to argue against a test). Try to vary it so that both members of the pair have an opportunity to write tests and one is not stuck implementing the tests. And always pass the keyboard after making your "move." If you find the task you are working on is complete, you can do a voluntary switch of the keyboard since you are moving onto a new task. Figure 19-3 shows an example of this.

Every arrow in Figure 19-3 represents a move. You can only check in when you are green, and you can check in as frequently as you like.

When you implement micro-pairing, understand that the control token of passing a keyboard back and forth might not be necessary. I commonly use workstations with two mice, two monitors, and two keyboards. In these setups, good teamwork is necessary as one person can jump in at any time.

Whether you choose promiscuous pairing or micro-pairing, frequent transitions are a surefire way to keep a team engaged. Both techniques are also excellent mentoring exercises to jump-start junior or new team members since the design is driven by

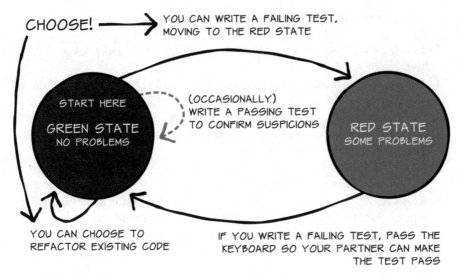

**FIGURE 19-3**   Test-Driven Development with Micro Pairing

the person writing the failing tests. When a team chooses to mix micro-pairing with promiscuous pairing, it's like riding on a roller coaster—intense but a lot of fun.

## Keys to Success

Pair programming should be a tiring activity. If you arrive home spent but upbeat, you've probably had a good day of pairing. Expect to do four to six hours of pairing per day, not eight or more. If you go home frustrated, your pairing session was likely less productive than it could have been.

Understand that not everything needs to be paired. Pairing is great for communicating design and for mentoring, but if you have a bunch of fairly straightforward bug fixes or are simply implementing a minor feature in an already fleshed out design, pairing might not be worthwhile.

Traditional pairing is not a bad practice. Having a strategist and tactician is a good idea and provides satisfactory results. For most people, however, staying engaged for long periods of pairing is difficult. Explanations for this could include social loafing (the tendency to slack off when working in a group) or the fact that having to interact with another person on what is ordinarily a solitary experience could be distracting or tiring. Whatever the cause, the fact is that people tend to check out. When you find that happening on your team, you should take action.

The first thing you should do is remove any other distractions. Distractions cause huge issues, and in a pair these issues are doubled. Consider turning off email, instant messaging, and mobile phones for a set amount of time. Then, dedicate ten minutes every so often for email and phone calls. Give people some escape or down-time. If you must have access to a phone while pairing, put a common phone in the team room so when the phone rings, everyone is distracted. That way, the distraction will end sooner.

Next, acknowledge that switching pairs frequently and having the workstation own the task may cause architectural direction problems. Use notecards to keep track of decisions and reference important information.

Look for other ways to tap into beginner's mind. If someone wants to learn a new skill, put him on a task where he can try something he hasn't done before. Belshee did this with success and documented it in his paper. Especially when paired with some-one who is highly skilled in a particular area, the inexperienced can learn quickly while bringing a fresh perspective to the task at hand.

If you go down the path of micro-pairing, understand that it is essential to switch the keyboard. No cheating. The keyboard must pass. This forces conversation and drives the design.

Successful pair programming, where people are engaged and the design is clean, is possible without the use of these techniques. If you can keep people focused with traditional pairing, great. If not, try some of the practices listed in this chapter. You might be surprised at how much more effective you can be.

# References

[COCKBURN]   Cockburn, Alistair, and Laurie Williams. 2000. "The Costs and Benefits of Pair Programming" (PDF). Proceedings of the First International Con-ference on Extreme Programming and Flexible Processes in Software Engineering (XP2000). http://collaboration.csc.ncsu.edu/laurie/Papers/XPSardinia.PDF.

[BELSHEE]   Belshee, Arlo. 2005. "Promiscuous Pairing and Beginner's Mind: Embrace Inexperience." Proceedings of the Agile Development Conference.

[PROVOST 01]   Provost, Peter. "Micro-Pairing Defined." Personal website. http://www.peterprovost.org/blog/post/Micro-Pairing-Defined.aspx (accessed 11 January 2011).

[HEDDEN]   Hedden, Trey, and John Gabrieli. 2006. "The Ebb and Flow of Atten-tion in the Human Brain." *Nature Neuroscience* 9, 863–865.

[WEINBERG]   Weinberg, Rick. "Jansen Falls after Learning of Sister's Death." ESPN. com. http://sports.espn.go.com/espn/espn25/story?page=moments/87 (accessed 30 January 2011).

[LACEY]   Lacey, Mitch. 2006. "Adventures in Promiscuous Pairing: Seeking Begin-ner's Mind." Proceedings of the Agile Development Conference.

[PROVOST 02]   Provost, Peter. Personal website. http://www.peterprovost.org/blog/post/The-Pair-Programming-TDD-Game.aspx (accessed 11 January 2011).

[CUNNINGHAM]   Cunningham, Ward. "Pair Programming Ping Pong Pattern." C2 website. http://c2.com/cgi/wiki?PairProgrammingPingPongPattern (accessed 1 April 2011).

# Chapter 20

# ADDING NEW TEAM MEMBERS

Established teams sometimes need to add new team members in the middle of a project. Whether the cause is attrition, company reorganization, accelerated deadlines, increased workload, or something else, it's crucial for new team members to be added thoughtfully and integrated quickly. Even in the best-case scenario, teams will temporarily slow down as they adjust to having new people in their midst and as new team members learn the ropes. When the wrong team member is added or the right member is added without a plan, this slowdown can be long and drawn out, proving Brooks' Law, which states "adding manpower to a late software project makes it later" [BROOKS].

The good news is that with some forethought and planning, teams can quickly return to a high-functioning state by helping new team members assimilate quickly to a new environment and a new system. Let's find out how one team dealt with the need to add manpower to comply with new dates in a contract.

## The Story

"I can't believe they're asking us to move up the release *and* add new features. Are you sure there is nothing we can do?" asked Charles.

"Nothing," said Stephanie, the team's product owner. "The new deadline and features are a contractual requirement, and we have no choice but to comply. The best thing for us to do at this point is to reshuffle the product backlog, write any new stories, and drop those that aren't required. We know our velocity, and this new work is at least pretty familiar to us. It's just a pain."

"Yeah, you're right Stephanie," said Mary-Kate. "We just need to keep our heads up and get through it."

For the next three days the team worked with Stephanie to get the product backlog in order. Several calls to the customer and some intense story workshops resulted in an updated product backlog and a release plan they were confident in. They knew, though, that management probably would still not like the result. Stephanie pulled together a meeting with management and the team to go over the findings.

Stephanie kicked off the meeting. "Thank you all for coming. We all know the reason we are here so let me cut to the chase and answer the question on the table, 'Can we hit the date and integrate all the new third-party functionality you are asking for?' The answer is hard to explain. It's both no and yes, and each has strings attached."

Chris, the general manager, went first, "Great news, Stephanie. Team, thanks for pulling this together. I'll let our VP know that you can commit to this."

"Hold on a minute, Chris," said Stephanie. "You haven't heard the strings. We can't commit to the new work and the accelerated timetable without adding a new person to the team. And not just any person. We need Dennis."

"Dennis is not available, Stephanie. You know that," said Chris.

"I do know that. But you asked me how we could make this happen. I'm telling you that to do it, we need Dennis. Dennis has the competencies we need. He understands how we work, and his personal values system is the right fit for the team. If we are going to make this happen, we need Dennis. This is a blocking issue for you to solve," said Stephanie.

After 30 minutes of negotiation, Chris caved.

"Fine, fine... You can have Dennis. We'll find a way to get the work done on his other project with someone else," said Chris.

Stephanie smiled. "Thank you. He's already prepped and ready to go. We've started transitioning him already."

"You sure don't waste any time, Stephanie. I know adding a new person isn't a cure-all, though. How will you get Dennis up to speed and still hit the compressed date?" asked Chris.

"Oh, we've got our ways," Stephanie said, and she left the office with the team.

"So, how are we going to get Dennis up to speed?" asked Charles. "Each of us has joined another project midstream at one time or another. It's never as easy as it seems and always slows the project down. How are we going to address this?"

Stephanie stopped to answer. "On another project I was on recently we had this come up. One of the team members devised a creative way to get the person integrated, and it's what I propose we do here.

"First, the new member was required to pair program with all the existing team members in turn to learn the system and ask questions. We are already pairing and working in a shared space, so this will be easy to implement. Understand, though, that it also means we can't expect anything productive from Dennis right out of the gate. After all, in pairing sessions he'll be watching more than he's writing code."

"Second, to help speed his development, we also need to write a written test and administer it weekly. I'm talking 20 to 30 questions that illustrate the system and our team makeup. We'll focus on the architecture, our processes, and our culture. We'll expect him to fail the test miserably at first, but by showing him what he doesn't know (and what we expect and want him to know), we can focus his learning on the elements that are most important to us. How's that sound?" asked Stephanie.

Mary-Kate went first. "So let me get this straight. We are under a compressed schedule, and we can't expect anything out of Dennis for a sprint or two? And you want us to write a test for him and then, I'm guessing, grade it or review it?"

Stephanie nodded her head.

"Stephanie, what benefits do you think this will give us?" asked Charles.

Stephanie pondered the question for a minute and came up with a story. "When I was in high school, I did a study-abroad program to Spain. I had studied Spanish for three years and had received good grades, so I thought that this trip to Spain would be no problem. Boy, was I wrong! I struggled with the language and butchered it pretty soundly for the first month. After a month, however, I noticed that my language skills had increased exponentially. When I came home after five months, I was fluent in Spanish. I learned that if you want to learn something, you have two options: Study it from the sidelines or immerse yourself in it—all of it—so that you pick it up much more quickly."

Stephanie continued, "We want to give Dennis the same kind of immersive experience. He needs to get right in the thick of things and write code in pairs with all of you. He needs to know what he's there to learn and what questions to ask (and we need to know that he understands what we're trying to convey): That's where the test comes in. At first, he will ask questions that you might find annoying, but after a month or so, we should see him really improving and, hopefully, contributing to the design and writing mainline code."

The team nodded in agreement.

"I guess we have a test to write and a schedule to develop to make sure Dennis is well immersed, then," said Mary-Kate. "Let's get started."

## The Model

Scrum teams pride themselves on being amenable to change. The team in our story was no different. They showed extreme flexibility in taking on a new deadline and a different scope. They also had the support of management, who understood the importance of team culture and having the right fit and was willing to make sacrifices to give the team the right new member.

Even with all that in place, though, you must be prepared for the fact that when any established team assimilates new members, that team naturally falls back into the forming and storming stages, as proposed by Bruce Tuckman in his 1965 article, "Developmental Sequence in Small Groups" [TUCKMAN].

Tuckman laid out four stages: forming, storming, norming, and performing. Consider, for example, a four-person rowing team.

In the first stage, forming, the team is learning how to work together. Everyone is "figuring people out." People are assessing who the perceived leader on the team will be. Politics and individualism play a large role as people try to highlight their own performance and establish themselves. On a rowing team, forming could be as simple as learning how to have the team put their oars in the water at the same time.

In the second stage, storming, the team is now beginning to show signs of cohesion—of gelling—as the interpersonal issues start to resolve. Though conflict still exists, the team is beginning to focus its energy on solving its collective problems and working things out together. On a rowing team, storming could be trying to get everyone to pull the oar back at the same time, regardless of the amount of force everyone is pulling with.

In the third stage, norming, the team is starting to really work well together. Team processes are becoming instinctive and the team members trust the way they are working. People are growing friendlier toward each other; the criticism they exhibit is more productive than destructive or political. There is clarity in what each person does, and the team is comfortable with it. The team members are following the rules they have established and are on their way to being a performing team. On a rowing team, norming could be when the team begins to enter, and win, a few competitions. The team is not at the top of its class just yet but is definitely a contender.

In the fourth stage, performing, the team has reached a high level of trust. The way the team works feels natural and fluid, and the team is in a state of flow, in "the zone" if you will. Relationships are tightly bonded, and each person is comfortable with criticism. The team addresses and solves problems as needed, and individuals are not afraid to ask for help or show weakness. The team is improving daily. In terms of a rowing team, performing would be competing for and even contending for the gold medal in the Olympics. Everyone's oar enters the water at the same time, each rower pulls with the same force, the oars exit simultaneously and at the same pitch, and the rowers shift their weight as one fluid motion instead of four distinct bodies.

Tuckman modeled his theory in the following way, as illustrated in Figure 20-1.

Although reforming and restorming are inevitable following a change to the team, teams should spend as little time as possible going through each stage (see Figure 20-2).

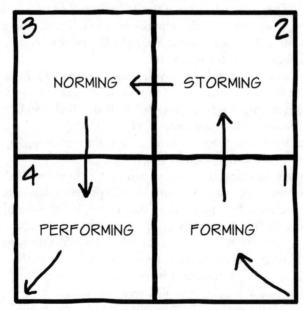

**FIGURE 20-1**   Tuckman's stages of group development

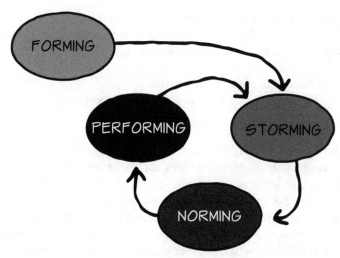

**FIGURE 20-2**     Ideally groups are able to minimize the time it takes to go through the phases again

In our story, Stephanie understood that taking on an additional person would temporarily slow down the team, as they reformed and stormed, but she also knew she could shorten the time the team spent in chaos by choosing someone whose values naturally aligned with those of the team, immersing this new person in the team's culture, and accelerating his learning through focused study.

Reforming a team is challenging and hard work. However, with the right attitude and willingness of the team—again, alignment of cultural values—it can be done. Take for example one of the high-performing teams I've worked on in the past. After a successful project, we split up to work on separate projects. Since then, we've gotten back together again for a few new projects. Whenever we've reformed, we've been able to reach a performing state within a week. And when we've had to add a new person to the mix (who we've chosen), it's taken us a little longer, but we've still returned to a performing state fairly quickly.

## The Exercise

The first step in fully integrating someone new into an existing team is to choose the right person. When you add someone to the team, look at his personal values system first. Is the person open to change? Flexible? Humble? A team player? Open to learning?

If you answer yes to these questions, then move on to the skills. Does the person have the skills needed to do the job? Values trump skills nearly every time because skills are so much easier to teach. In our story, the team chose Dennis because of his personal values system and his competencies. They knew he would integrate into the team culture nicely.

The next step is to write a test to help focus the learning. The team is responsible for creating the questions. The new team member is responsible for taking the test at the end of each week. Some of my favorite questions are as follows:

- Describe the architecture of the system.
- Tell us why pair programming and TDD are important.
- Who owns the code?

Mix technical questions with those that focus on culture and values.

The first time the team member takes the test, many of the technical answers should be blank, and some of the culture questions might be off base. By the end of the second week, however, the culture questions should be easy and the technical details should begin to appear. You should be worried if the newbie continues to answer questions such as who owns the code with, "I own such-and-such section of the application and Bobby owns this other section" instead of the correct answer for a high-performing team: The team owns the code.

# Keys to Success

Though keeping teams together for the long term is ideal, the reality is that companies often shift people from project to project. The best thing a Scrum team can do to prevent this from being a recurring theme is to make visible the pain that disrupting teams brings. The key to success when faced with integrating new team members is to accept that some backsliding will occur and to choose new team members wisely.

## Accept the Drop in Velocity

A change to team chemistry will result in some backtracking. If you have ever played or watched sports, you know that when a new player joins the team, the team dynamics are thrown off. The team, once a high-performing delivery monster, reverts to its basic form as it integrates its new team member. Consider what would happen if a sports team changed its starting lineup for every game. The results would be disastrous. Yet, businesses believe that somehow they can add or subtract members without affecting the team's output. Each time a team member enters or leaves, the team returns to Tuckman's *forming, storming, norming, and performing* stages. While this is inevitable, the goal is to get through these stages as quickly as possible and get back to being the high-performing team you were before the change. The other thing to consider when adding new team members is that it sometimes takes longer to get the new team member up to speed than there is time remaining on the project.

## Choose Wisely

Each team's culture is unique. As discussed in Chapter 3, "Using Team Consultants to Optimize Team Performance," you can choose a team consultant to help you for expert advice–type work or limited engagements. If the person is going to be a core team member, however, the chosen member should be like-minded and able to adapt quickly. For this reason, teams should try to avoid having team members forced on them based solely on availability. The right person is not necessarily the available person. After all, availability is not a skill set. While it may take a little longer to find the right person, doing so is crucial to the team's ability to return to a performing state quickly. Give people the authority to choose who will be added to (or subtracted from) their team. Forcing teams to accept a team member who doesn't mesh well with the existing team can have catastrophic effects, as outlined in Chapter 21, "When Cultures Collide."

## Risky Business

Adding new team members is especially risky when only one or two teams in your company are doing Scrum. Finding new team members from within non-agile groups who share the culture of the Scrum team is often difficult or impossible. The team members in our story were able to find a desirable new addition and had the support of management in freeing that person from previous commitments. Teams faced with uncooperative management or forced to accept a noncompatible new member aren't always so lucky. In these cases, teams often cannot find the way back to being a high-performing team. The next chapter discusses what to do when culture clashes force teams into a nonproductive state.

# References

[BROOKS]   Brooks, Frederick P., Jr. 1995. *The Mythical Man Month*. Boston, MA: Addison-Wesley.

[TUCKMAN]   Tuckman, Bruce. 1965. "Developmental sequence in small groups." *Psychological Bulletin*. 63, 6, 384–399.

Chapter 21

# WHEN CULTURES COLLIDE

Scrum teams strive to create an atmosphere where people can enjoy the process of producing excellent work yet still meet business goals and remain profitable. Getting a team to a level where this is possible is often a struggle, but with management support Scrum teams can reach a high-performing, rich mix of fun and accountability and can often out-deliver their peer teams.

The chemistry the team has created, however, is fragile. Its culture and ability to deliver effectively can be thrown off balance when someone is added to the team in the middle of a project. We saw in Chapter 20, "Adding New Team Members," that when the right team member is added in the right way, Scrum teams can quickly recover from such a change. What happens, though, when teams are forced to accept a new team member who is not a good cultural fit, someone who is not flexible, capable, or agile savvy?

We join ChemTeam, a high-performing team who, like the team in Chapter 20, needed to add a team member, but, unlike our previous team, was unable to hand-pick the new team member.

## The Story

ChemTeam had been working together for months, and the bonds that had formed between the team members were strong. The team was disciplined and focused, executing on its deliverables and delighting customers. The people on the team trusted each other and felt comfortable with the team's balance of conflict and camaraderie. They were a performing team.

One fateful day, in the middle of a project, a director in the company came to the team with a new business idea. This business idea, in his mind, would radically change their world. It nearly did. But not in ways he intended.

"Guys, great news!" he shouted. "We have an opportunity to work with Wirelacorp!"

Most of ChemTeam stared blankly back at the manager. "Wirelacorp? I've heard of them. Don't they provide Internet access in public locations?" asked Kamiar.

"Indeed they do," he said. "And we are *this close* to signing a contract with them that will allow our small business and user base to be able to access the Wirelacorp network, at no additional cost to our users!"

At this point, the team member's blank looks turned to ones of slight concern. The project that they had been working on was designed to focus only on the users the business had on its own network—it didn't include third-party interfaces or integrations for things like the Wirelacorp network. Not ones to be daunted by sudden change, though, the team immediately began to think of ways it could alter the service offering to take advantage of this opportunity.

Seeing her team beginning to get excited about the challenge, Shauna, Scrum-Master, spoke up, "We can do this," she said confidently. "Just give us a couple of weeks to clean up what we are working on. Then we can reprioritize our product backlog with you and the other stakeholders to give you a new release plan."

"No time!" said the director. "We have to get this working ASAP; this deal is critical to our business!"

"We would prefer to finish the work on this sprint before we change gears," explained Shauna. "But if this is truly urgent, we can abort this sprint, which will essentially result in us dropping what we're doing, and begin reprioritizing right away. Even then, if you want us to provide you *accurate-enough* estimates for you to build a go-to-market strategy, we need at least three days, and you will have to accept the priority of the backlog."

"I can only give you until the end of the day," said the director. "Do the best you can."

For the remainder of the day, ChemTeam assessed its backlog, the current state of the system, and the requirements to integrate and interface with Wirelacorp's network. The team proposed a timeline that represented the bare minimum to meet the needs of the business and that it felt comfortable in delivering. They then presented it to the director the next morning.

"Team, great work, but we need to bring this in by three months to meet the contract dates that we have been discussing with Wirelacorp," explained the director. "I need you to make this happen—tell me what you need."

The team members were visibly frustrated. They said they would come back in a couple hours with some plans on how they could pull in the schedule *without* taking on the technical debt that would come from hacking the system together.

It was now eight at night. The director was still in his office, waiting for the team to finish its deliberation. The team went to the director with the only solution it could come up with in the face of so many immovable obstacles. Shauna said, "We have a solution for how we think we can bring this in, but it is not ideal and may negatively impact us overall from a team and technical perspective. You need to understand this before we can continue."

As the director nodded eagerly, Shauna continued, "The only way to get this done more quickly than we estimated is to bring in more people, but not just any warm bodies will do. We have looked at the skills and competencies we need on this project and have identified two people who, if added, would enable us to reach our goal: Julio and Nancy. Julio is available; Nancy is not. For this to have the best chance of success, we need both of them."

"You can have Julio, but you absolutely cannot have Nancy. She is on a project critical to the business and cannot be taken away from it."

"Isn't this a project critical to the business as well? We have been working on this for eight months. And we are close to the final release," countered the ScrumMaster.

"All projects are critical," said the director. "And you cannot have Nancy. You can have Katherine; she is available."

Katherine was a seasoned developer. She had been considered by the team already but had been readily dismissed. While she had all the skills the team was looking for, she lacked the core values to work in a collaborative environment. Some of the team members had worked with her on past projects and had expressed concerns: She had fought her last team on the idea of daily standups, arguing that they were a waste of time, even though the rest of the team found the daily communication highly valuable. Shauna had also worked with Katherine on a past project. She had noticed that Katherine often rushed and had buggy code as a result. When the QA team members on the past project spoke with her about ways to create cleaner code, she attacked them, saying they did not know how to do their jobs. It was clear to the team that, while Katherine had the technical skills, her competencies and attitude about working on a team were vastly different than the cultural values established by ChemTeam.

Shauna shared these concerns with the director. He was not impressed. "You guys said you need two people on the team to make this work. These are the two I can give you. We all agree that Katherine can do the work. It's up to you to find a way to work with her."

The team members were no less skeptical, but felt they had no choice but to take Katherine. The team reluctantly agreed to the new schedule date and the new team members. Both Katherine and Julio started working on the project the following day.

ChemTeam tried to do things the right way. Its members knew they needed to baseline new team members and used the *adding new people to the team* approach (see Chapter 20). They created a survey and had both Katherine and Julio take it as a baseline measure of their knowledge of the team's process, tools, and project. The survey was to be repeated once a week so the team could track how well the new members had internalized both the process and the product. Both Katherine and Julio were enthusiastic at first. As time went on, it was clear from Julio's answers and his work that he not only understood the system but also had embraced the practices of the team.

Despite improvement in system knowledge, though, Katherine showed little improvement in the areas of process and culture. Katherine questioned the benefits of TDD, pairing, and working in a shared space at every opportunity. More often than not, work was interrupted to discuss the merits of a certain agile practice or principle. Her vocal skepticism was beginning to erode the team. Velocity decreased, quality suffered, and team morale fell to an all-time low. Shauna did her best to handle Katherine's criticism so the team could stay focused, but at the beginning of week four, Katherine snapped.

"I've answered this stupid survey week after week. I've already proven to you that I can build this system. I do not care that we are doing TDD. I hate working in this space, and I would be better off just writing code by myself in my office. This has got to be the most inefficient way of working ever! I could have written half of the system by now!"

Shauna tried one last time to bring Katherine around. "Katherine, as we have discussed many times, the reason the team is building the application using agile principles and practices is to avoid the pitfalls each of us has run into on past projects that were more traditional in nature. We are not perfect. This is hard work, both from a development standpoint and from a personal growth standpoint. We are all learning this as we go, and we make mistakes."

She continued, "Regardless of how we might feel individually, we are a team, and we need to continue to work as a team. The mere fact that we are doing TDD has lowered our bug count by a factor of nine compared to the other teams. Also, you and Julio have been able to get up to speed on this system in less than four weeks, and you now know it like the back of your hand. Without working in a shared space and pairing, this would have never happened."

"I cannot work this way. I will not work this way!" said Katherine as she stormed off.

By this point, Katherine's destructive influence had spread throughout the team. Many were beginning to argue the relative benefits of long-established practices. One day, a team member became so frustrated with the sudden infighting and bickering that he squeezed a can of freshly opened soda-water, spraying it on the walls, the computers, the desks, and, of course, the other team members. He stormed off, frustrated because of the team's deteriorating cohesion and trust. Something had to be done.

Shauna and the team members went back to the director without Katherine. They showed him the sprint and release burndowns that were clearly trending toward a lower velocity. They shared with him not only their frustrations but also the fact that bug counts were up and the unit test code coverage numbers were down. They recommended that they drop Katherine to salvage the project. They were turned down flat.

"Look, I know it's difficult, but it can't be helped," said the director. "My job is to get this contract signed. Your job is to make the deadline. You've told me you *need* two people to get this done. *She* needs something to work on. Work it out."

After the meeting, Shauna saw the pain on the faces of each team member. Even Julio looked beaten. She asked herself what was more important—the team and delivering the project or the fact that Katherine did not have anything else to work on?

Shauna decided it was time for action. She and the team outlined a plan that would address both the requirement of the director to give Katherine something to work on and the need for the team to return to its desired high-performing state. All that was left was to tell Katherine.

The next morning, Shauna pulled Katherine aside.

"Katherine, look, I see that you're not happy, and you see the team is not happy, right?" said Shauna. Katherine responded with a cautious *yes*, wondering where this was going.

"Well, I talked to the director about it. He said you can't come off the project because you do not have another project to move onto."

Katherine nodded in agreement.

"At the same time, if things continue as they are, this project is going to implode, and everyone, including me, will have a big black eye from it. I've got a plan on how we can avoid this *and* keep people happy in the short term," said Shauna.

The plan that Shauna laid out was to have Katherine remain on the team, but only on paper. Katherine would work in her office on non-system-critical tasks, away from the team space until the project and its associated time crunch was over. At that point, they could all discuss the issues and determine a long-term plan. Katherine agreed.

Katherine kept her distance from the team, only coming to the daily standup meetings—just down the hall from the director's office—to show that she was still on the project. The team was able to stay focused and its velocity returned. The code coverage numbers increased and overall project quality went up. Even Julio, who had a background in testing, was now writing code.

Four weeks went by before the director asked Shauna into his office.

"The team seems to have turned around, but I don't see Katherine. What part of the system is she working on?"

Shauna thought long and hard on how to answer this.

"She is working on non-system-critical tasks," she said. "I did this because the team was not going to meet the contract dates on time with the quality our customers demand. Also, several of the team members had threatened to quit the company rather than work with her. It was the right thing to do."

Visibly disturbed at being countermanded, the director exploded, "You took Katherine off the project even after I *told you* to keep her on?"

"Yes, I did," said Shauna with steadfast clarity.

Shauna sat as the director expressed his dissatisfaction with her. He ranted and raved about how what she did was insubordination and that she should be fired for it. After a few minutes, Shauna interrupted him.

"Let me ask you a question," said Shauna. "What is more important at our company, keeping people busy or delivering for our customers?"

"That's not the point," said the director, pounding his fist on the desk.

"It is the point. Please answer the question," pressed Shauna, now getting visibly frustrated. "Keeping people busy or delivering—which is it?"

Reluctantly, the director answered, "Well, delivery, of course, but that is no excuse for what…" Shauna interrupted yet again.

"I agree. I shouldn't have done what I did. Not because it wasn't the right thing to do but because you should have been the one to do it. Many times, I asked you to intervene. Each time I asked you said no. You were not willing to take action. It is my job as ScrumMaster to keep the team healthy and the project moving. You were limiting my ability to do my job, and you were not interested in hearing solutions or helping me fix the issue with Katherine, so I fixed it as best I could," Shauna finished.

"It's a bad precedent to set," said the director.

"A worse precedent to set is inaction by management," responded Shauna.

Shauna watched for a painfully long and silent moment as the director's face went from a deep shade of red to light red, and then to an almost normal skin tone. He took a deep breath and said, "Look, I understand what you did and why you did it. I have been under a lot of pressure with this deal and am just thankful that it's over."

"What do you mean, *it's over*?" asked Shauna.

"Didn't I tell you? Earlier this week the contract negotiations collapsed. We are not going to do the deal with Wirelacorp. It means we can go back to where we were," said the director.

"Uhhh," said Shauna.

"So, how long until we can deliver on the original functionality? Next month?"

And that is another story in and of itself.

## The Model

Let's look back at the story. The original team was a well-oiled machine. It had become accustomed to its own way of working and developed its own culture. Yet, the introduction of one uncooperative team member almost caused the team to implode. What happened?

In a nutshell, Katherine fit the culture of the larger group and company, but she did not fit the culture of the team. This culture was formed as the team grew and worked together on its own. Julio was open to trying new things and had the right mindset, but Katherine did not. Shauna and her team identified this disparity but were ignored by management. I call the type of behavior Katherine exhibited as part of the team *social deviance.*

Deviance in society can be defined as acting or doing things in a way that violates the established cultural norms. Cultural norms apply on many levels, from personal to family to work to society. For example, stealing violates larger *societal* cultural norms in the same way that, say, not performing certain development activities (such as test-driven development) violates established *team* cultural norms.

In 1938, Robert K. Merton published "Social Structure and Anomie" [MERTON]. In this paper, he proposed strain theory. Strain theory was an attempt to identify reasons for varying crime rates between different social classes. Merton identified two social structures: cultural goals, which were culturally assigned goals and aspirations, and institutional means, which outlined the acceptable means for achieving the goals. Merton theorized that cultural goals were what all people would want and expect throughout their lives, and institutionalized means were the ways to achieve

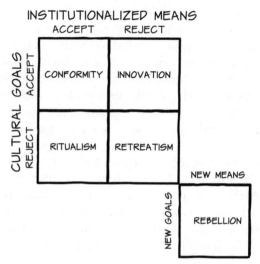

**FIGURE 21-1**    Robert K. Merton's topology of deviant behavior

the cultural goals, such as obeying established society standards. Merton stated that a balance would occur as long as individuals felt the cultural goals were being achieved by adhering to the "institutionally accepted mode of doing so." This is illustrated in Figure 21-1.

Merton identifies five attributes of strain: conformity, ritualism, retreatism, innovation, and rebellion. In conformity, people accept both the goals and means of society and chug though life. People who fall in the ritualism bucket have given up on the goals of society but continue conforming to the means to achieve them. Retreatism is where people reject both the goals and the means. When people reject both the goals and the means and replace them with new goals and means to reach them, they are in rebellion. In innovation, people accept the goals of society but use different means to achieve them, traditionally those of crime.

Take for example a university student. The student's cultural goal is graduation; the institutional means to achieve this goal are to attend class, study, and perform well on exams and papers.

- If a student does all this and graduates, the student has conformed.
- If a student does not study and does not pass exams, but keeps going to class anyway, the student is being ritualistic—he is going through the motions with no hope of achieving the goal.
- If a student knows that he will not graduate because his grades are subpar and as a result stops attending classes or studying, and instead plays video games in his dorm room, he has retreated.

- A student in retreat may tire of his drifter status (or have his funding cut off) and forego his education all together. He may begin to protest that education is overrated and that the goal of graduation is not one that people should strive to achieve. He will identify new goals (starting his own business, for example) and devise new means to achieve them. A student doing this is in rebellion.
- Lastly, if the student still has the desire to graduate university but is not able to do so using the accepted means (e.g., studying), he may resort to innovative, yet criminal, methods, such as cheating or plagiarism.

Businesses, too, have established societies and cultures. The societal rules and cultural norms are the institutional means. They propagate throughout the company, impacting and directing each employee. In business, cultural goals are often communicated as company goals, which employees of the company can achieve or fail to accomplish. Therefore, when thinking of businesses, I replace Merton's *Cultural Goals* with *Company Goals* and his *Reject* and *Accept* with *Fail* and *Succeed,* as illustrated in Figure 21-2.

With this small modification, let's consider how Merton's topology applies to a software organization where the company goal is to produce high-quality software by a certain release date, and the institutional means to do so are to work in a traditional, plan-driven way, hitting milestones and relying on up-front plans to steer the project:

- **Conformity**—Team members *follow* the institutional means and achieve the company goals.
    - Leads to high quality, morale, etc.
    - Employees have bought into the program.
    - People are engaged.
- **Ritualism**—Team members *accept* the institutional means but fail to meet company goals.
    - Low quality, low morale, etc.
    - Show up and do the job.
    - People are disengaged.
- **Retreatism**—Team members *do not accept* institutional means and fail to meet company goals.
    - Low quality, low morale, etc.
    - Show up but don't work.
    - Actively disengaged and know it.
- **Innovation**—Team members devise new means to be successful in achieving the company goals.
    - Can be negative (working the system) or positive (finding new ways to accomplish the same goals).
    - If it is positive, innovation leads to high quality, high morale, etc.
    - Unlike rebellion, only the means are different, not the goals.
    - Will cause friction in the organization.

- **Rebellion**—Team members devise new means and develop new goals that build on the company goals.
  - The means might be quite different.
  - Company goals are still met; team sets goals beyond company goals.
  - Team culture can be quite different.
  - Will cause friction in the organization.

Leaders and executives establish institutional means to achieve company goals. Sometimes, however, new means can be created and coexist within the institutional means established by business. In our story, Shauna's team had established its own means (TDD, pair programming, group space) to achieve the company goals. The mindset change that accompanies these means, however, had also caused them to think and work quite differently than the rest of the organization.

Shauna's team was unique inside the company. Most of the other employees were ritualistic: They accepted the means to do their work but typically failed at achieving the goals (e.g., delivery). This was evident by looking at factors inside the company. For example, bug counts were high, quality was low, morale was low, there was a medium amount of turnover, people had little or no passion for their work, they were not proud of their work, and most teams were not high performing.

Shauna's team had grown tired of failure and had decided to try something new, so they had adopted Scrum and XP. By using new institutional means to achieve the company goals, Shauna's team moved out of ritualism and into innovation, as shown in Figure 21-2.

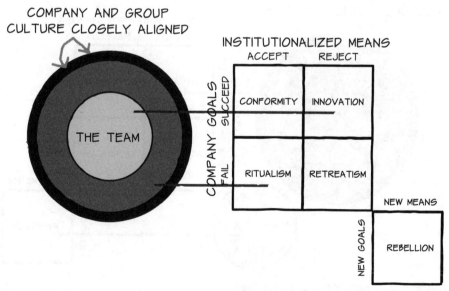

**FIGURE 21-2**    Shauna's team experiments with innovative means

As the team learned to work and turned into a high-performing team, it not only used new means but also began to establish new goals for itself based on its heightened understanding of Scrum and XP. These goals included the company goals of delivering software by a certain release date, but also included others centered around personal growth and becoming better at the craft of software development. The team's new goals included the following:

- Ship high quality software that meets customer needs.
- Allow the team to be responsive to changing business needs.
- Work at a sustainable pace while still delivering on schedule.

These cultural goals were unique to the team and did not span the company. The team's means were similarly unique and included the following:

- Work in a collaborative workspace.
- Pair program.
- Design using test-driven development.
- Collectively estimate and commit to the work.

As the gap widened between the team and the company in terms of means and goals, the team moved out of innovation and into what the rest of the organization would classify as rebellion (see Figure 21-3).

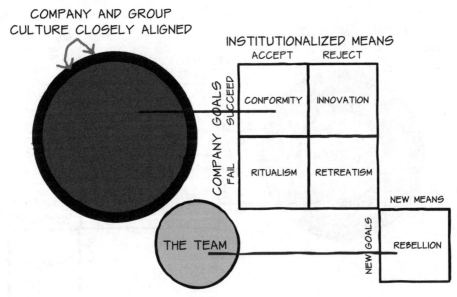

**FIGURE 21-3**   Team moving to rebellion

We find the team in this rebellious state at the beginning of the story. They are high-performing and achieving not only the company goals but the team's goals as well. Their director, however, is not in sync with the team. He throws a new set of objectives at the team in the middle of the project, ones that threaten the team's own goals. Though the team offers a plan that would allow it to continue to meet its goals while incorporating the new company goals, the director is less concerned with the team's goals than with the company's goals.

Enter Katherine. Katherine was a conformist in her company's culture. She accepted the established means and, though she seldom achieved them, did not reject the company's goals. When she was placed on a team with a radically different agenda, she rejected the goals and the means to achieve them. Her opposing viewpoint made her a deviant to the accepted social norms of the Scrum team. In response, she at first rebelled. She did not have new means or new goals to introduce, but she did attempt to bring the rest of the team back to the company goals and institutional means that she was used to working within.

Her rebellion created so much conflict within the team that it could not function. Too much of the team's focus and energy were spent on trying to work with Katherine. As a result, the work, the morale, and team performance suffered.

Once the team realized that Katherine could not fit into its culture, the team tried to remove her and her destructive influence. When that idea was rejected, the team asked Katherine to retreat, leaving the other members to work in peace and return to "normal."

While this worked for the team, it was a risky move for Shauna. The steps Shauna took to remove Katherine from the day-to-day team activities were a true last resort, one that might not be worth the risk to many of us. She could (and should) have taken different steps to move her toward conformity.

# Keys to Success

The best way to deal with culture clash is avoid adding members to your team that won't fit in. Ideally, teams should be able to control their own destinies, so that the team members themselves determine the composition of each team. The reality is, however, that sometimes we are forced to take people in that we would not have chosen on our own. When that happens, teams need to work with what they are given and stay the course in the face of obstacles.

## Control Your Own Destiny

The best way to keep from having a deviant in your midst is to ensure that the existing team has a say in choosing new team members for your team. I try to follow these simple rules of thumb on my projects:

- Let the team interview and pick its own members.
- Let the team decide the fate of team members.

When I was in university, I took several classes where the professor required us to deliver term papers and presentations as a team. The teams were self-forming and self-managing. Looking back, we were very agile. We picked our team members, we collaborated, we worked together, and we delivered together. We had team members who sometimes did not pull their weight—I can't blame them. I went to a school that was on the coast and had great surfing. These people spent time at the beach and came to us, usually at the end of the paper and presentation development cycle, and said, "Hey, can I get my name on this?"

As you can imagine, we said no, and they often didn't pass. We were empowered to decide the fate of our team members. If you did the work, you were allowed to share the credit. If you did not do the work, you failed. It was very simple at that point.

While we can't always work that way in business, we can educate management about the benefits of allowing teams to choose their own team members and ask for the power to move members off the team who are doing more harm than good. See Chapter 3, "Using Team Consultants to Optimize Team Performance," for more information.

## Work with What You Have

Let's face it. Teams are not always empowered to do what they think is right when it comes to their own health. So how can we keep the damage to a minimum when we have a new teammate thrust upon us? First, when a new member is added, take a moment to assess that person's conformity level and background. If the new team member is coming from a culture that clashes with your team and has a history of rebelling against, retreating from, or innovating to get around those norms, you should be encouraged. After all, rebellion itself isn't bad. On a team who is not yet performing well, a rebellious member can actually push the team toward desirable goals.

If the new team member is in conformance with or ritualistic toward a culture that clashes with your own, there is still no need to panic. You should expect, however, to have to do more to lay the groundwork on how your own culture works and what will be expected of a new team member. That might mean educating her about Scrum and agile principles and helping her to see the reason behind the choices your team makes. Do all you can to help new members conform to, rather than rebel against, the goals and means your high-performing team has established or is striving for.

Second, while doing your best to bring the person into your culture, be open to the new ideas and methods the person might bring to the team. I go back to many of Dale Carnegie's principles, as summarized in *The Golden Book*:

- Become a friendlier person.
- Win people to your way of thinking.
- Be a leader.
- Break the Worry Habit.
- Cultivate a mental attitude that will bring you peace and happiness.
- Don't worry about criticism.
- Prevent fatigue and worry and keep your energy and spirits high [CARNEGIE].

When I first read the Carnegie books, I was skeptical. It was not until I really analyzed how I approach and work with people that I understood how these basic principles really make you a better person to be around—and if you are a better person to be around, people will gravitate to you.

Though I understand why the ScrumMaster in our story, Shauna, arrived at her radical solution to Katherine, it was nonetheless risky, might have cost her job, and left the team shorthanded. If Shauna had implored team members to apply the Carnegie principles, or just followed them more steadfastly herself, the team might have been able to return to its performing state even with Katherine on board. Her decision to sideline Katherine, which was necessitated in part by the time crunch she was under, was a true last resort, not a practice I would recommend in most cases.

Instead, I might have counseled the team to allow Katherine more time to become accustomed to TDD as a way of programming before forcing her to pair. If *all* code was written by pairs, perhaps the team could have compensated by asking Katherine to do more testing work and less code development. Maybe if ChemTeam had stopped worrying so much about why Katherine wasn't adjusting and had tried harder to not take her criticism personally, its members could have stayed focused on the sprint rather than one team member's difficulties. If the team had tried to win her to its way of thinking systematically and slowly, everyone might have been less frustrated.

Shauna also might have asked other leaders on the team to help keep the team focused on the sprint itself, while she personally dealt with the impediment that was Katherine. Letting Katherine assimilate more gradually might not have helped the team's velocity, but it probably wouldn't have slowed the team down either. Focusing on the positive and minimizing the negative might have gone a long way to prevent blow-ups and soft drink explosions.

## Stay the Course

When faced with a new member who is a potential deviant, the following guidelines can help keep your high-performing team on track:

- Try to keep the deviant off your team. Help management understand that *people are not interchangeable components*. Team members should be chosen with care, not plugged in based solely on availability or even a particular skill.

- Educate new team members about the team's culture and give them *time and space to adapt*, so that they are not forced to rebel or retreat.
- If a new member does begin to deviate from the team's norms, *go back to the basics* and get people comfortable with Scrum (see Chapter 1, "Scrum: Simple, not Easy"). If this fails, identify what is causing the person to shift from the established culture of the team.
- Sometimes a new team member brings a deviant point of view that can ultimately be helpful (rather than hurtful) to the team. Help the team to understand that *it is not only the new team member that has to adjust*. When team make-up changes, existing team members might have to change some of their established norms to assimilate new members.
- If deviant behavior persists (or has been festering on your team for some time), it's time to involve HR, management, or the team itself in *removing the nonconforming team member* to a more suitable team.

Whether your team is able to choose its own team members or has to take what it gets, returning to normal after a new team member is added is one of the toughest challenges an established team has to face. Sometimes just knowing that temporary pain is to be expected and that there is a route back to a performing state can make the transition quicker and easier for all involved.

# References

[MERTON]   Merton, Robert. 1938. "Social Structure and Anomie." *American Sociological Review 3*. p. 672–682.

[CARNEGIE]   Carnegie, Dale. *The Golden Book*. http://www.motivationalmagic.com/library/ebooks/inspirational/GoldenBook.pdf (accessed February 13, 2011).

# Works Consulted

Baumer, Eric P. 2007. "Untangling Research Puzzles in Merton's Multilevel Anomie Theory." *Theoretical Criminology*. February 2007, Vol. 11, Issue 1, p. 63–93.

Featherstone, Richard, and Mathieu Deflem. 2003. "Anomie and Strain: Context and Consequences of Merton's Two Theories." *Sociological Inquiry*. November 2003, Vol. 73, Issue 4, p. 471–489.

Monahan, Susanne C., and Beth A. Quinn. 2006. "Beyond 'Bad Apples' and 'Weak Leaders.'" *Theoretical Criminology*. Aug 2006, Vol. 10, Issue 3, p. 361–385, 25p.

Murphy, Daniel S., and Mathew B. Robinson. 2008. "The Maximizer: Clarifying Merton's Theories of Anomie and Strain." *Theoretical Criminology*. November 2008, Vol. 12 no. 4, p. 501–521.

Chapter 22

# SPRINT EMERGENCY PROCEDURES

One of my all-time favorite TV shows as a child was *The A-Team*. My favorite character was Hannibal Smith. He had a saying, "I love it when a plan comes together." I do, too, which is probably why I love Scrum so much.

Sometimes, though, despite all our best efforts, plans fall apart. And I "pity the fool" (as Mr. T would say) who does not have a contingency plan when things unravel. Too many times on too many projects I've seen teams get into trouble. In this chapter I share a set of emergency procedures for you to follow when a sprint goes wrong, including the last-ditch option of sprint termination.

## The Story

"Guys, I've got bad news: The rumors were true," said Mike. "They've decided to split our division into two groups effective immediately. And I'm part of that shuffle. I'm going to be moving to the new group; the rest of you, though, are staying in this one. So the good news is that at least most of the team can stay together."

Mike's teammates visibly deflated. Mike always had good ideas on how to solve problems and issues. He was a key part of the team's success and would not be easy to replace.

"That's really bad news, Mike," said Billy. "It's just not going to be the same without you. I don't know how we're to fill your shoes."

"Well," said Mike. "Start figuring it out fast. When they said 'immediately,' they meant it. I was told to come back and pack my stuff. There is a moving crew coming tomorrow to relocate me to a different building," said Mike with great disappointment.

"What?" exclaimed Billy. "You're last day is *today?*"

Mike nodded.

"What are we supposed to do?" said Mark. "We're right in the middle of a sprint. What does this mean for our project?"

"I really don't know what to say, guys," Mike answered resignedly. "I made the case for a more gradual transition but got shot down. I didn't want to press the point with the general manager in front of a room full of people," said Mike.

"Well, maybe we can convince him if we approach him through the appropriate channels," said Billy. "C'mon, Mark, let's go fix this while Mike packs."

The pair approached the group manager, Pam. She explained that while she understood their dilemma, there could be no delay in Mike's move.

"Then we need to figure out what to do about this sprint," said Billy. "We're about halfway through our four-week sprint. There's no way we finish everything we committed to with Mike gone. Can't they wait a couple more weeks and give us time to wrap some things up?"

"I know this is bad timing," said Pam. "But in the big picture, it makes the most sense for the organization to make this happen now so everyone can adjust and begin being productive again as soon as possible. I know you're frustrated. I have been in this situation before. What we did was look at how our work was structured and how it aligned to the goal and find a way to approach the solution in a different way so that we could still achieve the sprint goal. It's a form of impediment removal. Is there any way you and the team can do something different to finish out the sprint and still call it a success?"

"Different? Nothing obvious springs to mind," said Billy. "I mean, we can look at the sprint goal and see if there are some stories we can adjust and still achieve the same result. We'll need to go back and refactor more than expected, but it might work."

Mark sat there thinking.

"I'm not so sure, Billy. We can investigate it, but we were running pretty lean this sprint even before we lost Mike, which by the way, Pam, is an awfully big impediment to remedy. Plus, the research is going to take time and might not result in a solution. Meanwhile we'll be falling further behind. Our best option would be to ask for help. By that I mean, maybe we can have someone come in and help us do the work so we keep our sprint goal. Pam, do you have any ideas on who might be available?" asked Mark.

"I wish I did, guys. This whole thing caught a lot of us by surprise. When I talked to the GM last week, the plan was to transition slowly, but this came down from the top, just last night," Pam explained.

"How about Javier? Can we get him? Or Amanda? They have the experience we need and would fit well with our team," asked Billy.

"Let me think about it. Right now, I can't think of a single team that isn't in the exact same situation as you. So, let's assume for now that I can't get you any help and you can't find a different way to accomplish your sprint goal. What's Option C?" asked Pam.

"Well," said Mark, "we can reduce the scope, meaning we cut out a few stories from the sprint backlog and put them on the product backlog. This will really irritate our stakeholders, though, one group of them especially. We told them we'd have a lot of functionality built out for them in this sprint, and we told them that weeks and months ago. We can't go back on that now; they'll kill us!"

"I agree. Looking at our sprint backlog, finding ways to cut scope isn't that easy," said Billy. "The cuts we'd need to make are so deep that it might even impact some of the stories we have worked on already. I would hate to have to remove nearly completed stories from the sprint demo just because they are dependent on other stories that we had to cut."

"Then, it looks like we need to cancel the sprint," declared Pam.

"Cancel?" asked Billy and Mark together.

"Yes, cancel—or abort. Cancelling a sprint is rare, but it applies in this case. You cancel when there is a change to the business that either negates the value of the sprint goal or leaves the team incapable of meeting the sprint goal. I think we're at that point. It's the only option that seems to make sense."

"The whole team chemistry is changed," mused Billy. "It's not just about the tasks Mike was going to do. It's that we need to rethink who we are without him. I want to make it very visible to the higher-ups how a move like this affects the team and the project."

"Yep," said Mark. "Like Billy says, it's not as much about the work Mike was doing or Mike per se. It's that when you disrupt a team in midproject, there's a cost. We've got to learn how to work together effectively without him. Plus, we've got some logistics to work out. We'll have to do a complete reset: Roll back our codebase to the last sprint and start planning over. And we've got to reschedule all those meetings, too."

"You're right," said Billy, "I'd forgotten about all that. I hope it's worth it to the company, the loss that everyone is going to take on this. It's going to take us a couple of months to get back to where we were in terms of velocity."

"Agreed. Let's hope this short-term pain has quite the long-term payoff," said Pam. "We've got a lot of work to do in the meantime. Let's go talk to the product owner and make our case."

# The Model

Cancelling a sprint is a big deal, by design. It is done only in extraordinary circumstances and always as a last resort. In our story, Billy, Mark, and Pam considered four options that Jeff Sutherland affectionately calls the *Scrum Emergency Procedures*. Sutherland has told me many times that when he was a fighter pilot flying sorties over Vietnam, he had strapped to his leg a set of emergency procedures on what to do in case of an emergency while on a mission. Scrum teams have a similar checklist available to them [LEFFINGWELL].

When something unexpected occurs that will affect the team's ability to realize the sprint goal, the team has four options:

1. Remove impediments.
2. Get help.
3. Reduce scope.
4. Cancel the sprint/abort.

Teams should first try either of the first two options. Reducing scope should be a last-ditch effort that is trumped only by outright sprint cancellation. The one thing you need to remember in all this is don't do it blindly. This is a negotiation, so each step is worse than the previous one by design. Talk this through, work diligently to find options, and remember that when the team is in dire straits, its members might not be thinking clearly. As the team members try to work through the options, encourage them to communicate—with each other, with their product owner, with management. These are not decisions the team or product owner (or anyone else for that matter) should make in a vacuum. Discuss the risks and impacts and do everything in your power to find a solution. Aborting a sprint is the last resort, used only for a ship-is-sinking-type event. Cancelling should *always* be your last choice.

## Remove Impediments

In Scrum we have something called the sprint goal. The sprint goal can be something as overarching as *improve performance* or *add additional payment functionality* or as focused as *allow customers to use an American Express card*. When considering what impediments could be removed to allow you to reach the sprint goal, focus on analyzing the issues and gathering ideas on how to correct the problems. The blocking issue could be something simple, like a broken build machine, or something more complex, like a distributed team imbalance. Regardless, work as a team to identify and remove or compensate for the issues whenever possible.

## Get Help

This one is pretty straightforward. If your team is looking at its sprint backlog and finds that it cannot meet the goal, and no clear workarounds exist, ask for help. Though this works in a pinch, it does have drawbacks:

- The person won't be part of the team. Including a newbie on the project for one sprint can come with complications.
- Your velocity for that sprint might be artificially inflated because the story was completed by an outsider or a team consultant instead of a core team member.

The best way to overcome these obstacles is through communication. Let your product owner know up front what is going on. Remind the product owner that the velocity may be inflated for that sprint and not to count on that level of velocity in future sprints. Help the non-team member get up to speed quickly and keep your team informed on what is being built and how it works by pairing or finding other ways to share knowledge.

## Reduce Scope

Teams often mistakenly reach for this option first because it is the easiest. Here's the thing. While some would say that the sprint backlog is more of a forecast than a

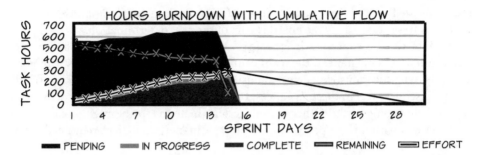

**FIGURE 22-1**   Cumulative flow diagram along with burndown

commitment, I firmly believe that when the team says it can deliver a certain amount of functionality in a sprint, it is a commitment made to the product owner and stakeholder group, who might well need to release that functionality at the end of the sprint.

Removing scope from the sprint backlog and failing to follow through on a commitment undermines trust. It's difficult enough to build trust among the team, the product owner, and the stakeholder/customer group. Any damage, no matter how slight, can degrade trust significantly. If it happens repeatedly, all involved will lose confidence in the team's ability to deliver.

Burndowns make scope cuts very visible. As Figure 22-1 shows, when you drop scope, the chart shows a big drop in work remaining and, if you do a cumulative flow diagram along with your burndown, a corresponding drop in pending work.

## Cancel the Sprint

When steps one through three fail or if they are not feasible, when you've hit rock bottom and need to press the reset button, you can cancel/abort the sprint. In fighter pilot terms, this would be the time for ejecting from the aircraft, leaving it to crash and burn while you float to the ground. As such, this is not something to take lightly. The Scrum Guide [SCHWABER] says that only the product owner may cancel a sprint; however, I find that it is always a collective team decision involving the product owner, the team, and stakeholders.

When a sprint is terminated, there are costs. All work is stopped; some of it might be lost. All meetings are cancelled. A whole new set of sprint meetings is scheduled. A new sprint planning meeting must be held immediately. Everyone affected is notified and the team begins anew.

The rule I live by is that the team resets the codebase as well, rolling its code back to the last sprint (the last known good sprint), and restarts from there. Why? Because while the team might well use some components that it had written before the sprint was cancelled, they don't know this at the time of the cancellation. The best option, therefore, is to return to the last known good state and begin again, even if the code is solid and could theoretically remain in the build. Without product owner acceptance and being tied to a sprint goal, it's just extra garbage in the code and should be deleted. A fresh start across the board is part of the cost of termination.

Sprints can be cancelled by the team or by management when, because of extraordinary circumstances, the team cannot or should not achieve the sprint goal. In highly dynamic industries, external business influences often lead to dramatically changing scope. (Yes, in these instances, the team should probably run short sprints of a week, but some don't.) Other reasons to terminate the sprint might include contract changes with a third party, running out of money, and client-requested scope changes.

At the end of the day, terminating the sprint reduces team morale and velocity. It breaks the stakeholder/team cadence and changes expected delivery points and forecasts as well. Extra communication is necessary to explain why the sprint was terminated. The team restarts with new planning meetings, building a new sprint backlog with a new goal and commitment. The team might need to address its estimated velocity as well.

In my years of working with Scrum projects, I have only had to terminate one sprint in one project. Why? A team member was suddenly moved to a new group after a reorg. It was neither pleasant nor fun, and our stakeholders were upset, but in the end, it was the best thing to do for the project.

# Keys to Success

It's hard to talk about success when we're discussing emergency measures. Any path you take will be painful. However, if you follow some general rules, you can minimize the pain.

- **Communicate**—I cannot stress this enough. This is where the values of Scrum come into play. It takes courage to take the steps needed to work through this rough patch, but communication needs to happen—and happen often.

- **Stay calm**—When things go south, it's hard not to panic. Remember that as a ScrumMaster, product owner, or team member, you need to manage the reactions of your customers and stakeholders. Take the high road and use this opportunity to highlight why Scrum is good. It offers options and flexibility, and its short cycles allow you to get on track fairly quickly, even after a catastrophic event like a termination.

- **Stay focused**—Look forward, not backward. Focus on cleaning up the sprint and getting on with getting on. The way you react will determine others' reactions. If you refuse to linger in the past but instead soldier on with a positive outlook, others will follow your lead.

# References

[LEFFINGWELL]    Leffingwell, Dean. Scaling Software Agility Blog website. http://scalingsoftwareagility.wordpress.com/2008/10/19/jeff-sutherland%E2%80%99s-sprint-emergency-landing-procedure/ (accessed 2 January 2011).

[SCHWABER]    Schwaber, Ken, and Jeff Sutherland. "Scrum Guide 2011 Edition." http://www.scrum.org/storage/scrumguides/Scrum%20Guide%20-%202011.pdf (accessed 1 August 2011). Also available at http://www.mitchlacey.com in the resources section.

# PART IV

# ADVANCED SURVIVAL TECHNIQUES

Chapter 23

# SUSTAINABLE PACE

*Our team works at a sustainable pace*—You hear it all the time, but what exactly does it mean? Is there a standard pace that all teams should strive to achieve? For example, my wife and I are both runners. Her sustainable pace is a seven-minute mile; mine, though, is more like nine and a half minutes. We can each sustain our own pace for many miles. But if I try to sustain her pace, if I try to run a seven-minute mile, for very long, I get sick—physically ill. Should I be training to reach her pace? Or is mine good enough?

And what does sustainable pace mean for your company? What if a team's sustainable pace is too slow to reach the company's goals? Should the team be asked to deliver, even if it means pushing its members to their limits, or beyond?

To help us better understand sustainable pace and its implications, let's join two functional project managers inside a large software company. The first, Hugo, is working as a ScrumMaster on a Scrum project. The second, Joana, is functioning as a program manager on a traditionally run project.

## The Story

"I don't know how much longer I can take this!" exclaimed Joana. She stood in the door to Hugo's office with an expression on her face that he was all too familiar with. He gestured to a nearby chair.

"You might as well get it off your chest," said Hugo. "More problems with your project?"

"They never end. This time it's the stakeholders! Whenever we try to clarify a requirement or get the acceptance criteria, we get the runaround. But still, they expect everything to be complete in time for their big release *and* at the end of every milestone. They vacillate, change their minds 20 times, and refuse to be pinned down. When they finally do figure out what they want, we're expected to make it happen in record time! 'Cram it in at the end,' they say," Joana explained.

"So what's new, Joana?" asked Hugo, smiling. "Seriously. I want to help but don't know how. Every time a milestone comes up, you come in here telling me how ridiculous it is to run a project this way and that you're never going to let this happen again. Every time, I agree. But as soon as the next milestone rolls around, you're back in here, in the same situation, facing the same problems. It can't continue, but it *will* continue until you do something different."

"I can always count on you to tell it like it is, can't I?" said Joana, smiling. "And you're right. This does keep happening over and over. We just get rested from our last wild push when it's time to work like dogs again! And it's getting worse. We're already working overtime every night, and we're six weeks away from the release. Last time, as bad as it was, we only had to burn the midnight oil for about three weeks. And it's not like we're putting out a product we can be proud of either. The shortcuts, the bugs, the problems are just piling up, but who has time to address them?" Joana sighed and leaned back in her chair. She looked down for a moment then continued.

"The team is losing faith in me and each other. Half of them are ready to quit, *again*. I really don't know what to do."

Hugo got up and walked to the whiteboard. He drew a quick sketch (see Figure 23-1).

"Part of the problem is the stakeholders. But let's talk about what's really dragging you down. You're not working at a steady pace," said Hugo, pausing to point at the drawing.

"See? You sit idle for a while, waiting for a decision or recharging your batteries from your last big push. Then you work at a pretty good pace for some amount of time. Then suddenly, you ramp way up and try to hold it at that level. Right?" asked Hugo.

"That's *exactly* it. We ramp up like we are now, working 60 hours a week. Then, once we hit the milestone, we crash. Sure, we might be in the office 40 hours a week, but we're really putting in something like 20 to 30 hours a week. After this next milestone, we'll probably need four easy weeks to recover from the burnout. It's not ideal, but I don't know what else we can do. We have to ramp up but, after we do, we need a break," admitted Joana.

"The uneven pace is killing you, though, Joana. Part of the reason you have to work an increasing amount of overtime is because you're recovering for longer periods of time between the spikes. The valleys will become deeper. It's a vicious cycle. You need to work at a steady, sustainable pace the whole time."

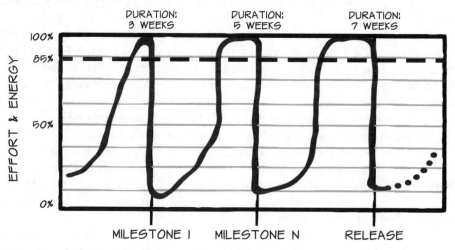

**FIGURE 23-1**   Peaks and valleys of variable pace

"It can't be done. Even if we wanted to work more during those valleys, we're often blocked by the stakeholders, who can't make a decision to save their lives, or their projects in this case," quipped Joanna.

Hugo smiled. "It can be done, but it's going to require two things. The first is a commitment from the team to refuse to take on requirements unless they're ready to be worked on. Keep them off the schedule until the decisions are made—and this includes acceptance criteria, architecture, everything. Before you say anything, I know how tough that's going to be. We're going to have to help the stakeholders, and the business, understand what's going on and how their inefficiencies contribute to these problems. They've been lulled into this false sense of security—no matter what they do, the functionality they request comes out when they want it. What they're going to have to learn is that if they haven't made decisions about functionality, they can't have the functionality by the date. You and I are going to take that on together," Hugo reassured Joana as she looked at him, bewildered.

"I'm almost afraid to ask what the second thing is," said Joana.

"The second thing we're going to have to do is teach your team how to avoid the wall," said Hugo.

"Come again?"

"Remember years ago when I ran marathons?" asked Hugo.

Joana nodded.

"Well, one concept I didn't understand until I experienced it myself was *the wall*. I thought I was ready for my first marathon. I had done the training, bought the shoes, had the venue all picked out. But I didn't realize how important it was to focus on my pace."

"Go on," said Joana.

"My mistake was that I had a time in mind, a goal. And as I neared the halfway point of the marathon I realized I wasn't going to hit that goal unless I went faster. I felt pretty good at that point (plenty of breath, muscles were loose) so I picked up the pace. Eight miles later, I knew I was in trouble. I began to feel sick. I tried to eat, tried to drink, but it only seemed to make me feel worse. I knew at this point I wouldn't meet my time goal, but I was determined to finish. I stopped a couple times, caught my breath, and tried to get my heart rate down. The rest breaks worked, but once I started running again I felt awful within minutes. Still I fought through it.

"Then, about 500 meters from the finish line, it happened. I hit the wall. I was disoriented, hallucinating. I threw up and collapsed. And I couldn't get back up. I was seeing stars, and I could just not function. There I was in front of all those people, with the finish line in sight. And there was nothing I could do but lie there. I never finished. I still have the newspaper clipping from that day, and I still get a hard time from the guys at the gym every year about it," said Hugo.

"So," said Joana, "If this project is a marathon, you're telling me we're not going to finish, and we're going to look like idiots trying?"

"Worse," Hugo explained. "You said earlier that the stakeholders are waiting until late in the project to make crucial decisions, right?"

"Yes," said Joana.

"What state of mind are you and the team in when you're asked to make your own decisions based on their last-minute requirements, decisions about design, architecture, and so on?" asked Hugo.

"We're pretty much too tired to process it. At that point, we're just trying to slog through and get it done," said Joana, frowning. "I hadn't thought about that."

"By trying to hit some arbitrary milestone and increasing your pace to something you can't sustain, you're going to hit the wall before the finish line, every time" said Hugo. "Unlike me, you might finish, but the end result will be buggy code, unhappy people, broken builds, and bad decisions. Sound familiar?"

"All too familiar," said Joana. "And I have five more weeks of this, then five more milestones after that. We'll have at least 30 or 40 more weeks of sheer torture before we're done," Joana said, putting her head in her hands. "This is impossible."

"You're right about that. Right now it is impossible," admitted Hugo. "But that's where the second thing comes in. Remember? There were two things we needed to do. The first was to put the pain of indecision back on the stakeholders where it belongs. The second is to find a pace that you can sustain, live with that for a while, and then train to go faster."

"Not following," said Joana, frowning.

"My first marathon ended badly. But I ran another one six months later and finished. I didn't get the time I wanted, but I ran a steady ten-minute mile throughout the race and, because I didn't go beyond my limits, I felt OK when I finished. Still tired, right? But in control, happy with my performance, and ready to race again another day," Hugo explained.

"So we need to figure out what a good pace is, and stick with it throughout the sprint—and throughout the project?" asked Joana.

"Yes, but there's more. Know what my time was on my last marathon?" asked Hugo.

Joana shook her head.

"Three hours flat," said Hugo. "That's a pace of seven minutes per mile, three minutes faster than my second marathon and two minutes faster than the goal I originally set for myself. Through training, practice, and discipline, I increased my sustainable pace and went faster than I'd ever dreamed possible.

"Joana, ultimately, it's your job to deliver, whether the pace is sustainable or not. And, as was the case with my first and second marathons, the pace you can sustain now is probably not going to be fast enough to meet the company's goals. When I realized this a few years back, I decided that to increase our sustainable pace, I needed to use Scrum and XP engineering practices on my teams. We use shorter iterations, continuous integration, test-driven development, pair programming, and more to improve our performance. I think that's the answer for you, too—help your teams understand agile practices and how they help. You'll be better able to gauge your progress, respond to problems, and maintain energy levels. Plus, your stakeholders will be better aligned with you, so you'll have fewer fires to deal with as you near a milestone."

Hugo paused while he let that sink in. "So, are you ready to take the leap? You in?"

Joana smiled, "Anything is better than the way we're working now. Show me the way, oh mighty marathoner."

Together they set about the hard work of changing minds and habits. The first thing they did was to appeal to management for permission to stop the project and began anew. They started using Scrum. They educated the stakeholders about their role and the expectations that were set for them to make the project go on time. They worked with the team to slowly add engineering practices that would make them a more effective unit. In the end, Joana's team found a comfortable pace that more than satisfied the company's needs.

## The Model

What we saw in the story is not uncommon. All too often, the norm for teams, especially those in a traditional development environment, is the burnout scenario that Hugo described and Joana confirmed. With the advent of more modern development methodologies, I've seen the numbers decrease over the past ten years, but even now, at least 50 percent of the customers I work with are still working beyond capacity for extended periods of time. These companies aren't heartless; like Joana they want employees to have a good work environment, but driving hard to meet milestones is the only way these companies know how to meet their goals. In the end, though, they are left with high employee turnover, buggy products, and fewer customers.

The problem doesn't magically go away when teams turn to Scrum, either. When they are new to Scrum, teams apply those same patterns of burnout and recovery inside a sprint. In a typical four-week sprint, the team might work below capacity for a week, at capacity for a week or two, and then beyond capacity during the final week, when they realize they are in danger of missing their sprint goal.

In the story, Hugo highlighted the peaks and valleys occurring on Joana's project. Valleys are periods when the team is in recovery mode (not productive), and peaks are times when the team is in crunch mode (overloaded). This pattern is represented in Figure 23-2.

In a more traditional software development process, the team must hit certain milestones (code complete, testing, beta release, and so on), as indicated by the vertical lines. If this were a picture of a suboptimal Scrum team, the vertical lines would indicate the end of various sprints.

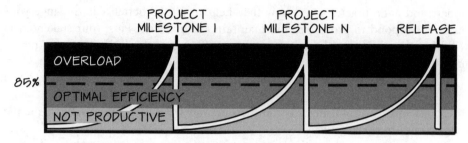

**FIGURE 23-2** Highs and lows of software cycles in milestones

Notice that, whether it is reaching for a milestone or a sprint review, the team starts out in a nonproductive state, spends some time operating at optimal efficiency, and then skyrockets into overload when it becomes obvious that the team cannot otherwise achieve the goal. Once the objective is achieved, the team falls off into a nonproductive state again, where its members catch their breath before ramping up again. This happens for a few cycles without causing the team much pain because the team is spending about twice as much time in an optimal state as it is in the unproductive and overloaded states. You can see this in Figure 23-3, which represents the typical distribution of time during the early cycles on a 12-week milestone schedule.

As the milestones (or sprints) progress, however, the distribution begins to shift. As bug reports and change requests pile up, the team's workload increases as its members try to keep the same rate of development while also fixing problems and integrating changes. Before long, the team is spending more time in an overloaded state and so needs more time to recover. The time spent in optimal mode begins to decrease.

Soon the team is caught in a vicious cycle. The more time the team spends working beyond capacity, the more time it needs to recover. And the longer it spends resting, the more time the team needs to spend in burnout mode to catch up. This is especially true on cycles of a month or longer.

I tracked this on my own projects. We found that as work progressed, our data looked more like the numbers shown in Figure 23-4.

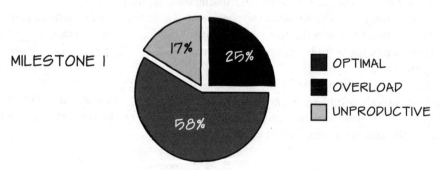

**FIGURE 23-3** Time spent in a sprint

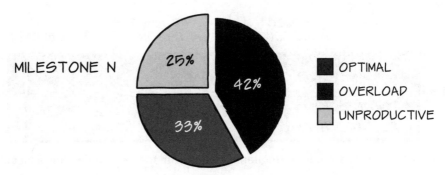

**FIGURE 23-4**  Overload increases, optimal decreases

Since then, I've observed that this trend is fairly standard across the board and that the longer the cycle, the more pronounced the imbalance. To understand why a steadily growing imbalance is so harmful to a project (and the end product), let's take another look at Hugo and his marathons. During his first marathon, Hugo hit a wall—he reached a physical state of exhaustion where he could not continue. Long-distance runners know that they must monitor their heart rates so that they stay in an aerobic state, where the body is creating energy by breaking glycogen into glucose and combining it with oxygen. When the body runs out of glycogen, it begins burning fat and producing lactic acid inside the muscles, causing the runner to hit the wall. To stay in an aerobic state, the runner keeps his heart rate in a certain range and must expend energy at a continuous rate rather than in bursts.

If the heart rate rises above a certain target, 85 percent of your target heart rate, the body begins to perform anaerobically, burning glucose without oxygen and operating far less efficiently. This is fine for exercise that requires only brief bursts of intense exertion, but problematic for long-term endeavors where a sustained level of energy is required.

A software team should strive for an aerobic state, where they are working at a steady pace and have an almost endless supply of energy. When they are instead forced to work in bursts of hyperactivity, they have a much more finite supply of energy available. As a result, they quickly become fatigued, begin making bad decisions, and as their metaphorical muscles begin to burn from lactic acid buildup, eventually stop out of sheer exhaustion. As these bursts grow longer so do the corresponding periods of rest, as teams feel the metaphorical burn of lactic acid in their own minds and bodies.

Maintaining a steady, aerobic state requires that we work in multiple sets of micro peaks and valleys to reach our sprint end or milestone marker. Figure 23-5 illustrates the peaks and valleys indicative of a sustainable pace. When we are in this state, we are operating at optimal efficiency, even at our peaks and valleys. Because we aren't tired or stressed or burned out, we're able to be our most productive.

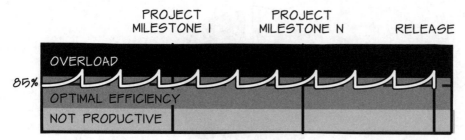

**FIGURE 23-5**   An illustration of frequent delivery with the same milestone schedule

So how do you get from a hectic pace that leaves employees burned out and over-worked to a steady, sustained pace that is optimal and productive? Let's revisit the story. When Hugo ran his first marathon, he tried to run beyond a sustainable pace and in so doing burned out and couldn't finish. By the time he ran his last marathon, however, he not only finished but managed a seven-minute mile. That kind of improvement wasn't a fluke. It took practice, training, discipline, and time. Likewise, if we want to create a sustainable pace that is robust enough to meet our goals, we're going to have to improve the way we run our projects. To do this we need to shorten our iterations, increase the amount of time we spend working in a team space, and monitor our burndowns to ensure a steady completion rate throughout each sprint.

## Shorten Iterations

The first thing you should do if you are experiencing burnout is shorten your cycle time, breaking the project into smaller chunks and delivering functionality more often. If you are working in one-month sprints, try two-week sprints. If you are using two-week sprints, try one-week sprints. You'll find that it's much easier to consume energy at a constant rate over a shorter period of time.

To examine why that's so, let's revisit the sustainable pace chart shown in Figure 23-5. Notice that before each milestone (or release date on a Scrum project), there are multiple peaks and declines in activity, all falling primarily inside the optimal zone. These short iterations allow for small bursts of energy, short recoveries, and frequent progress checks and adjustments in the form of sprint reviews and retrospectives. Psychologically, because the team can see the finish line from the beginning, it's much easier to work enthusiastically toward the end goal. Short iterations are the heartbeat of sustainable pace.

Working in shorter sprints might mean decomposing your stories into smaller bits and changing long-standing habits, but it has benefits that reach far beyond sustainable pace, including more frequent customer feedback. See Chapter 12, "Decomposing Stories and Tasks," for techniques and benefits associated with task decomposition.

## Monitor Burndown Charts

While *The Scrum Guide* published by Schwaber and Sutherland in 2011 says that burndowns are no longer a required artifact in Scrum [SCHWABER], I believe they are still essential tools in a team's arsenal. Your burndown chart can give you many clues as to how your project is progressing. What you want is a standard burndown across the board. It should look consistent with Figure 23-6.

However, for teams that run in an overloaded state, the burndown is much different. For these teams, what you see is a light flurry of activity (during recovery mode) followed by a large drop off in work being accomplished (in overload mode), as illustrated in Figure 23-7.

High burndown rates at the end of the sprint and slow burndown rates at the beginning are indicators that your team is attempting too much work at the end of the sprint. This might be because one team member is taking on too much work, it might be because the tasks are sized inappropriately, it might mean that the team is

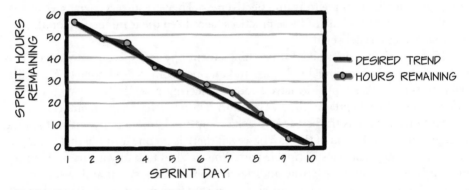

**FIGURE 23-6**   Example of a good burndown chart

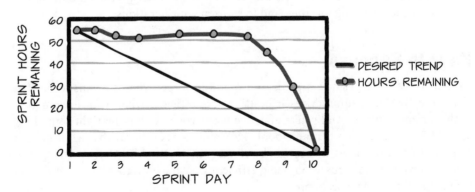

**FIGURE 23-7**   Example of a bad burndown chart  where the team updates everything at the end

in the habit of working sporadically throughout the sprint, or it could be some combination of factors. Spend some time evaluating what is causing your end-of-sprint bursts and take the steps necessary to correct them.

## Increase Team Time

In Chapter 10, "Core Hours," we learned why core team hours are important and how to establish them. Having a good set of core team hours is also critical to maintaining sustainable pace. Team members need to spend a certain amount of time in the same space together. With increased distance, even down a hall, comes distraction, and with distraction comes decreased communication—a lack of timely, shared information contributes to the huge spikes toward the end of a sprint. It's far too easy to zone out or be distracted by other tasks when you are working alone—it's far better to have four hours of team time daily than two, and if you can, even have more like six.

In Chapter 9, "Why Engineering Practices Are Important in Scrum," we discovered how important engineering practices, such as pair programming, TDD, and continuous integration are to team effectiveness. They are also cornerstones of sustainable pace. Habitual use of these practices helps keep the team focused on the stories that need to be delivered.

If you work in a distributed team, supplement physical space with virtual. This can include having continual webcams and an open conference phone line. On distributed teams, it's essential to have good engineering practices and pair programming sessions to help prevent the loss of information between team members.

Sustainable pace is the best way to achieve optimal productivity without risking team burnout. At the end of the day, however, there is no one formula that I can give you that will guarantee a sustainable pace. You need to talk to your team. Find out how each team member is feeling at different points in the sprint and overall in the project. Listen in daily standups for clues that someone might be overloaded or setting herself up for an end-of-sprint rush of activity. The best defense against hitting the wall is to keep a close watch on the team's pace, to increase the amount of time the team spends working together, and to shorten your iterations.

# Keys to Success

In their drive for efficiency, organizations tend to forget what it means to be effective. Tom DeMarco summarizes it best, "You're efficient when you do something with minimum waste. And you're effective when you're doing the right something" [DEMARCO, p. 122]. In the same book, DeMarco goes on to say that while effective organizations work toward their goals, albeit sometimes slowly, efficient organizations can become so focused on being efficient that they fail to notice that they are moving in the wrong direction.

In our story, Joana's team was trying to be efficient but was doing so at the expense of effectiveness. Recognizing that overloading the team only leaves your team and your customers unhappy is the first step toward adopting a strategy that leads to long-term success.

A sustainable pace is one in which each team member is committed to working at or near 85 percent, day in and day out. Learning to work at such a continuously high level takes some getting used to, especially if you are used to the extreme peaks and valleys associated with burnout. Besides changing the way you work inside the sprint, you'll likely face some organizational issues that can derail a team's pace, including team longevity, part-time team members, and unrealistic goals.

The first thing organizations need to realize is that to get teams working at optimal levels, management must give teams time to gel. A typical team comes together to work on a single project and disbands afterwards, and management expects high levels of output from the start. By the time the team has reached a performing state, the project ends and the team disbands (see Chapter 20, "Adding New Team Members," for more information on the four stages of team performance). The best teams are ones that have been together for multiple projects and have had time to form strong bonds and working relationships.

The second problem holding teams back is the split focus of their team members. To be highly productive, team members must be free to focus on the task at hand, and only the task at hand. Running a marathon requires single-mindedness, where the runner gives full attention to his body, his heart rate, and his energy levels. Runners don't try to run a marathon and do other tasks simultaneously. Yet we often ask our team members to be part-time on more than one project, thereby splitting their focus and degrading their performance.

One last key to success has to do with company goals. Team productivity can only be increased to a certain level—even the fastest runners can't complete a 26-mile run in 26 minutes. While ultimately you'll be on the hook for completing the work your company requires, if you find that doing so requires your team to work at an impossibly high pace, you're going to need to help management see the disconnect. Track your velocity and show them past release burndown charts of what the team is able to do once it gets to a high-performing state. Find data and research that shows the gains that other companies have seen. Find senior leaders inside or outside your company to speak or find a local community event or give them some books to read —anything—to help with the education of management.

Building software is a team sport. Alignment from leadership to the people doing the work helps ensure that there are fewer surprises, more satisfied customers, and most importantly, no team burnout.

# References

[DEMARCO]    DeMarco, Tom. 2001. *Slack*. New York: Broadway Books. p. 122.

[SCHWABER]    Schwaber, Ken, and Jeff Sutherland. Scrum.org website. http://www.scrum.org/storage/Scrum%20Update%202011.pdf (accessed 26 July 2011).

Chapter 24

# DELIVERING WORKING SOFTWARE

"Delivering working software every sprint is impossible!" I hear that refrain on a regular basis, most often from people who have never done Scrum before. I ask them how they know, and the answer is always the same: "We can't deliver in a year, so we certainly can't deliver in 30 days!"

At one point, I believed this as well. I encourage teams to use that feeling of impossibility as a motivator for the possible, to use that energy to prove that it can be done. More often than not, teams find that once they adjust their mindset, they can deliver working software every sprint. Let's look at one team that found a way to work toward a goal of potentially shippable software on a system that did not at first seem to lend itself to an iterative approach.

## The Story

Paul and his team set out to build a sales order processing and monitoring tool for a vehicle manufacturer. Paul had worked with Scrum and XP on previous projects, but for the rest of the team an agile approach was fairly new. Together, the team laid out four goals.

- Maintain high coding standards.
- Have a clean, manageable codebase.
- Build knowledge on the team.
- Be potentially shippable at the end of every sprint.

Paul and the team had no trouble devising a plan for addressing the first three goals. When it came to how to divide the work so that they could truly deliver working software each sprint, however, things got more difficult.

"I just don't get it," said Matt. "We'll need several sprints before we've got anything even remotely shippable. Do other teams really do this?"

Paul nodded. He knew how he wanted to approach the problem, but he also knew that it might take some convincing to bring the rest of the team on board. He thought for a moment about how to explain and came up with a simple example to describe the process without bogging down in the details of this particular project.

"Let me answer your question with another question," Paul began. "What is the purpose of slide presentation software?"

The team looked at each other like Paul was crazy.

"Come on, what is it?" pressed Paul.

"Well," said Darren with a degree of hesitation. "I would guess its purpose is to present slides in a meeting."

"Right!" said Paul, as he pulled up a standard presentation program and pointed to the screen. "So the purpose of this is to allow me to present material to you, like I'm doing right now, either on this screen or on another display. Do you all agree?"

The team nodded with hesitation.

"What is the *one thing* that this needs to do flawlessly, every time, no questions asked?" said Paul.

"Display slides; we just covered that," said Matt.

"Not just display slides… what else?" asked Paul.

"Well, to be useful, you'd have to be able to add content," said Darren pointing at the blank template.

"Right," said Paul. "So I need to be able to create slides and display them. We can all agree on that?"

The team nodded.

"Do I need animations?" asked Paul

"Sure you do," said Darren. "Your slides are so ugly that the animations are the only thing that keeps us awake!"

The team laughed.

"OK, OK. But seriously. Do I actually *need* the ability to do animations or sounds?" asked Paul. "What about graphics? Backgrounds? Multiple fonts?"

"If your primary goal is to just display content, no, you don't need all that other stuff. Where are you going with this?" asked Matt. "We are not building presentation software."

"No we're not. What we're trying to do is figure out how to approach our project. And to do that, we first need to think about the minimum functionality we need to reach our goal. The simplest thing the presentation software needs to do is enable users to create and display slides. Do they need templates, animations, or even multiple fonts? No. The absolute base requirement is one slide that can be created and displayed. Do you agree?" asked Paul.

"Well, yes, but it's not shippable. No one would buy it!" said Darren.

"True, but no one is suggesting we actually ship it. That's why they call it *potentially* shippable, right?" said Matt. "No one in their right mind would ever release presentation software that did the barest of bare minimums into a market crowded with robust options. To be marketable, the product would need to have more features, but it would be potentially shippable."

"I get it," said Darren. "We would need to expand on it, creating some functionality over time to get to a fully releasable point. But it could be shipped, theoretically, because it does meet the absolute base requirement."

"Good" said Paul. "So our goal would be to build the basic core of functionality fully and to make sure it flows through the system like a tracer bullet. We'd show the first piece to our stakeholders and get their feedback. Then we'd make adjustments and add incremental pieces of functionality to the presentation software. Eventually, it would grow into a full package that we can sell. We would be able to add additional functionality to it through updates, but we'd reach a point where it was marketable, and that's when we'd release."

"I'm still missing how this relates to our system," said Matt. "We're not building something simple like a presentation system, we're building a sales order processing and monitoring tool. It has to integrate with nearly 20 systems and there are, what, ten different types of customers, from accounting to shipping to manufacturing to sales? This is way more complex!"

"Yes. Our system is more complex, but that doesn't mean we can't use the same approach. I'm suggesting that we find a way to produce, by the end of the first sprint, a thin slice of functionality all the way through our system. This needs to be the core slice, the one people will use over and over again. What do you think that story is?" asked Paul.

"I think it's the base sales order path. People need to be able to put in an order and know that the right vehicle will ship to the right place as a result." said Darren.

"What is the most common vehicle?" asked Paul.

"Probably the basic cab and chassis," said Darren.

"Wait a minute," blurted Matt. "You're telling me that we're going to build a system that just processes an order for a basic cab and chassis? Next you're going to say the sales people can only pick one color or one engine, right?"

"That's exactly what I'm suggesting," said Paul. "We will build the most common flow through the system, which is an order for the base cab and chassis. Over time we'll add more stories that allow the entire company to do more. Stories like adding color choices, configuring for different engines, and the ability for the floor to update the status on the vehicle so shipping knows when it will be built. These things, these variables, are all dependent on this core story, though. Does that make sense?"

"I get it," said Darren.

Some other team members nodded yes. Matt did not.

"I'm still confused," said Matt. "Why on Earth would we do this? I'd think that we should just do our normal approach, which is to design the backend integration database, get that sorted out, build the integration components one by one, and then build the interface at the end."

"What would we deliver at the end of the first sprint?" asked Darren.

"Well," said Matt with a bit of hesitation. "I guess we'd show them the database designs."

"Remember, Matt, we're trying for working software here, and the threshold is potentially shippable, no matter how small the story," said Paul.

"Yeah, you're right, but won't this create a ton of work that just gets tossed out? I mean, we're probably going to hack that first story together and it will have mocks, which we won't use for the actual end product. What does this get us?" asked Matt.

Darren stepped up for this one.

"If I understand this Scrum thing, it's going to get us an opportunity to get feedback from our users in the review meeting, right, Paul?"

"Exactly!" exclaimed Paul. "The feedback is the most important part. We will show the users the base story. Then we'll work with them to order the remaining stories according to their highest value to the customer: Is it more important for the users to configure a different engine or a different color? These variables are things we can add in, but they build off this core base story. We're showing working software and getting real-time customer feedback. Since we're limiting our variables, the stories will remain small, which makes them easier to test and validate. From there we expand and then release with a minimal marketable feature set."

"I think I get it now," Matt said. "What you're saying, Paul, is that we build each layer of the system—even if it that means creating things we'll never ship with, like flat-file databases, mocks, basically the things that we will refactor out at a later date. We'll do the base story to validate that the system works end-to-end, and then we can expand on it as we go."

"You've got it, Matt," said Paul. "We'll build a thin slice and expand it as we go. It will be potentially shippable because it will meet our definition of done. We'll build acceptance, integration, and performance tests, document it, do everything we need to do to ship."

"I'm still not sure this will work," argued Matt. "My one big concern is rework. It seems like we're creating a ton of stuff we'll just have to throw away later. Isn't that wasteful?"

"No. It's risk mitigation. We'll be able to show the stakeholders a system at the end of the first sprint that works end-to-end for that base story. We'll get their feedback and make changes as needed. From this, we will increase the system capabilities, expanding the functionality and scaling it for more users," said Paul.

"OK. I'm willing to give it a try, but I can't commit to it wholeheartedly until I see this in action. I'll give it a shot for three or four sprints, but if I don't like it..." said Matt.

"You will," said Paul. "Trust me, you will."

The team tried the model Paul proposed and liked it. As the system expanded, and the number of stories expanded from the original base story, so did the team's confidence. After three months of running two-week sprints, the team was able to publish a release plan based on observed velocity. This in turn increased the confidence the rest of the organization had in the team—the team's predictions were based on historical velocity ranges and knowledge, so they were very accurate. The team delivered the system within the predicted date range without any of the usual integration glitches. In the end, everyone agreed that the team's commitment to delivering working software each sprint was the key to its success.

# The Model

It's not always easy to see the path to working software. In the story, we saw Paul's team struggle with how to build the system while achieving the goal of creating potentially shippable software every sprint. The team's understanding of working software was "completed, releasable components," rather than a working end-to-end scenario. Paul helped them to understand the value in building the system end-to-end from the beginning, starting with the smallest, most commonly used path through the system and all the tests and support in the team's definition of done (see Chapter 7, "How Do We Know When We Are Done?").

To get a team in the mindset of delivering working software every sprint, I have them focus on one of two factors: *core story*, which we saw in the story, or *number of users*. Then we move on to tackling system elements in terms of risk and, as the project progresses, expanding and validating further features.

## Core Story

One way to deliver working software is to identify one core story, fixing the other variables so that the core story runs through the entire system. As the project progresses, the variable components replace the mocks and flat files. Throughout the sprints, the team delivers working, potentially shippable software to its customers, validating that what is being created is indeed what the customers need, and revises the plan accordingly.

The core story is the absolute base requirement, the smallest slice of end-to-end functionality that is the most commonly used, as shown in Figure 24-1. In the story,

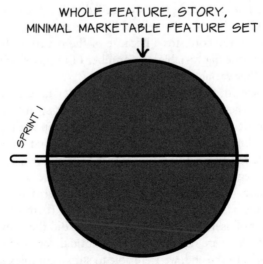

WHOLE FEATURE, STORY,
MINIMAL MARKETABLE FEATURE SET

SPRINT 1

**FIGURE 24-1**   Start with the base end-to-end functionality

the base was the slice of functionality that allowed sales people to enter an order for a single cab and chassis vehicle. All other factors were limited. The color was white, the engine size predetermined, the drive train and transmission only had one setting, the shipping address was constant, and so on. This enabled the team to create a single flow through the system, validate it with customers and stakeholders, and then build off that base story.

Constraining stories to their smallest possible size makes testing and validation much more manageable. As teams expand individual end-user functions (user interface design changes, updating a mock object, or even bringing a new integrated system online) and add them to the core, working software, they also add the tests and documentation that go along with the new function. The team in our story knows that users eventually need to be able to order a cab and chassis in a variety of colors. While this is a simple change in the UI, the backend integration to make this happen is much bigger than a drop-down box. Adding this small story expands not only the interface but also the backend components, acceptance, unit and integration test frameworks, documentation, and the like.

## Number of Users

Another way to shrink the size of the initial story, while still enabling end-to-end functionality, is to limit the number of users that can use or access the system. For example, I once worked as part of a team to build an authentication engine designed to support five million users. It was a three-tier system with a C++ plugin, a web service to manage the business logic, an interface for administrators to configure, and several databases that handled various calls based on the request coming into the system.

Our instinct was to build each component serially, integrating and testing everything at the end. We knew, though, that we needed to integrate and test as we went along to be potentially shippable. Therefore, like the example in the story, we, too, started by finding an initial core story. Because of the nature of this particular system, we chose to limit one big variable, the number of users, which changed the way we approached the other variables in the system.

We built a thin slice of functionality with the understanding that only one user would be able to use the system at the end of the first sprint. Thinking this way allowed us to employ devices that would never actually ship with the system, such as flat-file databases and mock integration points. This enabled us to gather customer feedback quickly. We ran stress and performance tests at every sprint, as well as an automated suite of integration and acceptance tests. Because we were working with a limited number of users, we were able to filter off select users from the front-end production load balancers based on their user ID and push them to this system. As we expanded the number of users, the system grew, and so did the complexity of the supporting objects. Flat files were replaced with dynamic databases; mock objects with real integration points. In the end, we were able to ship a complex system, within the release window, without the performance and integration issues that had plagued us on other projects.

## Start with the Highest Risk Element

Regardless of which approach you take, make sure you start with the highest risk elements. Building the highest risk technical solutions first may be second nature for an experienced Scrum team; however, like the team in our story, many teams have trouble figuring out how to both address their highest risks and also find ways to build incrementally. In the authentication model described in the "Number of Users" section of this chapter, for example, our team knew it should attack the C++ component first but struggled with how to do that while still delivering working software each sprint. Limiting the number of users enabled us to work on the highest risk component while still delivering working software.

When I think of the highest risk items, I like to associate them with the phrase, *the window of opportunity*. I often talk about this as an actual window—one so big that, at the beginning of any project, you could drive a bus through it. Each high-risk item is a metaphorical bus that needs to drive through the open window. The bigger the bus, the bigger the window needs to be.

Early in the project, it's relatively easy to drive the big buses through the window. As each day passes, however, the window closes a little more. If you don't find the big buses in your project early, and drive them through the window while it's open wide, you're going to have a huge disaster at the end as the bus crashes into the nearly closed window. That's why the highest risk elements need to be built early, in lockstep with limiting users and doing the smallest slice through the system. At the end of the sprint, you are validating that the bus has been driven through the window, showing *potentially* shippable software. As each sprint goes by, the buses you pass through your system, your high-risk items, get smaller just as the window does.

## Expand and Validate

As the project progresses, expand on the small slice, sprint-by-sprint, until you have a whole feature set or scenario, as shown in Figure 24-2. The expansion should be ordered by the product owner, who works with the stakeholders to identify the highest priority stories so the ordering in the product backlog is accurate.

Each element you build must always follow your definition of done. As more and more functionality is added, ensure that integration is working as expected. Invest in automation, as the costs of manual testing increase each sprint. (See Chapter 9, "Why Engineering Practices Are Important in Scrum," for more information on automation testing costs.) Always keep all unit tests up to date. Creating software that is potentially shippable might appear to slow down the team initially. However, the stability and predictability it brings ensures the team has a stable velocity, increasing everyone's confidence in the team's ability to deliver.

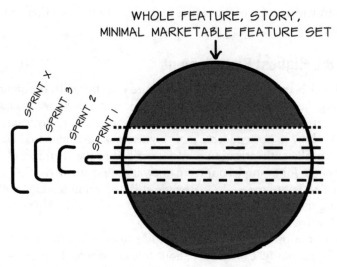

**FIGURE 24-2** Expand until the software meets customer needs

One possible outcome of always building working software is that you reach a point where the software solves the customer needs in its current state, before all the once-desired functionality has been implemented. Looking at Figure 24-2, as the team goes through each sprint and functionality is built, the demonstrable working software might reach a point where it is good enough to ship before it reaches the boundaries of the circle. That's not only OK, it's desirable. You are both saving money and also delivering what the customer needs.

The biggest advantage of working software is that teams can get real feedback from their stakeholders or users very early. This allows teams to incorporate changes, change directions, and rework designs when the system is small and relatively inexpensive to change. Therefore, keep your customers on the path of incrementally building the system with you, getting feedback, making incremental changes, and always remembering that working, potentially shippable software is the true measure of project progress.

## Keys to Success

One of the hardest things for new Scrum teams to do is to produce potentially shippable software at the end of every sprint. They are just not sure how to build a system incrementally. They tend to jump to building an entire package, a database for example, first, before they have a way to validate it.

Creating working software requires teams to change their thinking, accept the reality of rework, and focus on an end-to-end scenario.

## Change in Thinking

Agile coach and consultant Jeff Patton has a demonstration where he rips up a dollar bill. He says that the dollar bill is a user story, and he is going to break it into smaller pieces. As he rips the dollar into pieces, we understand that although the dollar is getting smaller, the individual pieces have no value. They only have value as a collective whole.

Teams often rip stories, and dollar bills, into pieces to make them smaller. However, these individual pieces often have no value; they are not potentially shippable. To create small pieces that still have value, you need to change your way of thinking. As Patton explains it, in the case of a dollar bill, this means splitting it into coins, say four quarters or ten dimes, instead of shards of worthless paper. In the case of software, it means making each small story a potentially shippable piece, one that can move through the entire system and has value.

Historically we have built entire software components all at once, integrating them near the end of the project. The problem with that is that each component on its own, like a piece of a dollar bill, has no value. The components only have value when they are integrated. This is a huge shift in mindset, one that is not easily broken. A challenge you will have in this model is fighting the urge to build a complete component of a system when the rest of the system does not work.

In our story, the team *and the customers* had to completely change the way they thought about communicating their needs and wishes (e.g., user stories), and building and delivering software. They realized they didn't have to worry about whether the software would actually ship; just that it was potentially shippable and demonstrable at the end of each sprint, and that it met the definition of done criteria. Though the system would not be fully released to production until it could support every scenario and a variety of users, limiting the stories initially and building onto the core story was the best route to working software. It was low risk and provided high degrees of transparency to the business.

Don't be afraid to think in ways that may not be familiar to you. Breaking out of a serial mindset requires some basic logical thinking that would apply in the real world—don't tear the dollar, change it into coins. Think it through, draw it out, and be willing to experiment with what works for your team and your project. Once you start delivering working software, you'll find it easier and easier to find iterative solutions to your most complex systems.

## Rework

When we start small, with flat files and mock objects in place of components, we know that eventually we'll have to refactor. As we add more and more backend functionality, we're going to throw away some code. We're going to have rework. We just don't know how much.

Dealing with this reality is difficult for many teams. Some rework is known—in the story the team knew that the flat files and mocks they created would later be discarded, but they were willing to do it because of the rewards: risk management, mitigation, and transparency. Other rework is more unpredictable. Customers are learning more about the system during the process, too. As they see how things actually work, they are able to better express their needs or even change their minds about what features they really want. Business direction can turn on a dime. New information can be discovered that can alter the course of a project. All these changes, while crucial to the success of the project, mean rework for the team—rework that should be managed and added to the product backlog for ordering and priority.

What teams (and many businesses) that make a commitment to potentially shippable software understand, however, is that it is much better to make many small changes throughout the project, and yes, even throw away some work, than to deliver a "complete" system after one year and then find out that it doesn't work as intended, is not at all what the customer wanted, or doesn't meet the needs of the current business environment.

## Focus on End-to-End Scenarios

End-to-end scenarios are what working software is all about. Without seeing how things will function at the end, even in a basic state, your customers and stakeholders will remain bewildered and big risk buses will continue to hide in the fog of ambiguity.

The value of end-to-end scenarios can be seen in the example of molding a piece of clay into a figure. At the beginning, you have two options. The first is to listen to all the requirements for the clay figure, and then go off to mold, paint, fire, and glaze it, eventually coming back with a hardened figure to present to the customer. The second option is to listen to the requirements and find a way to present the absolute base requirement, shape it roughly as prescribed. If you do that, you make a first pass and present the still malleable clay to the customer, asking *is this the basic form?* You continue down that path making slight modifications and returning to the customer to validate the changes. Eventually you reach a point (maybe sooner, maybe later) where the piece is ready to be fired.

Focusing on end-to-end scenarios gives you something tangible to show the customer while keeping the code malleable. It allows you to easily reform your understanding of the end product to better fit customer expectations. It keeps the window of opportunity open as long as possible, while still giving your customers something substantive and of value—something that could be fired and glazed as is, on demand.

Working software is not an impossible dream. It is the one goal that ensures that you are meeting your customer's expectations and delivering value each and every sprint. Whether you choose to focus on a core story or limit your users, remember to begin with the highest risk items, those buses that could otherwise remain hidden until too late in the process. Educate your customer about what you'll be delivering, why, and how they can help ensure that they receive the product they need, which may or may not be the product they originally asked for. Adjusting the way you think about software might be hard, but once you do, you'll find that incrementally delivering potentially shippable software is as easy as exchanging a dollar bill for ten dimes: Change, please.

## Work Consulted

Patton, Jeff. Personal website. http://agileproductdesign.com/jeff_patton.html (accessed 12 May 2011).

Chapter 25

# OPTIMIZING AND MEASURING VALUE

Do more. Do more. Do more. Teams hear it in their sleep. But there comes a point when, no matter how hard they push, teams just can't increase velocity under the current conditions. The reality is that other things—company meetings, documentation, email, product grooming, planning, you name it—are competing for the team's time.

The problem is that customers and stakeholders don't see all the behind-the-scenes work the team is doing. They see only their own backlogs and features. And they understandably want as many features for their money as they can get.

What is missing is transparency. Most Scrum teams use the burndown to provide visibility into what the team is working on. And it is a good visual indicator of progress—mostly. It turns out, though, that if you really want to understand how the team spends its time, you need more than that. By providing transparency and visibility into the work *types* the team is addressing, product owners and businesses can optimize for value.

## The Story

Sabela was working as a ScrumMaster with a product owner named Reisa. Reisa did a great job working with the stakeholders to prioritize the backlog. She was always available and had the answers the team needed. She was really good at her job. About four months into the project, though, Reisa started asking Sabela and the team if they could improve their velocity a little bit. The team was stunned. Sabela told Reisa that, for months, the team had been tweaking things and felt it was at its max output. Not convinced, Reisa continued to question the team on a regular basis, asking if there was any way to could get more work done in the two-week sprints.

The team wanted to please their customer. During its ninth and tenth sprints, the team tried to squeak out a higher velocity without sacrificing team values and engineering practices, and it worked. Their velocity output for the sprint jumped to just above the average for sprint nine, but during sprint ten it returned to the average it had been in the first eight sprints. Unfortunately, after a month of "pushing it," the team's average velocity was not affected in any significant way. At the end of sprint ten, the team finally asked Reisa what was behind her prodding.

Reisa told the team that she was getting pressure from her stakeholders *and* management to drive them harder. They wanted the team to move faster toward a mythical deadline known as *code complete*. "We understand that pressure," Sabela told Reisa, "but given the constraints we have, our current velocity is as good as it's going to get. We can't go any faster."

"What constraints are you talking about?" Reisa asked.

"There are constraints that we have to work under within the company. Not every task we do is for a story; sometimes we need to figure things out, go to meetings, review stuff with other stakeholders—basically just noise," replied Michel, a team member. "Constant requests from the database team take up most of our time—it's almost endless."

"I don't understand," said Reisa. "Please elaborate for me."

The team went on to explain to Reisa that the work it was doing basically fell into four simple categories: feature work, taxes, spikes, and preconditions. Feature work was the work that delivered actual value to the stakeholders of the system, what the money was meant to be spent on. Taxes were constraints put in place by the organization that were, essentially, the cost of doing business. Most of these were nonnegotiable standards that the team was required to adhere to. Spikes were used to understand and estimate the ambiguous stories. Teams often encounter stories that are quite large and have a lot of uncertainty. Instead of making a list of assumptions and estimating the story, the team set aside a certain number of hours to investigate what needed to be done to drive out the ambiguity and reduce the risk profile for that story or set of stories. Preconditions were defined as work that needed to be done for the team to call the sprint successful.

"I think I understand," said Reisa. "So, what can we do to increase our velocity?"

The team looked at her blankly.

"What do you mean, 'our velocity'?" Sabela asked. "Do you mean you want to see more feature work completed in each sprint, despite the constraints we described?"

"Yes, I want to see more feature work completed. What do we need to do to make this happen?" said Reisa.

Sabela picked up a one liter water bottle that someone had on the desk.

"Reisa, how much water can fit in this bottle?" Sabela asked. Reisa looked perplexed, but tried to answer.

"Well, one liter?" said Reisa.

"You tell me, is it?" Sabela responded.

Reisa confirmed. The one liter bottle that Sabela was holding could indeed hold one liter of water. The two continued the conversation and clarified that the bottle could also hold one half of a liter of water, but it could not hold more than one liter. To have the bottle hold more than one liter, the bottle would need to be re-engineered *or* Reisa would need to get a bigger bottle. Reisa understood this.

"Reisa, the bottle represents the team's velocity. We can carry one liter of work per sprint. Feature work is just *one type* of work that we need to do over each sprint, so feature work cannot fill the entire bottle, take up the entire velocity, because those other work types, things like taxes, spikes, and preconditions, need to fit in the bottle, too," Sabela said.

Reisa nodded in understanding.

"So, what you are telling me is that for the team to get more work done, more feature work, we need to either get a bigger bottle *or* reduce the other work types?"

"Yes!" shouted the entire team, visibly excited that it was starting to click.

"Why would I not want to just focus on feature work now and worry about the other work types later?" said Reisa.

"Because, just doing feature work does not ensure we have potentially shippable software. Calling a feature *done*[1] depends directly on some of the non-feature work we have in our bottle," Sabela explained.

"So it sounds to me like we need to lower taxes to clear more space for feature work," said Reisa thoughtfully. "That's probably not going to happen in our company culture, but it would help me tremendously to be able to show everyone exactly how the team's time is being spent. Can you make a chart so that I can bring this up with management?"

"I will," said Sabela. "The one tax that we might be able to remove concerns a few unnecessary meetings that we're having with another team. If we could come up with a more efficient way to share data, it might help free up some room in our bottle—but we'll need your help and management buy-in to make that happen. I'll note it on the chart."

Reisa shared the chart with the project customers and stakeholders. They were able to remove the unnecessary meetings and saw an improvement in the team's availability and velocity. Though they searched for more ways to make room in the "team bottle," they were unable to identify other opportunities for optimization. Once they saw how full the team's time really was, however, the barrage of "get velocity higher" statements and questions stopped.

The team continued to work with Reisa on what these four basic categories meant and how the team could integrate the model into its work moving forward. Reisa liked the visibility it gave her, and so did the stakeholders.

## The Model

Reisa's issue was that she did not understand where the team was spending its time. She knew that the burndown charts showed work getting done, and she knew that the work was coming from her product backlog. But she never understood why the team committed to such a low level of output—at least a low level as she saw it. She was getting pressure from stakeholders and management to have the team accomplish more work, and the team was pushing back. What was missing was the transparency and

---

1. See Chapter 7, "How Do We Know When We Are Done?," for more on the team's definition of done.

insight into what the team was *actually* working on when it wasn't working directly on features.

I, too, have battled ambiguity with customers, so I created this model. It is not revolutionary, but its simplicity enables teams to communicate to their stakeholders and customers how they are spending their time.

To provide the transparency and insight needed to make intelligent decisions, break the work down into these four categories:

- Feature work
- Taxes
- Spikes
- Preconditions

These buckets and their definitions have been built and refined over years of projects and dozens of project teams. I do not expect them to fit your business perfectly; however, they were written broadly enough that they should work for everyone. If you choose to refactor them, remember to keep the intent of the definition the same while changing the words.

## Feature Work

Feature work is the work that delivers actual value to the stakeholders. This often takes the form of user stories. I define feature work as the following:

*Functionality that will deliver business value to either a user or purchaser of a system or software package.*

Feature work can be attributed directly to ROI. Money spent on feature work should provide an overall return that is higher than the cost to build the feature.

## Taxes

Taxes, whether we're talking about income tax or corporate mandates, are often loathed by the people and teams paying them. I have found them to be both a saving grace and a gnarly burr in my side, almost simultaneously. Without them, infrastructure would degrade, and, when building systems, we would quickly fall out of compliance. They are a necessary evil. I define team taxes as the following:

*Corporate services or mandated requirements that pose a burdensome charge, obligation, duty, or demand on teams or groups.*

Based on this definition, when shipping software you find taxes imposed by both the company and the team. A sample of the taxes paid on the project discussed in the story follows:

- Security reviews
- Legal compliance reviews
- Scrum meetings
- Company or divisional meetings

These are only a handful of the items typically required to release software (such as security reviews) *or* that compete for the team's time (such as the Scrum meetings and company meetings). Businesses want to see value built as quickly as possible and sometimes forget that there is more to building software than just writing code and testing it. Financial systems, for example, require Sarbanes-Oxley compliance, so we should expect the taxes in that environment to be higher than those of a small, eight-person web development company that focuses on building interactive websites. The meetings with other teams that Sabela mentions in the story are an example of extraneous taxes that inflate the category and reduce overall feature delivery.

People often ask about the Scrum overhead. I lump that into taxes. Planning, retrospectives, and reviews are the taxes of Scrum.

## Spikes

A spike is used when the team cannot accurately estimate a story or feature set in its current form. A spike is a brief experiment to learn more about an area of application. There are many definitions for a spike. I use the following:

> *A spike is a brief, timeboxed activity used to discover work needed to accomplish a large, ambiguous task or story.*

All spikes must be timeboxed—a certain amount of time should be allocated to explore and further define work efforts that can't be properly estimated. The end result is a story or task estimate with a higher degree of accuracy.

An example spike would be something like "Investigate what the deployment process should be. Document and estimate the story in the product backlog." It would be impossible to estimate how long it takes to deploy without understanding what the deployment process is for the project and for the company.

One caveat about spiking work: The outcome of the spike, whether it be a set of tasks or more stories, cannot become part of the current sprint backlog. The new work items identified in the spike need to be prioritized with the rest of the product backlog by the product owner. Why? There are several reasons.

For one, the team has already committed to the goal and the work items on the sprint backlog, one of which was a spike. The team should not have committed to the tasks that would come out of that spike, because the team could not have known what the tasks would be. Therefore these tasks should not be added to the sprint. If the team did try to factor in the outcome of the spike, and set aside time to spend on some of the work from the spike, it would negate the benefit of a spike.

Another reason to not add spike outcomes to the same sprint is that the newly defined tasks may not be of higher priority or value to the product owner than tasks that already exist in the backlog. It is not up to the team to arbitrarily take on the work from the spike without consulting the product owner.

Bottom line: Spike in one sprint; work on the outcome in another, as prioritized by the product owner.

## Preconditions

The idea for preconditions was formulated when my first team asked, "Where do we put items that do not fall into the buckets of feature work, taxes, or spikes?" An example of a precondition is "Set up a build environment." While many are tempted to say "it should just happen," it's better to track the work because it is going to contend for the team's time.

We looked back at past work and found we had similar work items that fell into the *build environment* category, and from that we defined preconditions:

> *Preconditions are items that are not part of a story's tasks yet still must happen by sprint end. These are items identified by the team and negotiated with the product owner and ScrumMaster. Without completion of the items, the team cannot say "the sprint is complete."*

What this ended up being was the bucket for the team to put work in that it needed to do. This primarily contained work items like "pay down debt in acceptance test framework."

Preconditions should not be used all the time, nor should they dominate the sprint or product backlog landscape. They are commonly used as a way of positioning issues and efforts required to manage and regulate the team in a broad sense—issues such as morale, work environment, and so on.

As I reflect back on when this originated, and how I use it now, I find that I use preconditions less and less as more and more teams are mature and familiar with agile and Scrum. I would not consider this a hard requirement, but teams today still find preconditions helpful. You will likely have more preconditions in early sprints than later ones.

## Defects/Bugs

Some teams find it important to track defects separately from the feature work. This is OK. If your organization likes to see where defects go, by all means track them. You would do this by adding a category of "bugs" or "defects" and track it as illustrated in Table 25-1. This enables you to view it visually as illustrated in Figure 25-1.

**TABLE 25-1**   Type of Work Included in the Sprint Backlog

| TYPE OF WORK | TASKS | HOURS | CUMULATIVE HOURS |
|---|---|---|---|
| PRECONDITION | SETUP CI SERVER | 2 | 14 |
| SPIKE | FIGURE OUT HOW TO INCORPORATE PRODUCT LINE DATA IN THE PRODUCT LINE MAP | 4 | 18 |
| FEATURE | CREATE ANALYSIS TO ALLOW USERS TO ANALYZE OFFERINGS | 6 | 24 |
| FEATURE | CREATE DIMENSIONAL MODEL | 8 | 32 |
| TAX | REVIEW DATA CONNECTIONS WITH SECURITY TEAM TO ENSURE CORPORATE DATA USE COMPLIANCE | 2 | 34 |

## Structuring the Data

To structure the data, the team should start with a review of each task in the sprint backlog. Items should then have an identifier added to them that falls in one of the four buckets just discussed. A snippet from an example sprint backlog is listed in Table 25-1.

## Using the Data

Whether the data is stored in a spreadsheet or a database, you are now able to do analysis on the data *and* provide insight for the stakeholders of the system.

By drawing a chart like the one shown in Figure 25-1, you can see where the time is spent on a project.

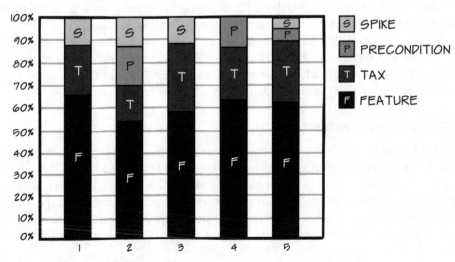

**FIGURE 25-1**   A chart makes it clear what proportion of overall work is spent on each type of work

In this example, we can see that the team averages close to 60 percent of its time on feature work, about 20 percent of its time on taxes, about 10 percent of its time on spikes, and that precondition work is done more intermittently.

From a financial perspective, the customers are paying $1.00 and are getting $.60 of value based on feature work. Spikes *might* provide value as they will inform future work, but they don't advance any features in the sprint. In sprint 5, we can see the taxes were nearly 30 percent—during that sprint, $0.30 of every dollar was spent on the cost of doing business.

# Keys to Success

With metrics like this at hand, you can readily provide your stakeholders with a tremendous amount of visibility into where their money goes. When implementing this model, remember to educate stakeholders about the model and work with them to find ways to maximize work-producing time. If you track this data for multiple teams, you also gain a new ability to spot trends and potential problems.

## Educate Stakeholders

I often find that stakeholders care about two things: money and time. One impacts the other. Too often stakeholders don't understand why solutions cannot be implemented instantaneously. A complete, high-level categorization of the activities competing for the team's time gives them a broader perspective: Time spent in one category of work directly impacts the others.

The model divides the team's time into buckets. Though the chapter provided some sample categories, you might need to identify different ways to characterize the team's work in your organization. It's important that you expose how the team spends its time; it's much less important to adhere to a rigid category list.

Showing your stakeholders and customers where their money goes and how much time and money the activities that surround software-building consume in your organization will go a long way toward ultimately gaining their acceptance of release dates, value, and the overall cost of physically doing the project.

## Work with Stakeholders

Once the chart is complete, remind the team and stakeholders that this behind-the-scenes look into the team's time is not meant to be used against the team. On the contrary, it is designed to help the team and the stakeholders identify ways to eliminate time-wasting activities or inefficiencies in the team's time that are beyond the team's control. For example, the stakeholders in the story were able to see how much time certain corporate taxes consumed and look for ways to move them out of the team's way.

You will never eliminate all non-work-producing activities. Some overhead is inescapable. And in some cases, you might not be able to identify any areas to streamline. That's OK. The point is to provide a transparent look at why the team moves at the speed it does. The actions that come out of the data will vary from team to team.

## Determine Trends and Patterns

If you use this model with multiple teams, you can use the data you collect to identify patterns and trends in the company. These can help you to forecast or spot trouble on new projects. Establish baselines, showing that by project type, a certain percentage of team time spent in each category is typical. When a team begins to venture outside the established patterns of the company, further digging into that team's deviation might be appropriate.

In the end, this model is about transparency and accountability. Implementing it on your project not only enables you to have insight into the work the team is doing, and where they are doing it, it undoubtedly raises blocking issues that are preventing higher performing teams from thriving in your company today.

# Works Consulted

Jeffries, Ron. "Essential XP: Card, Conversation, Confirmation." XProgramming. com. http://xprogramming.com/articles/expcardconversationconfirmation/.

Wake, Bill. "INVEST in Good Stories and SMART Tasks." XP123.com. http://xp123. com/xplor/xp0308/index.shtml.

# Chapter 26

# UP-FRONT PROJECT COSTING

It's budget planning time. Management has asked you what your new Scrum project will cost, when it will be done, and how many people you need. You know the answers you give will be forever forged in stone—how do you respond?

## The Story

Lindell was a project manager working on new features for the web component of the company's online service offering. She had been with the company for many years and, like the rest of her teams, had heard of Scrum but had never used it. One day, she was approached by the lead developer, Brian, to use Scrum on her next project. The conversation went something like this.

"Lindell, I think we should use Scrum on this project," said Brian.

"I'd like to use it as well, but Scrum wouldn't work for us. We have to lock down our people, date, and features up front. Speaking of which, management is breathing down my neck. I've got to get them something soon," Lindell glanced at her watch before continuing. "Management wants an up-front plan—and that kind of planning is not something Scrum teams do."

"I used to think that, too. I've been doing some reading, though, and then last week, I met this guy Mike at a user group meeting. He gave a talk about how they did project costing in his company. If I can get him to have lunch with us, would you hear him out?" asked Brian.

"Sure. If there's a way to use Scrum, I'm all for it," said Lindell.

"Great, I'll schedule something for early next week," said Brian.

The day could not come soon enough for Lindell who was getting more and more pressure from management to provide dates, the feature set, and the money needed for the project in terms of new hardware and people. As soon as they sat down to lunch, Lindell turned to Mike and pleaded, "Mike, I'm stuck! I have no clue on how to cost this project. I'd like to use Scrum, but I am not sure what to do. I feel like I have my back against a wall."

"I think I can help," said Mike. "Brian filled me in on some of your challenges. The first thing I think we need to do is review the feature set that is being asked for."

Lindell pulled out a 100-page specification document. Mike frowned.

"Do you have anything else or is this it?" asked Mike.

"This is it, for what it's worth. I mean, it's been signed off and approved, but I'm not even sure we all agree what it means in the end," admitted Lindell.

"Well, it's a starting point. What we really need is a product backlog. So, let's review the specification and create user stories from it. I even brought index cards," said Mike with a smile.

Lindell and Brian were both somewhat familiar with user stories from a course they had attended, so they had little trouble going through the document section by section and writing stories on index cards. After about 15 minutes, Lindell noticed a potential problem.

"Mike, I've been writing 'as a user' like I was taught, but our system has many types of users. Should I start writing things like 'as an accounting user' for the stories?" asked Lindell.

"Yes! Please! I'm sorry I did not explain that earlier," said Mike.

"No problem. I'm just happy to be doing something productive," replied Lindell.

After a couple of hours, they had created close to 50 stories. Mike had to get back to his office but offered to come back the next day to help them finish the costing.

When Mike walked in the next day, Brian had put all the story cards on the wall of the conference room. He and Lindell had already sorted them by functional area with the bigger, higher-level stories on the top and the smaller stories beneath them. To determine this, they had used their best judgment and discussed each story with one another, creating multiple groupings of functionality that they thought they could ship.

"This is great," said Mike. "Our next step is to figure out about how many points these stories are and what their priority is."

"The priority is simple," said Lindell. "They are all high priority. Points seems pretty abstract. Why can't we just skip that and figure out how many hours they are going to take?" asked Lindell.

Brian chimed in. "Using hours is too restrictive. Management will see a really rough hourly estimate and hold us to that number. Points give us a way to communicate size without tying it to a specific number of hours."

"It seems to me like we're wasting a lot of time that could be spent doing real planning," said Lindell.

Mike nodded, "I hear you, Lindell. We're only part way there, and it's hard to see from here how it will all come together. One thing I've learned in doing this is that we are all really good at estimating relative size, like determining which bag of groceries is heavier. If we were asked to determine the absolute weight of each bag, however, we would struggle. This is the reason I use story points, a relative measure, rather than hours, which is an absolute measure."

"All right," said Lindell. "We've come this far. Points it is."

"OK, where is your team? We need them here to estimate this," said Mike.

"My team? Ha! I don't get assigned a team until we get through procurement and resourcing. And I can't get through there until I have a budget and a plan. See, I knew Scrum wouldn't work."

"I know it's not ideal, Mike," Brian put in. "But all we've got right now is the three of us. Is it possible for us to estimate it… just for the costing process? We can always put better estimates on the stories once we have the team, right?"

"We can, yes, but I want you guys to understand that it works so much better when the people who do the work are the ones who estimate the work. If that's impossible, we'll just make do with what we've got. Are you familiar with using part of the Fibonacci sequence as the range of point choices? 1, 2, 3, 5, 8, 13, and if needed 20 and 40?"

"I've heard of it. But I don't really get it. Are those numbers hours, weeks? What?"

"They are measures of relative size," Mike explained. "Think of it like T-shirt sizes versus dress shirt sizes. T-shirts are relative, XS, S, M, L, XL, XXL. Dress shirt sizes are more absolute, with a neck and sleeve measurement."

When Brian and Lindell nodded, Mike continued. "So we treat our stories more like T-shirts. You pick a representative smallest story, an XS or 1-point story, and a representative biggest story (an XXL or 13)…maybe even a story that's in the middle (an M or L, 3 or 5). These become your *reference* stories. Then all the rest of the stories can be sized relative to those. A two-point story is *about* twice as big as a one-point story. An eight is about half as big as a 13. Get it?"

"Sort of."

"Let's start with this grouping here. Let's find our extra-small story, our one point."

Lindell and Brian agreed on a very easy, small story. "Now, show me one that's about twice as big." Again, Lindell and Brian had little trouble identifying a story for Mike. Soon, they were discussing the stories and assigning them points with minimal difficulty. It took the rest of the day, but Lindell and Brian finally made it through the entire wall of stories. Throughout the process, Mike was busy taking notes on each story discussed so Lindell and Brian could review them later.

"Let's take a break," suggested Mike. "So, Lindell, how do you feel this is working?"

"Wow! We sure flushed out a lot of assumptions. I mean, this story where we need to call the data set. Brian thought we were only using half of the data elements because the spec was out of date. Through discussing the story, I was able to remember a side discussion I had with someone at lunch recently who said that API had been rewritten and that rewrite would now allow us to use all the data we were looking for. I'm sure glad we caught that now!" said Lindell enthusiastically.

"That's one of the huge advantages to using this technique; the conversations really flush out assumptions and help get everyone on the same page early," said Mike. "What we need to do next is determine how many story points your team can accomplish per sprint. This is going to be a bit of a challenge since you don't have a team yet. Have either of you worked on a Scrum project in the company?" asked Mike.

"No, sorry, Mike. We're the guinea pigs," said Brian.

"Not a problem. When we first started, we estimated our velocity. It was not perfect—far from it—but it gave us a rough idea of what we needed to do to get through the project. It gives you a starting point," said Mike.

"Can you walk us through it?" asked Lindell.

"I have a paper on it that I can send you tonight, Lindell," said Mike.

"Perfect. So once we have our team's velocity, what's next?"

"We have to prioritize the stories you identified," said Mike.

"But Mike, these are all…"

"Top priority?" said Mike, "I know, but hear me out. Let's look at the groupings on the wall. Which group of stories is the most important, the one group you could absolutely not live without?" asked Mike.

"This set here," said Lindell. "But this one is a close second."

Before she knew it, Lindell had chosen a minimal marketable feature set [DENNE]. Mike moved the cards into a list format, with the most important stories on the top and the lower ones on the bottom.

"Great. In the backlog we see we have about 45 stories with a total point value at about 200. And you said earlier you had about seven months as your deadline—that's 28 weeks. So, let's say you run your estimation exercises and determine that the team can manage somewhere between 10 and 14 points per sprint. If they run 14 two-week sprints (28 weeks), how many points can they deliver?

"Somewhere between 140 and 196 points. So, not everything, but a good chunk."

"That's why prioritizing this list is so important. They'll do the most important stories in the time they have," said Brian.

"How do we get that number up to closer to the top of the range, the velocity number?" asked Lindell.

"You can add resources or improve efficiency, which is the job of your Scrum-Master. I suggest you have one, and, again, if you want to know why, I have a paper that explains it pretty clearly for management in terms they'll understand—money," said Mike.

"*Thank you,* Mike," said Lindell. "I cannot tell you how helpful this is. So we've narrowed down the scope and the velocity based on the team we get, but what about the cost?"

"How many people do you think will be on this project" asked Mike.

"I'm going for six people, but realistically we'll get five." said Brian.

"And what's worse is *none* of the people we get will be full time. They will all be split on other projects. If we are really lucky, we will have one fully dedicated person, but I am not holding my breath," said Lindell.

"How many hours will each team member have for your project on a given day?" asked Mike.

"Somewhere around six hours. That may be high, but it matches the average I've gotten on past projects," said Lindell.

1. CREATE USER STORIES    5. DETERMINE TEAM COST

2. PRIORITIZE STORIES    6. CALCULATE PROJECT COST

3. ESTIMATE STORIES    7. COMMIT, YES OR NO

4. DETERMINE VELOCITY

**FIGURE 26-1**    Project costing process

"Great! We will use six hours of availability per person on the project. Now, how do you do your billing? This is an internal project, right?" Mike asked.

"Yes, internal. Our loaded employee costs vary, but let's just go with $140 an hour," said Lindell.

"Great, so if we use $140, and you have five people, your cost should be around $700 an hour. If each person gives six hours a day to the project over a two-week sprint, the project will cost $4,200 a day or $42,000 per two-week sprint," said Mike. "What's your budget?"

"Our project budget is $800,000," said Lindell.

"So at $42k each, $800,000 will buy you 18 to 19 sprints. The problem is, you only have 14 sprints before your deadline. If your velocity stays 10 points per sprint, you can accomplish 140 points in 14 sprints, and it will cost $588,000 (($42,000/10)*140). That's well under your budget of $800,000 but doesn't deliver all the stories. You've got the money to add a person to the team, which would increase your velocity but still might not accomplish the entire backlog. Even so, we've accomplished what we set out to do," said Mike.

He went to the whiteboard and wrote the items shown in Figure 26-1.

The lightbulb went off for Lindell. She now understood how it all tied together. And even better, she thought she could give management more options and better information than she could have otherwise.

"Thanks, Mike," said Lindell. "You've been an incredible help. You know, I think this Scrum thing might work for us after all."

## The Model

In the story, Lindell was asked to determine what a project would cost in terms of time, money, and people (aka resources). This is a typical request that stumps many who are new to Scrum. Luckily, Lindell had help from Brian, who enlisted Mike to take them through the process of creating user stories out of a functional specification; sorting, prioritizing, and estimating those stories; and putting them together with an estimated velocity to determine what could be accomplished within the current budget and time frame.

## Functional Specifications

Functional specifications exist to give us a sense of certainty in the systems that will be built. They capture not only functional system details but architectural and component details as well. Unfortunately, functional specifications capture these details at the beginning of the project, when the least amount of information is available. Additionally, though they often describe desired system states, such as *the system shall have 99.999% uptime*, they do not say how that will be achieved. What's worse is that functional specifications traditionally outline a plan for the system to be built by function (design, development, testing) rather than by functionality (feature x, feature y, feature z).

Scrum projects forego functional specifications in favor of user stories and product backlogs. These high-level descriptions of functionality capture just enough information to let us know what will be built but do not fill in the details until closer to when the feature will be implemented. This emphasis on minimal up-front information and the team's commitment to grooming the product backlog during each sprint helps this living document remain pertinent and avoids wasted time spent on specifications that are out of date before they can be implemented. Product backlogs are made up of user stories. Your first step in costing your project is to build a product backlog by writing user stories.

## User Stories

User stories are abstractions. Abstractions live longer than details. Unlike functional specifications, stories leave the details for a future conversation between the product owner and the team. We saw Brian and Lindell use the functional specification to build a product backlog based on user functionality, not on job function. They wrote these not in a 100-page document, but on index cards that they could sort, tear up, and add to easily. While reframing each specification in the terms of a user story, they were able to uncover assumptions and identify hidden requirements that would have otherwise caught them by surprise further into the project. The cards contain just enough information to communicate the idea, or the concept, of what is to be developed, but they do not contain the details. The details are provided through conversation and are confirmed just before the start of the sprint as the team and product owner discuss the stories that will be implemented. Ron Jeffries calls this the three C's of user stories—card, conversation, confirmation [JEFFRIES].

Creating user stories from a functional specification can be a challenge. If you can, get rid of the functional specification and replace it with user stories and a product backlog. If you must maintain the functional specification throughout the life of the project, concentrate your effort on the product backlog. Part of the project overhead will be to map the product backlog to the specification and, as features are developed, communicate which part of the specification is complete.

## Estimating Stories

There are many techniques for estimation: historical data, individual expert judgment, decomposition, top-down, bottom-up, wideband Delphi, analogous, planning poker [GRENNING], and tools like COCOMO [BOEHM]. Regardless of which technique you use, people want as precise a number as possible. However, as mentioned in the "Functional Specifications" section of this chapter, teams don't know enough at the beginning of the project to be extremely precise, which is why we instead provide relative sizing estimates.

I prefer planning poker because it provides a little bit of everything—analogous, expert judgment, decomposition—and involves the entire team. Planning poker has several advantages. First, it focuses on the relative estimate size, not fixed hours or days. Next, it provides teams the opportunity to talk about what things mean. This helps spread information and knowledge about the system and prevents a single expert from dominating.

For example, let's say that a team of five people all estimate a story to be a two or three, and someone else estimates the same story to be eight or thirteen. That last estimate is likely showing some hidden assumptions that need to be shared. The conversation that ensues might increase the rest of the team's estimates, decrease the high estimate, or even cause the team to break the existing story into two different stories. Whole-team participation and knowledge-enhancing discussions are the key benefits to planning poker.

When estimating, teams typically estimate the work using story points—abstract units of measure. Why do they do all this? Because it's better to be roughly right than precisely wrong. In the story, Mike explained relative sizing by pointing out that it's much easier to look at two shirts and say, "This one is about twice as big as that one," than to try to determine the exact neck and sleeve measurements. Sure, you could figure it out if you wanted to, but the amount of effort required to get exact or precise estimates is economically prohibitive and generally not warranted. Getting roughly right estimates is all that is needed at this time.

Keep in mind that your relative sizes need to be similar enough to enable you and the team to make realistic comparisons. Comparing T-shirt sizes is simple. Trying to choose between a tuna or a killer whale (orca), or a compact fuel-efficient car or a long-haul shipping tractor trailer, is nearly impossible. The difference between their relative sizes is too great. Choose reference items that are more alike and easily visualized relative to one another: a small tumbler glass versus a pint glass or a small prop airplane versus a 747. Even relative sizing must stay within a certain scale.

Finally, remember that though Lindell and Brian estimated by themselves out of necessity, whenever possible all the people doing the work should be the ones estimating the work.

## Prioritizing Stories

At first, Lindell maintained that everything in the product backlog was equally important and so had equal priority. Mike (and you and I) knew this could not be true. If everything is the highest priority, then nothing is a priority. The first step in prioritizing user stories has to do with understanding what your users want. (Several excellent techniques can help you understand what users want, including the Kano Model of Customer Satisfaction, financial models like IRR, and Innovation Games® like Buy a Feature or Prune the Product Tree. I've included references at the end of the chapter to help you locate these resources.)

Once you have this information, you can use one of many techniques to prioritize your list. One quick way to determine priority is to just order the list from top to bottom, and label them 1-$n$. Nothing can be equal. You can also think in terms of minimal marketable feature (MMF) set, a term introduced by Denne and Cleland-Huang in the book *Software by Numbers*. They define an MMF as "units of software value creation. They represent components of intrinsic marketable value" [DENNE, p. 5]. I think of it as the smallest group of features that must exist to release the product.

In our story, as soon as Mike reframed the question in terms of minimal marketable feature sets, "Which group of features do you absolutely have to have in an initial release," Lindell was able to quickly prioritize her backlog in terms of what features and functionality the end users would absolutely need to have to use the system in production. Once Lindell identified the first set, she could then group the remaining features into additional releases to production that enhanced this minimal functionality.

## Determining Velocity

Without knowing the velocity of the team, it is essentially impossible to calculate what work will be done and by when. Lindell and Brian did not take the time to estimate their velocity while they were with Mike. They just pulled a random range out of the air to help them figure out how to calculate costs later.

Even though it's not ideal, it is possible to estimate a velocity range, even for a team that has never done Scrum before. Many of those techniques are detailed in Chapter 4, "Determining Team Velocity." The key is to update the plan with real data as soon as the team begins running sprints.

## Deriving Cost

In Chapter 8, "The Case for a Full-Time ScrumMaster," I discussed the loaded cost of an employee. Use that here if you don't bill for your time. If you work in a consultancy or have a capital expenditure budget that you are working from, you know what the billable rate is per person. Either way, you need to determine what the team costs.

This is accomplished by determining the number of hours the team thinks it can dedicate to the project per sprint and multiplying it by each person's hourly rate. It's really that simple.

For example, let's look at a team of five people.

| TEAM MEMBER | LOADED COST/HOURLY BILL RATE |
|---|---|
| ROGER | $100 |
| TIAGO | $220 |
| GEOFF | $150 |
| NIGEL | $150 |
| KAREN | $80 |
| HOURLY TEAM COST | $700 |

The team costs $700 per hour. Each team member averages six hours per day on this project and runs two-week sprints (ten working days). The team sprint cost is $42,000.

## Build the Release Plan

The final step in costing is to build a release plan. In our story, Lindell did some quick calculations to determine that at a certain velocity and sprint cost, the team would not be able to accomplish all the stories in the product backlog by the deadline. She and Mike were also able to determine that there was room in the budget to add more personnel, which might help the team accomplish more work prior to the hard deadline. The costing work she had done allowed her to present a more complete picture of the initial project realities and options for getting more done in the time allotted. Chapter 11, "Release Planning," provides details on how to build your own release plan, a required element when working with a PMO or external customer. Please refer to that chapter for details on how to build an agile release plan.

# Keys to Success

Costing projects up front is challenging, Scrum or no Scrum. *How much will it cost, when will these features be done, what will we get,* and *how long will it take?* Using Scrum doesn't change these questions, but it does change how you communicate your answers. Discussions of cost are reframed in terms of cost per sprint. Feature specifications are replaced by estimated, prioritized product backlogs. The questions of *when* and *how much* become questions of budget and velocity. You have to educate management about these terms to some degree for them to understand and accept your answers. In the end, though, you'll likely find that, like Lindell, you actually have more information and options to give them with Scrum than you did with function-based processes.

As you saw in the earlier discussions, the actual process of determining cost is not that complicated. What is complicated is building trust. After all, cost questions are usually concrete ways of asking the abstract question, how do I know you'll deliver what we've asked for? Most people have been burned in the past by teams that don't deliver, miss deadlines, and have less-than-desirable quality. From these failures, come the detailed questions, Gantt charts, and product specifications that dominate software development conversations. As you provide answers, don't forget that what you are really offering is assurance. Take the time to explain how the software will be developed and delivered. Frame every answer in terms of a range of what you believe can be accomplished, rather than a definitive number. If your answers were derived without the help of your team or with velocity estimates instead of real data, communicate these assumptions and prepare management for how actual data might alter your answers. At the same time, reassure them that you will provide that data as soon as it is available. Remind them that changes will occur and that your answers are an educated guess, not a promise set in stone.

Up-front costing is possible with Scrum. Try to involve your team and use historical data to come up with your projections. If that is impossible, you can simulate team discussions and estimates to answer initial costing questions. As soon as a real team is available, though, throw out the simulated numbers and replace them with real estimates and actual velocities. Change your projections to reflect the reality of your team and communicate the new numbers as soon as you have them. If you've done your job well during up-front costing discussions, management will not only be receptive to new numbers, they'll be expecting them.

Agile planning is straightforward. Tell your customers, stakeholder, and management what you know up front, inform them of any changes along the way, and deliver working software at the end of each sprint so that adjustments can be made. That's Scrum. That's agile. That's a process that builds trust.

# References

[BOEHM]   Boehm, Barry. 1981. *Software Engineering Economics*. Englewood Cliffs, NJ: Prentice-Hall.

[DENNE]   Denne, Mark, and Jane Cleland-Huang. 2004. *Software by Numbers*. Upper Saddle River, NJ: Prentice Hall.

[GRENNING]   Grenning,   James.   http://renaissancesoftware.net/files/articles/ PlanningPoker-v1.1.pdf (accessed 11 June 2009).

[JEFFRIES]   Jeffries, Ron. Xprogramming.com., http://xprogramming.com/articles/ expcardconversationconfirmation/ (accessed 31 December 2010).

# Chapter 27

# DOCUMENTATION IN SCRUM PROJECTS

We've all heard the common myth, *Agile means no documentation*. While other agile fallacies exist, this is a big one, and it could not be farther from the truth. Good agile teams are disciplined about their documentation but are also deliberate about how much they do and when. In this chapter's story we find a duo struggling to explain that while they won't be fully documenting everything up front, they will actually be more fully documenting the entire project from beginning to end.

## The Story

"Hey, you two," said Ashley, stopping Carter and Noel in the hallway as they passed by her office. "I've been sensing some resistance from you two over the initial project documentation. I need it by next Friday for project sign off, OK?" Ashley looked back at her computer and began typing again, clearly expecting a quick answer.

Carter and Noel looked at each other then back at their manager Ashley before replying. They had known this conversation was coming but didn't realize they'd be accosted in the hallway by an obviously harried Ashley when it did.

"Listen, we can document everything up front like you ask" Noel began as she and Carter moved to stand close to Ashley's doorway. "But we don't think it's the best approach. Things change and we cannot promise you that things will go as planned. Further..." Ashley stopped typing and looked up, interrupting Noel mid-stream.

"Look, I don't want to argue about something as basic as documentation. I just need it on my desk by Friday."

Carter spoke up.

"Ashley," he began. "Can I have five minutes to try to communicate a different approach? I know you've got a full plate, but I think it's important for you to understand this point before we table our discussion."

Ashley glanced at her watch, then nodded. "Five minutes. Go."

"When I was in college, I worked for our university newspaper," Carter explained. I worked as a sports photographer so I always went with the sports writers to the local football games. I would be on the field, and they would be in the stands.

"It probably won't surprise you to hear that not one of those sports writers came to the football game with the story already written. Now, they might have done some research on the players. They might have talked to the coaches about their game plans. They might have asked me to be sure to get some shots of a particular player. But they didn't write the article before the game even began.

"That's kind of what you are asking us to do with the software. You want the complete story of how this will unfold, including the final game score, before we've even started playing," said Carter.

"Well, that's how we get things done around here. Without the documentation, I can't get project approval, and I can't be sure that you guys understand what we need you to build," explained Ashley.

Carter continued. "Right. I get that. It's not unreasonable for you to want *some* information before we get started. And you should expect to receive frequent updates from us on what's going on with the project. After all, the reporters I worked with would take notes and write snippets of the article about the game as it was unfolding. They would come down at halftime to talk to me about the shots I had captured and the angle they were working on based on how things were going so far.

"But to ask us to tell you what the software will look like, exactly how much it will cost, and precisely when we'll be done is like asking us to predict the final score of the football game. We can tell you how we *think* it's going to go, but when things are changing and unfolding, it's difficult to predict all the details."

Ashley nodded. "But things aren't always that volatile with our projects. We know basically what we want this to look like. It's only some things that we aren't sure of."

"Right," said Noel. "And if you've got a project where we can nail down most of the variables and have a clear picture of the final product, we can give you more documentation.

Carter nodded, "To go back to my sports writer analogy, there were times when one team was clearly dominating—the game was a blowout. In those cases, the reporters had their stories mostly written by halftime. They'd already come up with the headline, filled in a lot of the details, and were just waiting until the end of the game to add the final stats and score.

"Most times, though, the games were close and the outcome uncertain. In those cases, the reporters would keep filling in the skeleton of the story with the events as they happened in real time. They would come down to the field at halftime, and we would talk about the unfolding story and how they were writing it. We'd strategize and say 'if the game goes this way, we'll take this approach. But if it goes that way, will take this other approach.'

"Likewise, the level of detail in our documentation should depend on how certain we are that things aren't going to change."

Ashley leaned back in her chair with her hand on her chin, deep in thought. Noel decided to go in for the kill.

"Ashley, remember when the Deepwater Horizon platform exploded and the oil started spilling in the Gulf of Mexico? Or the 9/11 attacks in the US? The London train bombings or the Moscow airport attacks? Or the quake and tsunami in Japan? Or when Reagan or Kennedy were shot?"

Ashley nodded.

"Well, you would notice a trend in all these events. In the initial accounts, the media headlines conveyed the big idea, but not many details. All they could tell us at first was generally what had happened (oil spill/terrorist attack/quake/tsunami/assassination attempts), when, and where. Why? Because the events were still unfolding and that was all anyone knew for sure. As the reporters on the scene learned more, they added the new facts to the story and changed the headlines, and the stories, to reflect the new information.

"All those little updates and facts and details, though, were important to capture in real time, even if they later had to be updated to reflect changes and new information. Without them, much of the information about the events would have been forgotten in the chaos surrounding it. The reporters didn't try to write more up front than they knew. Instead, they recorded what they did know as they went along. Later, after the details had solidified, they went back through the various articles and wrote a larger, encompassing synopsis that outlined the specific event from the initial failures to the current state," Noel said.

"That's what we're suggesting we do: make our documentation a story in progress. Is this making sense?" asked Carter.

Ashley sat forward.

"I think I get it now. What I originally heard you say was 'I can't give you documentation.' But what you're actually saying is that you will document certain things up front, most things in real time (updating them as necessary to reflect reality), and some things after the fact. But what does that mean in terms of software exactly?"

Noel spoke up, "One of the things we need to write for this project is the end-user manual and the customer support reference manual for the call centers. I think you'll agree we should not write those *before* we write the code, correct?"

Ashley nodded.

Noel continued, "Right, so when should we write them? In the past, we have written them at the very end of the project. When this happens, we scramble to find the little details because we forget to write them down, or we say 'we'll remember that' and we never do. The details are essentially lost, and a significant amount of time is needed to find them and document them, if they can be found at all. In the meantime, we're holding up a release of a functioning system all because we've forgotten exactly what every feature does in the system, and we are re-creating everything so we can create these manuals.

"What we need to do is document as we go, as soon as we can without doing too much. That way when we get to the point where the UI stabilizes, let's say, we can create even more detailed user guides, but we will not have lost our details. And if things change along the way, we will update what we have written to reflect it. It's a balance between stability and volatility. The more volatile something is, the more careful we need to be in what level we document. If it's stable, we can do something like a large database diagram model in a tool. If it's volatile, we might just draw a picture on the whiteboard—again, both are documents, database models to be exact, but they are very different in terms of formality," finished Noel.

"So, are we on the same page?" asked Carter.

"Yes," said Ashley. "I get it now. I think this is a good approach and something that I will advocate, provided you give me regular feedback so I can update senior executive management. But I still need the big headlines by Friday. Agreed?"

"Agreed," said Carter and Noel together.

And that was that.

## The Model

Many people can quote the part of the Agile Manifesto that states, "working software over comprehensive documentation," but they fail to mention the very important explanatory component that follows: "While there is value in the items on the right, we value the items on the left more" [BECK]. Scrum teams still value documentation; they just change the timing of that documentation to be more consistent with their level of knowledge.

For example, imagine you are in your university world history class. You get to the point in the class when it's time to discuss Western European history. Your professor says to you, "Now I want each of you to buy my new book *Western European History: The 30th Century*. Come prepared for an exam on the first five chapters in two weeks."

You would probably look around the room, wondering if what you just heard was correct and ask a fellow student, "Did he just say *30th* century history?"

Common sense tells you that without time machines, it is impossible to read a factual account of future events—they haven't happened yet! Sure there are predictors and indicators that suggest what *might* happen, but nothing is certain. This then begs the question. If this approach is wrong for a university class, why is the exact same approach accepted when developing software?

Before we've begun any work on a project, we are often asked for exact details as to what will be delivered, by when, and at what cost. To determine these things, teams often write volumes of documents detailing how the system will work, the interfaces, the database table structures, everything. They are, in essence, writing a history of things that have yet to occur. And it's just as ludicrous for a software team to do it as it would be for your history professor.

That doesn't mean we should abandon documents, and it doesn't mean that we should leave everything until the end either. A certain amount of documentation is essential at each stage of a project. Up front, we use specifications or user stories to capture ideas and concepts on paper so that we can communicate project goals and strategies. When we sign off on these plans, we agree that what we have documented is the right thing to do.

The question, then, is not, should we document, but *what* should we document and *when*. The answer has everything to do with necessity, volatility, and cost.

## Why Do We Document?

Every project needs a certain amount of documentation. In a 1998 article on Salon.com titled "The Dumbing-Down of Programming," author Ellen Ullman notes how large computer systems "represented the summed-up knowledge of human beings" [ULLMAN]. When it comes to system documentation, we need to realize that we're not building or writing for us; we are writing for the future. I think Ullman summarizes it best with this snippet from the same article:

> *I used to pass by a large computer system with the feeling that it represented the summed-up knowledge of human beings. It reassured me to think of all those programs as a kind of library in which our understanding of the world was recorded in intricate and exquisite detail. I managed to hold onto this comforting belief even in the face of 20 years in the programming business, where I learned from the beginning what a hard time we programmers have in maintaining our own code, let alone understanding programs written and modified over years by untold numbers of other programmers. Programmers come and go; the core group that once understood the issues has written its code and moved on; new programmers have come, left their bit of understanding in the code and moved on in turn. Eventually, no one individual or group knows the full range of the problem behind the program, the solutions we chose, the ones we rejected and why.*
>
> *Over time, the only representation of the original knowledge becomes the code itself, which by now is something we can run but not exactly understand. It has become a process, something we can operate but no longer rethink deeply. Even if you have the source code in front of you, there are limits to what a human reader can absorb from thousands of lines of text designed primarily to function, not to convey meaning. When knowledge passes into code, it changes state; like water turned to ice, it becomes a new thing, with new properties. We use it; but in a human sense we no longer know it.*

Why is this important? Because we need to realize that, in a human sense, we use the system and we know the system. That is why we document.

So, what is essential to document and what is needless work? Much of that depends on the type of system you are building and the way in which you work. Teams that are co-located need to document less than teams distributed across continents and time zones. Teams that are building banking systems need to satisfy more regulatory requirements than teams building marketing websites. The key is to document as much as you need and nothing more.

## What Do We Document?

The list of essential documents is different for every project. Going through my list of recent projects, some frequent documentation items include the following:

- End user manual
- Operations user guide
- Troubleshooting guide
- Release and update manual
- Rollback/failover manual
- User stories and details
- Unit tests
- Network architecture diagram
- DB architecture diagram
- System architecture diagram
- Acceptance test cases
- Development API manual
- Threat models
- UML diagrams
- Sequence diagrams

We didn't write all these before the project began. And we didn't wait until the final sprint to start them either. We did them as the information became available. Many of the user stories, for instance, were written up front. But some of them were changed, and others were added as the project progressed and requirements became clearer. Our unit tests were written as we coded. And at the end of every sprint, we updated the end user manual to reflect new functionality. We included in our definition of done what we would document and when we would write it (see Chapter 7, "How Do We Know When We Are Done?").

## When and How Do We Document?

So if we don't do it all up front and we don't save it all for the end, how does documentation happen in an agile project? Documentation, any documentation, costs money. The more time it takes to write and update, the more it costs. What agile projects strive to do, then, is minimize write time, maintenance time, rework costs, and corrections.

Let's look at three approaches we can take when documenting our projects.

- Document heavily in the beginning.
- Document heavily in the end.
- Document as we go along.

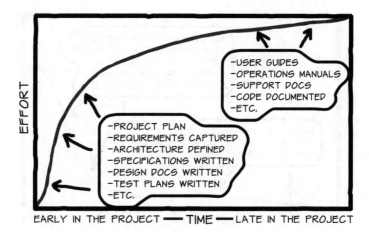

**FIGURE 27-1**    Traditional project with up-front documentation

## Document Heavily in the Beginning

Traditional projects rely on early documentation. As you can see from the diagram in Figure 27-1, a typical waterfall team must capture requirements, build a project plan, do the system architecture, write test plans, and do other such documentation at the beginning of the project. If we were to overlay a line that represented working software, it would not begin to move up until the blue line started to flatten.

The benefit of this approach is that people feel more secure about the system being built. The major drawback is that this sense of security is misleading. In point of fact, though a great deal of time, effort, and money has gone into writing the documents, no working software has been created. The chances of getting everything right up front are marginal on stable projects and next to zero on volatile projects. That means factoring in costly rework and extra time. Chances are good that these high-priced, feel-good documents will turn into dusty artifacts on the project bookcase.

## Document Heavily at the End

When we document heavily at the end, we document as little as possible as the software is developed and save all the material needed to release, sustain, and maintain the system over time until the end of the project. Figure 27-2 illustrates this approach.

The benefits of this approach are that working software is created quickly and that what is eventually written *should* reflect what the system does.

The problems with this approach, however, are many. People often forget what was done and when and what decisions were made and why. Team members on the project at the end are not necessarily the people on the project in the beginning; departing team members take much of their knowledge with them when they go. After the code for a project is complete, there is almost always another high priority

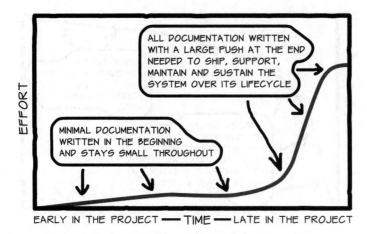

**FIGURE 27-2**    Documenting heavily at the end of the project

project that needs attention. What usually happens is that most of the team members go on to the new project, leaving the remaining team member(s) to create the documentation for the system by themselves. Countless hours are spent hunting for data and trying to track down and access old team members, who are busy with new work and no longer have time for something "as insignificant as documentation."

Though saving documentation until the end is cheaper in the beginning because more time is spent on actual software development, it is usually expensive in the end because it can hold up a release or cause support and maintenance issues, as it will likely contain gaps and faulty information.

## Document as We Go

Agile projects do things differently. We acknowledge that while we can't know everything up front, we do want to know some things. We also maintain that documentation should be part of each story's definition of done, so that it is created, maintained, and updated in real time, as part of the cost of creating working software. Figure 27-3 illustrates the document-as-we-go approach.

The product owner works with the stakeholders and customers to build the requirements while the team works with the product owner to achieve emergent design and architecture. The team also keeps the code clean, creating automated tests, and using code comments and other tools to slowly build other required documentation for the system, such as the user manuals, operations guide, and more.

The one drawback is that it does take a little longer to code when you document as you go than it would to fly through the code without having to write a comment or update an architectural diagram. This is more than offset, though, by the benefits. There is less waste, less risk of eleventh-hour holdups, and more emphasis on working software. Much of the documentation is updated automatically as changes are made

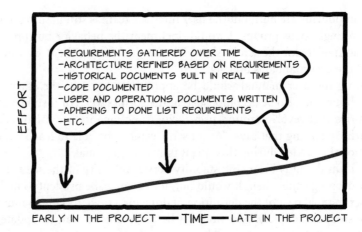

**FIGURE 27-3**   Documenting as you go

to the code, reducing maintenance and rework costs. Just as news reports capture the details of a story for posterity, real-time documentation of decisions and behavior in real time minimizes gaps in knowledge and creates a living history of the software for future teams and projects.

## Documenting in an Agile Project

So we agree that in most cases, agile teams will want to document as they go. So what exactly does that look like on a typical software project? To illustrate, let's use a document that is familiar to almost everyone: the user manual. A waterfall approach would be to write the entire manual at the end. We've discussed why this is a plausible but risky solution. The more agile way to approach a user manual is to include "update the user manual" as one of the acceptance criteria for a story that has to do with user-facing functionality. By doing that, the manual is updated each time working software is produced.

Let's say, for example, that I'm writing the user manual for an update to Adobe Lightroom (my current favorite piece of software). I'm in sprint planning and the product owner explains that the story with the highest priority is "As an Adobe Lightroom user, I can export a series of photographs to Adobe Photoshop so I can stitch them together to make a panorama." As we're talking through that story, I recommend that we add "update user manual to reflect new functionality" as one of the acceptance criteria for that story.

As I write the code or as I'm finishing the feature, I would also edit a document that provides the user instructions on how to use the feature. Depending on how stable the feature is, I might even include screen shots that walk the user through how to do this for both Lightroom and Photoshop. If the feature is less stable, meaning the core components are built but the user interface team is still hashing out the user interface through focus groups, I would document the behavior but probably only include placeholders for the screen shots. The key here is that the story would not be done until the user manual is updated.

Updating the user manual would be appropriate to do at the story level, as I described, but could also be accomplished at the sprint level. For instance, if we have several stories that revolve around user-facing functionality, we might add a story during sprint planning that says, "As a user, I want to be able to learn about all the new functionality added during this sprint in my user manual."

What I am doing is balancing stability versus volatility of the feature to determine how deep I go and when. It would not, for example, be prudent to make updating the user manual part of the definition of done for a task. Too much might change before the story is complete. Nor would it be acceptable to wait to update the user manual until right before a release. That's far too late to start capturing the details of the new behaviors.

When determining when to document your own systems, you must balance cost, volatility, and risk. For more on determining your definition of done, refer to Chapter 7.

## Starting Projects without Extensive Documentation

One challenge you will have is to help stakeholders and customers understand why you are not documenting everything up front. Tell them a story like Carter did at the beginning of this chapter (or share that story with them). Remind them that while documenting heavily up front drives down the perceived risk, you never know what you don't know until a working solution is in place.

Eschewing extensive documentation up front does not mean you are off the hook for a project signoff piece. But it does mean that the piece will look different to your stakeholders than it has on other projects. Rather than give them the specific artifacts they request, answer the questions they are asking in regards to schedules and requirements in the most lightweight way possible for your project and situation. A PMO might, for instance, ask for a Microsoft Project plan, but what the PMO really wants to know is what will be done by about when. By the same token, a stakeholder might ask you for a detailed specification, when what she really wants to know is, "Are you and I on the same page with regards to what I'm asking you to do?"

Signoff and approval will occur early and often. The product owner will hold many story workshops to build the product backlog, will work with the team to build the release plan, and will then communicate that information to all interested parties, soliciting enough feedback to ensure that the team will deliver what the stakeholders had in mind (which is rarely exactly what they asked for). The documents the product owner uses to do this are only a mode of transportation for ideas and concepts, and a document is not the only way to transfer those ideas. Up-front documentation can just as easily take the form of pictures of whiteboard drawings, sketches, mockups, and the like—it does not need to a large formal document.

The beginning of the project is when you know the least about what you are building and when you have the most volatility. What your stakeholders need is the piece of mind that comes from knowing you understand what they need and can give them some idea of how long it will take to deliver. Expend the least amount of effort possible while still giving them accurate information and reassurance. At this point in the project, everything can and will change.

## Keys to Success

The keys to success are simple:

- **Decide**—Determine what you need to document for your project and when it makes the most sense to produce that documentation. Some things, such as code comments, are easy to time. Other items, such as threat models, are more difficult. Work as a team with your product owner to determine the must-have documents at each stage of your project.
- **Commit**—Once you have a documentation plan, stick to it. Put it in your definition of done. Hold yourselves accountable. Documentation is never fun, even when it's broken into small chunks. Remind your team that a little bit of pain will eliminate a great deal of risk come release time.
- **Communicate**—If this is the first project to move forward without extensive up-front documentation, people will be nervous. Help them out, especially at the beginning of the project, by sending frequent updates, pictures of whiteboards, and any other documents that are produced. Do like your math teacher always told you and show your work. Seeing working software and physical artifacts goes a long way toward calming the fears of even the most anxious executives.
- **Invest in automation**—Documentation is easier and ultimately cheaper if you invest a little time in automating either the system or the documentation itself. For example, if you can create an automated script to compile all the code comments and parse them into documentation, you've saved a manual step and instantly made your documentation more in sync with the actual code. It's also much easier to document acceptance test results and API documents automatically than it would be to do manually. On the flip side, you might find that automating the features themselves can save you a lot of documentation work. For example, a manual installation process might require a 40-page installation guide; an automated installation process, on the other hand, probably only needs a one-page guide and is better for the end user as well. Whenever possible, automate either your documentation or the features it supports. The results are well worth the investment.

Being agile does not equate to *no* documentation; it means doing timely, accurate, responsible documentation. Make sure that documentation is equally represented in your team's definition of done alongside things like code and automation. Remember that when change happens, it's not just the code that changes—the entire software package that you are delivering changes, documentation included. Lastly remember that as much as you might wish otherwise, documentation is a part of every software project. When you do a little at a time and automate as much as possible, you'll find that while it's still an obligation, it's not nearly as much of a chore.

# References

[BECK]   Beck, Kent, et al. "Manifesto for Agile Software Development." Agile Manifesto website. http://agilemanifesto.org/ (accessed 16 January 2011).

[ULLMAN]   Ullman, Ellen. Salon.com. http://www.salon.com/technology/feature/1998/05/13/feature (accessed 18 November 2010).

# Chapter 28

# OUTSOURCING AND OFFSHORING

When the work piles up and the costs mount, shifting a portion of the work to out-side teams, especially ones that can be hired at a reduced rate, can seem like a good idea. However, what starts out as a well-intentioned shifting of a project can turn out to be a nightmare.

Outsourcing and/or offshoring, though sometimes unpopular, are here to stay. And because that's true, too many of us find that we have to make the best of a less-than-optimal situation. That was the case with Jonathan, a newly hired lead devel-oper at a Silicon Valley software company known for its agile development practices. Let's see how he reacts when he learns that he is to manage two newly outsourced teams.

## The Story

Jonathan had been working at his new company for three months. He was happy to be associated with an employer who valued agile principles and with teammates who knew how to deliver quality software. It was a far cry from his last job, with an employer that just didn't get it and a team stuck in ScrumBut [GUNNERSON]. That all changed the day his manager Emma invited him for coffee and a talk.

"I won't beat around the bush, Jonathan," Emma began as they walked toward the coffee stand. "I've got some good news and some potentially bad news. I'll start with the bad. I just got out of an executive management meeting. We are going to shift your project to our overseas office. The good news is that you've been such a great leader that the senior vice president asked specifically for you to run it. Are you up for it?"

Jonathan tried to keep his face neutral, but his first thought was that moving the project overseas would be the worst possible solution. He turned to Emma.

"Emma, is there any way we can keep it local? The team here has made great headway over the last few months," asked Jonathan.

"I wish I could say yes. The problem isn't your team; it's that our flagship product is slipping behind schedule. To get it back on track, we're diverting all local resources to help, including the people on your team. At the same time, we want to keep your project moving, so we've decided to contract with some overseas groups. A side ben-efit is that the move will save us money; we'll be able to get the outsourced team for 80 percent less than we are paying the local teams," Emma explained.

Jonathan had experience in outsourcing and offshoring work before, at his last company, which was one of the main reasons he changed jobs. He was not happy about the news, but being a new hire he understood his place and what he needed to do.

"I've been through this before, Emma, and I have to be honest. I'm not sure it's a good idea," said Jonathan.

"Which part, having you lead the effort or shifting the project?" she asked.

"Both," said Jonathan. "Now I'm not saying every company is like this, but I do want to share with you the outsourcing experience at my last company so that you can understand my hesitation. A couple of years ago, I was lead developer for an in-house team. We were cranking along pretty well. Because we always met our targets, management thought we had extra capacity, so they added more work to the pile. We became stretched so thin that a single snap would have ripple effects through every project in the company, delaying everyone. It was not a pretty sight.

"Management's solution was to have local teams partner with offshore teams. It seemed harmless enough, right? It worked like this: The architect on the team, a couple other guys, and I would go through and build a prototype, document it, and then send everything off to the team to build and implement. We ran it all in sprints so they delivered stuff back to us every couple of weeks.

"The problem was that 80 percent of the code they sent back was in such bad shape that it was easier to rewrite it than to explain to the offshore teams how to fix it. This went on for months. One by one, my teammates quit out of frustration—the fun had gone out of their jobs, and they felt, rightly or wrongly, that they were the clean-up crew for the offshore team. When I left a few months ago, I was the last original team member. Since then, that company's been having a support nightmare. There's no one left locally who knows the code, and because the turnover was just as high on the overseas team, there is no one left there to ask questions of either. All they've got is buggy code and mad customers.

"Management at that company looked at the initial figures and decided it was a cheap and easy solution. And sure, it cost less hour per hour, but the work they got back was inferior to what we would have delivered had we all been local. And it cost them a whole lot of good employees, including me. If you decide to do this, I'll give it my best shot, but I firmly believe this is the wrong thing to do. Outsourcing this work will not get us to where we need to be faster; in fact, it will slow us down and cost us more in time, money, employees, and customer satisfaction."

Emma stood there stunned. She used the distraction of ordering coffee to give her time to think. When they picked up their coffee and took their seats, she looked up at Jonathan and cautiously replied.

"You bring up some good points, Jonathan, points I have not considered because I have never had to outsource work. Can you tell me some more of how you had things set up and what you would do differently? I ask because I know the decision has been made to push work out. But, and this is a big but, we can still influence how we structure it," Emma explained.

"Yes, there are some things we can do to help make it less painful. We were based here in the valley, and the outsource shop was in India. They were 13 hours ahead of us, which made it uncomfortable for both parties to communicate. Either I had to work late or they had to work late. It just didn't work. It would be much better to stay closer to the same time zone, which in our case would mean contracting with an overseas team to our south—Argentina is only four hours ahead of us, so communication would be much easier," said Jonathan.

Emma was frantically writing notes. "What else?" she asked.

"Well, next I would embed team members together. What I mean by this is that if we outsource the work, we need to plan ahead. We need to have the outsource team come to our offices to work with the local team before those guys shift over to the flagship project. This enables us to have a good knowledge transfer and gives the overseas team a chance to ask the local team questions around direction, architecture, strategy," said Jonathan.

Emma was a bit stunned. "You want me to fly the *whole* team in?" she asked. "Isn't that a bit expensive?"

"Of course it is," said Jonathan. "It's one of several hidden costs of outsourcing. And it won't just happen once. After the initial transition, we'll need to spend time doing the deeper knowledge transfer that can only occur with pairing and time. That will mean flying a few people at a time from overseas to here for a one-month stay, then sending them home and flying a few more people in. Eventually everyone down there will have the opportunity to work with the local team before the local team switches to the flagship project. It costs a lot more than just what you see on paper— and you won't have the local team switched over to the flagship product as quickly as management thinks. The alternative, though, is to take the approach my other company took and just swap them out now and pay for it later in buggy, unintelligible code and unhappy customers. It's our choice."

Emma was visibly discouraged. She had not considered these factors.

"What else do we need to consider?" asked Emma.

"Well, if I'm going to run this, we need to plan on a hefty travel budget. I will be going down to Argentina once a month at a minimum to spend time with the team. Communicating only via email will only slow us down and make things worse. Once they get on their feet, we can look at less travel, but it will be a long while before that happens," said Jonathan.

"What if we can't make this happen the way you want?" asked Emma.

"I don't know. I can't imagine this ending well if it's set up poorly and underfunded."

"All right," said Emma. "What I need you to do is write this up for me and prepare a presentation for management so we can present our case. Can you do that?" asked Emma.

"I'll have it ready by next week," said Jonathan. "I came to this company based on its reputation. The management team is well known in the valley for putting people and customers first. I'm confident that once management sees the potential problems, it will fund the solutions. Of course, I'd still rather keep it local. But if we do have to outsource it, at least we can do it correctly."

# The Model

Most software companies use outsourcing not because they want to lay people off, but because they have too many concurrent projects and not enough staff to support them. Management looks at the options and decides that outsourcing is their best solution. What they might not consider or understand is what that could mean for their teams, their code, the final product, and their bottom line.

Outsourcing and offshoring are challenging using any framework, but when you add agile practices such as pairing, core team hours, and daily standups, offshoring an agile project quickly becomes a complicated and somewhat expensive endeavor. That being said, I'm not suggesting you use a traditional approach for offshoring; on the contrary, you need to be very disciplined and have frequent checkpoints, greater transparency, and other agile practices to make success more likely.

Before you make the jump to outsourcing, consider the true costs. If you still decide to do it, or the decision has been made for you, work to structure the outsourcing correctly for the best chance for success. Let's look first at the costs and then at strategies for dealing with the realities of outsourcing.

## Consider the True Costs

When it comes to cost, it's tempting to look only at the per-hour cost per person. If a developer in your country costs $100 per hour and an overseas developer costs $20 per hour, it appears much cheaper to use an overseas team. But as Jonathan pointed out in the story, management must factor in the hidden costs of offshoring. These include transition costs, increased overhead, long-term retention, managing the work, and making sure the new team follows the development practices/processes that are valuable to the local teams.

### Transition Costs

One big hidden cost of outsourcing is transition. As Jonathan highlighted in the story, it will cost time and money to get the new team up to speed. People need to get together to transition effectively, which means bringing some or all of the remote team into a central office to work with the original team. And it's not just a one-time knowledge dump. Getting the new team to understand a system in depth involves having at least some of the team members travel to pair with the old team members. It is best to have people cycle back and forth—meaning have some of the local team travel to the remote site and have some of the remote team spend time with the local team. Depending on the size of your project, the knowledge transfer can take weeks, months, or even a year.

Research shows that transition costs can range from 5 percent to 57 percent of the total project cost [OVERBY] [ROTTMAN]. Studies also show that while there might be a cost savings in using overseas teams, it is often removed by transition costs. In fact, the outsourcing venture might ultimately cost more than using local teams [YU].

## Increased Overhead

In Chapter 8, "The Case for a Full-Time ScrumMaster," I discussed how to determine the loaded cost of an employee. We calculated that most employees spend only 40 percent to 60 percent of their time on task during any given project, meaning they spend three to five hours per day doing productive work. The rest of the time is part necessary overhead, part noise and waste.

Outsourced projects have built-in communication challenges that take away from available productive time. In teams I've worked on, and many of the teams I've coached, people on outsourced projects spend an extra hour every day on additional meetings, email, and phone calls, as teams struggle through cultural and language barriers. This increased overhead must be factored into the overall project cost.

## Long-Term Retention

Overseas teams tend to have high turnover rates. Once trained, people understand they are more valuable and will often leave for a better paying job. One company I worked with in India said their turnover rate was nine months for each employee. If the organization you work with has a similar turnover rate, that means that by the time you finish transitioning the project, you're going to have to absorb the costs associated with bringing in new team members. Turnover rates might be higher for your local teams as well. The longer the transition time, the more difficult it will be for your local team members to stay engaged with the project.

## Cultural Challenges and Managing the Work

Day-to-day work tends to be more difficult on an outsourced project. You have to coordinate meetings, phone calls, and video conferences. You need to be more exacting with your email communications. All these obstacles have solutions, but the solutions come with increased costs.

Cultural challenges also come into play as you attempt to work together. In *Succeeding with Agile*, Mike Cohn suggests that teams create coherence—or "stick together" [COHN] (called "group cohesion" in the social sciences). To demonstrate the difficulties of understanding other cultures, Cohn relates how Geert Hofstede from IBM identified "five key dimensions along which cultures varied" [Hofstede as cited in Cohn, p. 359]. The data is illuminating and reveals what most of us know already. Chinese teams are less likely to challenge authority in a public forum; American teams are more likely to call it like they see it. Indian teams might say yes when they really mean "I hear what you are saying but don't agree." Overcoming cultural obstacles takes time, training, and patience, which ultimately means more cost to the project.

## Development Practices

A friend told me that management once outsourced a key component in one of his projects to a company in another country—supposedly a top-notch consulting firm. He managed the remote team (as well as the local team), but knew there was trouble with the remote team. After weeks of them coding with no code drops, he finally insisted that they send him the partially completed code. What was received was a solution with a single Program.cs file, which contained a single method, Main(). That method was hundreds upon hundreds of lines long. The out-of-country team had a dozen developers working on that single method, a method that didn't even work. He subsequently fired the remote team.

It's not as if these practices are limited to outsource firms; I've witnessed this behavior in US-based firms as well as those in Europe, China, Japan, and India. But if you've got a high-performing Scrum team, you've long since abandoned those kinds of practices in favor of agile engineering and best practices that make software reliable and easy to maintain. You expect, therefore, to work with new teams that develop software to the same standards and using the same beneficial practices. Those teams won't come cheap.

You also need to decide how you want to work with the offshore teams. You might choose to use work package deliverables, where each team builds a set of features on its own. Or you might choose to work around the globe, where the code moves from site to site to site. These added complexities make having standard engineering practices such as continuous integration and test-driven development even more critical to your success. Training teams that don't already do this to use these practices takes time and money.

## Dealing with Reality

If your company is considering outsourcing, show them the list of hidden costs described in this chapter. Maybe you'll be lucky and the powers that be will reconsider. It's more likely, however, that you'll be stuck with an outsourcing situation at some point in your career. It doesn't have to be the death knell for your project, as long as you don't go in blindly. When considering offshoring a project, you need to factor in all the costs, including vendor selection, transition costs, travel, losses in productivity, and increased project management. So how do you account for all these costs and give management some idea of what their real cost will be?

### Budget and Cost

When estimating the budget for an outsourced project, I've found it helpful to show only the best- and worst-case scenarios; I do not guess at a most likely cost because too much information is unknown about the entire experience (team dynamics, code quality, the product itself, etc.) to determine what is most likely.

Your first input is the total project budget. The budget might be an external number (if you are soliciting a bid) or an internal number (if you have a fixed cost you are trying to hit either in terms of loaded costs of a team or actual funds that you have to manage).

List the broad cost categories in one column. In the example in Table 28-1, the first cost item I list is vendor selection. If you already have a vendor, that cost wouldn't apply to your project. From there, I list what percentage (variable) of that item in the budget is usually spent on that category. For example, the best-case scenario for vendor selection is 0.5 percent; in the worst-case scenario, the percentage goes up to 1.5 percent. I do this for each potential hidden cost item.

You'll notice that some of the categories in Table 28-1 are identical to the costs I highlighted in the model (transition costs, for instance). Others, such as increased project management and losses in productivity are large buckets for several related costs. For example, losses in productivity include increased overhead, the need to get up to speed on development practices, and an anticipation of high turnover rates. You can use these categories or choose ones more specific to your own situation.

The percent variables I list are based on my experience. I suggest you start with your own data and, if needed, look at industry trends. For example, if you have a big team, your travel variable could be significantly higher than that shown in Table 28-1. Some costs, such as bugs and turnover, are harder to estimate, as you'd need to have some idea of the quality you will receive back from the offshore team and what their turnover is likely to be. That's why it's important to continue to track these costs over time, so that you can not only demonstrate the real cost of outsourcing but also create a better estimate for the next project.

Of course, you might also find that with tight engineering practices and a good effort at engineering, you actually do save money. If so, great. It's still important to know for certain what the real cost of outsourcing is in your situation. Gather data

**TABLE 28-1**   Offshore Cost Variable Model

| | OPTIMISTIC (BEST CASE) | | | PESSIMISTIC (WORST CASE) | | |
|---|---|---|---|---|---|---|
| | BUDGET | VARIABLE | HIDDEN COSTS | BUDGET | VARIABLE | HIDDEN COSTS |
| VENDOR SELECTION | $1,000,000 | 0.5% | $5,000 | $1,000,000 | 1.5% | $15,000 |
| PROJECT TRANSITION COST | $1,000,000 | 2.5% | $25,000 | $1,000,000 | 5.0% | $50,000 |
| TRAVEL | $1,000,000 | 5.0% | $50,000 | $1,000,000 | 15.0% | $150,000 |
| LOSSES IN PRODUCTIVITY | $1,000,000 | 3.0% | $30,000 | $1,000,000 | 8.0% | $80,000 |
| INCREASED PROJECT MANAGEMENT | $1,000,000 | 7.0% | $70,000 | $1,000,000 | 15.0% | $150,000 |
| | | | | | | |
| TOTAL HIDDEN COST | | 18.0% | $180,000 | | 44.5% | $445,000 |
| PROJECT BUDGET | | | $1,000,000 | | | $1,000,000 |
| TOTAL PROJECT OUTSOURCE COST | | | $1,180,000 | | | $1,445,000 |

and go into each new outsourced project with as much information as possible. That way, you won't be caught off guard by the cost of doing business offshore.

## Time, Distance, and Culture

The country where the outsourcing takes place is not the issue; you can find high-performing teams all around the world. The reason I am not a proponent of outsourcing, aside from the hidden costs, has to do with the fundamental challenge with distributed teams. Successful agile projects depend on high-performing teams. It's difficult to function as a unit when teams are spread out across time zones, don't share the same culture, and feel disconnected from one another by distance.

That being said, I have seen successful Scrum teams that outsource. Just not many. The ones that are successful have invested time, money, and patience in creating long-term relationships among the local and outsourced teams, have taken the time to understand each other's culture and point-of-view, and have been well-versed in agile principles and practices before they begin.

In the next section, we look at ways to ensure that your outsourced project runs as smoothly as possible, both for the local teams and the offshore teams.

# Keys to Success

The keys to success listed in this section are all based on one underlying ideal: No matter how far apart you are, do all you can to make it feel like you're a single team, working in one co-located space.

## Choose the Right Offshore Team

There are two dimensions to choosing the right offshore team: hiring agile teams and going north/south.

### Hire Agile Teams

When you outsource an agile project, hire a team that is already agile. Otherwise, you'll spend a great deal of time and money trying to educate the outsourced team on agile practices and principles, which might be very foreign to the team's own company culture. And don't depend on a line item in a marketing presentation that says, "We're agile." Go watch the team in action. See how the team members work and make sure their idea of being agile is consistent with your local team's philosophy. And most importantly, talk to former clients. This often gives you an idea of how agile the outsourced team really is.

### Go North/South

If you're going to go offshore, try to choose a team within three time zones of your local teams. This usually means going north/south instead of east/west. If you are in the UK, outsource to Portugal, Spain, an African nation, or maybe even Eastern Europe. If you are based in North America, look to South America. North/south really saves on the late-night conference calls and the time lost waiting for answers. When time zones are a factor, quick questions that could be answered in five minutes in a shared team space could potentially derail the project for a day.

## Allocate the Work in the Least Painful Way

When looking to break up your work, you have several options. One common approach I see is for teams to use "work package" deliverables. A work package is an allocation of a specific feature or set of features that the outsourced team works on. Though you need a local team coordinator to facilitate and coordinate the work, this approach generally does not require entire teams from both locations to meet on a daily basis.

Another option that many companies use is to have multiple teams work on the same codebase. When considering this option, understand that certain engineering practices and standards need to be in place, such as quality gates or check-in requirements, notations, a common definition of done, and more. By having teams working on the same codebase during their non-overlapping workdays, you can ostensibly accomplish more work in less time.

A third approach I've seen companies try is to offshore specific functions such as testing, UI, data modeling, or varying layers of a system. This is probably the worst of the options outlined here because the feedback loops and integration loops are horrendously long.

The best approach when allocating the work is to give the offshore team independence by providing them with a complete feature or feature set to work on and build end to end. It's also the most expensive. Stakeholders and customers (or product owners) will have to travel and spend significant amounts of time working offshore with the team. Another advantage of dividing the work into distinct features is that if the offshore team produces something of subpar quality, it is easy to jettison the poorly implemented feature in its entirety.

## Stick with the Scrum Framework

When you outsource work, don't abandon the Scrum practices that have been successful for your co-located team. While it might be more difficult to coordinate these activities, they are essential for long-term success.

### Daily Standup

Continue to have daily standups, preferably via teleconference. If you've followed my advice and stayed within three time zones, this should be relatively painless. If you're up against a 12- to 13-hour time difference, finding a time during working hours each day for both teams to meet is going to be difficult. Share the pain by alternating weeks: One week, one part of the team is on duty late; the next week it's the other part of the team. In other words, if you are in Asia and your team is in Canada, you'll be working late, say at 9 p.m., for one week. The next week you'll get to meet at the more normal time of 9 a.m., while your team in Canada gets the late-shift daily standup. It's essential that you keep having the daily standups, even when it's difficult or painful.

## Sprint Reviews

Keep sprint reviews live via video conferencing. Don't demo via email. Schedule a time for a demo and then alternate which team has to have the awkward time. Use a staggered approach like with the daily standup: One sprint, the review is at 9 p.m. on a Friday; the next time it's at 9 a.m. on a Friday. Yes, people will complain, especially the stakeholders. Kindly remind them their support is needed, that the team deals with this daily, and that this is the best way to deal with the reality of outsourced projects.

## Retrospectives

Don't skimp on retrospectives. In fact, they might be the most important tool you have to build a cohesive team. You still need to alternate the times and have at least 30 minutes to 1 hour of overlapping retrospective time. You might also choose to have each team do a local retrospective, using group time to review what was discussed and to determine how to remove the identified impediments/issues.

## Build a One-Team Culture

We've talked about the importance of a well-run transition. But if your team is going to remain involved in the project with the offshore team, you have to find ways to work together long term. Start the project with an in-person kick-off meeting with the entire worldwide team. (Add this to your growing list of software costs.)

You need to plan team building activities and regular visits. You should also bring offshore people to the central office and vice versa on a rotational basis to build team cohesion. At these joint meetings, work toward building a common development environment and codebase. This helps with packing and unpacking the code.

## Use Pairing to Create Shared Understanding

It is essential that the team members know each other and understand the codebase they are collectively building. The best way to accomplish this is to have dedicated pairing sessions. Many technologies exist to enable long-distance pairing (VNC/Live-Meeting/Windows Live Shared Desktop, to name a few). Use them. Let management know up front that you will need to work in pairs and that these pairs will be based on work, not proximity.

As with everything else, pairing is more challenging when teams do not share many (or any) common work hours. Even if it's painful, find two hours at least three times per week when pairs can work together on the code. As with meetings, share the pain of staying late or arriving early by alternating the times each week.

## Continuous Integration

Pairing is a good start, but you also need a way to know how the codebase is doing in real time, whether your code spans the globe or is a work package done in a single office. To help ensure that everyone knows the current state of the code, maintain a continuous integration server (and institute a good branching strategy). CI becomes more of a challenge when you factor in bandwidth issues between countries, available hardware, and the number of people involved, so don't go into this lightly—think the strategy through and factor in the things that you might take for granted, like a gigabit Internet connection, readily available telecommunication equipment, and electricity.

## Keep in Constant Contact with Technology

Two things I insist on with offshore teams are a dedicated uplink, such as an "always on" phone line, IM, or video portal. The uplink allows a live connection between teams throughout the day. If someone in Seattle has a question for the team in Brazil, they need only pick up the handset and ask the question. It mimics rolling back in your chair and shouting out the question to the local team. It's quick, it's easy, and it's always on.

The webcam is another must-have. You should be able to see your long-distance team members—and they should be able to see you. If you need to talk to them, you can see that they are at their desks and talk to them instantly.

Another one of my favorite technology tools is the push-to-talk mobile phone. This works great for teams that are in the same country but, for whatever reason, don't have webcams or a dedicated phone line. This enables them to have that instantaneous, spontaneous connection to their teammates.

If your company fights you on implementing any of these technologies, push back hard. Remind them that it was their decision to outsource the work and that these tools are essential to the project's success.

## Be Prepared to Travel

Travel is essential when outsourcing work. If the company has not allocated a budget for travel, don't do outsourcing. It will never work. Frequent in-person meetings are the only way to establish a true team environment and build trust among team members.

Travel is also an essential tool to nip problems in the bud. Every culture is different, even within your own country. When you are dealing with another country, culture differences magnify. Words, mannerisms, and even body gestures in one country can mean something entirely different in another. Nothing degrades team trust faster than having two teams that are not versed in each other's cultures. When trust issues surface, take action immediately, and take it in person. You might even have to move the whole team—pick one—to the other location. Get them to work together for a week or two to rebuild trust. Do this frequently. Yes, this will be expensive, but the time wasted when two teams don't trust each other is far more costly, especially when your customers are the ones to suffer the consequences.

## Have a Project/Team Coordinator

If you do decide to have multiple teams working with the same code, help reduce problems by assigning each team a project coordinator. I worked with one team who had its code circle the globe daily. The code went from Eastern Canada to China to Western Europe daily. In each location, a different team worked on it. Each location's team had a coordinator who was responsible for unpacking the code in the morning so the team could work on it and then repacking it at the end of the day to transition it to the next team. The coordinator also relayed the backlog to the next team and tracked his or her team's progress.

While not optimal, having a project coordinator on each team responsible for managing the flow of code enabled these teams to spend a combined 14 productive hours on the code per day.

## Never Offshore When...

There are certain times when a company should not offshore a project, no matter how careful the attempt.

- Don't outsource the first release of complex, high-technology-risk projects.
- Don't outsource if your local team struggles with development practices (TDD, CI, refactoring) or is undisciplined.
- Don't outsource without corporate support for the travel budget and technologies necessary for success.
- Don't outsource with an agile offshore company if you have no experience with agile yourself. You can't succeed with an offshore agile project if you have yet to do an onshore project.

As much as I dislike the practices of outsourcing and offshoring, I am realistic enough to understand that it is likely something every company will face. Do all that you can to fight it. Demonstrate the real costs. Look for people within your own organization who can share their struggles with offshoring. Present a well-reasoned case for keeping the project local.

When all that data fails to sway management, don't despair. With a hefty travel budget, a willingness to use technology, a faithful adherence to the Scrum framework and agile engineering practices, and the right offshore team, you can still succeed. It just takes a little more effort, a lot of extra patience, and several million frequent flyer miles.

## References

[GUNNERSON]   Gunnerson, Eric. "ScrumBut." http://blogs.msdn.com/b/ericgu/archive/2006/10/13/scrumbut.aspx (accessed 6 December 2008).

[OVERBY]   Overby, Stephanie. 2003. "Offshore Outsourcing The Money: Moving Jobs Overseas Can Be a Much More Expensive Proposition Than You May Think." *CIO Magazine*. September 1. 16(22).

[ROTTMAN]   Rottman, Joseph, and Mary Lacity. 2006. "Proven Practices for Effectively Offshoring IT Work." *IT Sloan Management Review*. 47(3), (Spring), 56–63.

[YU]   Yu, Larry. 2006. "Behind the Cost-Savings Advantage." *MIT Sloan Management Review*. 47(2), 8.

[COHN]   Cohn, Mike. 2010. *Succeeding with Agile*. Upper Saddle River, NJ: Addison-Wesley. p. 359.

## Work Consulted

Saran, Cliff. "Badly-Managed Offshore Software Development Costs Firms Millions." Computer Weekly. http://www.computerweekly.com/Articles/2004/06/15/203138/Badly-managed-offshore-software-development-costs-firms.htm (accessed 23 January 2011).

# Chapter 29

# PRIORITIZING AND ESTIMATING LARGE BACKLOGS

You've just finished a great story-writing workshop with your stakeholders. You're excited about the new product and are anxious to get started. Until, that is, you get back to your office and look at the mountain of stories that you've somehow got to estimate and prioritize. All your excitement disappears as you face the hard truth: You have no idea where to start.

The sheer size of new product backlogs can be overwhelming. That's why you need to attack them with something even bigger. I'm talking about a club that's about 14 feet wide and 10 feet high. You need to find yourself a big wall.

## The Story

Gordon was the product owner for a new, two-year project. He had worked with Scrum before and had a great relationship with the team and its ScrumMaster, Lynne. The problem was the product backlog. Already at 300 stories and growing, and with more than 20 competing stakeholders, the backlog was going to be a bear to estimate and prioritize. As Gordon began to work through the stories, he quickly became overwhelmed. He sought out Lynne for some advice.

"Lynne, you've got to help me out on this one," he said. "I can't get a handle on this backlog. I need to involve the stakeholders, but I'm afraid a prioritization workshop with all 20 of them will just degenerate into a big fight that accomplishes nothing. I'd tackle it myself, but it's so huge, I don't even know where to start. Any ideas?"

"I do have an idea, actually. We had a similar problem on the Jet project," said Lynne. "We had hundreds of stories, a couple dozen stakeholders, and a lot of questions."

"What did you do?" asked Gordon.

"Well, the first thing I did was print out all the story cards into something that we could use. You've done that right?" asked Lynne.

"Yup, got them all right here on index cards," said Gordon, patting his bag.

"Great. Next, we need to find a room with a great big wall," said Lynne. She gestured toward the conference room down the hall. "That one will do."

Together they walked down to the empty conference room and looked at the space.

"Well, it has a big empty wall," said Gordon. "And it's fairly easy to book. Dare I ask why I need a big wall?" asked Gordon.

"You'll see," said Lynne. "As soon as you can get it coordinated, book two meetings in this room, preferably the same day. In the morning, it'll be just you, me, and the team. In the afternoon, you can bring in the stakeholders to join us. We'll meet back here then, and I'll walk us all through the session. Bring your story cards. I promise you'll walk out of here with all the stories prioritized and estimated."

A week later, Lynne, Gordon, and the team met in the conference room.

Lynne asked Gordon to read the first five stories aloud then pass them out to the team members. The team members had a few questions about a couple of the stories, which Gordon fielded. One question came up that Gordon didn't know how to answer.

"That's OK," said Lynne. "Mark it with a red dot and note the question on the back. We'll come back to it this afternoon."

"OK," Lynne continued, addressing her team. "I want you guys to put those five cards on the wall, big stories go to the right; small stories to the left. Don't worry about exactly how many points. Just throw them up there. If it has a red dot, make your best guess for now. We'll refine this later anyway."

After a little haggling, the cards were in place. Gordon read the next five cards, and the team placed them on the wall. The team soon got into a rhythm and was able to quickly place the cards on the wall spots that everyone felt comfortable with. After three hours, all the cards had found their way onto the wall.

"OK," said Lynne. "We have an hour left before lunch. I want us to correlate what we see on the wall to points. Let's start with these stories on the left. If you were going to separate the one-point stories from the two-point stories, where would you draw the line?"

The team moved a few stories left and a few to the right until they felt comfortable that the stories on the far left were one-point stories. Lynne then taped a line from top to bottom to separate the ones from the twos.

"OK," she said. "How about two-point versus three-point? Where's the line?"

Again, the team debated for ten minutes or so, and then settled on a dividing line. Lynne added another taped line. They did this again to divide the three-point stories from the five-point stories, the five-point stories from the eight-point stories, and the eight-point stories from the thirteen-point stories. Lynne then asked for one final dividing point.

"Which stories are bigger than 13?" she asked.

The team had little trouble grouping all the big stories together on the far right. Lynne added one final divider. She released the team for lunch and turned to Gordon.

"So, we've got basic points assigned to all the stories in your backlog. That's important because how much a story costs could well affect its priority. Some of the huge stories might need to be broken down, but that will depend on what we find out in part two of our meeting, when the stakeholders come in. We'll have them move the cards into priority order and ask them any questions that you couldn't answer."

"Won't it mess up our estimates once we start moving these around?" asked Gordon.

"Nope," said Lynne. "We determined smallest to largest by moving cards from left to right. We'll illustrate priority by moving cards up and down. High priority stories will be high on the wall; low priority stories will be low on the wall. We'll just ask the stakeholders to keep the cards inside the taped lines where they found them."

"What will the team do during all of this?" asked Gordon.

"They should watch and see what the stakeholders move up and down, and listen as to why. Some of those answers will influence the sequence of the work. They should take notes as well, and might ask some of the questions on the red dot cards. You and I, though, will have to limit the discussion to a couple of minutes, to make sure we get everything prioritized before we leave," Lynne explained.

"And what do we do if the stakeholders disagree and get hung up on a story? Or keep moving the same story up and down?"

"You and I will watch for those types of discussions. If we can't resolve the dispute fairly quickly, we'll mark any stories that have serious conflicts with a yellow dot, note the two strongest dissenting stakeholders on the back, and move on. You can take the conversation about these more controversial stories offline with the two stakeholders who felt the most strongly about any particular story. There shouldn't be too many of those."

The stakeholders came in after lunch and were briefed on the process. After some initial hesitancy and a few tense moments, they soon were moving cards up and down inside the taped lines. When stories were similar, Lynne encouraged them to group them near each other and move them together.

After a few hours, the prioritization was complete. Lynne and Gordon thanked everyone for their participation and promised to follow up on the yellow dot cards.

"Just one more thing before we go," said Lynne. "Do you see these high priority stories over here on the far right of the wall?"

Everyone nodded.

"These are stories that you guys want to have done very quickly, yet they are so big, we can't even put estimates on them yet. I propose we spend a little time with these stories, breaking them into more manageable pieces. We can then re-estimate and reprioritize these smaller stories. There are only about 20 of them, so it shouldn't take too long.

Two hours later, Gordon and Lynne sat back in their chairs and stared at the wall. The last of the stakeholders had just left and they were finally alone.

"Well, I promised you an estimated, prioritized backlog," said Lynne, smiling. "What do you think?"

"I can't believe how well it worked!" said Gordon. "Everyone feels like they've had a say, I only have a few outstanding issues to discuss, and we're ready to get started with our first sprint. I feel like the weight of the world is off my shoulders. How can I thank you?"

"Don't thank me," said Lynne. "Thank the wall. The really big wall."

# The Model

Working on big backlogs can be a challenge. There's just so much to keep track of! And when the backlog is raw (not estimated and prioritized), it can be hard to know where to begin. While planning poker is a fantastic tool for estimating user stories, it's difficult to imagine tackling a pile of hundreds of stories, one at a time. That's exactly what Gordon was facing in the story: He was overwhelmed by the sheer size of the effort.

Lynne's suggestion, and my proposal, is to use a technique I call The Big Wall. It's similar to Lowell Lindstrom's Affinity Estimation [MAR], which I was introduced to in 2008, with one distinct difference: The Big Wall technique allows you to consider both size and priority.

The Big Wall is a quick and effective estimation and prioritization technique that enables teams to, at least initially, rise above discussions of two versus three and five versus eight and just group things in a purely relative manner along a continuum. It enables stakeholders to assign a general prioritization to a large group of stories without getting hung up on whether one story is slightly more important than another. The only tools you need are a stack of user stories (get them from your product owner, or if you are the product owner, print them) and a big empty wall, about 14 feet long by 8 to 10 feet high. Then you need to gather your stakeholders and team and plan to spend a day or so getting physically involved with your stories.

Height determines priority. Stories at the top are higher priority; stories at the bottom are lower priority. A story's priority can be based on ROI, business value, or something as vague as "it's just important and I don't know why." Width is reserved for size. Stories on the left are smaller; stories on the right are bigger (or if you're in, say, Japan, you can reverse this and move from right to left if it's more logical). The important thing is to envision one line going horizontally and one going vertically. Team members and stakeholders should ask themselves where, relative to the other stories, does this one fit?

If you already have an estimated backlog, you can just do the prioritization section of this exercise. If your product owners and stakeholders have already given you a prioritized backlog, you can just do the estimation section of this exercise. (Your product owner will likely want to revisit the prioritization after the estimates are done. After all, cost has a big impact on priority.) If you are like the characters in our story, you can do both sections. Let's look in detail at how this would work, beginning with the team's role.

## Team

Given a raw product backlog, you should start with estimation. One way to do this is to emulate the team in our story and start with a blank slate. Instruct the team that the far left of the wall should hold the smallest possible stories, and the far right should contain the biggest possible stories, without regard to numbers. The team puts stories somewhere on the wall based on those two poles. The advantage to doing it this way is that there is no preconceived notion of what a two- or three-point story is; it's truly relative based on how big the wall is, which is why it's nice to have a really big wall.

On the other hand, your team might feel more comfortable if you give more structure to the wall by identifying reference stories. Ask the team to identify five reference stories: a representative one-point, two-point, three-point, five-point, and eight-point story. Don't worry about creating a bigger reference story; anything bigger will usually be broken down as it rises in priority. Finding reference stories should take less than an hour.

Once the team has identified the five stories, place them on the wall in the locations that reflect their sizes (again, smaller to larger, moving from left to right). Leave some room on the right side of the wall for stories bigger than eight. Ask team members to take the remaining stories and compare them to the size of the reference stories, and then place them in the appropriate spot on the wall. For instance, if a story seems to be a bit smaller than a five but much bigger than a three, put it just to the left of the five-point reference story. If it seems bigger than a five but much smaller than an eight, put it just to the right of the five-point reference story and left of the eight-point reference story. The closer in size it is to the reference story, the physically closer it should be to the reference story. There is no real science to this, it's just the team looking and saying, "This is more than a two, but it's not a three, so it belongs in the middle." That is good enough.

Whichever way you choose to get there, once you've placed the stories on the wall, discuss with the team where the logical breaks are between story sizes. Like we saw Lynne and Gordon do in the story, put a line of tape where the team determines the stories separate into point groups. Soon you'll have a wall that looks something like the wall in Figure 29-1. Now that you've estimated your stories in terms of size, you need to assign them a priority.

## Stakeholders

Your customers and stakeholders will look at the stories in a much different way than the team just did. They're not as interested in how many points a story has; they are most interested in finding the stories that relate to them and making sure those stories get done. This may put the stakeholders in conflict with one another. This is OK—in fact, it's ideal because it reflects reality and helps the product owner make tough decisions.

The first thing I do is explain to the stakeholders why we are here and what we want to accomplish. This little speech goes something like this: "I have met with each of you and have created a set of stories that reflect your wants and needs. The team has spent the morning grouping these into relative sizes. The stories to the left are smallest. The stories to the right are the largest. What I'd like you to help me do is

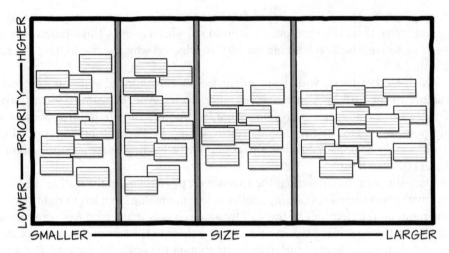

**FIGURE 29-1**   Stories arranged by size

determine the relative priority of all these stories. I'm going to ask you to move these stories up or down inside the taped lines. The higher up a story is on the wall, the higher its priority to the business. If you place a story at the top, I will ask you for justification as to why it's up there. You may also ask each other why one story is more important than the other. In the end, we'll know how all the stories relate and have an idea of what functionality we'll have early in the project and what functionality will happen later. The team will observe and might ask questions to help them better understand a story."

Remind the stakeholders that if they move a story lower on the wall than someone else did, they need to mark it with a yellow dot. This alerts everyone that we might need to have a conversation about the story's true priority. I also encourage/ expect people to ask, "Who moved this one down (or up)?" or to say aloud, "I think this one needs to move. Who wants to disagree?" This enables a conversation to happen between the interested parties without facilitation. If a discussion goes on too long without resolution, the facilitator (usually the product owner), should collect the card, note the two stakeholders who cannot agree, and make a note to meet with them privately later.

While the team is in the room for this exercise, they are not active participants. They are observers, taking notes on the behavior, the interactions, and the reasons why certain stories are rising or falling in priority. They can also answer any stakeholder questions, if needed. If there are stories that the team couldn't size with confidence because it required answers from a particular stakeholder, the team can also ask questions about those stories, as time allows.

The goal of prioritizing as a group is to help all stakeholders understand the priorities of various stories and how the others view it. The exercise should take between

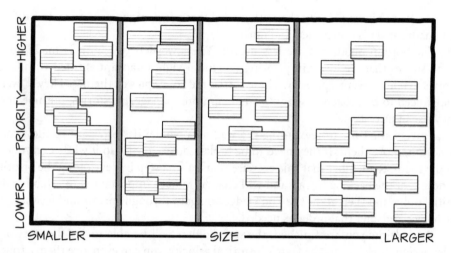

**FIGURE 29-2**    Prioritized and estimated backlog on the wall

two and six hours, depending on the number of stories and the number of stakeholders. The end result should look something like the picture shown in Figure 29-2.

When the dust has settled and the group steps back to look at what they've done, your wall will break down roughly into four quadrants, as shown in Figure 29-3.

The stories in the top-left quadrant are high priority and small. They'll end up in the top of the product backlog. The stories in the top-right are high priority and large. You should break most of those down into smaller stories because they'll be coming up in the first several sprints. As the stories are broken down, you may find

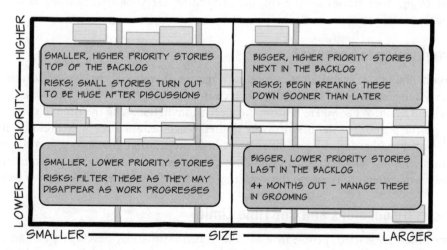

**FIGURE 29-3**    The four quadrants

that some are higher priority than others and that a few might even move to a different quadrant. This is expected and normal.

The bottom quadrants are less urgent. The lower-left quadrant is made up of small stories that are lower in priority. The lower-right quadrant is filled with large stories that are lower in priority. These stories are your epics or themes. They'll eventually need to be broken down into smaller, more manageable stories, but not until they rise in priority.

Leave some time to reexamine the wall as a whole. If stories are in the wrong quadrant, move them. If they need to be broken down, try to do it while everyone is in the room. Remember that this exercise is just a first step in developing the priority ordering of the backlog. It can and will change. What's important is to establish the initial order and then allow the knowledge you gain through sprints and feedback to influence and alter that order as needed.

By the time you are finished, the stakeholders will be able to see the start of a release plan. If you know the team's historical velocity, you can even give them a rough range of which stories in the upper-left quadrant will be finished (see Chapter 4, "Determining Team Velocity," and Chapter 11, "Release Planning").

Don't be overwhelmed by a raw product backlog. You can estimate and prioritize even the most out-of-control product backlog fairly quickly if you have the right people, a lot of ink and paper, a little time, and a really big wall.

# Keys to Success

Using a big wall seems like a fairly easy technique, and it is, but it does have some drawbacks. If you want to pull this off successfully, you need to consider and be prepared for preplanning, setting time limits, parking unresolved issues, creating (and destroying) user stories on the fly, and reminding everyone that nothing is set in stone.

## Preplanning Is Essential

No one likes to be surprised by a meeting's agenda. If your stakeholders walk unprepared into a room with a wall full of index cards they might just turn and walk right back out again. When you're writing the meeting invitation, take the time to communicate the purpose of the meeting, the desired outcome, any necessary prework, the scheduled breaks, and the general rules. A little preparation goes a long way toward minimizing the amount of hand-holding you have to do during the meeting and ensures that everyone comes to the workshop prepared for what they'll encounter there.

## Focus Discussions and Set Time Limits

Once they get started, people love to talk. When estimating, developers can go off into the weeds, discussing the merits of this or the other approach. When prioritizing, stakeholders can spend 30 minutes arguing over why a particular story is of more value than another, especially when they are politically motivated. Your job is to notice these tangents and redirect the conversation to the topic at hand.

When team members get stuck on implementation or architectural issues, bring the focus back to the relative size of the story. If you're using T-shirt sizes, remind them that you're looking for a relative size. If it's too big or poorly understood to estimate, they should give it an XXL, which is the appropriate size for stories that need to be broken down or discussed prior to being worked on.

When stakeholders start debating marketing strategies or customer satisfaction goals, remind them to consider the product as a whole. It might help to structure the discussion in terms of the minimal marketable feature sets, the minimum amount of functionality that an end user needs, for specific (requested) delivery windows (as introduced in Chapter 26, "Up-front Project Costing"). Consider as well the MMR, or minimal marketable release [ANDERSON]. The minimal marketable release, as identified by Anderson is *"a set of features that are coherent as a set to the customer and useful enough to justify the costs of delivery."*

Don't let healthy debate turn into a time-eating tangent. Keep people talking, but make sure they're talking about the right things and that their conversations are moving the process forward, not stalling it unnecessarily. If all else fails, get an egg timer.

## Use a Parking Lot for Unresolvable Disagreements

A parking lot is a place to put stories when the discussions seem to be endless. After all, it's not that the discussions or arguments are bad; most of them are valid. The problem is people have a hard time leaving the argument to focus on the larger backlog. One solution is to put those discussions/stories in the parking lot to revisit later. A parking lot is typically represented by a flip chart or small section of the whiteboard that is designated "Parking Lot." It is a temporary place to store index cards or write topics that need to be parked for now and picked up later. Use it anytime a process bogs down over an argument or off-topic discussion.

If the team is simply unable to say "it's a little bigger" or "it's a little smaller" and its members really need time to go to the weeds, park the story by physically relocating the index card. If the stakeholders need to sit down with you to really dig into the relative priority of two stories, park those stories as well. If a topic comes up that is interesting but doesn't move prioritization forward, park it and move on.

The stories and ideas in the parking lot can be handled at the end of the meeting or even after the meeting has been completed. A few unresolved stories should not distract from the huge pile of unsorted stories.

## Bring Extra Cards/Paper for Stories Created in the Room

This might seem like a no-brainer, but when you're focused on the big picture you tend to forget the little things—extra cards, pens, sticky notes, and paper. Understand that you're going to be ripping up stories and writing new ones during this exercise, so make sure you have the supplies you need to do it.

Above all, make sure people know that it's OK to just dispose of a story if it is badly written, needs to be broken down, duplicates another, or just doesn't need to happen. Stories aren't gold. They're ideas on paper. Feel free to destroy some and add others.

## Remind Them That Things Will Change

While it might seem like it at the time, a story's size or priority is not a life or death decision; nothing is carved in stone. Stories might be resized; priorities might shift. The product backlog is a living document that must be groomed each sprint. Initial estimates and priorities are important to capture, but they are only a starting point. If the team and stakeholders get hung up, remind them of this crucial fact: "Look. This is a preliminary estimate (or priority). We can revisit it later as we learn more and as things develop."

The work looming inside a large, raw backlog doesn't need to weigh you down. With a little cooperation, a whole lot of patience, and a wall big enough to hold all those stories, you can bring that backlog down to size in just one day.

# References

[ANDERSON]   Anderson, David J. 2010. *Kanban*. Sequim, WA: Blue Hole Press. p. 152.

[MAR]   Mar, Kane. "Scrum Trainers Gathering (4/4): Affinity Estimating." Personal website. http://kanemar.com/2008/04/21/scrum-trainers-gathering-44-affinity-estimating/ (accessed on 30 June 2008).

# Chapter 30

# WRITING CONTRACTS

We know the standard contracting model—customers want to see in writing what they'll get, at what cost, and by what date. But how do contracts work with a Scrum delivery model? After all, Scrum teams deliberately avoid fixed scope, cost, and date contracts, preferring to fix only one of those elements and leave the others variable. So how can Scrum teams work with clients who expect to have all three elements fixed in a contract? In our story, we see two colleagues face a customer who has been burned by fixed-everything contracts in the past, and discover the pay-as-you-go solution they propose to earn the business.

## The Story

Julio worked for a large consulting company based in Los Angeles. Julio, as the account manager, helped procure business and write contracts but was not that experienced in Scrum. One night at a dinner party, Julio met and chatted with a potential new client named Richard. He discovered that Richard, a director of a large talent agency, was deeply dissatisfied with his current booking software but was leery of paying for yet another system that didn't meet his needs.

"Julio," Richard said, "I'm sure you've got a great shop. But you can't guarantee me that I won't be wasting my money. Everyone says they know what I need. But in the end, I just spend a small fortune for software that isn't right. We're just going to live with what we've got."

"I know what you're talking about, and I know how frustrating it is to pay for something that doesn't work the way you want it to. We do things differently. What we can do is deliver a small portion of your system at a time, and offer you the opportunity to pay only for the software you accept. Because you're paying as you go, your risk is minimal. Can we meet at your office next week so my colleague and I can explain what we offer that others don't?" asked Julio.

Richard agreed to the meeting. The next day, Julio spoke to his colleague, Rob. Rob had many years of experience running Scrum projects and helped deliver the work Julio brought in.

"I think I know how we can approach this," said Rob. "I've just finished working with a cruise company in Long Beach on a booking website. They, like Richard, had been burned before and were pretty skeptical that we could deliver. We were able to deliver new functionality every two weeks. After every delivery, the clients reviewed the work in progress and had the opportunity to adjust what we worked on next based on what was going on with their competitor's website. They were extremely happy."

"That's what I've told Richard," said Julio. "We can give him immediate results. I'd like you to go with me to meet him and help explain how Scrum works. Tell him about how with Scrum, we can go twice as fast for half the cost as anyone else. This will really help him solve his problems," explained Julio.

"Whoa! Hold up!" exclaimed Rob. "We can't tell Richard Scrum is going to solve all his problems because it isn't true. Scrum is a framework that helps us deliver working software to our clients, sure, but it isn't some magic pixie dust that you can sprinkle on your problems. If anything it highlights problems faster and forces people to fix them—that's the beauty."

"I don't think I can sell Richard on how we're going to come in and expose his problems! He's stressed out enough as it is," replied Julio.

"That's not what I mean by *highlights problems*. For example, I was able to show our management how having people split across multiple projects was a waste and was lowering quality. As a result, I got a dedicated team, so our quality and productivity are improving—we need to bring this same sort of awareness to Richard. However, to say Scrum makes things like this happen is a vast oversimplification. At the sales call, let me handle the Scrum questions; you just close the deal," said Rob.

"OK. I see your point. I'll let you explain how we will run this project using Scrum. If I can get him to commit, I might need you to help me put together a contract that will assure Richard he'll actually get something for his money while giving us some reassurances, too."

The day of the meeting arrived. After the initial pleasantries, Richard got right to the point. "Let's cut to the chase. What can you do that this list of other vendors has failed to do?" asked Richard, pointing to a whiteboard where he had written the names of the past consulting companies he had worked with.

Rob jumped right in. "We can give you the freedom to change your mind without charging you a fortune."

"How's that?" asked Richard.

"I worked for one of the consulting companies on your wall for a couple of years. I left because I noticed that we always failed to mention one key component in the project: It's software! Things change! And contracts should allow for that change. Instead, most contracts are the opposite. Most companies bid the lowest possible price and then charge a fortune for every change. These are software companies; they know that change is inevitable. In fact, they count on it to make money. But you are not a software company; you're a talent agency. You expect to pay something close to the contract price for software that works the way you want it to. Instead, you end up paying a lot more than you thought you were going to, and you're told it's your fault because you're the one who made all the changes."

"You've hit it on the head. So, how are you different?" asked Richard.

"You've got a bunch of software that doesn't work the way you envisioned, right?" asked Rob.

"Right."

"At the beginning of each project, you described how your current system was not working, talked about a few things you wanted instead, and answered a whole bunch of questions. Then the companies on this wall went away, did some software magic, and delivered you a brand new system several months later. Is that pretty accurate?"

"Yep," Richard answered.

"And once you started working with it, it didn't do what you needed in this section, didn't work like you had pictured in this place, and just didn't measure up overall. You paid for some costly changes to try to fix it, but in the end what you got was a clunky, buggy system that resembles what you asked for but is nothing like what you wanted, or *meant*."

"Right. Every time, once we saw the end result, we knew it wasn't quite right and could then describe what we needed instead. But we were out of budget and frankly out of patience," Richard explained.

"You're not alone. People know what they want when they see it—but it's hard to describe it, hard to even think of all the angles, right?"

Richard nodded yes.

Rob continued, "One of my customers is a big cruise company in Long Beach. Everyone there knew the current system was not working, but no one could agree on what exactly needed to be built or the problems the solutions were supposed to solve. It was a big mess. We could have taken a more traditional approach to building their system, which I think you're familiar with, Richard."

"Oh, you mean me paying and the vendor not delivering? I'm *very* familiar with that model," said Richard.

Julio laughed and interjected, "What we did instead was write a two-stage contract. The first stage is similar to a traditional discovery phase in a project. The second is a pay-as-you-go development plan, with deliveries every two weeks."

"What do you do in the discovery phase and how long does it last?" asked Richard.

"It's a fixed-cost phase that lasts about two weeks," said Julio.

Rob explained, "During discovery, I will come to your site for two weeks. I'll bring with me two people from the team that will do the work for the second phase, if we get the work that is. During that time, the three of us will interview everyone with some say in how the software should work: users, stakeholders, accounting, you name it."

"Accounting? Why in the world would you interview them for an engagement booking tool?" asked Richard.

"They hold the money and want to forecast revenue on future engagements," explained Julio. "That makes them a stakeholder. We also need to understand their expectations with regards to capital expenditure and their impression of IT shops."

"Interesting," said Richard, scratching his chin.

"Once we've met with everyone, we'll develop a set of user personas and use that to build a product backlog with user stories. The last thing we do before the end of the first phase is estimate the product backlog," said Rob.

"Back up," said Richard. "User personas? User stories? Product backlogs? I don't know what these things are."

Rob and Julio spent some time explaining these basic Scrum artifacts and the concept of agile estimation. After awhile, Richard could see the connection between end customer value and stories, and how they changed based on the emerging functionality of the system.

"So," concluded Rob, "at the end of the discovery phase, we'll give you an estimated product backlog and a potential release plan. The plan will be based on how much work the team will likely deliver each sprint, at a certain degree of confidence, and, of course, the information we have to date. We'll offer you the ability to change your mind without penalty, as long as you swap items of equal size. You'll have the estimated cost of the functionality, and a detailed plan for what we believe we can deliver."

"What happens at the end of that discovery phase? Is there a requirement that I use your company for phase two if I don't like what I see?" asked Richard.

"Absolutely not," said Julio. "Our job in that first phase is to build a backlog with user personas and stories. That is the deliverable, along with our release plan. You can take that backlog to a number of other vendors to get their bids if you like. At that point we simply are another company competing for your business. You may find our costs to be a little higher up front, but we don't gouge you for changes in the end."

"What happens if you're great at making a plan but not so good at following through? What if I choose you to build the product and you don't deliver?" asked Richard.

"I think this is the best part," explained Julio. "The contract will say that if you are not happy with the quality of what we build, you give us one sprint's notice and we are done. It will also say that if at any time you decide you have enough functionality, you give us one sprint's notice for us to close the project down. It's truly a pay-as-you-go plan. Oh! One more thing. If you do not accept the work, meaning you don't agree that what we built in the sprint was what you asked for, you don't have to pay for that sprint."

"So, what stops me from saying I don't accept the work and getting it all done for free?" asked Richard.

"Trust," said Julio. "It's as simple and as complicated as that. You'll go into phase two knowing that we are working in your best interests—we've worked to understand your business and are there to help you succeed. We want long-term partners, not one-off customers. We may not have the largest customer base, but we have the most loyal. We are strategic about who we hire and the customers we take on. If potential customers do not align to our company values, we refer them to a larger consulting shop. It's that important to us."

In the end, Rob and Julio were able to work with Richard to structure a contract that he could be confident in and they could all trust.

# The Model

Customers want maximum functionality and quality at the lowest possible cost and in the shortest possible time. Worse, they expect us, the IT professionals, to guarantee all these factors, with 100 percent confidence at the beginning of the project. Who can blame them? Like Richard in our story, our customers have been burned too many times by failed projects, cost overruns, missing functionality, and bug-ridden code.

So why can't we deliver what we promise? Two reasons: Change and timing.

Before we can get into writing contracts to support agile projects, we first need to understand, and come clean, on how a lot of traditional contracts are written. I've been guilty in the past of doing what I've written in the following section, "Traditional Contracts and Change Orders," and I've seen this repeated hundreds of times, most recently about two weeks before this chapter was finalized.

## Traditional Contracts and Change Orders

Customers are no different than you and I. We all want to know what we are getting for our money, and when we are going to get it. Because of this, I see most traditional contracts starting like this:

1. Companies/customers publish or send a request for a proposal. This RFP lists all the features/work that the customer desires. In most cases, the work will not be in priority order—it *all* needs to be done.
2. There is a short question and answer window where you, the contractor can ask detailed questions, flesh out assumptions, and attempt to discover the budget. As you work on your proposal, you will naturally try to fit your overall project cost into the customer's budget range—if you don't know the range, you'll make your best guess.
3. Your final proposal will come in as close as possible to the lower end of the budget, or if you don't know the budget, lower than what you think your competitors would submit, and you put in everything the customers think they want. You do this so that you can win the business. Figure 30-1 depicts an actual customer contract—imagine trying to read it, let alone *understand* it.
4. Your proposal *might* include your change order process. It should as it's a key component of how you'll handle changes when they surface. You know going in that change orders might be the only way to break even or make money off the low bid you offered to secure the business. Why? Because we all know that there's no way to uncover all the assumptions and figure out how what the customer really *meant* to ask for in the small, pre-execution RFP window. Things are going to change.

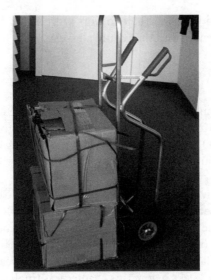

**FIGURE 30-1**   This traditional contract weighed more than 100 pounds/50 kilos

Now, change order processes are interesting beasts. They are absolutely necessary on a traditional contract, yet the mere act of having to ask for changes and going through a complicated process will frustrate customers and, over time, degrade trust.

Why have change orders if they degrade the trust of your customers? Because without them, most software companies would go out of business. On one project I ran, for example, the statement of work was "loose" because the account manager just wanted it to be done. We spent six months on it, and the system was so immense, it was impossible to capture everything it would do. By the time the project ran out of budget, the customer said they *needed* significant changes for it to be accepted, even though it met the loose requirements laid out in the statement of work. As a result, our company did a couple hundred thousand dollars' worth of work for free. Believe me when I say that our next contract included a detailed change order process.

If vendors agree to make all changes for free, the sheer volume of changes is like death by 1,000 cuts. By the end of the project, all those small changes will add up to a staggering cost that the vendor has to eat. To protect against that, vendors who want to stay in business develop a good change order process and stick to it.

A good change order process is going to be fairly lengthy and very detailed. For example, the Washington State Department of Transportation Construction Change Order Process Guide is 68 pages [WSDOT]. It is a very well thought out document that clearly illustrates how the process works and how to do it. Why does the state do this? To protect its interests. Author Dave Nielsen wrote an article, "How to Control Change Requests" [NIELSEN], in which he describes several detailed ways to handle change requests. The point I'm trying to make is a good change order process will likely be large and detailed. Trying to handle changes more informally on a traditional project is a recipe for disaster.

Consider this simple example: making cookies. My wife, Bernice, asks the kids and me what we want for dessert. We're on our way out the door, so we yell back, "Cookies!"

Bernice calls out, "What kind?"

One of the kids responds with, "The kind with sugar." (She is a total sugar freak and doesn't want any healthy-type food.)

Now my wife is confused. We've just left the house and my mobile is off. She knows our favorite cookie is chocolate chip, but we seemed to have just asked her for sugar cookies. So, aiming to please, and assuming we must be bored with the old standby, my wife bakes the sugar cookies, complete with sprinkles. We return to find them cooling on the counter.

"Yuck," say the kids. "What are these?"

"Sugar cookies, like you asked for," says Bernice, perplexed and feeling a bit unappreciated.

"We didn't ask for sugar cookies," whine the kids. "We wanted chocolate chip. You know that's what we always make."

"Well, this is what I heard you say and what I made," says my frustrated wife. "If I make more, it'll cost you." And off we go.

The failure here was poor communication between the customers (the kids and me) and the team (my wife). The kids thought that when they said "the kind with sugar" for cookies, Bernice would understand that we meant chocolate chip. But what she heard us ask for was sugar cookies. With no further way to clarify our needs, Bernice did the best she could and made sugar cookies. The kids were disappointed. She was frustrated. No one got the result they wanted.

In the world of software, people don't have relationships like families do—trust is fragile and easily broken. Building the wrong thing for our customers erodes their trust in us. Washington State DOT and Nielsen don't love huge processes, but they implement these complicated change orders in an attempt to improve communication and to get it right. Plus, if they do get it wrong, they can prove that they followed the agreed-upon process and that what they built accurately reflects the approved change order.

In every instance that I can think of, change orders are necessary on traditional projects. And large, detailed change orders are the best way to ensure some sort of accuracy. Yet, no matter how good your change order system is, you will still lose trust with your customers as soon as they go through the process. In their minds, you should have understood their request to begin with. (Like my kids expected their mother to understand they meant chocolate chip cookies, your customers feel that you should understand their requests because, to them, they are clear and easy to follow.) Instead, your customers have to spend time re-explaining what they want through a lengthy change order, it's costing them more money, and the release date

**FIGURE 30-2**   Change Order boat

is likely to slip. Worse yet, the final product still may not be exactly what they envisioned, even after going through the process, but they have to pay for it nonetheless.

Another reason change order processes degrade trust is the fact the most companies have figured out that they can bid on the lower end of the cost scale, betting on the fact that the customers will change their minds. A change order process is necessary on traditional contracts because vendors are taking all the risk. This business strategy, one that takes advantage of the fact that all customers will change their requirements as they discover what they really want, can leave a really sour taste in the customer's mouth. Take the picture shown in Figure 30-2 as an example.

Notice the names of the boats in the picture. The big one is called *Change Order*; the smaller one behind it is called *Original Contract* [BOAT]. From the customer's perspective, the vendor promised them a certain product at a certain cost. What the customer got was a product that's kind of close to what they wanted but cost them much more than the original bid and probably came in behind schedule, too. Meanwhile, the vendor is sailing off into the sunset with a big wad of cash. And we wonder why they don't trust us!

Change, though, isn't the only reason why we struggle to meet customer expectations on traditional contracts. We are also handicapped by timing.

## Timing

Customers ask for dates, cost, and commitment right from the start. The timing of these requests, at the beginning, puts both the vendor and a customer in a bad position from the onset of the contract, because there is no way to be precise that early in the process. Vendors and teams ask customers to spell out *exactly* what they want before they're exactly sure, while customers require vendors to guarantee a set of functionality, at a certain cost, and by a certain time based on a set of requirements built on a soft foundation.

The fact is, vendors just don't know enough at the project's start to make those kinds of promises. To understand why the timing is such a problem, we only need to look as far as the Cone of Uncertainty, which Barry Boehm introduced in 1981 and Steve McConnell reintroduced in 1997 in his book *Software Project Survival Guide*. It is pictured in Figure 30-3.

The cone demonstrates that at the beginning of any project, we have the most uncertainty, with a variance of 4x to 0.25x in range. This means that what we estimate to be a six-month project could actually end up taking anywhere from 1.5 to 24 months! Yet, when we are in this state of heightened uncertainty, teams are forced to write a contract saying exactly what they'll deliver, by when, and at what cost, with no variance. It's no wonder people end up with huge boats! However, very few projects start at the far left of the cone. In a contracting situation, the customer will have some notion of their requirements, which puts them somewhere between the *Approved Product Definition* and *Requirements Complete* milestones.

In Scrum, what we do is try to move from uncertainty to certainty in as short a cycle as possible. As explained in Chapter 1, "Scrum: Simple, Not Easy," we learn as much about the system and how it should be designed as early as possible by providing working software based on emerging requirements sprint after sprint. Design and requirements assumptions are flushed out early, allowing us to move to certainty quicker and with more confidence.

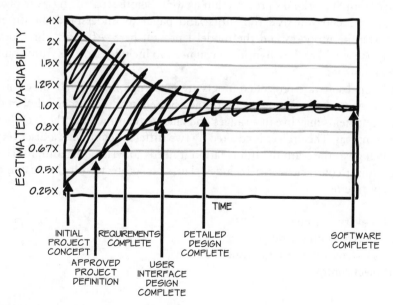

**FIGURE 30-3**  The Cone of Uncertainty

Even Scrum projects, however, would be unable to predict exactly what the final cost, functionality, and delivery date will be on day one of a Scrum project. That's why a different contracting model is needed, one built for change and designed to limit promises made in the time of greatest project uncertainty and maximize early learning.

I call that contracting model *Ranges and Changes* and describe it in detail in the next section. While the model might not be appropriate with all clients and in all situations, it does work extremely well with customers who are engaged, understand the problems with traditional projects, and are interested in refining the product as it is being developed. If you have customers who are not engaged or are just looking "for the date" or "just the cost," this model will not work for you.

## Ranges and Changes

The ranges and changes model was born from a project I bid in 2007. The resulting contract was just like the one Julio and Rob described to Richard in the story. The project was an overwhelming success and proved to me that the contract I had developed could work for other clients. And it did. Though we've tweaked it a bit over time and to suit certain situations, my colleagues and I have used the ranges and changes model at various companies across North America and Europe. The model shares certain features with "Money for Nothing and Change for Free," presented by Jeff Sutherland at the Agile 2008 conference [SUTHERLAND]. In fact, after hearing his presentation, I adjusted my own model based on some of his ideas.

In this section I describe the ranges and changes model and discuss some key takeaways from Sutherland's presentation as well. Before structuring your own contract, I recommend you read the Sutherland paper to understand the differences between what he proposes and the model I present here. After all, the model you ultimately use will likely be a hybrid, as you need to include elements from your company's own policies.

Traditional software project contracts are made up of things like milestones, the description of work, project goals and objectives, deployment schedules, and warranties. These items may live in a ranges and changes contract, but they get there in a very different way. The project is covered by two different contracts: a discovery contract, which gives the team the information it needs to write a meaningful contract, and the project contract, which includes clauses to protect both the customer and also the contractor.

- Discovery contract
  - Ascertain the ranges
  - Determine cost and timeline
- Project contract

The first contract covers only the discovery phase, which helps the team determine the **ranges** necessary to write a meaningful contract. The resulting contract includes the parameters for execution and the all-important **changes** clause.

## Discovery Contract: Ascertain the Ranges

The discovery phase is covered by a fixed-fee, fixed-length contract with one goal: Allow the team to gather enough information to discover and communicate what it can deliver (a product backlog), by when (an initial sprint release plan), and for how much (cost per sprint). The contract typically covers two or three team members for about two weeks. If the customer chooses to go with another vendor at the end of the fixed-length discovery contract, these deliverables can be reused.

The first deliverable is the product backlog. Building the product backlog for a customer is a three-step process: identify user types or personas, write user stories, and estimate the stories.

*Identify User Types or Personas.* The discovery team should determine who the users of the system are, what their interests are, how they will use the system, and their expectations. This helps the people writing the stories understand who the users are and creates a more user-centric view of stories. When I do this, I interview as many users of the system as possible to understand their current interactions, what they like and dislike about the current system, and what their *number one* thing would be to fix.

*Write User Stories.* The discovery team is responsible for writing user stories following the *"As a <user>, I can <action> so that <result>"* template. I like to invite the customer to the user story workshop along with the team. The team members and customer representatives can brainstorm ideas and write stories. Even if the customer chooses not to write any actual stories, having someone from the customer side is beneficial because it gives the team an opportunity to ask the customer specific questions regarding user stories that help clarify and make the story point estimates more accurate. The user stories make up the product backlog.

*Estimate the Stories.* The discovery team estimates the resulting user stories in story points. This helps the stakeholders and customers understand the story cost, a consideration when prioritizing the stories in the backlog. Make sure the customer is available for questions during estimation. (We talk more about ensuring customer availability in the "Keys to Success" section of this chapter.)

## Discovery Phase: Determine Cost and Timeline

Once the team has worked with the customer to gather information, the team works on its own to determine the cost and timeline. This is a four-step process: determine team velocity, calculate cost per sprint, build a release plan, and establish payment options.

*Determine Team Velocity.*   If you have an established team and are bidding on a project that is similar to work the team has done before, you should have a good idea of the team's expected velocity. If you don't, you need to forecast or estimate the team velocity. Either way, you communicate velocity to your customer as a potential range. Understand that your customer will expect you to achieve somewhere near the top of that range on most sprints. Refer to Chapter 4, "Determining Team Velocity," for more information.

*Calculate Cost Per Sprint.*   In Chapter 8, "The Case for a Full-Time ScrumMaster," I discussed the loaded cost of an employee. Use that here if you don't normally bill for your time. If you work in a consultancy or have a capital expenditure budget that you are working from, you know what the billable rate is per person. Either way, use the loaded employee costs to calculate the cost per sprint. Sum up the loaded cost per person per hour, multiply it by the estimated hours per sprint the team will burn, and you have your cost per sprint.

*Build a Release Plan.*   The release plan is your bread and butter—it lays out a low range and a high range of what you and your team can deliver. In the release plan, you should have a guaranteed number of points the team will deliver each sprint and by the end of the project, so that anything you achieve beyond those numbers is perceived as additional value to the customer. Fix the variable (budget, time, scope) that matters most to your clients. If they have a set budget, you can show them how many sprints that will buy them and the range of functionality that will be delivered by the time those sprints are complete. If they have a set date, you can show them how many sprints you can run by that date, how much that will cost, and the range of functionality you can deliver in that number of sprints. If they are most concerned with functionality, you can show them the range of how many sprints it will take to complete the functionality and the range of cost they will incur depending on whether your sprint count is in the low or high end of the range. Please read Chapter 11, "Release Planning," for more information on building a release plan.

*Establish Payment Options.*   The final step is to determine the payment terms that will work for you and your customer. You can offer them the option to pay by point (potentially more cost to them) or to pay by sprint, with a guaranteed minimum number of points delivered each sprint. You can also offer a cost-per-point range that the customer can pay. If the team delivers 10-14 points, it costs $X per point, but if the team manages 15-19 points, it costs $Y, and so on.

## Project Contract: Delivering the Goods

At the end of the discovery phase, you have several deliverables for your potential client: a set of user personas, an estimated product backlog, a release plan, and a project contract. The resulting contract references the estimated product backlog and preliminary release plan. It guarantees that you will deliver a **range** of points each sprint (based on your predicted velocity) for a certain cost, or at a certain cost per point. It includes the team's definition of done and an explanation of how the work will be delivered to the customer. It also includes language that indicates under what conditions the customer can reject a sprint's worth of work. You also need a clause in the contract to discuss change, the **changes** section of the contract model.

*Changes.*  Even a Scrum contract has to include a clause about changes. My contracts allow the customer to reshuffle the work on the product backlog, or add new stories, as long as the total number of points on the product backlog remains the same and the total for each sprint still fits inside a predetermined range of what the team can deliver. At an Agile 2008 conference, Jeff Sutherland presented, "Money for Nothing, Change for Free." In it, he described his approach to change with the cleverly named "change for free" clause. (We look more closely at the "money for nothing" clause in the "Keys to Success" section later in this chapter.)

Sutherland's change for free clause stipulates that the customer must be working with the team and that the product owner is responsible for prioritization. Under those conditions, the customer can add new stories at no charge as long as a story of equal or similar value is removed. An example I use to help people understand this concept is in relation to a one-liter bottle. This bottle is designed to hold one liter of any liquid: water, oil, vinegar, soft drinks, cream, you name it. At the beginning of the project, the customer decides to add olive oil and white vinegar. Change for free means the customer can choose to add some amount of water to the bottle as long as he removes an equal amount of olive oil or white vinegar. Otherwise, the bottle will overflow.

At this point, your contract is nearly complete. You just need to add four crucial elements: customer availability, acceptance window, prioritization, and termination clauses. We discuss these four elements in more detail in the next section.

# Keys to Success

A contract based on good information and customer interaction goes a long way toward building trust with your customer. But besides cost ranges and allowances for changes, a good Scrum contract includes stipulations for the elements that make or break a Scrum project. These include customer availability (for feedback, for acceptance, and for product backlog maintenance) and a clear understanding of how to maximize the Scrum advantage of keeping the project in a potentially shippable state. Let's take a closer look at how to include these elements in a Scrum contract.

## Customer Availability

Include a set number of hours per week to which the customer can commit to being available. You don't want to fall into the trap of having an active customer up front only to have them disappear as the project progresses. Short sprints require near-daily customer availability. Longer sprints have the advantage of offering more sporadic customer availability but also run the risk of having all the customer time focused toward the beginning and end of the sprint. Even though the demands on the customer are higher with shorter sprints, I prefer shorter sprint durations because it keeps the customer engaged throughout the project.

## Acceptance Window

The acceptance window is the amount of time the customer has to accept functionality delivered in that sprint. You can choose to have the window be as short as "during the review meeting" or "*x* hours or days after the review meeting." The clause should also illustrate what the default behavior is if the window passes and the customer has neither accepted nor rejected the work. In most cases, the default should be automatic acceptance.

I prefer a short acceptance window, ideally a day or less. Longer acceptance windows start to intrude on the next sprint, as some work cannot go forward without acceptance or modification of the work that has occurred to date. If the feature is reviewed outside the acceptance window and found to be lacking something, this new work goes onto the product backlog as a new story to be prioritized (and will cost the customer money, which is why *customer availability* is essential). Features reviewed inside the acceptance window that are lacking are generally rejected (and cost the vendor money to fix).

That's the other provision I include: If the customer rejects any work delivered in a sprint, the customer doesn't have to pay us for that work. Will people try to take advantage of this? Yes. If you choose to include this provision, choose your customers wisely. Learn to say no to customers who you can't trust.

## Prioritization

Unlike a traditional RFP, a product backlog must be groomed regularly—kept in priority order and estimated in points on a regular basis. Make sure that the contract includes time spent with the customer estimating new stories, breaking down large stories, and helping them determine any shifts in priority. Help the customer understand that they are allowed to adjust the priority of the stories in the product backlog as they desire but that doing so may have an impact on how much the team can accomplish by a certain date.

The team may want to sequence the work a certain way, to achieve optimal flow for development. This may or may not align with the order in which the customer would like to see features delivered. Mike Cohn writes in *User Stories Applied* [COHN, p. 99] that the customer wins every time. I agree. It is our job, though, to help customers understand that the requested sequence of the work might increase estimates, thereby causing things to not get done (aka less functionality for the same amount of money). At the same time, though, there is no cost for adding things to the product backlog, as long as something comes out in its place.

## Termination Clauses

My contracts say that the customer can terminate the contract at any time and for any reason. We finish out the current sprint and have one additional sprint to clean things up as needed, such as transfer codebases, paperwork, and the like. This builds trust and forces the team to really drive toward potentially shippable each sprint.

Similarly, Sutherland's money for free clause acknowledges the fact that the software may reach a shippable state before all features have been enacted [SUTHERLAND]. As such, the customer can determine whether to stop development after any sprint and just ship the software as is. Monetary protection is built in for both the customer and the vendor. So how does this work? The customer has a prioritized list of work. At some point during the execution of the contract, the cost of doing the remaining work will be prohibitive and return little or no value. Sutherland calls this the ROI cutoff. Once the customer determines that the project has arrived at the ROI cutoff, the remaining work is scrapped. Because the project is, in essence, shipping early, money will be left over in the contract. With the money for free clause, the customer keeps the majority of the remaining funds, but the vendor also receives a percentage (in Sutherland's case, 20 percent) to cover the costs of ending the contract early.

## Trust

Once you get used to working with them, contracts that take into account the realities of a Scrum delivery model might just be the best contracts for vendors and customers. Structuring your contract to allow for change is the best way to do business. Giving customers the freedom to pay for each set of functionality as it's delivered, add or change stories as long as a story of equal value is removed, and cut the contract short or terminate it altogether at will pay off in terms of repeat customers and referrals. After all, in the end trust is the most important thing a software development company will ever build.

# References

[COHN]    Cohn, Mike. 2004. *User Stories Applied*. Boston: Addison-Wesley.

[WSDOT] Washington State Department of Transportation website. http://www.wsdot.wa.gov/biz/construction/pdf/guidetochangeorderprocess.pdf (accessed 2 December 2010).

[NIELSEN]    Nielsen, Dave. "How to Control Change Requests." PM Hut website. http://www.pmhut.com/how-to-control-change-requests (accessed 2 April 2010).

[BOAT] Construction Marketing Ideas website. http://constructionmarketing-ideas.blogspot.com/2009/04/real-change-order-boats.html (accessed 1 March 2010).

[SUTHERLAND]    Sutherland, Jeff. "Agile 2008: Money for Nothing." Scrum Log. Jeff Sutherland website. http://scrum.jeffsutherland.com/2008/08/agile-2008-money-for-nothing.html (accessed 2 December 2010).

# Appendix

# Scrum Framework

Scrum is a framework for managing complex projects (see Figure A-1), such as software development. Scrum uses a prescribed set of roles, meetings, and artifacts and divides a large amount of work into small chunks called sprints. It is based on and employs agile principles (see Chapter 1, "Scrum: Simple, Not Easy," for more on Scrum's underlying principles).

I like to think of the balance between the roles, the meetings, and the artifacts that make up the sprint cycle as like that of a finely tuned race car. Tiny incremental adjustments can lead to exceptional wins; at the same time, a slight knock or issue with the car and its engine can lead to less output, slower speeds, and rapid engine wear. How does this relate to Scrum? Let's explore each component in detail.

## The Roles

Scrum consists of three roles: the ScrumMaster, the product owner, and the development team (I also refer to the development team as *team* or the *core team* throughout

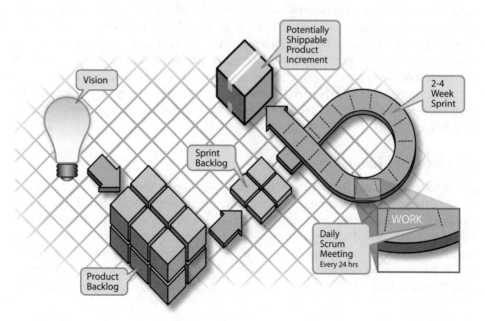

**FIGURE A-1**   The Scrum framework (download a copy at http://mitchlacey.com)

the book). Together they work in the interests of the customers and stakeholders to turn the vision into a workable product or service. If they were parts of a race car, the development team would be the engine, the product owner the driver, and the ScrumMaster all the lubricants and sensors.

## ScrumMaster

A race car has gauges and sensors to help monitor the engine and oil to help lubricate it. Without oil, the engine would grind to a halt, destroying itself in the process. The oil is everywhere, keeping the parts of the engine working smoothly, cooling them, and ensuring they perform well under stress.

The ScrumMaster is like that. He has embedded sensors and gauges that allow him to identify when the team is not performing to its ability, and he has the skills (lubrication) needed to assist in correcting the issues. Being the ScrumMaster is a hard job. A good ScrumMaster is someone who notices nonverbal cues, is comfortable with conflict, is an effective communicator, can build trust and earn respect, and understands team dynamics. A good ScrumMaster can "evolution-ize" development. He can build trust not only in the team but with customers as well. For more on choosing the right ScrumMaster see Chapter 5, "Implementing the Scrum Roles."

## Product Owner

If the ScrumMaster is the oil and sensors in the engine, the product owner is the driver. The product owner points the car in the correct direction and makes the minute course adjustments necessary to stay on course and deliver results. She represents customer and stakeholder interests. Her job is to establish, nurture, and communicate the product vision to the team and the other stakeholders, manage the project return on investment and financials, and make decisions about when to create an official release (with customer and stakeholder input). The product owner is the one person ultimately responsible for the success or failure of the project. She decides what is developed, when it is developed, and whether that which has been developed meets expectations.

## Development Team

The development team (or *core team*, or simply *the team*) is the engine of our race car. All the driving and lubrication in the world are no use without an engine. The development team executes the product owner's vision with the help of the ScrumMaster. The team is comprised of the people needed to deliver the work—developers, testers, architects, designers—anyone who is needed. A development team is ideally made up of full-time people dedicated to the project. (Reality sometimes makes this impossible. See Chapter 3, "Using Team Consultants to Optimize Team Performance," for ways to create a high-performing team under less than ideal circumstances.) The team is responsible for managing its work, its commitments, and the execution of those commitments.

Most Scrum material says that the ideal team size is seven, plus or minus two people. I prefer even numbers as it facilitates better XP engineering practice integration, so my rule would be six, plus or minus two. The team is just that, a team—roles and titles should be removed as it helps build the camaraderie around the team. The goal is to remove the mindset of "I'm a developer and I only write code" and shift the attention to "I'm a team member who is responsible for delivering this work *and* I cannot do it alone." On a Scrum team, testers may write code and developers may write tests—cross-functionality is a good thing.

# The Artifacts

Scrum is not an artifact-heavy development process, but three artifacts are crucial to success: the product backlog, the sprint backlog, and the burndown.

## The Product Backlog

The product backlog is the master list, prioritized by business value and risk, of all the features and functionality needed to implement the vision, and in the end, the product or service under development to achieve that vision. The product owner is responsible for managing the product backlog, keeping it up to date, prioritized or ordered, and clear. Unlike a requirements document or product specification, the product backlog is never complete. Instead, it is a living document that expands or contracts in response to changes in priority, value, or risk. Items can be added or deleted from the product backlog at any time. Once added, they are prioritized (or ordered) by the product owner in relation to the other items: bugs, features, enhancements, nonfunctional requirements, and so on.

Priority is determined by business value and risk (or whatever ordering makes sense for your company and project). The highest priority items are slated for development first; the lowest are completed last (see Figure A-2). The team works with the product owner to estimate the size of the product backlog items (PBIs), relative to one another. That size can be expressed in points, T-shirt sizes, or any other non-time-specific unit. The key is to stay away from time-based estimation for PBIs. Those specifics will come later (see Chapter 11, "Release Planning," for more on estimation).

High priority stories should be small and clear so that they can be brought into the sprint. Lower priority items can be large and fuzzy. As high priority items are completed and lower priority items begin to rise to the top of the backlog, the bigger stories need to be broken down into smaller chunks, a process called decomposition (see Chapter 12, "Decomposing Stories and Tasks").

ORDERED PRODUCT BACKLOG

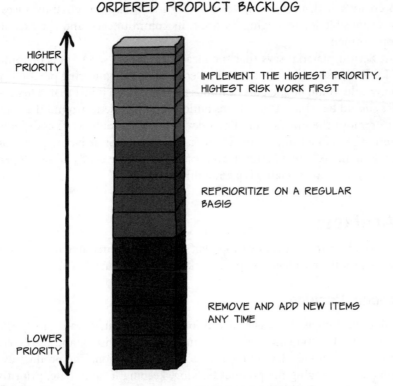

HIGHER PRIORITY

IMPLEMENT THE HIGHEST PRIORITY, HIGHEST RISK WORK FIRST

REPRIORITIZE ON A REGULAR BASIS

REMOVE AND ADD NEW ITEMS ANY TIME

LOWER PRIORITY

**FIGURE A-2**   Keep the product backlog ordered and prioritized

## The Sprint Backlog

The sprint backlog is the output of the planning meetings (described below). It is essentially the list of tasks that the team needs to complete during the sprint to turn a selected set of product backlog items into a deliverable increment of functionality. Unlike PBIs, sprint backlog tasks have a time-based (hourly) estimate. Since the team is doing the work, they are responsible for keeping the sprint backlog up to date.

During a sprint, new tasks might be discovered and tasks that have already been identified might be adjusted. This is perfectly normal behavior. The team simply adds the new tasks (and an estimate of the work remaining on that task) to the sprint backlog or adjusts the wording (and if necessary the estimated work remaining) for tasks in progress. As the team completes tasks, the task should be marked as done on the sprint backlog. The sprint backlog shows team members what is complete and what remains. This data helps team members run an effective daily scrum meeting.

While changes to the sprint backlog are expected, the ScrumMaster should be watching for patterns about the type or amount of work that is added or adjusted. If a pattern emerges, it can teach a team quite a bit about the system as it is built and possibly the team itself.

## The Burndown

While *The Scrum Guide* published by Schwaber and Sutherland in October 2011 says that burndowns are no longer a required artifact in Scrum, I believe they are still essential tools in a team's arsenal. Scrum requires that teams communicate how much work is remaining and how task completion is trending throughout the sprint. The best tool I've found to track this is the sprint burndown, a graphical, real-time picture of what work is remaining in the sprint. It is calculated by graphing the number of hours remaining (y-axis) against the number of days remaining (x-axis). Burndowns can be handwritten or created with a tool such as Microsoft Excel. To update the sprint burndown, the ScrumMaster or the team plots the number of hours remaining on the chart at the end of each day. Connecting those points shows a graph of the work still outstanding as the days of the sprint go by. You can visualize whether the team is on track to complete all the work remaining by extrapolating the line to the last day of the sprint.

# The Meetings

In Scrum, we have four meetings: the planning meetings, which occur on the first day of each sprint; the daily scrum, or daily sprint, meeting, which occurs every day; the sprint review meeting; and the team retrospective.

## Planning Meetings

Each sprint begins with a two-part sprint planning meeting. For a one month or four-week sprint this two-part meeting should last eight hours. For a two-week sprint, plan for about four hours. As a general rule of thumb, multiply the number of weeks in your sprint by two hours to get your total sprint planning meeting length.

Part one of the sprint planning meeting is a review of the product backlog. This is the time for the product owner to describe *what* she wants to see built for the next sprint. During this part of the meeting, it is not uncommon for the team to banter back and forth with the product owner, asking clarifying questions and driving away ambiguity. By the end of sprint planning part one, the team selects a sprint goal: a one-sentence description of the overall outcome of the sprint. This helps later when questions about depth and breadth come up: If the work does not directly tie to the sprint goal, then it is not done during the sprint.

During part two of the sprint planning meeting, the team decides *how* the work will be built. In this meeting the team begins decomposing the product backlog items into work tasks and estimating these in hours. The product owner must be available during this meeting but does not have to be in the room. In fact, many teams find it helpful to work without the product owner during this detailed part of the meeting. Many teams find they enjoy discussing many implementation possibilities without worrying that the product owner will panic or misunderstand. If the product owner does remain in the room, the ScrumMaster needs to take charge of this part of the meeting, keeping the team focused and free to explore possibilities without being limited by the product owner's own ideas or opinions.

## Daily Scrum Meeting

The most frequent meeting that occurs in Scrum is the daily meeting, otherwise known as the daily scrum or daily standup. Regardless of what it is called, the purpose remains the same: Give the team the opportunity to sync daily, at the same time and at the same place.

The daily scrum meeting is a daily planning meeting where the team answers a standard set of questions. The three questions most often used are as follows:

- What have you accomplished since the last meeting?
- What will you accomplish today?
- What impediments or obstacles are in your way?

Some teams add a fourth question. For more on the fourth question, see Chapter 18, "The Fourth Question in Scrum."

The daily scrum meeting is not a deep-dive problem solving meeting; it is meant to identify what people did, what they will do, and their issues—nothing more. Any other issues need to be taken offline as action items for the ScrumMaster to resolve or the team to discuss further, depending on the issue. At the same time, the daily scrum is not a status reporting meeting. People should be talking to each other, not reporting their activities to the ScrumMaster. Its purpose is to keep people focused on what they did and will do. The ScrumMaster's only function is to facilitate the meeting, not act as a detective or taskmaster.

The team determines when the meeting will take place, but it should be every day at the same time and place. All team members are required to attend every day. Other people may be invited to attend, but it is important to understand that this meeting is for *the team*, not for executives, managers, dev leads, or anyone else. If non-team members do attend, they are in "read only" or "listen only" mode. They are not allowed to actively participate, but can watch, listen, and learn.

Done well, daily scrum meetings improve team communication, identify issues and impediments, and build a sense of "team." Read more about how to run an effective daily scrum meeting in Chapter 17, "Running a Productive Daily Standup Meeting."

## Sprint Review

On the last day of the sprint, the team holds a sprint review meeting. This meeting (the length, like the sprint planning meeting, depends on sprint length) allows the customers an opportunity to review the progress made on the project to date and provides them a venue to give direction or guidance to the team with regards to the project. During the demo, the team recaps the goal of the sprint and presents the work that is done.[1] It is not uncommon for customers to praise the team in this meeting, nor is it uncommon for the customers to ask for changes. After all, the reason we do Scrum is to provide quick feedback loops and multiple opportunities to inspect and adapt; this is one of those loops. Any new requests should be put on the product backlog and prioritized. In this meeting, the team should ask for customer acceptance. Sometimes, customers say that some functionality was not delivered or was not delivered as expected. In those cases, work may be put back on the product backlog. If this is a recurring pattern, it should be noted by the ScrumMaster and addressed with the team.

For more on effective sprint reviews, see Chapter 15, "The Sprint Review."

## Sprint Retrospective

The sprint retrospective follows the sprint review. It provides the team an opportunity to identify ways in which it can improve its work process and execution of the Scrum framework. The meeting is mandatory for the team members and the ScrumMaster. Since this is a meeting for the team to identify ways to improve, I find it best to keep the product owner out of the meeting.

The ScrumMaster typically facilitates the meeting, helping the team build a list of prioritized improvement items they can implement in future sprints. These items should be reviewed at subsequent retrospectives so the team knows how they are doing and if improvements are happening. Once again, the duration hinges on the sprint length.

In this meeting, the team should answer (at least) the following two questions:

- What went well during the last sprint?
- What could be improved in the next sprint?

Everyone should participate. The ScrumMaster should not be going around the room asking people for their answers—instead the team should be actively writing its answers on a whiteboard. Once the team members have finished answering, they should work together to prioritize the items and begin deciding whether the items will be addressed. Retrospectives that do not have a lot of activity or that do not drive

---

1. See Chapter 7, "How Do We Know When We Are Done?," to understand what this means.

change are frustrating for everyone involved and often lead to the team questioning their value. The value comes through the opportunities for change identified in the retrospective. If the opportunities are not acted on and the team does not improve, there is a larger issue. For more on running effective retrospectives, see Chapter 16, "Retrospectives."

# Putting It All Together

The parts and rules by themselves are easy to understand. Putting them together in the most effective way, however, poses challenges. Moving back to the race car analogy, each part must be finely tuned for optimum performance. The chapters in the book dive deeply into implementation details and real-life strategies for optimizing performance, moving faster while remaining in control, and dealing with the knocks, blowouts, and backfires that come from trying to race in the competitive world of software development.

# INDEX

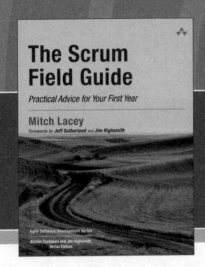

# FREE
# Online Edition

Your purchase of **The Scrum Field Guide** includes access to a free online edition for 45 days through the **Safari Books Online** subscription service. Nearly every Addison-Wesley Professional book is available online through **Safari Books Online**, along with thousands of books and videos from publishers such as Cisco Press, Exam Cram, IBM Press, O'Reilly Media, Prentice Hall, Que, Sams, and VMware Press.

**Safari Books Online** is a digital library providing searchable, on-demand access to thousands of technology, digital media, and professional development books and videos from leading publishers. With one monthly or yearly subscription price, you get unlimited access to learning tools and information on topics including mobile app and software development, tips and tricks on using your favorite gadgets, networking, project management, graphic design, and much more.

## Activate your FREE Online Edition at
## informit.com/safarifree

**STEP 1:** Enter the coupon code: GBWPYYG.

**STEP 2:** New Safari users, complete the brief registration form.
Safari subscribers, just log in.

If you have difficulty registering on Safari or accessing the online edition,
please e-mail customer-service@safaribooksonline.com